THE INSIDERS' GUIDE® TO

VIRGINIA'S CHESAPEAKE BAY

Including Virginia Beach, Norfolk & The Eastern Shore

THE INSIDERS' GUIDE TO
VIRGINIA'S CHESAPEAKE BAY

Including Virginia Beach, Norfolk & The Eastern Shore

by

Suzy Adams Dixon

and

Sally Kirby Hartman

THE INSIDERS' GUIDE

The Insiders' Guides Inc.

Co-published and marketed by:
Richmond Newspapers, Inc.
333 East Grace Street
Richmond, VA 232219

Co-published and distributed by:
The Insiders' Guides Inc.
The Waterfront • Suites 12 &13
P.O. 2057
Manteo, NC 27954
(919) 473-6100

•

SIXTH EDITION
1st printing

•

Copyright ©1995
by *Richmond Newspapers, Inc.*

•

Printed in the United States
of America

•

Richmond
Newspapers, Inc.

Director, Supplementary Publications
Jim Boyle

Manager
Ernie Chenault

Account Executive
Mike Morrison

Project Coordination
Bonnie Widener

Sean Conteras, Ronnie Johnson,
Susan Reily and Ben Shulte, artists

The Insiders' Guides® Inc.

Publisher/Editor-in-Chief
Beth P. Storie

President/General Manager
Michael McOwen

Vice President/Advertising
Murray Kasmenn

Creative Services Director
Mike Lay

Partnership Services Director
Giles Bissonnette

Project Artist
Mel Dorsey

Online Services Director
David Haynes

Fulfillment Director
Gina Twiford

Sales and Marketing Director
Julie Ross

Controller
Claudette Forney

ISBN 0-912367-74-1

Preface

Whether you're spending a few days or a lifetime here, we hope this book helps you enjoy your stay in Virginia's Chesapeake Bay region. Since the majority of the attractions are at the mouth of the bay where it spills into the Atlantic Ocean, we've concentrated on the area there called Hampton Roads. This region of beaches, historic sites and some of the best seafood on the East Coast includes Norfolk, Virginia Beach, Portsmouth, Suffolk and Chesapeake.

Since these cities are divided by water, bridges and tunnels, this can be a tricky region to explore at first. But it's worth getting out the map and wandering to the different cities since each is unique. In this edition of The Insiders' Guide we've tried to make it easier for you to find your way around.

Rather than segmenting the book by city, we've arranged it by topic. Since we're talking about a unified region, this approach seemed to make the most sense when it came to categories such as History or the Military. However, within sections like Restaurants, Attractions and Recreation you'll find a handy city-by-city breakdown of where to go and what to do. Although we've included a special section called Kidstuff, throughout the book you'll find suggestions for entertaining children.

Since the Chesapeake Bay's beauty isn't confined to the populous Hampton Roads' region, you'll find plenty of suggestions in this book for exploring some of the more remote areas along the bay. You could spend days winding along the backroads of the historic Eastern Shore or get the pampering of a lifetime at a Northern Neck resort. To really get away from it all try a boat cruise to Tangier or Smith islands. This year's edition of The Insiders' Guide has a new section designed to help boaters plan their own excursions in the bay.

Our goal was to create a book that will become a well-thumbed companion as you explore this area. Even people comfortably settled into the region will find numerous suggestions for activities they've never tried before. We hope The Insiders' Guide will be the first place you turn when you show off our region to company. When you're ready for new adventures, check out the Daytrips section for ideas on nearby destinations that are well worth visiting.

Although we know this area well, when we sat down to write about it, we were amazed at its diversity. We hope you have as much fun as we've had exploring Hampton Roads.

If we've left out your favorite place, please let us know so we can check it out before the next edition of The Insiders' Guide is published.

About The Authors

Suzy Adams Dixon, a lifelong resident of southside Hampton Roads, is the owner of an advertising and public relations firm specializing in real estate. As a freelance writer, she has been a frequent contributor to area lifestyle magazines, including *Metro Magazine*, *Hampton Roads Magazine* and *Port Folio*. She is also the former editor of a bi-weekly real estate magazine, *Home Search*, published by the *Virginian-Pilot/Ledger-Star*.

Her best work to date is son Scott, a graduate of both University of Virginia and the Colgate Darden School of Business, now sharpening his own Insiders skills with his new bride, Monique, in Virginia Beach.

Following a bout of mid-life crisis, Suzy and her husband Rick live the enviable empty nester lifestyle between Norfolk's West Side and Tampa, Florida, where both continue to perfect the advanced art of casual exploration of the Insiders favorite haunts.

Sally Kirby Hartman first discovered Hampton Roads when she moved to Norfolk in 1985. She is public relations director for The Norfolk Foundation and a freelance writer who specializes in magazine and public relations work. She formerly was associate editor of *Virginia Business* magazine and editor of *Tidewater Virginian* magazine. She has won writing and editing awards from the National Federation of Press Women, Virginia Press Women, Arkansas Press Women and the Council on Foundations. Before becoming a diehard Virginian, Sally spent most of her life in Arkansas. She graduated from the University of Arkansas with a journalism degree and for several years was features editor of the *Arkansas Gazette*. She and her husband, Ron, have one son, Luke.

Acknowledgments

There are far too many people involved in this project to thank individually. However, you all have our gratitude for the information and tips you so eagerly shared. And, we appreciate the encouragement from everyone who asked how the book was going during these past few hectic months.

Sally thanks Gayle Donovan for the photo on the back cover. She also appreciates the help she received from Amy Jonak at the Norfolk Convention and Visitors Bureau, Kim Cosner at Brickell & Associates, Keith Toler at the Portsmouth Convention and Visitors Bureau, Beth Baker at the Norfolk Naval Base Public Affairs Office, H.L. and Linda Wilson of the Bibliopath Bookshop & Bindery, Mare Carmody of Eagle 97, Hubert Young of Young Properties, Peggy Haile at the Kirn Memorial Library, Patricia Rawls at the Business Consortium for Arts Support, Jim Raper of Zuni, Jim and Lisa Bacon of Richmond, Mike Kensler of the Chesapeake Bay Foundation and Suzanne Taylor of Virginia's Eastern Shore Tourism Commission. Sally especially thanks her husband, Ron, and son, Luke, for their patience, understanding and willingness to explore new places here at home.

In addition, Suzy thanks Cynthia Carter West, Norfolk Scope; Kristine Sturkie, Public Affairs Office, NEXCOM; and Pricilla Trinder, Prudential Decker Realty.

The Chesapeake Bay chapter could not have been written without the assistance of Gail Coleman, Cale Realty Company in Gloucester; Horace Williams and Patty McMichael; The Mathews Chamber of Commerce; and Maggie and Aubrey Ellis.

Suzy especially thanks her husband, Rick, for his unselfish contributions of research, astute observations and dishwashing during the writing of this guide, son, Scott, for sharing his enormous wealth of nightlife knowledge, and mother, Eleanor, for her spunky words of encouragement.

The Supplementary Publications Department of Richmond Newspapers would also like to thank Suzanne Taylor, Virginia's Eastern Shore Tourism Commission, The Norfolk Convention and Visitors Bureau, The Virginia Division of Tourism, Virginia Beach Convention and Visitor Development and The Virginia Department of Economic Development.

Photo: Richmond Newspapers

These crabs are caught in a crab pot off the Chesapeake Bay.

Table of Contents

Directory of Maps

Virginia's South Hampton Roads Area

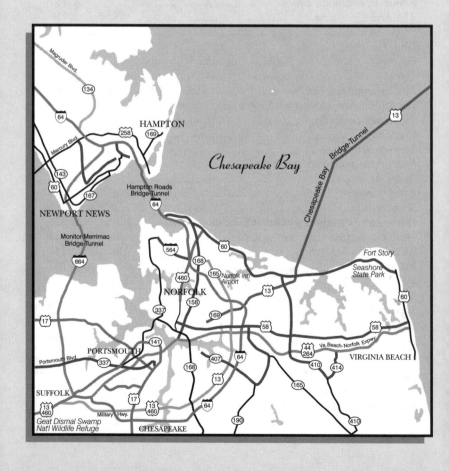

Downtown Norfolk

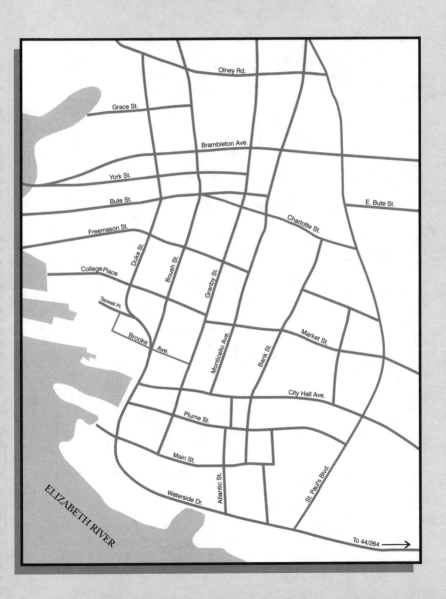

Virginia Beach

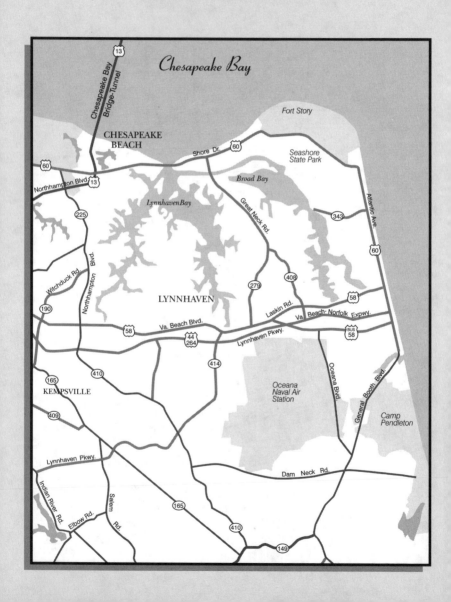

Greater Suffolk

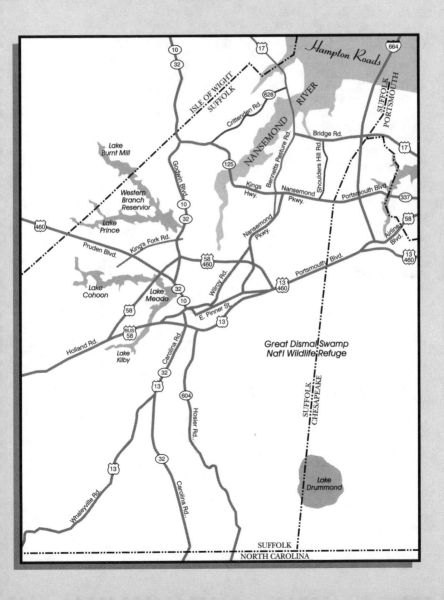

Greater Portsmouth

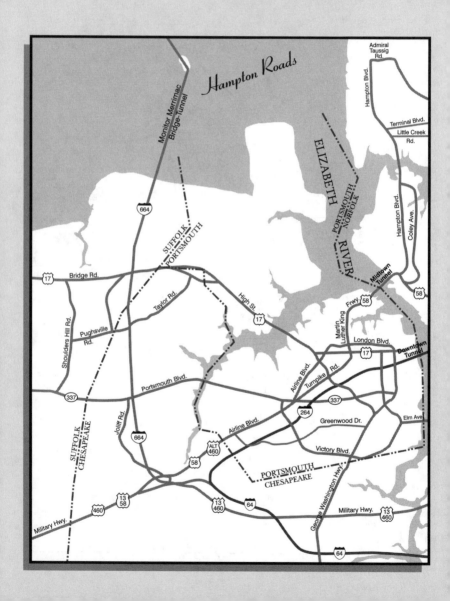

Greater Chesapeake

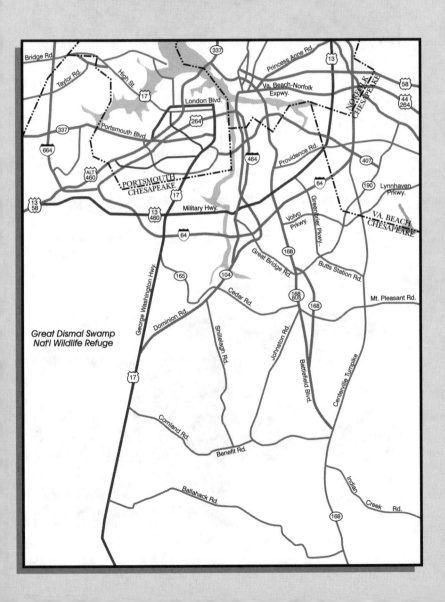

A couple takes a stroll under a romantic sunrise at Virginia Beach.

Inside
Area Overviews

Virginia's Chesapeake Bay region surrounds one of the country's most ecologically significant resources and one of its most scenic spots. Southeastern Virginia is where the bay begins its 200-mile journey from the Atlantic Ocean to Annapolis, Maryland. From its start near Norfolk and Virginia Beach, the bay continues its journey northward between Virginia's picturesque eastern and western shores.

Anchoring the southern end of the Chesapeake Bay is the Hampton Roads region. With both the bay and the Atlantic Ocean lapping at its shores, this is an area of beaches and tidal wetlands that also happens to be home to nearly 1.5 million people.

As a visitor or newcomer to Hampton Roads your mind will be boggled by all the terms you hear to describe this area: Southeastern Virginia, Hampton Roads, Tidewater, Southside, South Hampton Roads and Virginia Peninsula. To add to the confusion, residents often use specific names of the nine cities and six counties that make up this vast region of Virginia located where the Chesapeake Bay spills into the Atlantic ocean.

Ask residents where they're from and you'll get a boatload of answers depending on the circumstances. If they're in Illinois or New York, they'll probably say "Southeastern Virginia." If they're visiting Roanoke, Richmond or some other part of Virginia, they might say "Hampton Roads." If the question is asked at the opera, a corporate meeting or elsewhere in the region, the answer is likely to be "Portsmouth," "Virginia Beach" or another specific locality.

All the terminology is accurate. But in today's politically correct times there are some names for this 2,499-square-mile region that are "more correct" than others.

Geographically, this is Southeastern Virginia. Officially, it is the Norfolk-Virginia Beach-Newport News Metropolitan Statistical Area. This is the 27th most populous MSA in the country and the largest MSA between Washington and Atlanta. Hampton Roads is bigger than Sacramento but smaller than Indianapolis. Until 1983 the region was broken into two MSAs — South Hampton Roads and the Virginia Peninsula. The two areas are physically divided by the James River and the body of water known as Hampton Roads. To some extent, residents still feel loyalty to one side or the other.

The politically correct term for this region is Hampton Roads. In the 17th century this name was given to the body of water where the James, Elizabeth and Nansemond rivers flow into the Chesapeake Bay to form the world's finest deep-water harbor. The name "Hampton" honors Henry Wriothesley, the Earl of Southampton, who supported the colonization of Virginia in the early 17th century.

In past decades, the term "Tidewater" was frequently used for this coastal plain as well as adjacent regions that stretch along the York and James rivers.

But since "Tidewater" conjures up negative images of mud flats and brackish water, its use has been discouraged in recent years.

In the 1980s, economic developers started touting "Hampton Roads" as the name for the entire region, which includes Norfolk, Portsmouth, Chesapeake, Suffolk and Virginia Beach on the south side of the Hampton Roads Bridge-Tunnel. To the north are Hampton, Newport News, Poquoson, Williamsburg and the counties of James City, Gloucester and York. In 1993 the MSA expanded to include Isle of Wight County on the southside, Mathews County on the Peninsula and nearby Currituck County, NC. Since 1990 all the region's mail has been postmarked with "Hampton Roads" rather than the names of individual cities and counties.

For at least a decade, Hampton Roads has ranked second to Northern Virginia as the state's fastest growing region. It has six of the state's 10 largest cities, and Virginia Beach is No. 1 in population.

The region, which is crisscrossed by a half-dozen major rivers, feels more unified today than it did 10 years ago. New tunnel crossings link cities separated by rivers, and longtime tolls have been eliminated on them. Today it's common for residents to commute to work through a tunnel from Suffolk to Newport News or Hampton to Virginia Beach. Frequently when they're driving along Interstate 64 or other major arteries, residents aren't sure what city they're in. In October 1994 another barrier to regionalism fell when long-distance charges were removed between the Southside and the Peninsula and Cape Charles on the Eastern Shore. Soon the calling range will extend to Williamsburg. In the summer of 1995, the region's lone remaining toll road — the Norfolk-Virginia Beach Expressway — is destined to become a free ride.

To simplify matters for this Insiders' Guide, which concentrates on the five Southside cities, we'll use the names of specific cities if possible. When talking about the region, we'll call it Hampton Roads.

A Vast Region

Semantics aside, Hampton Roads is a fascinating, multifaceted area that prides itself on its remarkable history. The earliest recorded mention of the region was in 1607 when the first permanent colonists in the New World landed at Cape Henry in what is now Virginia Beach. Hampton Roads survived occupation during the Revolutionary War and the War Between the States. It stepped into modern times with quick buildups during World War I and World War II when thousands of military personnel and defense workers came here to work. Many of them liked the area enough to become permanent residents.

If there's one thing Hampton Roads is noted for, it is military might. The region's strategic East Coast location has

Insiders' Tips

Hampton Roads is about 90 miles southeast of Richmond and 185 miles south of Washington. Its borders touch the Atlantic Ocean, Chesapeake Bay and the North Carolina state line.

Photo:Norfolk Convention and Visitors Bureau

Norfolk is the home to Norfolk Naval Base, the world's largest Navy base.

helped it accumulate the world's largest concentration of naval operation. It also has bases representing every branch of the U.S. armed forces as well as the Armed Forces Staff College and the headquarters for the North Atlantic Treaty Organization (NATO). Nearly a third of the region's workers earn a paycheck from the Department of Defense or a private defense contractor.

Mainstays of the economy include shipbuilding and repair, service jobs, tourism and the port. Traditional industries, such as growing peanuts and tonging for oysters, remain the livelihood for some residents. Coal exports are as important to the busy Port of Hampton Roads as they were in the 1890s. These days the area is also a major port for container cargo as well as products such as grain, cocoa beans and rubber.

In recent years new industry has come into the region. There are high-tech Japanese companies in Chesapeake producing computer disks and copy machine parts. In the past five years Hampton Roads has become a hub for the service-oriented "fulfillment industry." Various companies use thousands of workers to process credit card transactions, take orders for merchandise and handle insurance claims.

Tourism is one of the most important segments of the economy. Each year more than 2.5 million visitors flock here to enjoy miles of shoreline extending along the Chesapeake Bay and the Atlantic Ocean. Besides soaking up the sun, visitors can tour a variety of museums and historic homes. They can fish for flounder or sea bass, relax on harbor cruises or exert themselves by windsurfing, parasailing or bungee jumping.

Excellent health care is a plus for Hampton Roads. The addition of Eastern Virginia Medical School in 1973 attracted experts in most medical fields, including heart transplants. The medical school has a well-respected in-vitro fertilization program that produced the United States' first test-tube baby in 1981. Recently, the school's researchers have been on the trail of a cure for diabetes. Area physicians, many of whom are on EVMS' faculty, attract patients from around the world for corrective urological surgery, sex-change operations and reconstructive surgery.

Diverse People

If you're a newcomer, you'll find plenty of company in Hampton Roads. Most residents have moved here from somewhere else. The region ranks second to Orlando, Florida, in the mobility of its residents. Some of these "come-heres" are retirees enjoying the good life along the area's waterways. Others are drawn by work at military bases, defense contracting firms or other private employers. During the 1980s the region added nearly 200,000 new jobs, and many workers who came then are still here.

Interspersed among the newcomers are natives who are fiercely proud of their region and the strides it has made in the past decades to improve itself. Because they're accustomed to the ebb and flow of military personnel, most old-timers quickly accept newcomers.

If you've just moved here, you may be surprised at how readily the Hampton Roads community will welcome your time and talents. The region is filled with tireless volunteers working for everything from the Virginia Opera to Habitat for Humanity. Even before you unpack, you may find yourself recruited to help plan a festival or raise funds for the children's hospital. Getting involved in committee work will speed up the process of feeling at home.

Although Hampton Roads doesn't have the ethnic enclaves of Boston or Baltimore, its citizens hail from diverse places. Its military residents have lived all over the world. There are thriving Filipino and Hispanic communities as well as a growing number of residents from India. During the last decade, the region had one of the country's fastest-growing Jewish populations. The 1990 census showed that 68 percent of the region's residents are Caucasian. However, in the last decade the region's African American population grew slightly faster than that of Caucasians.

City Rundown

Hampton Roads cities pride themselves on their individuality. Some were created centuries ago; others were formed as recently as the 1970s. They run the gamut from urban to suburban and downright rural. Sum up the strengths of the five southside cities, and you a have a vibrant region with something to offer everyone.

Norfolk

The region's oldest city dates back more than 300 years. During the past decade the city has seen decaying water-

---

Insiders' Tips

The region is blessed with a mild climate that can make a beach stroll a pleasant post-dinner activity on Thanksgiving and Christmas. There are four distinct seasons but rarely drastic extremes in temperature. The average January temperature is 40 degrees. The August average is 78 degrees.

front warehouses replaced by The Waterside festival marketplace as well as hotels, parks, attractions and new office buildings. In 1991 Norfolk gained a new 23-story Marriott hotel and adjacent convention center. In 1993 Harbor Park baseball stadium opened to much acclaim as the new home of the Triple-A Norfolk Tides. In 1994 the city finished its crown jewel — the $52 million National Maritime Center (Nauticus). Now it is ready to start construction on a gigantic downtown shopping mall that will have anchor luxury stores Nordstrom's and Macy's when it opens in a few years. Already under construction downtown is a branch campus of Tidewater Community College.

Norfolk, with a population of 250,300, is Virginia's second-largest city. Its downtown is the region's financial hub. Within a two-block radius are regional headquarters for all the major banks in the state. One of the gleaming downtown highrises is headquarters for Norfolk Southern Corp., whose rail lines run through 20 states and Canada. Old Dominion University (ODU), Virginia Wesleyan College, Eastern Virginia Medical School (EVMS) and Norfolk State University (NSU) have their campuses here. Norfolk International Terminals is the state's largest marine terminal.

The city is home to Norfolk Naval Base, the world's largest Navy base. Norfolk is also the region's cultural core and is home base for the Virginia Symphony, Virginia Stage Company, Virginia Opera and numerous smaller arts groups. On the weekends, Norfolk is one of the most fun places to be with free festivals and other events scheduled on about 100 days of the year. Most are held at Town Point Park, adjacent to the Waterside.

Virginia Beach

With 409,900 residents, Virginia Beach is Virginia's most-populous city. This often surprises visitors focused on the city's resort strip and its 38 miles of Atlantic Ocean and Chesapeake Bay beaches. Although tourism is the city's No. 1 industry, there's much more to Virginia Beach than waffle houses, T-shirt shops and sunbathers.

Virginia Beach has more office buildings than any other city in the region as well as Lynnhaven Mall, the region's largest shopping center. Since this is a city with no traditional downtown, offices and stores have cropped up in suburban office parks. The city has numerous manufacturers and distributors. Stihl chain saws are made here, and Lillian Vernon Corp. ships millions of catalog orders from its distribution center.

Virginia Beach also maintains its traditional agricultural base. Ride the roads

Remember that the wind blowing off the ocean or bay can make winter temperatures feel much colder. In summer, high humidity can make you swelter. With an average rainfall of about 56 inches, be sure to pack an umbrella, especially during winter and spring.

Insiders' Tips

out to Pungo and Sandbridge, and you'll be amazed to learn you're still within the city limits. Stretching for miles are horse farms and fields of soybeans and strawberries. This agricultural heritage dates back centuries before the current city of Virginia Beach was formed in 1963 from the merger of vast Princess Anne County and the tiny resort community of Virginia Beach.

The city also is home to The Christian Broadcasting Network and spin-off operations. Rev. M.G. "Pat" Robertson lives on the elegant grounds of CBN, where the "700 Club" show is produced. CBN is home to the fast-growing Family Channel and Regent University as well as a hotel with a AAA four-diamond rating. Other educational institutions in the city include Tidewater Community College and Virginia Wesleyan College.

Portsmouth

With 103,800 residents, this is one of the region's most charming cities. The Olde Towne Historic District adjacent to downtown has the largest collection of historic homes between Alexandria, Virginia, and Charleston. Portsmouth has more houses on the National Register of Historic Places than any other Virginia city.

Adjacent to the restored 18th-century neighborhood are several museums, including a delightful one for children that in late 1994 completed a major expansion and relocation. On the banks of downtown's Elizabeth River is Portside,

an outdoor festival marketplace. A double-decker ferry regularly churns the waters between Portside and Waterside, across the river in Norfolk.

The federal government is the main employer in Portsmouth. The Norfolk Naval Shipyard, the world's largest ship repair yard, is here. Also in the city is the Portsmouth Naval Hospital, the Navy's first hospital. Already the largest Navy hospital on the East Coast, the hospital is in the midst of a multi-year expansion. Portsmouth also has a major Coast Guard installation and a branch of Tidewater Community College.

In addition to government operations, Portsmouth has the Portsmouth Marine Terminal and a strong manufacturing base. Among the products made in the city are Hoechst Celanese fibers.

Suffolk

With 430 square miles, Suffolk is Virginia's largest city in land mass. The city is renowned for its peanuts, which flourish in its rich soil, and calls itself "The Peanut Capital of the World." The peanut is the backbone of the city's long-standing agribusiness sector, which includes four shelling companies and six major processors. Planters Peanuts started in the city — as did its mascot Mr. Peanut. Planters, a major employer, roasts peanuts in its plant and gives Suffolk a pleasant aroma.

Besides peanuts, Suffolk manufactur-

Did you know that:

- Norfolk has the world's largest Navy base.
- Portsmouth is home to the world's biggest ship-repair yard.
- Suffolk is the Peanut Capital of the World.
- The Port of Hampton Roads exports more coal and imports more cocoa beans and rubber than any other U.S. port.
- The United States' first in-vitro baby was born in Norfolk in 1981 with the help of Eastern Virginia Medical School.
- Norfolk is mile zero for the 1,095-mile Atlantic Intracoastal Waterway, which takes boaters to Miami.
- With nine underwater tunnels, the region ranks second to Japan as the world leader in tunnels.

ing plants produce Lipton tea and Hills Bros. coffee. The city has a mammoth distribution center that ships merchandise for QVC, the country's largest TV home shopping channel. Suffolk also has a branch of Paul D. Camp Community College.

Suffolk, which has 53,100 residents, maintains a traditional downtown. It also is gearing up for development in outlying areas near the Monitor-Merrimac Memorial Bridge-Tunnel, which opened in early 1992. The tunnel links Suffolk with Newport News, and eager developers have staked their claims on thousands of prime acres near the tunnel. Already Suffolk is leading other cities in percentage increase in residential building permits.

Chesapeake

Once the site of the East Coast's largest plant nursery, Chesapeake has been Hampton Roads' boomtown during the past nine years. Although Chesapeake maintains a strong agricultural base, in recent years it has sprouted subdivisions,

shopping malls, office parks and manufacturing plants. The city has Virginia's fastest-growing school district.

Like Virginia Beach, the city of 164,000 has no traditional downtown. Its business hubs are clustered around exits off Interstate 64. Two manufacturers have their North American headquarters in the city. Sumitomo Machinery Corp. of America, makes industrial drives while Volvo Penta North America produces marine engines. Sumitomo is one of several Japanese manufacturers with plants in Chesapeake. The city also has numerous distributors and service companies. Among the largest is Household Finance Corp., which built its East Coast processing center in Chesapeake several years ago.

Chesapeake has two of the region's newest shopping malls — Greenbrier and Chesapeake Square. As a booming shopping hub, it keeps adding new retail centers and restaurants. The city has a branch campus of Tidewater Community College. Popular recreational areas include the Great Dismal Swamp National Wildlife Refuge and Northwest River Park.

Photo: Virginia Beach Convention and Tourist Development

*The Norwegian Lady statue commemorates the wreck of a Norwegian ship off
Virginia Beach's shore in 1819.*

Inside
History

Water and war. These two factors are intertwined in the history of Virginia Beach, Norfolk and the neighboring cities of Portsmouth, Chesapeake and Suffolk. Since the 17th century, the region's location on the Chesapeake Bay and the Atlantic Ocean have made it a prime trading partner with the world. Having one of the finest deep-water harbors has pushed Hampton Roads into a key player in every war from the Revolutionary War to the Persian Gulf conflict of 1990.

Until April 26, 1607, this wooded coastal plain, commonly known as Hampton Roads, was home to about 18,000 Native Americans. The Algonquin, the Nansemond and the Chesapeake tribes thrived on oysters and fish harvested from the ocean, the bay and their many tributaries as well as on crops sprung from rich soil. On that spring day in 1607 when the Indians' world changed, three small ships carrying 104 Englishmen led by Adm. Christopher Newport sailed to what is now Cape Henry in Virginia Beach. Twenty-eight explorers ventured ashore, fell to their knees and thanked God for carrying them safely to land. That night they were attacked by the Chesapeake Indians.

The next day the newcomers hiked for 8 miles, frightening Native Americans tending a smoldering fire. The explorers raked aside coals and sampled their first delicacy in this new land — roasted Lynnhaven oysters. The third day the group ventured about 50 miles to Jamestown Island where they established the first permanent English settlement in America. They later returned to hammer a wooden cross at their landing spot at Cape Henry, where the Chesapeake Bay flows into the Atlantic Ocean.

Capt. George Percy, a member of the expedition, wrote of his first encounter with Virginia, "There we landed and discovered fair meadows and goodly tall trees with such fresh water running through the woods so I was almost ravished at the first sight thereof."

To the British, Virginia's land was so abundant that they eagerly granted colonists 100 acres to establish plantations. By 1634 Virginia was divided into eight counties, and several settlements had sprung up along the region's river banks. Within four years smaller counties were created. Suffolk fell into Upper Norfolk County, which became Nansemond County a few years later. The rest of South Hampton Roads ended up in Lower Norfolk County, which later yielded Princess Anne County, Norfolk County and several cities. By 1703 Virginia had a population of 60,606 living in 25 counties. Norfolk County had 2,279 residents; neighboring Princess Anne County was home to 2,017 people.

Norfolk was chartered as a town in 1682 when 10,000 pounds of tobacco was paid to Nicholas Wise Jr. for 50 acres to lay out a town. Norfolk, which became a borough in 1736, is the region's oldest city. Suffolk was incorporated along the Nansemond River in 1742. Portsmouth, across the Elizabeth River from Norfolk,

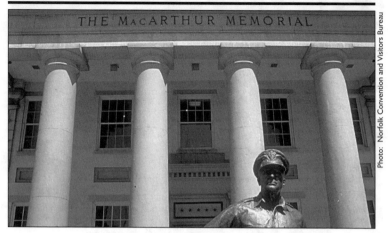

Photo: Norfolk Convention and Visitors Bureau

Norfolk's Douglas MacArthur Memorial Museum is the resting place of the famous military general. The city is his mother's childhood home.

officially became a town in 1752 when 65 acres was set aside for a community named after the famous English seaport. Virginia Beach, Chesapeake and the modern city of Suffolk are the region's newest municipalities. Virginia Beach and Chesapeake were created in 1963 by merging large counties with smaller towns. The current city of Suffolk was formed in 1974 by merging a smaller town of Suffolk with vast Nansemond County.

In the 17th and early 18th centuries, tobacco was the mainstay of the local economy. Farmers grew the cash crop along the region's numerous rivers, cured it and shipped it overseas from their private wharves. By 1736, foreign trade had helped make Norfolk the largest town in Virginia, with 1,000 residents. Thirty-three years later its population had swelled to 6,000.

During this time the region was plagued by pirates who plundered ships coming into the port. The most famous was Blackbeard, who built his headquarters in what is now Virginia Beach.

In 1763 George Washington surveyed land in what is now Chesapeake and Suffolk for the Dismal Swamp Land Co. He dug the first spade of dirt to create a canal through the Great Dismal Swamp, a 200,000-acre wilderness area.

As the region's prominence as a world port grew, local docks bulged with turpentine, cheese, corn, lumber and other products awaiting export. Besides Europe, the region had a thriving trade with the West Indies. In 1767 Andrew Sprowle, a merchant and shipbuilder, started Gosport Shipyard near Portsmouth. By the late 1700s three-fourths of Portsmouth's land owners worked in the maritime trade as merchants, shipwrights or other craftsmen.

Revolutionary War

The region's harbor and its proximity to Williamsburg, meeting site of the First Continental Congress in 1774, made it an important player during the Revolutionary War. Since Virginia had the strongest navy of the 13 original colonies, this area's harbor was vital to winning freedom for the colonies.

That fact wasn't lost on the British. In November 1775 Lord Dunmore, the last royal governor of Virginia, captured Portsmouth and boasted that Norfolk was defenseless. Less than a month later, the British were defeated at the Battle of Great Bridge, near the current site of Chesapeake's city hall. Lord Dunmore's only victory had already come during a battle at Kempsville in 1775, in what is now one of Virginia Beach's most populous neighborhoods.

New Year's Day 1776 was the most fateful day in Norfolk's history. In the afternoon British soldiers opened fire on the city and continued their assault for 11 hours. With the wind whipping flames, two-thirds of the city was destroyed. By the end of February, colonists had torched the rest of Norfolk. The government of Virginia ordered the second burning to prevent sheltering Lord Dunmore and his soldiers. Of more than 1,300 Norfolk buildings only the brick walls of St. Paul's Church remained. Even they were marred by a cannon ball wedged in one side. Norfolk held the dubious distinction of being the most devastated community in the colonies during the Revolutionary War.

To try and protect the harbor, in early 1776 the Commonwealth of Virginia ordered the construction of Fort Norfolk. Across the Elizabeth River from it, the commonwealth established Fort Nelson in Portsmouth.

During the war the Gosport Shipyard in Portsmouth was one of the busiest places in the colonies. The British burned the yard in 1776 but the colonists quickly built new wharves and scaffolding so they could produce new ships. Although the British were routed from Hampton Roads by the burning of Norfolk in 1776, they returned in 1779 and took over Ports- mouth. They promptly proceeded to ransack homes and burn ships anchored in the harbor. Suffolk also was burned in 1779 during a raid that originated in Portsmouth. The traitor Benedict Arnold set up headquarters in Portsmouth in 1781 before moving 50 miles away to Yorktown with Lord Cornwallis, who surrendered there a few months later.

After the war, the region started the arduous task of rebuilding. Former residents were aided by European immigrants, many of them merchants, who saw opportunity in America. Within a few years Norfolk regained its role as a major world port. Suffolk came alive when it was designated as a port of delivery in the Customs District of Norfolk and Portsmouth.

During this time of reconstruction several major projects were built. The Cape Henry Lighthouse, which had been started before the Revolutionary War, was completed in 1791 under orders from President George Washington. Today the Virginia Beach landmark is the oldest public works project in the country. In 1794 the federal government took over Gosport Shipyard, although it didn't actually buy it until 1801. The yard later was named the Norfolk Naval Shipyard even though it was located in Portsmouth.

In Norfolk, Congress authorized Washington to build a new fort to protect the harbor. In 1795 the government paid 200 pounds of sterling for the dilapidated Fort Norfolk. Permanent brick buildings were constructed around 1810 in anticipation of another war with the British. The region had rebounded from the Revolutionary War when trade restrictions imposed because of the War of 1812 torpedoed foreign trade.

In 1825 there was great fanfare in the region when the Marquis de Lafayette, the French general who had aided the country during the Revolutionary War, visited here as part of his farewell tour of 24 states.

By 1851 the Norfolk and Western Railway had laid track in the region and managed to put a roadbed through the Dismal Swamp.

Prosperity had returned by 1855 when the area was devastated by yellow fever. In June mosquitoes breeding in the hold of a steamer from St. Thomas escaped and wreaked havoc, particularly upon Portsmouth and Norfolk. Within two months all business in Norfolk stopped. Hotels, homes and warehouses were turned into hospitals as up to 100 residents a day died. Only one ship was allowed into the harbor, and its sole cargo was coffins. When those ran out, residents were buried in boxes or blankets sometimes in mass graves. By the end of the plague four months later, 2,000 were dead in Norfolk — one-third of the population. In neighboring Portsmouth yellow fever killed more than 1,000 residents.

At War Again

The region again flexed its military muscle during the War Between the States. On April 12, 1861, it didn't take long for news to arrive that the Confederates had fired on Charleston's Fort Sumter. That day the Confederate flag was raised at the blockhouse on Craney Island near Portsmouth. On April 17, Virginia became the eighth state to secede from the union. Three days later Union soldiers fled the Navy yard in Portsmouth, burning buildings and 11 warships as they escaped.

One of the first battles was the little-known Battle of Sewell's Point in May 1861. There were no fatalities as local Confederates skirmished with federal troops stationed across the water at Fort Monroe in what is now Hampton.

By November, 1861, more than 20,000 Confederate soldiers were stationed in Portsmouth at the Navy yard, which was at work on eight Confederate vessels. The most famous was the USS *Virginia*, which was forged from the partially burned hull of the ironclad USS *Merrimac*. The *Merrimac's* historic battle of the ironclads with the USS *Monitor* took place March 9, 1862, in the waters between Norfolk and Hampton. Four hours later the *Monitor* retreated to Fort Monroe, the last Union stronghold in Hampton Roads. Later that year the *Merrimac* ran aground at Craney Island and was blown up by its crew. Fourteen years later its hull was salvaged and hacked up with a few pieces remaining as relics.

In May 1862, the Confederates ordered residents of Portsmouth, Suffolk and Norfolk to evacuate. They burned the Portsmouth Navy Yard to save it from federal troops landing at Ocean View, a Chesapeake Bay community that is now part of Norfolk.

At the start of the war, Suffolk was a training ground for Confederate soldiers from Georgia and South Carolina. But soon the town was occupied by Union soldiers, just like nearby Norfolk and Portsmouth. This was a humiliating time for these three cities. Federal troops ransacked homes and forced ferry passengers to trample on the Confederate flag.

After Confederate Gen. Robert E. Lee surrendered in Appomattox, Virginia, in 1865, the Hampton Roads area began the arduous task of reconstruction. There was no money in Portsmouth's treasury, and the city's Navy yard was in shambles. Norfolk buildings were dilapidated, and the city's foreign trade was nonexistent. There were only 300 residents left in Suffolk, which had boasted a population of 1,395 in 1860.

In the two decades after the end of the war, the region did an about-face. Brick three-story buildings soon lined the streets of downtown Norfolk as carts loaded with oysters, chickens and other provisions rolled toward the city's many hotels and popular farmer's market. Steamships regularly called on the port, and a new rail line linked the city with distant parts of the country.

Although cotton was the main export commodity after the war, that changed in 1883 when the Norfolk and Great Western Railway shipped its first load of coal from western Virginia to Norfolk. To keep pace with demand, the railroad built a new coal pier at Lambert's Point in Norfolk. In 1886 the railroad brought in 504,153 tons of coal. By 1889 trains were hauling more than 1 million tons into Norfolk. At Lambert's Point workers loaded coal on ships bound for overseas or other parts of the United States.

Two other railroads — the Chesapeake & Ohio and the Virginian — also hauled coal into Norfolk and Newport News, making Hampton Roads the world's largest coal port. A constant line of coal trains became a common sight for local residents.

During this period, Virginia Beach also witnessed major changes. In 1880 a wooden clubhouse was built at 17th Street and the Oceanfront to entice beachgoers. Three years later a railroad line from Norfolk to Virginia Beach provided an easy way for city dwellers to get to the new Virginia Beach Hotel, which held 75 guests. Soon steamers were transporting vacationers down the Chesapeake Bay from as far away as Washington, D.C., and Baltimore.

In 1887 the hotel was enlarged to hold 400 and renamed the Princess Anne Hotel. The luxury resort boasted electric lights, elevators, saltwater baths and the top bands of the day. Guests included Presidents Benjamin Harrison and Grover Cleveland as well as inventor Alexander Graham Bell and actor Lionel Barrymore. The hotel burned in 1907, was replaced in 1922 and burned again in 1955.

By 1888 leading Norfolk area citizens had begun building large cottages with

---

Recently discovered in Suffolk are 408 significant archeological sites dating back 10,000 years. Most are located along the Nansemond River or the edge of the Great Dismal Swamp.

Insiders' Tips

sweeping verandas along a new board-walk on the beach. In 1906 Virginia Beach incorporated as a city and continued growing as a resort with the opening of Seaside Park Casino. The resort was re-nowned for its Peacock Ballroom, which bragged it had the largest dance floor on the East Coast. During the 1920s and '30s the lively resort featured such well-known band leaders as Tommy Dorsey, Duke Ellington and Cab Callaway. Their bands drew big crowds for the ballroom's popu-lar 10¢ dances (or three for 25¢).

Jamestown Exposition

One of the biggest regional events of the early 20th century was the Jamestown Exposition, held near Norfolk in 1907 to commemorate the 300th anniversary of the settlement of Jamestown. The Expo-sition site was 340 acres at Sewells Point, 10 miles from downtown Norfolk. Local organizers, who had raised $1 million in stock to help fund the Exposition, spent several years erecting a mini-city on marshland and pastures. To celebrate the event, 21 states built replicas of famous buildings such as Independence Hall in Pennsylvania and the Old State House in Massachusetts. Entire halls were de-voted to manufacturing, transportation and art.

The Exposition opened April 26, 1907, with a 100-gun salute as President Theodore Roosevelt arrived on the *May-flower*, the presidential yacht. During a parade 14,000 soldiers saluted Roosevelt, who called the event the greatest military pageant witnessed in the country since the War Between the States.

Although foreign dignitaries con-verged on the exposition during its seven-month run, the elaborate event was not financially successful. A decade later, just months after the start of World War I,

the Exposition site was included in 474 acres purchased by the federal govern-ment for $1.2 million. Its destiny was to become Norfolk Naval Base — the world's largest Navy base. Its develop-ment started with $1.6 million allocated in 1917 to build piers and buildings. About 20 of the original Jamestown Ex-position buildings are still in use on the Navy base.

World War I

In 1914, as the world stood on the brink of war, the Army took over 343 acres of Cape Henry to build Fort Story in what is now Virginia Beach. Fortified with 16-inch howitzers, during World War I Fort Story was known as the "American Gibraltar." It was considered the Atlantic coast's most strategic heavy artillery forti-fication. As the Army expanded onto sur-rounding land, the fort's prominence con-tinued to grow.

The impending world war first touched Portsmouth in 1915 when two German ships were interned in the city. After war was declared in 1917 the Navy yard saw unprecedented growth as three drydocks, four destroyers and a battleship were built. To keep pace, thousands of workers from throughout the country flooded the city. The city's naval hospi-tal, established in 1827 as the Navy's first hospital, quickly expanded into the larg-est naval hospital on the Atlantic coast. In 1915 Portsmouth had a population of 38,000. By 1918, it was home to about 57,000 residents. At Norfolk Naval Ship-yard, employment surged from 2,700 be-fore the war to 11,234 in 1919.

Norfolk also experienced dramatic growth during the war. Within a month in 1917 a training camp for 7,500 soldiers had been completed at the old Jamestown Exposition site. After hastily erecting bar-

The Norfolk Mace

The most prized possession in Norfolk is its sterling silver mace. The ceremonial symbol of power was presented to the Borough of Norfolk in 1754 by Virginia's Lt. Gov. Robert Dinwiddie. South Carolina is the only

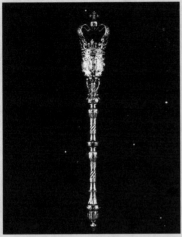

other American owner of a British-made mace from the 18th century.

Norfolk's mace is 41 inches long and weighs 6½ pounds. Inscribed on it are the initials of silversmith Fuller White of London. It also bears an etching of a lion, showing it is pure silver, as well as emblems of England, Scotland, France and Ireland. During the burning of Norfolk in 1776, residents hid the mace in what is now the Kempsville area of Virginia Beach.

The mace was used in 1836 to celebrate the 100th anniversary of Norfolk's charter as a borough. It made an appearance in 1857 during the 250th anniversary of the landing at Jamestown. In 1862 Norfolk's mayor hid the mace under his hearth to protect it from Union soldiers occupying the city during the War Between the States.

No one paid much attention to the mace after the war. In 1894 Norfolk's police chief found it lying in disrepair in a back room of the police station. Norfolk National Bank (now NationsBank) arranged to repair the mace and store it. In 1925 a group of Norfolk 3rd graders raised money for a bag to protect the mace.

The mace now resides in a second-floor gallery in The Chrysler Museum, which is open Tuesday through Sunday. During city parades and other official occasions, police officers lead processions by solemnly carrying a replica of the mace.

racks, warehouses and mess halls, the Navy built a bulkhead, dredged channels and filled in enough areas to add 300 acres to the Navy base. After a year's work the base had built a submarine base, landing fields for airplanes and dirigibles and hundreds of buildings.

Like Portsmouth, Norfolk also had an influx of workers from throughout the country. Besides the military, Norfolk gained numerous private manufacturing plants. In 1910 the city's population was 67,452. By 1920 it had swelled to 115,777.

World War I gave a great boost to the region's port. With northern ports in New York and other large cities unable to handle increased demand, Norfolk and nearby Newport News filled the gap.

Their proximity to the Atlantic and eight area rail lines attracted an endless parade of ships from throughout the world. They came primarily for coal that arrived day and night from West Virginia. Other export commodities included tobacco, cotton and seafood. Norfolk's port also was used heavily by the Naval Overseas Transportation Service, which sent 288,000 soldiers and their provisions to France.

The postwar years were a jolt for the region as it recovered from the days of heady prosperity. To keep solid economic footing, Norfolk residents approved a $5 million bond issue in 1922 that created a grain elevator and terminal. The city built a modern downtown farmer's market that cost $500,000. It annexed 27 square miles of adjacent land, including the Navy base and Ocean View resort area.

During the Great Depression, which started in 1929, the region weathered the economic slowdown with help from the Navy. Naval operations gave Norfolk's economy a $20 million a year boost. The port also held its own. When coal exports plummeted, sugar exports picked up the slack. In Portsmouth a drop in employment at the Navy yard after World War I was offset by jobs modernizing 15 Navy ships. The 2,538 workers the yard had on the payroll in 1923 had grown to 7,625 by 1939.

Virginia Beach continued to court the resort trade with the completion in 1927 of The Cavalier, a luxury resort near the oceanfront. Agriculture was the mainstay of what is now Chesapeake, while peanuts and lumber remained the backbone of the economy in Suffolk.

World War II

Once again thousands of workers descended on the region during World War II. The Norfolk Naval Shipyard payroll jumped by more than 36,000 workers from 1939 to 1943 as nearly 1,000 workers a month joined the war effort. Employment reached a record high in 1943 with nearly 43,000 workers. To make room for the construction of the 101 ships and landing craft the yard turned out during the war, it expanded from 352 acres to 746 acres in Portsmouth. During the war, the Navy yard did nearly $1 billion in business — half of it going for workers' wages.

In Virginia Beach and Princess Anne County, three military bases were added

Insiders' Tips

For decades, drivers stopped at the busy intersection of Hampton Boulevard and Princess Anne Road in Norfolk wondered about the vacant patch of land on the corner. With the dedication of Yellow Fever Memorial Park in 1993, the barren spot was given new life. The lot in residential West Ghent was a mass burial ground in 1855 when a third of Norfolk's population died during a yellow fever epidemic. With the help of a $10,000 fund-raising effort by a local Brownie troop, the park has been outfitted with benches, a plaque and year-round plantings of yellow flowers and a fourth was consolidated from smaller operations. The Army leased a Virginia National Guard rifle range to start Camp Pendleton. The Navy built the Oceana air base and the Dam Neck base, which today handles data systems and missile operations. In 1945 the Navy merged four smaller bases into the Little Creek Amphibious Training Command. Off the coast of Virginia Beach, German U-boats patrolled the coast and occasionally sunk Allied ships.

During the war the region benefited greatly from the $12 million the Navy earmarked for construction at the Navy base and the Navy yard. Wooden buildings slapped up during World War I were replaced with solidly built brick and stone structures.

By 1941 apartments and houses were going up faster that they had in the past 20 years. The federal government, the Navy, the Norfolk and Portsmouth housing authorities, and private developers all hustled to build new homes. Although Norfolk had two new high schools, they quickly became overcrowded with military dependents. Some schools had to operate in shifts. City buses, restaurants and hospitals filled to capacity, and Norfolk had to quickly expand its water supply. To the rest of the nation, Norfolk was a prime example of wartime overcrowding.

From 1940 to 1944 Norfolk's population swelled by 44,000. As defense workers searched far and wide for housing, adjacent Norfolk County added more than 40,000 new residents. Portsmouth gained 13,000 residents; Princess Anne County grew by 5,000.

Although ship building and ship repair were the area's claim to fame during the war, the region's fertilizer plants, furniture manufacturers and other industries also were expanding. During the war, the threat of German U-boats off the coast torpedoed much of the area's commercial foreign trade. But the port made up for that by shipping tanks, bombs and other military supplies to Europe and North Africa.

Postwar Years

After World War II — the fifth major war to have an impact on the region — thousands of wartime workers stayed in Hampton Roads. To keep from falling into a postwar slump, city leaders started aggressively modernizing the region. Norfolk initiated a campaign to annex neighboring counties, a move frequently met with opposition by people living near the land-hungry city.

Intercity transportation was a key issue during postwar years. Ferries still connected many parts of the region. To speed car travel, the Elizabeth River Tunnel opened in 1952 between Norfolk and Portsmouth. The success of the region's first underground roadway led to another tunnel between the two cities in 1962. In 1957 Norfolk linked to Hampton via the new Hampton Roads Bridge-Tunnel. At the time its 6,860-foot tunnel was the longest of its type in the world.

As marvelous as those accomplishments were, they paled in comparison to the Chesapeake Bay Bridge-Tunnel. Construction on the 17.6-mile roadway started in 1961. It took 3½ years before Virginia Beach was linked with the isolated Eastern Shore of Virginia. For drivers the bridge-tunnel cut 90 minutes off the drive from Virginia Beach to New York. The feat cost $200 million and required two mile-long tunnels, three bridges, four man-made islands and a causeway. The bridge-tunnel is considered one of the seven modern wonders of the world. Today it is at the start of another round of construction that will add new bridges to the tunnel complex.

Mergers were major news in the early 1960s as large counties and small cities struggled to combat Norfolk's annexation mania. As a result, in 1963 the resort town of Virginia Beach annexed rural Princess Anne County and instantly became a city of 125,000. The same year South Norfolk merged with agricultural Norfolk County to form Chesapeake. In 1974 Suffolk merged with Nansemond County to create the new city of Suffolk. The mergers left south Hampton Roads with five cities and no counties and signaled a new era of growth and prosperity.

In recent years the region's history has been shaped by the rejuvenation of Norfolk and Portsmouth and the coming of age of Virginia Beach, Chesapeake and Suffolk. In the 1960s civic leaders banded together to create Eastern Virginia Medical School. The state's third medical college opened in 1973 in Norfolk and is in the heart of a burgeoning medical center that includes two hospitals and several research institutes affiliated with the medical school.

The Witchcraft Trials

By the early 17th century Virginians were swept up in the frenzy of witchcraft trials that gripped Salem, Massachusetts.

In 1655 Lower Norfolk Court, which contained what is now Virginia Beach, Norfolk, Portsmouth and Chesapeake, enacted a law stating that anyone making a charge of witchcraft was liable for a fine or court censure if the charge couldn't be proven. As a result witchcraft counter-lawsuits seemed to come out of the woodwork.

The star case was that of Grace Sherwood, a resident of the Pungo area of what is now Virginia Beach. Grace, a carpenter's wife and mother of three sons, was charged with witchcraft in 1697. When she sued her accuser for defamation, the case was settled without trial. In 1687 Grace and her husband James sued another couple for slander for accusing Grace of being bewitching the couple's cotton.

Grace was named in two other suits, including one that accused her of riding and whipping the plaintiff and sneaking out a key hole like a black cat. In 1706 after several searches, the county court ordered Grace to "be tried in ye water by Ducking." The dunking took place in July 1706 in the Lynnhaven River.

Grace was tied with ropes with her right thumb touching her left big toe and her left thumb tied to her right big toe. Trussed like a turkey, Grace was tossed in the river in front of hundreds of curious onlookers. Because she did not sink, Grace failed the trial by water and was immediately jailed. She later was released and sent home to live without further recorded incident.

Although Grace Sherwood died in 1740, her legacy lives on in Witchduck Road, a major thoroughfare in Virginia Beach. The site of Grace's dunking is known as Witchduck Point. The house where she's rumored to have lived was standing until only a few year ago when a fire destroyed it.

During the 1970s and early 1980s dilapidated buildings along Norfolk's downtown waterfront were razed to make way for The Waterside festival marketplace, Town Point Park, elegant condominiums and Dominion Tower. The new National Maritime Center (Nauticus) and Harbor Park baseball stadium now anchor either end of the rejuvenated waterfront. A mile away blocks of substandard housing were torn down to create the upscale Ghent Square area. Nearby turn-of-the-century homes in Ghent attracted new residents eager to restore their splendor. Today the city is committed to the revitalization of Park Place, a low-income urban neighborhood, and Ocean View, whose hodgepodge of homes, motels and businesses occupy prime property along the Chesapeake Bay. It also is building a $270 million downtown shopping center and a downtown branch of Tidewater Community College.

Through the years Portsmouth, which has one of Virginia's largest collection of historic homes, has worked to ensure the preservation of Olde Towne. To complement this historic district, the city has gone through major improvements since the 1970s. Recently it has enhanced its downtown business district with wide brick sidewalks, period lighting and landscaped road dividers. Portsmouth's latest coup is the Children's Museum of Virginia, which in late 1994 expanded to 27,000 square feet downtown. The city's seawall along the Elizabeth River is home to Portside, an outdoor collection of restaurants and shops.

In the late 1980s Virginia Beach joined the revitalization movement with a $94 million face lift in its resort area. The effort added mini-parks, attractive lighting, benches and landscaping along Atlantic Avenue and the 2.9-mile oceanfront boardwalk. The city continues its efforts with plans for a new amphitheater, golf courses and other amenities.

In Chesapeake, Virginia Beach and Suffolk, which are blessed with many miles of farmland, the emphasis has been on new development during the past few decades. Agriculture remains important to the cities, whose major commodities include peanuts, soybeans, strawberries and hogs. However, the temptation to sell the family farm has turned many former fields into subdivisions and office parks in the past decade.

The entire region was an economic hotspot during the early 1980s when federal spending was on the upswing. With military rapidly expanding, eager defense contractors moved in to do business and

For quick insight into Norfolk, pick up a copy of "Walking Tours of Historic Norfolk." The brochure is produced by the Norfolk Convention & Visitors Bureau. Inside is a handy map of significant buildings downtown and in the Freemason and Ghent neighborhoods. The free guide also includes a synopsis of Norfolk's history as well as photos and tidbits about historic structures. Copies are available at the convention bureau, Gen. Douglas MacArthur Memorial, Moses Myers House, Chrysler Museum and d'Art Center.

Insiders' Tips

thousands of workers left tougher economies for the greener pastures of Hampton Roads. As a result neighborhoods, shopping centers and office parks sprung up across the land as the region added 200,000 new jobs during the 1980s.

Development moves at a less manic pace today as the region works to balance its economic prosperity with preservation of its environment. Water still plays a vital role in shaping Hampton Roads' history, as does war. During the Persian Gulf war in 1990 and 1991 more than 40,000 military personnel left the region for the Middle East. In addition, thousands of civil service workers and employees of area defense contractors also headed to the Persian Gulf. Half the warships in the Gulf were homeported here. When the war ended, the region celebrated with enthusiastic homecomings that harked back to World War II as bands, banners and tearful relatives welcomed home their heroes.

Today Hampton Roads' heritage is still visible despite the area's high-rise office towers, interstate highways and suburban homes. Its economy, although greatly diversified in recent years, remains rooted in the military and the port. Tourism, started along the Virginia Beach oceanfront in the late 19th century, is a cornerstone of the region's economy. And peanuts still give identity to Suffolk.

Like Hampton Roads' early explorers, many newcomers land here because of the area's proximity to the Atlantic Ocean and Chesapeake Bay. They like what they see and decide to make it their home.

Inside
Getting Around

Welcome to Hampton Roads, where getting from place to place requires going under, over, around, across or, in case of a thunderstorm, through water.

While our bridges, tunnels, major arteries and interstates have undergone extensive renovation and expansion in recent years, it is still wise to know the best times to venture out, especially if you're heading for major shopping centers or beaches. Because this is home to the largest military installation in the country, it is common wisdom to leave the driving to those headed to the bases in the morning, from 6 AM to 8 AM, and away from bases in the afternoon, from 3 PM to 5 PM. This translates to morning journeys north on Expressway-44 (read "distressway")/Interstate 64, and afternoon jaunts south on those same routes. The congestion periods hold for all tunnels connecting Norfolk to Portsmouth and Hampton. Helpful automated signs along the interstate system will alert you to pending backups, which can delay you an hour or more. If lights are flashing, you might consider following the alternate routes indicated by checkerboard directories on interstate signage. While normally longer in mileage than your original route, they will guide you around traffic gridlock to your escape route.

Most local radio stations are diligent in reporting backup alerts during rush

Photo: Virginia Beach Convention and Visitor Development

Biking is one of the best ways to get around the beach.

periods; AM 530, the state-operated station, broadcasts updates all day, though the signal doesn't carry too far beyond the interstate. For information anytime, day or night, you can also call (800) 792-2800.

For newcomers with a fear of merging, traveling on Hampton Roads' interstate system can be quite a thrill. Because of the diabolically designed entries and exits, use extreme caution when entering or exiting the interstate. Once safely in the flow, it may be helpful to note that you are actually going south when on Interstate 64 East and north on Interstate 64 West.

Enamored with the number "64," the Virginia Department of Transportation has named all the major connectors with that suffix. If I-64 is the wheel that circles the area, these are the "spokes": 464 is a quick, usually desolate, shot between Norfolk and Chesapeake; 664 is a new connector between 64 and the new Monitor-Merrimac Tunnel to the Peninsula; 564 zips you from I-64 to the Naval Base; and 264 takes you from the heartbeat of Downtown Norfolk to 64 where it magically changes to 44, the expressway to the Virginia Beach oceanfront.

Speaking of tolls, for those of you used to shucking out the quarters and dimes, as of summer 1995, you won't have to. By then, tolls on interstates in the region became a thing of the past.

The rules of the road in Hampton Roads are simple and straightforward. Seat belts are required for all vehicle occupants, and children younger than age 4 or less than 40 pounds must be secured in a child restraint or booster seat. As throughout Virginia, right turn on red after stopping is permitted unless otherwise indicated. One new law on the books is one you Type A drivers should note: It is

against Virginia law to cut through a parking lot to avoid a traffic light or stop signal. You'll just have to wait your turn like the rest of us.

Good news may lie ahead for those of us who must strap ourselves in our urban assault vehicles during rush hour. The grand sum of $6 million has just been approved to fund a three-year study that will place the area's traffic problems under a microscope and find state-of-the-art solutions. The end result might be anything: a new tunnel solely for high-speed rail; highways that monitor traffic via computers; a high-speed rail line and highway running from I-95 south of Richmond to Norfolk. Who knows? The best part about this study is that for the first time, there are no presumed outcomes, only the promise of an all-inclusive menu of possible changes and major road projects that solve congestion problems and link Hampton Roads to the rest of the world, even if that means utilizing technology that currently doesn't exist. Now, if that study will just explain why it's necessary to halt traffic to change light bulbs inside the tunnels, we'll all rest easier behind the wheel.

How To HOV

Spanning the distance from Virginia Beach to Norfolk and Chesapeake to the Naval Base is Hampton Roads' answer to rush hour frustrations — the HOV-2 system. The median on I-64 between the Rt. 44/I-64/264 Interchange and I-564 has been designated for vehicles with two or more persons headed westbound to the Naval Base in the morning, eastbound in the afternoon. Readerboards along the interstate system alert you to the traffic direction of the reversible lanes. Entry and exiting is limited, so unless you are really headed to or from the Base, sticking to the regular interstate with the masses might be your best option. All the details of HOV-2 are available from the Virginia Department of Transportation at 925-2584.

Let Someone Else Do The Driving

To avoid traffic trauma, you might want to consider putting someone else behind the wheel. Although buses are not the transportation vehicle of choice for the majority of Hampton Roaders, Tidewater Regional Transit, our local bus service, can scoot you along major highways for a base fare of $1.10 plus 50¢ for each additional zone. For some interstate-weary business and military folks, there is some interest in TRT's new Express Bus Service with 22 spanking new buses that will zip you to Downtown Norfolk or the Naval Base from two convenient Park & Ride locations: Pembroke Mall and Timberlake Shopping Center. A call to 623-RIDE can get you the complete schedule and pickup points.

If you're headed to someplace a little off the normal beaten track, a taxi is the answer. Unless you're at the airport, don't expect one to be just waiting for your fare. It's best to call one of the many companies listed in the phone book, and plan on adding enough time for them to arrive. Initial charges average $2.50 plus $1.25 for each mile thereafter.

From Memorial Day through Labor Day, if charm, not speed, is your fancy, you've got a ticket to ride on one of TRT's darling trolleys. While limited in travel, you can hop aboard for a trip along five Virginia Beach routes (50¢ to $1.75) or take a tour through historic Norfolk or Portsmouth ($3.50). Full information and trolley tokens are available at TRT booths at Waterside in Norfolk, Portside in Portsmouth or 27th at the Boardwalk in Virginia Beach.

The Resort Strip

Amazing what $94 million dollars can do. What we Insiders still call "The Strip" has been stripped of its gaudy redneck look and is being transformed to a squeaky-clean family resort. The widened Atlantic Avenue with its new street lights, charming street signs and plantings are a vision of a resort city determined to put its money where the tourists are.

Take note, this is a tourist alert! A Code has been entered into Virginia Beach law making "cruising" illegal. Cruising is the debatable pleasure of traveling up and down Atlantic Avenue to show off a hot vehicle or pick a date out of the pedestrian crowd. Now it's a no-no, and friendly Virginia Beach officers, staked out at control spots from the Rudee Inlet Loop through 31st Street, will be delighted to autograph a ticket if you're spotted traveling past a traffic control point two times in the same direction within any three hour period. The Cruising Law is in effect from 2 PM until 4 AM, April 15 through September 30, and was initiated to alleviate gridlock during the busy vacation period. Signs are clearly posted along the violation area, lest you forget.

Airports

NORFOLK INTERNATIONAL AIRPORT
Norview Ave.   857-3351

When headed for "ORF" — airline lingo for the Norfolk/Virginia Beach area — you'll most likely set down in an airport situated in the midst of acres of our gorgeous Norfolk Botanical Garden, quite a beautiful entry to our fair region. Norfolk International, home of the only permanent customs facility between Washington, D.C., and Atlanta, Georgia, is just 6 miles from Downtown Norfolk, and 15 miles from the Virginia Beach oceanfront, so getting from the airport to your destination is a quick and relatively painless trip.

More than 3.4 million harried passengers passed through electronic surveillance at Norfolk International last year alone. Served by most major carriers now in the midst of a fare war, you can hop a most affordable nonstop flight to Atlanta, Baltimore, Boston, Charlotte, Chicago, Cincinnati, Dallas-Fort Worth, Detroit, Manteo, N.C., Nashville, New York, Philadelphia, Raleigh-Durham, Richmond, St. Louis, Tampa and Washington, D.C.

Major carriers (as of this writing) include:

American	(800) 433-7300
Continental	(800) 525-0280
Delta	627-2145
Northwest	(800) 225-2525
TWA	(800) 221-2000
United	(800) 241-6522
USAir	(800) 428-4322

Commuter service is provided by American Eagle, Business Express, Northwest Airlink, TWA Express, United Express and USAir Express. Air charter service is provided by Piedmont Aviation Services, Inc.

The airport has completed an expansion that refurbished the main passenger terminal, added 10 new gates and built a new control tower. During the refurbishing, the Armed Services YMCA opened a Military Welcome Center in the airport. This is a lounge with a television and free coffee and soft drinks. Outside in the main lobby is a military information booth that has a staff person on duty who will also answer questions from civilians.

If you must park at the airport, there are two multilevel, covered parking garages and one open lot for long-term parking, and short-term open lots at both arrival and departure sides of the terminal. Overall, there are 4,000 spaces, so the parking nightmare typical of many other large airports just isn't a factor here. Expect to pay $1 an hour up to a maximum of $14 for short-term, 75¢ an hour up to a maximum of $5 per day for long-term. If you're lucky enough to find a curbside parking place, meters ask for 25¢ for 10 minutes. Cars with handicapped license plates park free.

If you're without personal transportation, taxis circle like vultures at the arrival side of the terminal, so you shouldn't have any trouble hailing one. The cost is about $18 to Downtown Norfolk and about $25 to the oceanfront in Virginia Beach. Taking the Norfolk Airport Shuttle costs about $11.50 to Downtown Norfolk and $15.50 to the oceanfront. To find a shuttle from the airport, check at the glassed-in booth in the median outside the baggage claim area. Some hotels also offer courtesy transportation to and from the airport; you might check on this when you make reservations. If you do need to make specific arrangements, here are a few numbers:

Norfolk Airport Shuttle	857-1231
Beach Taxi	486-4304
Yellow Cab	460-0605, 622-3232, 399-3077
Black & White	489-7777
B&W Cabs of Chesapeake	543-2727

And, for the truly decadent traveler:

Celebrity Limousine Service	853-5466
Executive Car Service	622-7441
Atlantic Beach Limousine	471-0068
Hollywood Limousines	481-9333

CHESAPEAKE MUNICIPAL AIRPORT
1777 West Rd.   *421-9000*

Owned and operated by the City of Chesapeake since 1979, this small airport is located just south of Great Bridge and is capable of handling small jets on its 4,200-foot runway. The facility is open to the public every day from 8 AM to sundown and has 100-octane, low-lead jet fuel. Pilots arriving after hours can call the number above 24-hours a day to make suitable arrangements.

Mid Eastern Airways (FBO) is responsible for the operation of the facility, which offers charter, flight school and major maintenance. Hanger space and rentals are also available, with a small pilot's lounge with all the basic layover amenities.

Pilots, take note. The identifier is W36, and there is no landing fee.

HAMPTON ROADS AIRPORT
5192 W. Military Hwy.   *488-1687*

With two asphalt runways and four reciprocals, Hampton Roads Airport offers runways from 3,500 to 4,000 feet. Mercury Flight Center is FBO at this general aviation airport in Chesapeake just past Bowers Hill off South Military Highway. Flight school, maintenance, hanger facilities and tie-downs are available. The airport is open from 8 AM to 5 PM daily and until 8 PM in the summer. It has 100-octane, low-lead fuel.

The Identifier is PVG, and no landing fee is required.

SUFFOLK MUNICIPAL AIRPORT
200 Airport Rd.   *539-8295*

This city-owned airport, which started in 1943, is on the outskirts of Suffolk. Three runways are in operation; two at 5,000 feet and one at 3,600 feet. Hours of operation are 8 AM to 8 PM from April through October and from 8 AM to 5 PM the rest of the year.

There are hangars, tie downs and a maintenance facility as well as 100-octane low-lead fuel. The airport's identifier is SFQ. The number above is available 24-hours a day. There is no landing fee.

Train Service

AMTRAK
9304 Warwick Blvd.
Newport News   *(800) 872-7245*

Service to Washington, D.C. includes daily departures at 7:55 AM and arrivals at 7:17 PM, Monday through Friday and 9:22 PM on Saturday and Sunday.

Travel By Water

THE ATLANTIC INTRACOASTAL WATERWAY

There's more to Hampton Roads travel than gridlocked interstates and backed-uped tunnels. You can escape it all when you travel on water. It may not be as quick as land or air travel, but it certainly is one of the greatest pleasures of living in this region of river, ocean and bay.

Connecting the area to destinations north and south are the Dismal Swamp Canal and the Albemarle & Chesapeake Canal, which form alternate routes along the Atlantic Intracoastal Waterway between the Chesapeake Bay and Albemarle Sound. The Atlantic Intracoastal Waterway provides pleasure boaters and commercial shippers with a protected inland channel between Norfolk and Miami, Florida.

The Dismal Swamp Canal, the oldest operating artificial waterway in the

United States, is on the National Register of Historic Places as a Historic Landmark, as well as being noted as a National Historic Civil Engineering Landmark. It is the primary course for recreational craft making a lazy journey from Deep Creek in Chesapeake down to the Pasquotank River in Elizabeth City, N.C., which in turn spills out to the Albemarle Sound. If you travel this route (along with the Yankee rich and famous steering their boats to warmer climates in fall and the reverse come springtime), be sure to stop at the Mariner's Wharf city docks for a visit with the famous Rose Buddies, Elizabeth City's self-appointed welcoming committee for visiting cruisers.

The second headwater canal is the Albemarle & Chesapeake, primarily used by commercial vessels. It weaves through the locks at Great Bridge out to the less protected waters of Currituck Sound and on through the locks at Coinjock, N.C., to the Albemarle Sound.

Both canals and the rest of the waterway are maintained by the United States Army Corps of Engineers. When navigating these waters, you should have both bow and stern lines ready when going though any locks, and reduce speed to

A Pronunciation Guide

Here's a quick way to tell newcomers from Hampton Roads natives. Just ask them to pronounce the name of area cities. OK, Virginia Beach and Chesapeake are pretty easy to fake. But Norfolk, Portsmouth and Suffolk can trip you up if you're not careful.

The region's British heritage remains emblazoned on many of its city and street names. The following guide will have you speaking like a native in no time.

Botetourt: bot-a-tot. Lord Botetourt was the Virginia Colony's governor from 1768 to 1770. In Norfolk there are at least two streets and an apartment complex named for him.

Boush: bush. This major downtown Norfolk artery has been called Boush Street since 1762. It was named for Samuel Boush, who was elected as the first Norfolk mayor but died in 1736 before he took office.

Greenwich Road: grin-ich. The name of this Virginia Beach road fouls up many a new broadcaster trying to talk intelligently about traffic tie-ups.

Monticello: Thomas Jefferson may have called his estate outside Charlottesville mont-a-chel-lo, but Monticello Avenue in Norfolk is pronounced mont-a-cell-o.

Norfolk: naw-fik. If you go calling this city Nor-folk, that's a dead giveaway that you're not from here. The name is borrowed from the British, who have a Norfolk County. Say the name rapidly, and you'll sound fine.

Portsmouth: ports-muth. Portsmouth, England was the namesake for this city. If you hear someone calling it porch-muth, you will have found a bona fide native who's lived here a lifetime.

Suffolk: suff-ik. This city also has a namesake in England. Like Norfolk, this is a city whose name should be said quickly.

eliminate wakes when approaching, motoring through or leaving the locks and bridge structures. You should also stay on the lookout for natural hazards, such as submerged stumps, rocks or logs.

For more information, including charts and available anchorages, contact the U. S. Army Corps of Engineers in Norfolk at 441-7606.

THE CHESAPEAKE BAY BRIDGE-TUNNEL

No discussion of the waterways of Hampton Roads would be complete without a mention of the Chesapeake Bay Bridge-Tunnel, acclaimed one of the Seven Wonders of the Modern World. Considered the world's largest bridge-tunnel complex, it consists of more than 12 miles of trestled roadways, two mile-long tunnels, two bridges, almost 2 miles of causeway, four man-made islands and 5.5 miles of approach roads, totalling an absolutely amazing 23 miles.

The bridge-tunnel connects Southside Hampton Roads to Virginia's Eastern Shore, and those headed north to New York can save 95 miles and 1½ hours by taking a ride across the mighty surge of the Atlantic Ocean and the waters of the Chesapeake Bay. If it is your first trip across the span, you might just want to add those hours back into your itinerary and stop off at the first island for a snack at the Sea Gull Restaurant, a walk down the busy fishing pier, or to snap up a T-shirt at the goodies-packed souvenir and gift shop.

Emergency road service is available, and there are call boxes every half-mile. One-way crossing toll is $10.

As of this writing, a second bridge that will parallel the first span is on the drawing boards. The new bridge would serve southbound traffic from the Eastern Shore, and completion is anticipated by April of 1999.

Gourmet seafood dishes are served in many area restaurants.

Inside
Restaurants

Let's face it. Hampton Roads is not the best place on earth to go on a diet. You've got your seafood, your corn-fed beef, your antipasto, your Peking duck and your burrito combo platter. You've got so much temptation whipped up by so many prime-time chefs that you could eat out three meals a day, seven days a week and never duplicate the menu.

Yes, when it comes to the practiced art of satiating hunger, the cart of many colors — and flavors — is ready to wheel in your direction. Whether you're in town for a night, a week's vacation or to snag a permanent address, you'll soon discover that only your taste buds know for sure where you'll wind up with a napkin in your lap. While delicacies from the deep take top banana in many of our most favorite places, you can broaden your appetite horizons by sampling some of the best ethnic, Mexican, Chinese and good old Southern cooking this side of the burn-off-those-calories-video line.

With so many restaurants to sample, we'll keep this intro brief, but we must mention the grand finale of every meal . . . the check. Most places accept plastic as payment, although American Express is not welcome at quite a few establishments who hope you leave home without it. Personal checks are likewise not a just dessert for many tabs. Be advised to check out each restaurant's specific payment policies when making reservations.

A word about reservations is in order, too. If it's Memorial Day weekend at Virginia Beach, don't expect to waltz in unannounced to a waiting table. Ditto any holiday or, for that matter, any night during peak summer season. Most better restaurants require, or at least recommend, that you make reservations for your dining party, and that (believe us!) has no bearing whatsoever on the time you may actually be seated. This is no way implies that your restaurant of choice does not want to pamper your every culinary desire, it's just that the party of 12 just ahead of you may be savoring the umpteenth mini-cup of cappuccino. So, wherever your destination for the evening's repast, be prepared to linger at the inevitable well-stocked bar for an aperitif before your name is announced for din-din.

We have chosen to take you through the wonderful world of caloric intake by category rather than city by city. That's because, if you're like us, if you have a taste for mu shu pork, you don't want to have to flip through 47 pages of Cajun spiced American nouvelle to locate the best Chinese places in the area. We'll try to give you the decorative flavor of each establishment, along with the most popular menu items, and throw in a few totally subjective opinions along the way.

Next to each restaurant's name, you'll notice a nifty little dollar sign signal, the Insiders' secret code for what you might expect to pay for a divine dinner plus reasonable cocktail intake or sensible bottle of wine. These all apply to an evening's meal, and you can work the math to subtract about one-third for a lunchtime visit:

Less than $20	$
$21 to $35	$$
$36 to $50	$$$
$51 and more	$$$$

One last note before we're seated. The tour we're about to take is current as of this meal, but we do have chefs that have wings under their white smocks. What's pasta today may be pai fan tomorrow. But menu u-turns and restaurant name-changes are all a part of the thrill of the food chase.

American

Norfolk

CARRIAGE INN
313 W. Bute St.
$$ 622-4990

Built in 1850, this brick carriage house has housed restaurants off and on for decades. It reopened in 1993 after a few years' hiatus. The Inn is in Freemason, Norfolk's most historic neighborhood, so be sure to take a post-dinner stroll. The restaurant features mostly sandwiches at noon with a few daily specials to tempt you. There's an extensive dinner menu of steaks, seafood, chicken and pork. The bread pudding is an excellent end to any meal.

CHARLIE'S CAFE
1800-A Granby St.
$ 625-0824

Hearty breakfasts and comfort food are the hallmarks of this small Ghent eatery that attracts a diversified clientele from police officers to young professionals. Even though Charlie left in 1993, the new owner kept his trademark menu. Omelettes, waffles, pancakes and fluffy biscuits hit the spot at breakfast, which is served all day. At noon burgers, meat loaf and sandwiches share the spotlight with home-cooked specials like chicken and dumplings and pot roast.

DO-NUT DINETTE
1917 Colley Ave.
$ 625-0061

If you're a fan of vintage diners, this is the place to go. The dinette opened in the 1940s. Current owner Sheila Schneider Mullins took over in 1987 from her parents who'd run the dinette for decades. There are only 16 stools, most of them occupied by regular customers. Breakfast and lunch are served daily. The morning meal features eggs, sausage, hash browns and irresistible donuts just pulled from the hot oil and dripping with glaze. There's always a lunch special such as fried chicken or fresh seafood. The dinette has some of the best prices in town.

DOUMAR'S
20th and Monticello Ave.
$ 627-4163

Doumar's is a Norfolk landmark that shouldn't be missed. It's been at the same location since 1934 and still has car hops. When they hang a tray on your car window loaded with burgers, fries and milkshakes served in real glasses, you'll think the calendar slipped back a few decades. The food is good and cheap. Doumar's opens for breakfast and keeps serving until late night every day but Sunday. Its standouts include pork barbecue and the best limeades in town. Be sure to end your meal with ice cream in a homemade cone — after all, Abe Doumar, the restaurant's founder, invented the ice cream cone in 1904. (See the sidebar in this chapter.)

ELLIOT'S

1421 Colley Ave.
$$ **625-0259**

This is the granddaddy of the trendy Ghent restaurants. Elliot's has been going strong since 1978 with an unbeatable menu of burgers, pastas, seafood, chicken and beef. Popular items include mile-high nachos and "the works" brownie loaded with ice cream and fudge sauce. Besides the food, Elliot's is known for its eclectic interior that has a giant silver moon, funhouse mirror, old Norfolk photos and lots of flea-market memorabilia. Elliot's has expanded several times and has a sunny, glassed-in side room and patio seats along the sidewalk. Both are great spots for people-watching in warm weather. Lunch and dinner are served daily with brunch offered on Sunday. Elliot's is a winner of *Port Folio's* dining award.

FREEMASON ABBEY

Freemason and Boush Sts.
$$ **622-3966**

This aptly-named restaurant is in a former Presbyterian church built in 1873. Before becoming a restaurant in 1988, the building was an Odd Fellows meeting hall. Although the Abbey retains its original exterior, inside it has been remodeled into a modern two-level restaurant. The menu includes seafood, pasta, quiche, sandwiches, chicken and steaks. Perenalli's greens is a notable salad and makes an ideal lunch when accompanied by crab soup or gumbo. Each Wednesday is lobster night with a New England lobster dinner served for a reasonable price. Other nights also have bargain-

priced specials such as prime rib or steamed shrimp. Lunch and dinner are served daily, with brunch offered on Sunday. Reservations are accepted.

THE GRATE STEAK

235 N. Military Hwy.
$$ **461-5501**

Mention beef in this region, and The Grate Steak springs immediately to mind. For years this has been the main choice for chowing down on cooked-to-perfection steaks. The reason: You charbroil it yourself over a giant grill. This is a fun place to go with a group. Select your cut, plop that baby on the grill and let it sizzle. (Just don't wear a sweater while you're cooking or it will definitely need a trip to the cleaners to get out the smoky smell.) Potatoes, bread and a hefty salad bar make sure you're stuffed when you leave. There's also a regular, cooked-in-the-kitchen menu. Lunch is served on weekdays with dinner available daily. The Grate Steak is a winner of *Port Folio* magazine's Popular Choice award.

GREENTREES CAFE

112 Bank St.
$ **625-2455**

Longtime caterers Herschel and Helene Blum relocated in 1994 to this downtown location in the shadow of some of Norfolk's tallest bank buildings. Their pleasant cafe quickly hit the spot with downtown workers looking for a way to avoid another humdrum lunch break. An outdoor patio is a pleasant spot in spring and fall. Our favorite lunch is GreenTrees salad sampler, which lets you mix and match from several choices. There's always an interesting soup on the menu, some innovative entrees and a variety of sandwiches. Desserts are tempting. GreenTrees is only open on weekdays for breakfast through late afternoon lunch.

KELLY'S TAVERN

1408 Colley Ave.	623-3216
1936 Laskin Rd.	
Virginia Beach	491-8737
Crossways at Greenbrier	
Chesapeake	523-1781
$	

Kelly's is one place we go that makes us toss health to the wind and go for the hamburger with fries. The grilled chicken sandwich is a perennial favorite. Kelly's has been in Norfolk's trendy Ghent neighborhood since the late 1970s and in recent years expanded to Virginia Beach and Chesapeake. All restaurants offer sandwiches, salads and appetizers. The newer restaurants also have some full dinners. Kelly's serves lunch and dinner daily, with the Beach location featuring a Sunday brunch. The Beach establishment also takes reservations.

LONE STAR STEAKHOUSE

450 N. Military Hwy.	
$$	466-0124
2712 N. Mall Dr., Virginia Beach	
$$	463-2879

The name says it all for this Texas-style chain restaurant that's actually based in Kansas beef country. Tossing peanut shells on the floor and line dancing to country music help create the ambiance for the steakhouse. Steaks are huge, and you can pick yours out in the kitchen or trust the staff to find the biggest, juiciest one. Lone Star is open daily for dinner.

LOAVES AND FISHES BY DAIL

339 W. 21st St.	
$$	627-8794

After years of running Dail's seafood, the Dail family opened a restaurant in the Ghent area Palace Shops in late 1992. There's more than the seafood you'd expect on the menu. Look for chicken salad, roasted turkey, pasta and home-cooked specials such as meat loaf and chicken and dumplings. For lighter meals try Dail's sandwiches, soups and salads. Daily specials run the gamut from linguine and red clam sauce to meat loaf. Homemade pies are tempting. You can still buy fresh seafood here as well as some produce and baked goods. Sunday brunch is a treat at Dail's.

MAGNOLIA STEAK

Colley Ave. and Princess Anne	
$$	625-0400

This former "down Southwest cafe" has revamped itself into a restaurant that puts the spotlight on Angus beef. Steaks range from a 22-ounce porterhouse to filets for more delicate appetites. Although the steaks come highly recommended, you'll find a good variety on the menu from walnut-encrusted catfish to seafood and a some Southern and Southwestern specialties. A recent lunch featured a hefty slab of spicy meat loaf and a wonderful side dish of collards spiced with ginger and curry. The atmosphere is elegant at this long-standing Ghent eatery that serves both lunch and dinner.

MAUDE'S

Town Point Center	
$	640-7120

This is one of our favorite spots for a quiet business lunch. With the National Maritime Center (Nauticus) just across the street, Maude's is a perfect place to get fortified for the day of maritime exploring. It's on the second floor of Town Point Center at Boush and Plume streets (look for Maude's sandwich board outside). Owner Heather Whitehead is a chatty Australian with a knack for cooking. Specialties include lamb or buffalo burgers, roasted eggplant sandwiches and a chicken salad dressed up with feta cheese, vegetables and a mustard vinaigrette. Maude's, which is open for breakfast and lunch on weekdays, will tempt you with a big lineup of daily specials. There's a parking garage directly across the street.

MIKE'S COLLEY DELI
1603 Colley Ave.
$ 622-6214
A Colley Avenue fixture since 1941, Mike's is a traditional Kosher deli with a variety of sandwiches and side dishes. It's open daily for lunch and early dinners.

NO FRILL GRILLE
7452 Tidewater Dr.
$ 587-0949
The name of this restaurant says it all. It opened in 1988 to serve good, basic food at a reasonable price: barbecue ribs, hamburgers, milkshakes and big salads. The place has a '50s feel and is open for lunch and dinner every day but Sunday. A sister restaurant is Dog-N-Burger, a tiny takeout place at 2001 Manteo Street in the Ghent area.

OH! BRIAN'S
7512 Granby St.
$$ 480-7267
This Ward's Corner restaurant has drawn a loyal following since its opening in 1990. Its hallmarks are fresh fish and pasta. Popular entrees include an Italian fish stew and crab cakes. Homemade bread and desserts — including apple and cherry crisps — round out the offerings. Early bird specials are a bargain. Lunch and dinner are served every day but Sunday. Oh! Brian's has been a recent Popular Choice winner in *Port Folio* magazine's dining awards.

PHILLY STYLE STEAKS & SUBS
7456 Tidewater Dr.
$ 588-0602
One Philadelphia expatriate we know swears this eatery turns out the most authentic cheese steaks and subs he's had since he left the City of Brotherly Love. Owners Joe and Debbie Hatch opened in 1983 and still import their sandwich rolls from up north. They serve lunch and dinner every day but Sunday.

Photo: Virginia Beach Convention and Visitor Development

Waterfront dining is a pleasure in Hampton Roads.

REGGIE'S BRITISH PUB

The Waterside

$ 627-3575

This British pub has a great view of the Elizabeth River from the second floor of The Waterside, and on nice days, Reggie's balcony is a pleasant spot to dine. The menu is a blend of British and American. It offers Cornish pasties, fish and chips and shepherd's pie as well as sandwiches, steaks, chicken and salad. Desserts include Norfolk County apple dumpling and chocolate mousse pie. Lunch and dinner are served daily. Live music is a plus on weekends.

REISNER'S DELICATESSEN

144 Janaf Shopping Center

$ 461-8548

Founded in 1943 by Austrian immigrant Allen Reisner, this deli is still run by Reisner's daughter, son-in-law and grandchildren, who carry on the family tradition of serving some of the best deli food in town. The hot pastrami and Swiss sandwich ranks with the Reuben as Reisner's best sellers. However, health-conscious diners will also find a grilled chicken breast sandwich. Side dishes include onion rings, corn fritters and potato pancakes. All desserts are homemade, including Kahlua milk chocolate cheesecake. Reisner's is in Janaf shopping center on Military Highway and sells a good variety of bottled wine. It closes on Sunday.

SCHLOTZSKY'S DELI

700 N. Military Hwy.	*455-BUNS*
246 E. Main St.	*627-Buns*
2704 N. Mall Dr., Virginia Beach	*340-BUNS*

$

Hearty sandwiches are the hallmarks at this chain deli that's one of our favorite spots for a quick lunch. Sandwiches come on freshly made sourdough, rye, whole wheat or jalapeno cheese buns. Our all-time favorite is "The Original," which piles three meats and three cheeses, black olives, onions, lettuce, tomatoes and mustard on sourdough. Salads and pizzas round out the menu.

UNCLE LOUIE'S

132 E. Little Creek

$$ 480-1225

This sophisticated 10-year-old restaurant is tucked away in the back of Uncle Louie's gourmet shop. It is surprisingly spacious with an excellent seasonal menu that runs the gamut from seafood to sandwiches. Steaks cut from Angus beef are the house specialty. If you're really starving, get things started with the "mother load," an aptly named dish of potato skins buried under cheese, bacon and sour cream. Besides homemade desserts, Uncle Louie's has 110 coffees, thanks to its affiliation with First Colony. Stop in during the afternoons for a pot of tea and some scones, finger sandwiches and other traditional teatime fare. Uncle Louie's is open daily for breakfast, lunch and dinner.

Virginia Beach

ARTY'S DELI

Collins Square
$ 340-2789

Arty's Deli opened in 1987 with a traditional Kosher menu highlighting such favorites as corned beef and brisket cooked on site. Last year it moved across Virginia Beach Boulevard to a new location. Arty's pastrami sandwiches, chicken soup and chicken salad have big followings. Arty's serves breakfast, lunch and dinner every day but Sunday.

BAJA RESTAURANT

3701 Sandpiper Rd.
$$ 426-7748

Despite its Mexican name, this restaurant specializes in homemade pizza and seafood. The Baja has been a casual Sandbridge beach eatery since 1974. It overlooks Back Bay and has a screened dining area. Fresh fish usually includes flounder, tuna and catfish. The Baja is known for crab cakes. During the summer it serves lunch and dinner daily. In the off-season it shuts down on Sundays. Dinner is served six days with lunch only on Friday and Saturday.

BLACK-EYED PEA

675 Phoenix Dr., Virginia Beach   486-2760
1432 Greenbrier Pkwy., Chesapeake   523-5977
$

This is our hands-down favorite chain restaurant, and it was a happy day for us when it arrived in Hampton Roads a few years ago. The Dallas-based restaurants whip up home-cooking like we grew up with — gravy-slathered chicken-fried steak, juicy pot roast, lumpy mashed potatoes and blackberry cobbler topped with ice cream. We don't eat that way much anymore, but when we do the "Pea" is where we head. Giant glasses of iced tea are perfect for washing down all that Southern food. For the cholesterol-conscious, salads, baked-potato dishes and sandwiches also are on the menu. The Black-eyed Pea is open for lunch and dinner.

THE JEWISH MOTHER

3108 Pacific Ave.   422-5430
$

The Jewish Mother is a Virginia Beach landmark that's been around since 1975. It's a fun, New York-deli type place with a big lineup of sandwiches. Lox and cream cheese, latkes, blintzes and homemade soups are on the menu. The Jewish Mother serves a variety of salads and breakfast items, too. With more than 20 desserts in a showcase up front, it's hard to pass up the sweets. Children eat their sandwiches off Frisbees they can take home. Live entertainment at night brings in some national bands. Breakfast, lunch and dinner are served daily.

KITCHIN'S KITCHEN

26th and Atlantic
$ 428-1296

Founded in 1941 as an open-air snack bar along the oceanfront, Kitchin's Kitchen is a local favorite. Hearty breakfasts draw a crowd of regulars. Lunch specialties include fresh-ground hamburgers. Cook Sue Gergen creates a different homemade soup each day as she has done since 1949.

MARY'S COUNTRY KITCHEN

616 Virginia Beach Blvd.
$ 428-1355

Since 1958 Mary's has been dishing out big breakfasts and home-cooking. It still has the same owners who specialize

Sailing Up For Supper

When Hampton Roads seamen cast off from their docks early in the evening, it's a sure bet that they're setting sail for one of our many restaurants that make a boater welcome. All along the Bay, rivers and creeks, waterfront eateries dot our coastline. While many welcome sailing parties that come unannounced, it's often wise to phone ahead to ensure a berth at your destination.

Starting in Virginia Beach's Long Creek, you can pull into Chick's Oyster Bar, 481-5757, for some delectable steamed seafood in a casual atmosphere, or into Angler's Cove, 496-3690, another seafood favorite with a rustic feel. At nearby Lynnhaven Inlet, you have your choice of always chic Henry's, 481-7300, or dress down and make a wake to Bubba's, 481-3513.

The ever-popular Rudee Inlet has it's triple-R treats awaiting intrepid ocean sailors. There's the River House with its own slips, but call the harbor master at 422-2999 if your proposed port o' call is Rockafeller's or Rudee's.

Traveling up towards Norfolk, you'll find the waters along Shore Drive quite hospitable to hungry seamen. Chef supreme Monroe Duncan will welcome you in for New World cuisine at Monroe's, 588-0100, and a few yards away, you can paddle into the Fisherman's Cove, 362-CRAB, and pop onto the big deck to take a crack at hot, steamed crabs. The Blue Crab, 362-8000, is next along the waterfront, and then find Tracy's, 362-2100, both specializing in tasty, fresh seafood.

You'll find excellent choices port and starboard on the Elizabeth River which parts Downtown Norfolk and Portsmouth. The premier pull-in would be The Waterside Marina, 627-3300, from which you can take your pick of the many food tastes that await inside, notably the Maryland-based seafood palace known as Phillips, along with Waterside Live!, a conglomerate of restaurants and nightclubs. If you're feeling crabby, head down the prom-enade to the Riverwalk, 622-6664, at the Omni Hotel for their incredible "Crab Bash" held during the summer.

Across the Elizabeth, in Portsmouth, you can pull into the Holiday Yacht Harbor, 399-0991, and head to Amory's Wharf, an elevated restaurant that offers a panoramic view of Crawford Bay as well as the Elizabeth. For a more casual fast feast, head downriver to Portside, 393-5111, where vendors will tempt you with everything from crab cakes to burritos. Farther up towards Hampton Roads harbor is our personal favorite, Scale o'de Whale, 483-2772, which sits perched on the end of the pier and welcomes boating patrons on a first-come basis.

In Chesapeake, Lock's Pointe, 547-9618, offers a fine dining room with a casual glassed-in patio Smithfield Station, 399-2874, welcomes travelers at the confluence of Cypress Creek and the Pagan River in Smithfield. And, lastly, Suffolk offers its own casual boat-up dining at Bennett's Creek Marina, 484-8700, on the body of water with the same name.

in barbecue, meat loaf and luscious desserts such as German chocolate cake and banana cake. Early bird specials are real bargains.

OUTBACK STEAKHOUSE

1757 Laskin Rd.	422-5796
1255 Fordham Dr.	523-4832
$$	

This steakhouse may aspire to live up to its Australian ambiance, but its menu is pure American with beef and more beef. From New York strip to prime rib and sirloin, the steaks are big and cooked to perfection. It didn't take long after the Outback's opening in 1993 for word to spread of its "bloomin' onion" appetizer — a huge batter-fried onion served with spicy remoulade. Meals come with salad, vegetable and bread. The Outback serves dinner daily and also has a Sunday lunch.

POLLARD'S CHICKEN

100 London Bridge Blvd.	
Virginia Beach	340-2565
3033 Ballentine Blvd., Norfolk	855-7864
326 E. Bayview Blvd., Norfolk	587-8185
717 Battlefield Blvd., Chesapeake	482-3200
$	

Despite the giant plastic chicken out front, there's more than fried hen on the menu at this local chain of family restaurants that's been around since 1967. North Carolina-style barbecue, chicken and dumplings and Brunswick stew are as popular as the chicken. Daily specials feature country-style comfort food such as livers and gizzards. Homemade desserts include five-layer coconut cake and bread

pudding. Lunch and dinner are served daily.

PUNGO GRILL

1785 Princess Anne Rd.	
$$	426-6655

This restaurant prides itself on its eclectic menu. On a typical day diners can enjoy crab cakes, pasta, lasagna, catfish, Thai and Jamaican chicken and 12 different vegetables. The Grill, which opened in 1988, is in a restored 1919 house in the heart of Pungo in rural Virginia Beach. It works local produce into the menu when it's available. Homemade desserts include chocolate mousse, hummingbird cake and lemon meringue pie. Lunch and dinner are served everyday but Monday. Reservations are encouraged.

THE RAVEN

1200 Atlantic Ave.	
$	425-9556

Since 1968, The Raven has been a beachfront mainstay. Its offerings include French dip sandwiches and the Raven champignon — a burger dressed up with bacon and sauteed mushrooms. During off-season Wednesday nights, all-you-can-eat crab legs and shrimp pack in the crowds. Lunch and dinner are served daily.

ROSIE RUMPE'S REGAL DUMPE

14th St. and Atlantic Ave.	
$$	428-5858

If you're looking for entertainment

If you're in Virginia Beach and longing for a great meal that comes to you, call Takeout Taxi at 456-5678. The delivery service will rush over with meals from one of 14 different restaurants.

Insiders' Tips

with your food, this is a definite option for dinner. Rosie Rumpe's opened in the Sandcastle Oceanfront Motel in the summer of 1993 and survived its critical first two tourist seasons. It is decked out like King Henry VIII's favorite tavern and takes you on a time trip to the 16th century. During the two-hour dinner and show you chow down on soup, salad, rolls, dessert and an entree choice of steak, chicken or fish. Costumed minstrels sing, make jokes and may drag you into the show. The prices are fixed, and reservations are recommended.

Chesapeake

CARA'S
123 N. Battlefield Blvd.
$$ 548-0006

Opened in 1992 along the Atlantic Intracoastal Waterway, this restaurant has expanded Chesapeake dining options. Its menu is heavy on seafood but also includes chicken, Angus beef and huge specialty salads. Cara's is in the Island Wharf shops and has a deck overlooking the waterway. Everything is homemade, including breads and desserts such as Mississippi fudge pie and peanut butter pie. Sunday brunch is served along with lunch and dinner daily.

CHEER'S
1405 Greenbrier Pkwy.
$ 424-4665

Modeled on its Boston namesake, this casual eatery opened in 1990 on the outskirts of Greenbrier Mall. Its menu is varied and includes sandwiches, salads, beef, chicken and seafood. Popular entrees include barbecued ribs and a Boston chicken and shrimp combo served over fettuccine in cream sauce. There is a fresh fish daily special as well as a cheesecake

of the day. An inexpensive express lunch is available for the working crowd. Lunch and dinner are served daily with brunch available on Sunday.

Portsmouth

THE MAX
435 Water St.
$$ 397-1866

The Max specializes in what its owner calls "semi-gourmet meals," such as seafood Miranda and chicken piccata, but now there are nachos, fried clams and pizzas on the menu as well. Desserts are homemade. The restaurant overlooks the Elizabeth River. The Max serves lunch and dinner daily with a buffet brunch on Sunday.

MOM'S BEST DELI
340 Broad St.
$ 399-1199

One of our favorite stops for a quick sandwich, this small deli also turns out some good home cooking and recently moved to a new location. Daily specials include chicken and dumplings and corned beef and cabbage. Homemade salads and desserts also are notable. The deli has gained local fame for its chocolate chip cookies and meringue pies. It serves lunch on weekdays.

NEW YORK DELICATESSEN
509 Court St.
$ 399-3354

The deli has been in downtown Portsmouth since the 1930s and in its current quarters for about 20 years. Kosher foods include Reuben and pastrami sandwiches, lox and bagels and chicken soup. Desserts include homemade cream puffs. It serves breakfast, lunch and early dinners and closes on Sunday.

Crab Talk

Watermen and restaurateurs have their own lingo when it comes to the region's favorite mollusk — the blue crab. Here are some terms you may hear:

Backfin — Also called the "paddle" fin, this appendage is where the tastiest crab meat lies. The flat backfin serves as a swimming aid and, when it's time for the crab to molt, it develops the white, pink or red lines crabbers rely on to help them spot peelers.

Busters — A crab who's getting rid of, or busting out of, its old shell.

Doublers — Male and female crabs riding tandem during the mating process. This may last for days while the female molts, is impregnated and develops a new protective shell.

Jimmies — A very hard male crab with a slender apron. (Crabs reveal their sex and state of maturity in several ways, including the shape of their abdominal apron.)

Papershell — A crab who molted about 12 hours ago, but whose shell is already toughening.

Peeler — Often used as bait, these are crabs on the verge of molting with a soft shell ready and waiting under the hard one.

She-crab — A young female crab with a V-shaped apron. These crabs are favorite ingredients in local soups that often include cream and sherry.

Softshell — Just molted, this tired, vulnerable crab is sought by fish and fishermen alike. Softshell crabs are a real delicacy that shows up on menus in late spring and summer where they are battered, cooked and eaten whole, legs and all.

Sooks — Mature female hard crabs who have molted for the last time, characterized by a dark bell-shaped apron.

Sponge crab — A female crab carrying her egg mass on her abdomen.

Suffolk

BUNNY'S RESTAURANT
1901 Wilroy Rd.
$ 538-2325

Bunny's is Suffolk's home-cooking standout. It's been dishing up fried chicken, crab cakes and chicken pot pie since 1971 from its location near Wilroy Industrial Park. This is a no-frills place with a big lineup of vegetables such as stewed tomatoes, candied yams and butter beans. Meals come with homemade hushpuppies. Bunny's is open daily for breakfast, lunch and dinner. Breakfasts feature Belgian waffles, eggs and pancakes.

FRONT STREET RESTAURANT
434 N. Main St.
$$ 539-5393

Housed in a historic home near downtown Suffolk, Front Street is open for lunch on weekdays and dinner on Wednesday through Saturday. Dinner entrees range from steaks and scallops to trout and chicken. Specialty dishes include scalloped oysters and chicken cordon bleu stuffed with brie and ham. The lunch menu features mainly salads and sandwiches.

THE PEANUT RESTAURANT
6001 Holland Rd.
$ 657-9846

Located on Route 58 beside a cotton patch, this restaurant prides itself on home-cooked daily specials such as pork chops, ham and chicken and dumplings. Vegetables include butter beans, homemade onion rings and collards. Peanut pie and banana pudding are on the dessert menu. Check for weekend all-you-can-eat shrimp specials. The restaurant, which also sells country crafts, serves lunch daily and dinner on Wednesday through Saturday.

Bakeries

Norfolk

BON APETIT
2708 Granby St.
$ 625-4777

This tiny Mediterranean bakery turns out an amazing amount of bread, baklava and specialty pastries. Its products show up in local stores and restaurants, but individuals also can stop by for a coconut macaroon or a bag of croissants. The bakery is part of a small Mediterranean grocery whose wares include filo dough, grape leaves and feta cheese. It is closed on Sunday.

FRENCH BAKERY & DELICATESSEN
4108 Granby St.
$ 625-4936

This bakery has been run by the Habib family since 1913 and has been in this location since 1942. The Habibs pride themselves on using the same recipes as when the bakery was founded. They pro-duce all types of French pastries, including eclairs and French cigars. One popular seller is the orange donuts. The bakery is open Monday through Saturday. For lunch it serves submarine sandwiches on homemade bread.

NAAS BAKERY
3527 Tidewater Dr.
$ 623-3858

Naas has been around for at least 50 years. Its current owners have run the business since the early 1970s and gained a loyal clientele. The bakery is known for its danishes, coffee cakes and butter cookies. It is open daily, and there are tables for dining.

RICH & TONY'S
161 Granby St.
$ 627-2345

This bagel shop stocks 18 different types, ranging from banana nut to oat bran and spinach wheat. Most bagels are made right here. Lunch includes deli sandwiches and salads. The restaurant is open daily for breakfast and lunch.

YORGO'S BAGELDASHERY
Selden Arcade, Main St.
$ 623-6609

Since it's opening in Selden Arcade in 1993, Yorgo's has captured the fancy of the downtown lunch crowd. About a dozen different New York-style bagels are continually pulled from Yorgo's oven. While they're great slathered with cream cheese, the bagels are even better turned into a sandwich. Our favorites are smoked turkey with prosciutto on an onion bagel and hummus on a whole wheat bagel. Chili served with bagel chips is just right on a gloomy winter day. Salads and homemade cookies also are on the menu. Yorgo's is open daily.

Virginia Beach

BAKER'S CRUST
704 Laskin Rd.
$ 422-6703

Bread is the name of the game at this trendy bakery/cafe that opened in 1993 in the Hilltop North shopping center. Choosing from the 18 homemade varieties on hand is a daunting task helped only by eating the generous samples doled out. You'll be tempted to take home crusty French baguettes as well as loaves flavored with pumpernickel, cheese or figs. There's ample seating to savor a hoagie on fresh bread or a nouvelle turkey with cream cheese and apricot on whole wheat. Salads come in a boule of French bread. Luscious desserts and a variety of coffees round out the menu. The Baker's Crust is open for breakfast, lunch and dinner.

BONJOUR BAKERY AND DELI
336 Constitution Dr.
$ 473-9107

This European bakery first fired up the ovens in 1986 and is run by a Lebanese baker who whips up luscious baklava, eclairs, chocolate mousse cigars and other French pastries. You may have to search to find this spot. Although it is in a shopping center across from Pembroke Mall, it is dwarfed by a neighboring Kmart. Bonjour Bakery is open Monday through Saturday and serves lunch. Featured items are sandwiches on homemade bread.

THE MUFFIN PAN
Indian River Rd. at I-64
$ 366-5747

There's a Swiss pastry chef at the helm of The Muffin Pan in the Founders Inn and Conference Center on the grounds of The Christian Broadcasting Network. You don't have to be a guest of the inn to savor the Napoleons, pastry swans with chocolate hearts and other delicacies. Gourmet soups, salads and sandwiches also are served daily. The Muffin Pan is open from the crack of dawn to midnight.

PASTA E PANI BAKERY
1065 Laskin Rd.
$ 422-8536

This Italian bakery is loved for its breads, particularly the crusty sourdough. It also has semolina and white bread and rolls. Other products include fresh pasta, ravioli, Italian sauces, cheeses and cold cuts. The bakery also makes a wonderful biscotti. Its a branch of the nearby Pasta e Pani restaurant. The bakery is open Tuesday through Saturday.

REAL BREAD COMPANY
1554 Laskin Rd.	491-8065
1053 Independence Blvd.	363-2119
222 W. 21st St., Norfolk	627-3101
$	

Despite their hefty weight, the Real Bread Company's all natural breads always have a light texture. And, they're made with high-protein Montana wheat ground on site. Breads contain no eggs, oils or fats and are Kosher approved. From its original location in Hilltop East shopping center in Virginia Beach, the bread company has grown like fast-acting yeast dough. No longer do loyal customers have to drive 25 miles to stock up on country raisin bread, challah or Tidewater sourdough. There are now three southside outlets with one also in Hampton. All are takeout operations that generously let you sample their wares. Also in stock are homemade cookies, muffins and gourmet desserts.

SUGAR PLUM BAKERY

1353 Laskin Rd.
$ 422-3913

This nonprofit bakery has a tremendous following in Virginia Beach. It started in 1987 to provide training and jobs for young adults with mental retardation. It serves that mission well while turning out what one person we know calls "the best cookies I ever ate." There are more than 200 items in the bakery, making it one of the region's largest.

Among the best sellers are chocolate mousse cake, six-grain bread and buttery wedding cookies.

The bakery's small cafe is a great place to savor a sweet roll and coffee. Sugar Plum also serves lunch, which features a variety of salads and sandwiches and a soup of the day. The menu changes seasonally. The bakery is open Tuesday through Sunday.

Barbecue

Norfolk

PIERCE'S PITT BAR-B-QUE

The Waterside
$ 622-0738

This is a spin-off of Pierce's outside Williamsburg, probably the best-known barbecue restaurant in Virginia. The Norfolk location is in the food court of The Waterside. It specializes in minced pork barbecue and traditional side dishes like baked beans and cole slaw. Pierce's is

Photo: Virginia Beach Convention and Visitor Development

Food vendors line the Virginia Beach Boardwalk with their summer delights of everything from ice cream to hot dogs.

open daily for lunch and dinner. It is a winner of *Port Folio* magazine's Popular Choice award.

Virginia Beach

THE BAR B QUE GRILL
1601 Hilltop W. Shopping Center
$ 428-7758

This immaculate cafe gives a down-home touch to the tony Hilltop area. The grill's owners hail from Florida but their barbecue style has a Texas twang. Pork, beef and chicken barbecue anchor the menu. Dinner plates come with two side orders and two corn fritters. There are 14 side dishes available, including Brunswick stew, baked beans and stewed apples and yams.

Fried fritters are laced with whole corn kernels and lots of black pepper. Each day there are homemade soup and dessert specials. In true Southern style, the iced tea comes presweetened unless you specify otherwise. The restaurant is open for lunch and dinner every day but Sunday.

THE BEACH BULLY
39th St. and Baltic Ave.
$ 422-4222

This casual tavern-style restaurant provides a change of pace for beach goers tired of the resort city's predominant seafood. The Beach Bully opened in 1985 four blocks from the oceanfront. You'll recognize it right away by the fleet of portable barbecue grills surrounding the building. Barbecued beef, pork and chicken are all on the menu. Platters come loaded with two side orders of homemade specialties, including hand-cut french fries. One popular offering is the baby back rib dinners. The restaurant is open daily for lunch and dinner.

Chesapeake

JOHNSON'S BARBECUE
1903 S. Military Hwy.
$ 545-6957

Arkansas-style barbecued slathered in a tangy red sauce is the reason to come here. You'll find your pork minced or served as meaty ribs. Chicken and beef also are treated to Johnson's special touch. Fixings include potato salad, cole slaw and baked beans. Don't miss the homemade sweet potato or apple fried pies. They're so popular they sell out quickly. Lunch and dinner are served every day but Sunday.

MR. PIG'S BAR-B-Q
445 N. Battlefield Blvd.
$ 547-5171

Mr. Pig's has been Chesapeake's main barbecue restaurant since the late 1980s. Vinegar-sauced North Carolina barbecue is the house specialty, however, the restaurant also does a brisk business with its fried chicken. Brunswick stew, boiled potatoes and chicken salad are among the other menu offerings. The restaurant serves lunch and dinner but closes on Sunday.

Portsmouth

RODMAN'S BONES & BUDDY #2
3562 Western Branch Blvd. 397-3900
RODMAN'S BONES & BUDDY #3
5917 Churchland Blvd. 483-2000
$

Although these restaurants only opened in the 1980s they have a rich history. One of the owners was the founder of The Circle, a Portsmouth dining landmark. His partner is renowned for operating Rodman's barbecue. "Buddy & Bones" pays tribute to two deceased Ports-

Doumar's

With its car hops and antique ice cream cone machine, Doumar's revels in its history. Founder Abe Doumar was lured to Norfolk in 1907 by the Jamestown Exposition, which promised to attract thousands of new customers to eat his ice cream cones.

Doumar, who came here via St. Louis and Coney Island, invented the ice cream cone during the 1904 St. Louis Exposition. He started out in Norfolk's Ocean View area and by 1913 had opened a second location on the Virginia Beach boardwalk with his brothers. Since 1934 the only Doumar's has been in Norfolk at Monticello Avenue and 20th Street. This is a classic drive-in built in 1949, and time has stood still since then.

As soon as you pull up, a car hop trots out with a menu and orders you to flip on the headlights when ready to order. Within a few minutes she hauls out limeades, cherry Cokes and milk shakes in real glasses. Hamburgers are swaddled in wax paper spiked with a toothpick. Everything comes on a tray that hangs on the car window. Switch on the lights again, and the waitress whisks the tray away.

Doumar's nephew Albert runs the drive-in with his son Thad. On most days at either 3 PM or 7 PM one of them fires up Abe Doumar's original machine and creates hand-made cones. Two car hops have each been on duty for more than 40 years. Some cooks have been there just as long making Doumar's famous pork barbecue and other sandwiches.

Prices are unbeatable, and the atmosphere is great. There's room to dine inside where walls are lined with blown-up photos of Doumar's early days. There are several photo albums to peruse, and the owners will be happy to show off their cone-making technique if it's time to make a batch. Customers can also buy a big jar of homemade cones to take home.

Photo: Norfolk Convention and Visitors Bureau

At Doumar's Drive-In visitors can enjoy ice cream cones made from the world's first cone machine, invented by Abe Doumar.

Doumar's is open from 8 AM to 11 PM Monday through Thursday. It keeps serving until 12:30 AM on Friday and Saturday nights but closes on Sundays. The drive-in is a popular gathering spot for antique car owners who feel right at home here.

mouth restaurant owners who bore those nicknames and served the "square dog," now a staple of Rodman's menu. (Just so you won't be confused, the original Rodman's is in Suffolk and is strictly a catering operation.)

Rodman's has loyal customers who lap up the barbecued pork and chicken. Side dishes include Brunswick stew and navy bean soup. Its hushpuppies are some of the best around. Featured menu items include sliced Smithfield ham sandwiches and, of course, the square dog. This is a sliced grilled hot dog served with lettuce, tomato and a lump of Smithfield ham just as Bones and Buddy would have offered it. The restaurants serve both lunch and dinner every day except Sunday.

Suffolk

HERB'S BAR-B-Q
868 Carolina Rd.
$ 539-9785

This is your classic barbecue joint — the kind you have to be told about to find. Herb Brinkley has run the business since 1951 and maintains a menu that has changed little since then. Barbecue pork comes either sliced or minced on a sandwich or a platter. The combination plate is served with barbecue, cole slaw, corn bread and Brunswick stew. Herb gives cornbread a different twist by serving it as delicious fried nuggets. The restaurant maintains a rustic look, and it still has curb service under the metal canopy out front. It closes on Sunday.

Coffeehouses

Norfolk

BREWBAKERS
806 Spotswood Ave.
$ 625-2739

This cozy Ghent cafe opened in 1974 and quickly gained a following for its salads, soups and sandwiches. The coffee is always fresh, and you'll find a full menu to go with it. Among the top sellers are a sourdough bread bowl filled with soup and a stuffed baked potato served with a salad. Homemade desserts are excellent.

FIRST COLONY COFFEE HOUSE
2000-1 Colonial Ave. 622-0149
1550 Laskin Rd., Virginia Beach 428-2994
$

Java lovers take note: California chic finally arrived here when this coffee paradise opened in Norfolk in 1992. Since then it has spread to the Hilltop East shopping center in Virginia Beach with plans to take the country by storm with a chain of coffeehouses. The founders are the Brockenbrough brothers who run First Colony Coffee Co., which has blended beans in Norfolk since 1902. With First Colony's gourmet coffees already nationally famous, the Brockenbroughs figured it was time to test the waters with their own coffeehouse. Gleaming antique coffee dispensers and a copper-top bar create the mood for the classy but casual place.

White bean chili, and olive and cream cheese sandwiches will tempt you at lunch

Photo:Virginia's Eastern Shore Tourism Commission

Locals and vacationers alike take advantage of the fresh seafood that the Chesapeake Bay region has to offer.

and dinner. Desserts are divine and imported from New York. Biscotti is just right for dunking. Linger over the house blend or check out the wilder coffee and tea flavors of the day. On your way out, grab a bag of beans for the road. Locations are open daily for the breakfast crowd as well as night owls.

THE PERFECT GRIND
The Waterside
$ 622-3203

If you're in downtown Norfolk and longing for a terrific cup of coffee, head for this tiny beanery under the escalators at Waterside. You'll find an abundance of coffee choices as well as tea and hot chocolate. Specialty pastries will tempt you. The Perfect Grind is open daily from early morning until Waterside closes.

PRINCE BOOKS AND COFFEEHOUSE
109 E. Main St.
$ 622-9223

Take an established bookstore, move it to a historic building and add a coffeehouse with an innovative menu. The result is one of the most inviting spots in downtown Norfolk. Housed in the Beaux-Arts Life Building, the coffeehouse always has a coffee of the day brewed and a variety of espressos, cappuccinos and caffè lattes. The outstanding food prepared Mediterranean style makes even non-coffee drinkers love this place. Our favorite is the grilled panini — Italian-style sandwiches served on seasoned focaccia bread. Salads, muffins and desserts also are on the menu. Seating is limited in the coffeehouse, which is open from morning until evening.

Virginia Beach

CUPPA JO'S COFFEE HOUSE
301 25th St.
$ 437-4436

This trendy coffeehouse is tucked away near the oceanfront. Besides the variety of coffees you'd expect, there is a variety of desserts and a few entrees. Cuppa Jo's opens late morning and stands ready to serve a pre-midnight nightcap.

Steinhilber's Thalia Acres Inn

The year is 1922. It's the Lynnhaven Golf and Country Club, and you have traveled hours for a gentlemanly round, far away from the big city of Norfolk, to the rural Town of Lynnhaven in Princess Anne County, long miles from the sleepy outskirts along the Atlantic Ocean known as young upstart Virginia Beach. Life is lazy, slow and genteel. And then comes the Depression.

During the early '30s, Depression takes its toll. The Country Club flounders, and in comes a young man from the city to buy the property. The young man is Robert Steinhilber who, along with brothers Walter and Herman, has successfully run a popular eatery on Main Street in Norfolk. While they negotiate, the Club burns to the ground, save the thick concrete foundation and, in 1935, Robert and Herman buy the 140-plus acres out in the country and turn it into a country resort. They build stables to board horses, patch up a driving range, erect log cabins for overnight guests, create riding trails and set up picnic tables for those city folk who need to escape from the hustle and bustle of city living. Robert takes his bride, an avid horsewoman from Berkley, and they build a restaurant so people who visit will have a fine place to eat. It is now Thalia Acres Inn . . . and then it is World War II.

The trees around the Inn are thick with the war. Just around the bend is a prisoner of war camp, set up as a processing station for German POWs. Steinhilber is a German name, and not to be trusted by those who had never met the gentle man. The military claims the building and the grounds and it becomes an Officer's Club along with drill and tank testing fields, while the young Steinhilbers watch powerless, biding time.

In the early '40s, much worse for wear, Thalia Acres Inn is returned to the rightful owners. The war has ended and life resumes. The area now has merged into the City of Virginia Beach, the restaurant is enlarged and suddenly there is the newfangled passion for family flight to suburbia. The country club to driving range to tank testing site becomes . . . homes . . . built on land sold by Herman to crystal-balled investors, hungry for the heavily wooded property. Once a long driveway of oyster shells and grass, Thalia Road becomes a yellow-brick pathway, entry into the prestigious neighborhood tucked away on the Lynnhaven River.

Steinhilber's Thalia Acres Inn flourishes, and expands. Tourists flock to Virginia Beach and hear wonderful things about the fine dining in this tucked away restaurant along the Lynnhaven. They come. But, they themselves are not all so wonderful. They're too rude, too pushy and too boisterous for Pop Steinhilber's liking. He is defiant, closing the restaurant during the summer season to avoid the pressure to serve patrons who show no respect. He becomes a legend.

Today, Steinhilber's is still part yesterday, part today, where kind respect for those serving and those served is a way of life. Now operated year round by Robert Steinhilber's children, Steve and sister Jeanne, you can hear the echoes of the past when you sit on the lower level where the locker rooms and rathskeller once roared with country club members and World War II officers. If you choose to drive down what was once an oyster shell driveway to the gracious hospitality and old world charm that awaits at roads end, you might ask your server for a favorite story or two. Many have been there for over 35 years. And oh, the tales they can tell

GLORIA JEAN'S COFFEE BEANS

Lynnhaven Mall, Virginia Beach   463-5890
Greenbrier Mall, Chesapeake   420-6561
$

Gloria Jean's breaks through the clutter of commonplace mall fare with some outstanding coffee. There are also desserts and coffee-related merchandise to tempt you.

HAPPY HOG COFFEE & TEA GALLERY

3101 Virginia Beach Blvd.
$ 340-4144

Sip your favorite steaming brew while surrounded by original art. The Happy Hog gives the region's growing coffeehouse trend a new twist. It opened in 1993 with just a few muffins, biscotti and donuts to accompany the main wares of coffee and tea. This is a pleasant spot to relax. The *New York Times* and other big-city dailies are on hand, the deep green decor is soothing and the art changes monthly. Open Tuesday through Saturday for breakfast and lunch.

PJ BAGGAN JAVA CAFE

960 Laskin Rd.
$ 491-8900

This gourmet cafe and wine shop also does an excellent job with coffee. PJ's creates dynamite gourmet sandwiches, salads and desserts. (Our top pick is the avocado sandwich dressed with cream cheese, havarti, cheddar, avocados and veggies.) And, the restaurant caters to wine lovers with one of the biggest stocks around. The coffee lineup includes basic beans as well as fancy cappuccino and espresso. The cafe is open daily for breakfast, lunch and dinner. You'll always find three urns filled with the brews-of-the-day with plenty of others you can order by the pot. The atmosphere is upscale, and you'll want to linger here. Since PJ's is directly across the road from the Surf n Sand theater, it's a great place for post-movie conversation.

RUMLEY'S COFFEE AND TEA CO. LTD.

32nd and Pacific
$ 422-1260

Coffee lovers may be overwhelmed by the 30 varieties of beans in this tiny shop. Tea lovers will also find their niche here, too, particularly if Rumley's happens to be serving high tea in the afternoon. There are a couple of tiny tables for sipping your java. Rumley's is open daily.

Portsmouth

BRUTTI'S

467 Dinwiddie St.
$ 393-1923

Besides the coffee, the "bagelnutz" is the claim to fame here. This Brutti's invention is a mouth-watering nugget of bagel dough stuffed with flavored cream cheese and then cooked. Baguettes baked on site are the basis for sandwiches. Bagels also are baked daily. Espresso and cappuccino round out the menu. Brutti's is just off High Street and is open daily for breakfast through an early dinner.

SOTTO VOCE ESPRESSO
331 High St.
$ 393-9121

This relaxing spot has a large selection of coffees and sandwiches, bagels and desserts to accompany them. An eclectic decor and old *Look* magazines to read make this a terrific place to linger.

Chinese

Norfolk

BAMBOO HUT
2200 Colonial Ave.
$ 640-1649

Always good, always fast, always reasonable — that's Bamboo Hut, and, while they may slide somewhat in the category of international "fast food," it's hard to beat their Beef and Broccoli or their Mu Shu Pork. With both Mandarin and Szechuan menu offerings, they've spread out to multiple locations throughout the region, which more or less is a clue to their popularity among Insiders. Note: This is strictly a take-out operation, or you can have your order delivered. You'll find them here in the heart of Ghent and in:

Virginia Beach:
2832 Virginia Beach Boulevard
Lynnhaven Mall
Larkspur Square
2407 Pacific Avenue
1801 Pleasure House Road
College Park Shopping Center

Norfolk:
6400 East Virginia
Beach Boulevard
7450 Tidewater Drive
Chesapeake:
455 North Battlefield Boulevard

CHINA GARDEN
854 N. Military Hwy.
$$ 461-3818

The combination lunches and dinners here are tough to top, but, if you insist, you can order from the page after page of their extensive menu, or heap your plate time and again from the lavish lunch buffet spread. Peking duck by Chef Lu is a house specialty, and you'll really enjoy the Chinese brunch tradition of dim sum served here on weekends. You can find other China Gardens at Pembroke Mall at the Beach and 303 High Street in Portsmouth.

MAJESTIC HOUSE
1119 N. Military Hwy.   466-0450

This is our all-time favorite Chinese restaurant (and the one that always has lots of Chinese-Americans eating there). An innovative all-you-can-eat menu eliminates the traditional soggy buffet line in favor of cooked-to-order entrees. For one reasonable price you can choose as many entrees as your palate can stand. Each will be fresh from the wok, cooked to your specifications and delivered to your table. You can keep ordering until you beg for mercy. For those who know their limits, the regular menu is still in force. The Majestic has the best hot-and-sour soup and spicy Szechuan cooking in the region and prides itself on its New York-style Chinese food. It's open for both lunch and dinner.

SHINE SHINE PALACE
The Waterside
$$ 623-0778

Choose from Hunan, Cantonese or Szechuan fare from the menu, and dine in a most opulent setting for chopsticks with spectacular views of the Elizabeth River from the top floor of The Waterside festival marketplace. The smells that greet you as you enter are enough to snap those taste buds to attention, and we can almost guarantee you'll be satisfied not only with the splendid food but with the service as well.

SZECHUAN GARDEN
121 West Charlotte St.
$ 627-6130

Some like it hot, and none serve it spicier than Szechuan Garden, a local favorite for both lunch and dinner. Our most favorite dish on the menu is the gan bien string beans, spicy and tender. (One Insider we know picked up several orders to add to their dinner party menu!) Their sesame pancakes are hard to top too, and they offer a full selection from secret Hunan, Cantonese and Mandarin recipes. Their Beach counterpart is at 2720 North Mall Drive.

SZECHUAN IN GHENT
1517 Colley Ave.
$$ 625-1551

Ghent has many restaurant choices, but this is a favorite. The interior decor is surprisingly elegant for a Chinese eatery, but the extensive menu and cordial service match the best of them. Peking duck for two is a house specialty, but we're partial to the triple seafood delight. A special vegetarian menu is available, too.

KIN'S WOK
222-H W. 21st St.
$ 623-2933

Judging by the sleek Mercedes squealing away with their windows fogged from the steam of those little white boxes, you can easily surmise that Kin's Wok has sweet and soured its way into the hearts of nearby Chinese food lovers. With an extensive menu of over 200 items, you'll have to be prepared to carry it out . . . there are only a few tables for eat-in patrons. Portions are enormous, and chicken or shredded pork with string beans are delish. For those Chinese food lovers in the Ward's Corner area, there is cause for celebration. Kin's Wok 2 has opened at 7545 Granby Street, 423-2828, offering the same extensive menu as its Ghent sister.

HUNAN EXPRESS
6586 - D Tidewater Dr., Tidewater Shoppes
$ 853-8187

When Hunan Express first opened,

Get Crabby!

Although you'll find crab on almost every restaurant menu, you may want to buy a bushel for your own pick-and-eat feast. Be aware that crab prices fluctuate wildly depending on how prolific the catch. Before planning your menu call ahead and find out if crabs are on hand. They are usually most abundant in spring and summer.

Among the places to buy a bushel or half-bushel of crabs are: Colley Avenue Seafood Market, 4106 Colley Avenue in Norfolk, 423-2489; Channel Crab, 714 Stapleton Street in Norfolk, 622-3724; Chesapeake Bay Crab House, 2592 Campostella Road in Norfolk, 454-0653; Loaves and Fishes by Dail, 339 W. 21st Street in Norfolk, 627-8714; Wicker's Crab & Seafood, 3138 Victory Boulevard in Portsmouth, 487-4201; and Leggett's Seafood, 340 N. Main Street in Suffolk, 539-5331.

the only way you could have your Chicken of Four Seasons was to fly it home. Now, with the addition of 96 tables, it's an official new full-service eatery, and good eatin' it is. We Insiders will now give you the answer to your question about that gorgeous dish being served at the next table. It's the Four Seasons Bird Nest, made of sliced chicken, thinly sliced strips of beef, jumbo shrimp, sea scallops, baby corn, snow peas, mushrooms and assorted veggies done in a rich brown sauce and spread over a nest formed with crispy fried noodles. Perched on the top of the nest is a bird carved from the rind of a melon. What a dish. What a great restaurant.

Virginia Beach

FOON'S
4365 Shore Dr.
$$ *460-1985*

One great benefit of the authentic Hunan and Szechuan dishes here at Foon's is that they are all prepared without MSG. Outstanding on the menu are Szechuan shredded beef, Peking duck and soft-shell crab with ginger and scallions.

FORBIDDEN CITY
3544 Virginia Beach Blvd.
$$$ *486-8823*

This is one of the priciest Chinese restaurants in town, but once you slide into that "forbidden booth" and close the privacy curtains, you can pretend you're not really in Virginia Beach after all. Having completed an extensive renovation, including the addition of a bar for patrons awaiting a table or takeout, the exceptional General Tsao's Chicken has received its marching orders again.

PEKING DUCK INN
5204 Fairfield Shopping Center
$ *495-9110*

Check the chalkboard when you enter this aroma-filled restaurant to see what delicacy Chef Michael Chou has prepared from fresh local ingredients. And do please order the eggrolls for a grand surprise. They're not your usual, run-of-the-mill cabbage crispies. One type, for example, is a soft flour pancake filled with duck, plum sauce and scallions, just a hint of the light, fresh tastes that await no matter what you order.

Continental/French

Norfolk

ANTIQUITIES
Norfolk Airport Hilton
$$$ *466-8000*

White linen and attentive wait staff all add to the luscious menu featuring continental Euro-American favorites (including wild game) in this elegant, candlelit, beautifully appointed restaurant lurking behind the stark exterior of the Norfolk Airport Hilton. From beginning to end, you'll be enchanted by maitre d' Earl Branche, a distinguished member of Hampton Roads' old guard of restaurant professionals, who will prepare a delectable Caesar salad as well as strawberries Fifi, flambeed tableside in Grand Marnier. This is a place to truly act out the word "dining," as lingering at the table is not only welcome but encouraged.

Virginia Beach

LA CARAVELLE
1040 Laskin Rd.
$$$ *428-2477*

Rich French-Vietnamese offerings in

an elegant candlelit setting await you at this much-touted restaurant decorated in the country French manner inside the Seashire Inn. Duckling in Grand Marnier sauce, salmon in champagne sauce and tornadoes Caravelle are among our favorite entrees.

LE CHAMBORD
324 North Great Neck Rd.
$$$ 498-1234

A wonderful feast for the eyes as well as the stomach, Le Chambord is one of the most charming restaurants in the area and rightfully claims membership in *Port Folio* magazine's Golden Fork Hall of Fame. Its crisp decor and comfortable seating urges patrons to linger over divine entrees like quail stuffed with crab or Chateaubriand Bearnaise with red onion confit. Lunches offer a lighter bill of fare, with some marvelous salads, perfect with a glass of wine for a noontime break. Owners Frank and Luisa Spapen have been justly awarded the American Automobile Association's Four-Diamond Award, one of only two such honorees in the region. (Ship's Cabin in Ocean View is the other.) To capitalize on the casual-dining craze, Spapen has opened The Bistro & Rotisserie next door to Le Chambord, serving affordable bourgeois dishes like pork chops and garlic-mashed potatoes. Watching the master chefs at work under the huge, copper-hooded Bistro kitchen is a real treat.

THREE SHIPS INN
3800 Shore Dr.
$$$ 460-0055

This is one of the most romantic restaurants in the region as far as we're concerned. On a winter's evening, reserve early for a table beside the enormous fireplace, where you will be pampered by knowledgeable servers tempting you by describing the preparation of their duck with black cherry sauce or the brace of quail. A place not just for dinner, but for a most enjoyable evening.

Ethnic

Norfolk

ANTHONY'S
2502 Colley Ave.
$ 622-7411

Owner Anthony Chiperas just can't get enough of this location on the outskirts of Ghent. His father and uncle operated a restaurant at the same spot starting in 1943. In 1990, Chiperas revived the restaurant but closed for lack of a liquor license. In 1994 he returned determined to survive.

Mediterranean foods are the stars here, with baby lamb ribs being one of the best sellers. Entrees are creative and range from souvlaki to moussaka and linguine. Anthony's is open for lunch and dinner and closed on Sundays.

GERMAN PANTRY
5329 Virginia Beach Blvd.
$ 461-5100

This tiny, authentic German cafe has been in business since the late 1970s. New owners maintain a traditional menu that includes a variety of wieners and wursts as well as pork chops with sauerkraut. Daily specials feature such hearty fare as spatzle with goulash served with an excellent green salad and hard roll. Breads are imported from Canada but most everything else is made on premises, including Black Forest cake.

The Pantry has a small German store selling greeting cards, magazines and cooking supplies. Lunch and dinner are served everyday but Monday.

INDIA HOUSE

5760 Northampton Blvd.
$ 460-2100

India House was a 1993 newcomer to the local restaurant scene and immediately became one of our favorites. The extensive menu lets you choose from traditional tandoori and curried dishes as well as more exotic fare. Besides beef, seafood and lamb dishes, there's a good vegetarian lineup. If you're not sure what to order, try the lunch buffet. India House is open daily for lunch and dinner.

THE MONASTERY

443 Granby Mall
$$ 625-8193

This is one of the city's most venerable ethnic restaurants. Adolf and Anna Jerabek opened it in 1983 after moving from Czechoslovakia via New York. House specialties include roast duck and an excellent goose in the winter. Schnitzel and goulash are also featured on the 38-item menu. Daily specials range from salmon to roast lamb. Guests are welcomed with a plate of cheese, apples and bread. They will be tempted to end their meal with the Jerabeks' homemade Black Forest cake, strudel or chocolate fondue. The Monastery is open for lunch Tuesday through Friday. Dinner is served Tuesday through Sunday by waiters dressed as monks.

Reservations are suggested, particularly if the symphony, opera or other arts group is performing in downtown Norfolk. The Monastery has won so many Golden Fork awards from *Port Folio* that it has made it into the magazine's hall of fame.

NAWAB

888 N. Military Hwy.
$$ 455-8080

It was a happy day for Norfolk gourmands when this Indian restaurant opened in 1992 on the outskirts of Military Circle Mall — typically a haven for all-American chain restaurants. Nawab was the first regional restaurant to specialize in Indian cuisine. Its vast menu ranges from tandoori dishes cooked in a clay oven to curried chicken or squid. The menu is extensive and includes mulligatawny soup and a good mix of seafood, lamb, beef, vegetarian and chicken dishes. Nawab's bread is the traditional papadam wafer made from lentil flour. The restaurant is open daily for lunch and dinner. Nawab's lunch buffet is reasonably priced and is a good way to sample Indian cuisine.

ORAPAX INN

1300 Redgate Ave.
$ 627-8041
Hilltop West, First Colonial
and Laskin Rds. 428-3137
$

This is one of our mainstays. When we can't decide where to go for dinner we usually end up here. The inn opened in 1970 in residential West Ghent and branched out to Virginia Beach in 1994. This casual restaurant is renowned for its Greek specialties, including pastitsio, spanakopita, Greek salads and a gyro platter. It has some of the best fried calamari around.

Meals come with an irresistible homemade bread and melted butter for dipping. Salads are served with a bottle of the tangy house dressing for you to pour. Popular entrees include the spinach pizza and moussaka. There are daily specials. The Orapax is open for lunch and dinner and has delivery to nearby neighborhoods. It closes on Sunday. In September the owners shut down for most of the month for their annual pilgrimage to Greece. The Orapax is a recent People's Choice winner in *Port Folio* magazine's Golden Fork Awards.

TABOULI

4140 Granby St.
$ 627-1143

Middle Eastern fare is the star of this intimate Norfolk restaurant. Its namesake tabouli is some of the best we've ever eaten. Featured items include kababs, falafel and salads. You won't find your typical gyros sandwiches here. Adventuresome diners will be enamored with Tabouli's Turkish specialties. Their more cautious companions can feel at home with a cheese and herb pizza and sandwiches. Tabouli is open for lunch and dinner everyday but Sunday.

TAKIS GYROS

The Waterside
$ 627-5087

This Greek eatery is one of our favorites for lunch. It is in the food court of Waterside and serves great gyros, Greek salads and spanakopita. Other traditional foods on the menu include souvlaki and baklava. Takis is open for lunch and dinner daily.

Virginia Beach

ANATOLIA

2158 N. Great Neck Rd.
$$ 496-9777

Anatolia is a stylish restaurant that excels in gourmet Turkish cuisine and has the region's broadest selection of Middle Eastern food. Its owner is a former Greenwich Village restaurateur who decided to head south and opened the restaurant in 1990. The extensive menu includes lamb and beef kebabs; chicken, shrimp or lamb sautees; shrimp dishes and vegetarian specialties. A wood-burning brick oven turns out some of the best pita bread you'll ever eat. Early bird dinners are a bargain. Anatolia is in the Great Neck Square Shopping Center and is open for lunch and dinner daily with hearty breakfasts

served on weekends. If you go on Friday or Saturday nights you'll definitely need a reservation since that's when belly dancers entertain during dinner.

BANGKOK GARDEN

Loehmann's Plaza, Virginia Beach Blvd.
$ 498-5009

The region finally gained a full-fledged Thai restaurant when Bangkok Garden opened in 1993. It is owned by a Thai native who's run a Hampton restaurant for several years. Fiery food will whip your palette into shape. You'll find the seafood stir-fried or bathed in a lemon grass broth. One top choice is the pork seasoned with mint, lime and a potent chili powder. The staff dons Thai costumes at night and occasionally treats customers to traditional Thai dancing. The restaurant is open daily for lunch and dinner.

THE STREET COOK

Lynnhaven Pkwy. and Princess Anne Rd.
$$ 471-7810

This Mediterranean restaurant has a cuisine its owner describes as "a little Greek, a little Italian and a little Virginia Beach." It turns out great seafood crepes, veal Erica and poulet Florentine among other entrees. Homemade desserts include a chocolate torte and baklava. The Street Cook is open for lunch Tuesday through Friday and for dinner Tuesday through Sunday. Reservations are accepted.

Italian

Norfolk

LA GALLERIA RISTORANTE

120 College Pl.
$$$ 623-3939

Valet parking outside, mahogany, veined marble and hammered copper inside . . . a tiny hint of the spectacular evening you'll have dining at La Galleria in downtown Norfolk. This place can only be classified as an "event," and has to its credit mucho awards for its wonderful food as well as its decor. Recognized as one of the 10 most beautiful restaurants in the country by two national trade magazines, fine northern Italian specialities are prepared superbly and served with panache. Get your taste buds activated with a white pizza from the wood-burning oven, then move on to polla alla Sorentina (chicken stuffed with spinach, zucchini and mozzarella in wine sauce) or vittello La Galleria (veal with fresh tomato sauce). The bar that floats off-center in the restaurant is gorgeous, and its a popular spot for gathering after work or dinner.

FELLINI'S
123 West 21st St.
$$ 625-3000

Credit owner Mike Cavish with introducing "new pizza" to the palates of Hampton Roads residents and visitors. Cancel that chain restaurant pizza and order one of his Thai Chicken, BLT (the "L" is spinach!) or Cajun pizzas, prepared to order in the open kitchen you can see from any table in the intimate house. A favorite hangout for locals who know every server and bartender by name, plan to push your way through the crowds to the bar on a weekend night. There's more than pizza, though. Their pasta dishes are phenomenal, and they prepare one of the best and biggest Caesar salads in town. You can get the same Fellini's taste at the Beach, too, via their speedy home-delivery service. Place your order by calling 422-3500. Note: At press time, Fellini's was planning a move to 4910 Colley Avenue.

MAMA'S ITALIAN KITCHEN
182 West Ocean View Ave.
$ 587-4262

You had better be hungry! The servings are mammoth and can only be described as comfort food, Italian style. An Ocean View landmark for generations, you may have to wait a bit in the unrushable atmosphere, but all your Italian basics like spaghetti with sausage and lasagna, along with some exotics like Pasta Putanesca (pasta with anchovies, pine nuts and herbs), are well worth the "weight."

IL PORTO
333 Waterside Dr. (The Waterside)
$$ 627-4400

If expansion is a sign of success, Il Porto in The Waterside is on a garlic roll. Since its opening in 1983, it has expanded two separate times to accommodate diners who adore their Northern Italian cuisine. Savor the homemade pasta, veal and seafood while you watch ships slide down the Elizabeth River. Two spacious patios are available for dining when weather permits.

REGINO'S
114 East Little Creek Rd., Ward's Corner
$ 588-8012

The pizza comes in one size . . . humongous. And it's amazing how you can eat the whole thing, it's so delish (although we have heard rumors that they will prepare a medium size if you insist). Antipasto and lasagna to die for are also here in this long and narrow eatery tucked away in Wards Corner. You may have to wait outside the door on a busy evening, but the aroma of garlic that hits you when you step inside makes any wait well worth the time. Just to spread the love of garlic, Regino's operates a sister restaurant at Hilltop Plaza at the Beach, 491-1613.

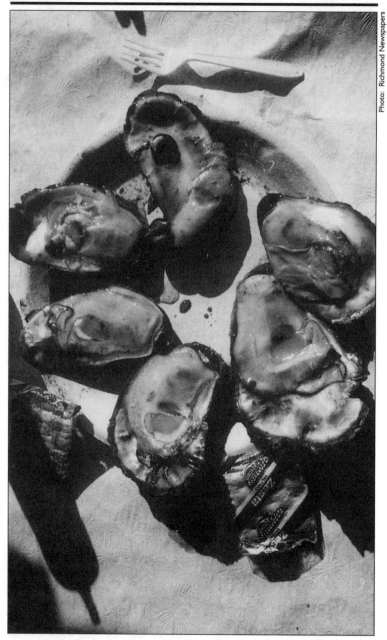

Photo: Richmond Newspapers

Seafood is the king cuisine served in restaurants in Hampton Roads.

SPAGHETTI WAREHOUSE
1900 Monticello Ave.
$ 622-0151

We're talking volume at Spaghetti Warehouse, a great family place housed in a totally rehabbed old warehouse located on the outskirts of Ghent. Volume number one: The food literally hangs off the platter no matter what you order. The other volume: the number of patrons lined up to take their turn at the vast menu, especially on weekend nights. It's a bit noisy for a romantic bottle of Chianti, but a super place if you have teenagers who never seem to be filled up.

Virginia Beach

IL GIARDINO RISTORANTE
910 Atlantic Ave.
$$$ 422-6464

While it isn't really necessary to dress up to eat here, you'll want to look your best to impress all the beautiful people you'll bump into. There's no doubt you'll be tempted by the dazzling array of appetizers, but do share one. You'll want to save room for the entree . . . a little veal, perhaps? A supper here may be the very best meal you have at Virginia Beach, both for divinely prepared dishes and superb service. We suggest you also meander into their European-style outdoor cafe, where you'll certainly want to linger over espresso. Afterwards, there's a happening piano bar, and the lounge stays open until 2 AM to maintain its social cachet.

AERO'S SEA GRILL
981 Laskin Road
$$ 428-0111

You just can't have too much garlic in your bloodstream. That's why a trip to Aero's is so vital to keep you going. Start your feast with Zuppa di clams, order a Caesar salad prepared tableside and then launch into a full or half order of fabulous homemade pasta, or perhaps one of their exceptional veal dishes. The atmosphere, along with the food, is totally delightful. FYI: The restaurant is owned by Michael Scaramellino of La Brocca fame. His son, Michael Jr., whose middle name is Aero, is manager in charge.

ALDO'S RISTORANTE
1860 Laskin Rd.
$$ 491-1111

Not only will you eat well here, you'll look good doing it. This is a charming place, with a never-ending turnover of equally charming patrons, all waiting for their personalized platter of homemade pasta graced by light and tasty sauces, one better than the next. Their fantastic pizzas, baked in a wood-burning pizza oven, are likewise yummy. Popular for lunch and dinner, it's a fun place when you're in the mood for a taste of Italy.

BELLA PASTA
1423 North Great Neck Rd.
$$ 496-3333

Take your pick here from Northern and Southern Italian dishes, with a few creative American specialties like Chateau Bella, a marinated tenderloin, tossed in for universal appeal. Order your chicken or veal prepared in such time-honored styles as piccata, marsala, parmigiana or scaloppine. But first you must demand their fabulous Crostini, ovals of Italian bread fried in olive oil and slathered with garlicky cream cheese, basil and strips of red peppers. Pass the breath mints, please.

CIOLA'S
1889 Virginia Beach Blvd.
$$ 428-9601

What masquerades as a good-old roadside diner is the laboratory for the

Italian chemists who can whip up some of the most tummy-pleasing dishes this side of Italy. From pasta to lasagna, the portions are generous and consistently excellent, all cooked to your order. A long-time Virginia Beach landmark, neither the interior decor nor the quality of the food has changed in many a year, a fact for which many of Ciola's fans are quite grateful.

PASTA E PANI
1065 Laskin Rd.
$$ 428-2299

The running battle here is which is more delicious — the homemade pasta or the pani (bread). Simplicity is the key, whether it's a pizza from the wood-burning stove or delicately flavored pasta entrees. There's also a separate deli where you can bag some of their specialities along with cheeses, meats and other Italian groceries.

DIVINA ITALIAN RESTAURANT
1297 General Booth Blvd.
$$ 422-2712

Our advice is very simple: Rush through your dinner to get to dessert. Lap up the saltimbocca, with veal and pro-sciutto, or chicken Marsala, then rush headlong into tiramisu, that confection of ladyfingers, sweet mascarpone cheese, espresso and liqueur or a rich Napoleon. Settle back with an espresso or cappuccino and relax. Your meal has been divine, and remarkably affordable too.

LA BROCCA
608 Birdneck Rd.
$$$ 428-0655

"Dancing shrimp with cognac" should give you a clue to the fine dining experience that's tradition at La Brocca. Since La Brocca means wine carafe, you can expect an exceptional wine list, and if you're in doubt about your selection, owner Michael Scaramellino and his son are at the ready with the proper suggestion. The medieval decor with its Portuguese tapestries and lattice work gives the restaurant a dark, intimate ambiance, perfect for a romantic dinner for two.

Portsmouth

CAFE EUROPA
319 High St.
$$$ 399-6652

If you ever have a yen for veal cooked to absolute perfection, a trip to Portsmouth's Cafe Europa is almost the only sensible choice. A charming little cafe, all lace curtains and candlelight and long known for it's Italian and French cuisine prepared to ultimate perfection by chef and owner Michael Simko, it is a multi-time Golden Fork winner for the quality of food, atmosphere and service.

Japanese

Virginia Beach

AJI-ICHIBAN
309 Aragona Blvd.
$$ 490-0499

It's natural, pretty and fresh, with no fat or sugar. It's sushi, and it's the new power food for the late 20th century. Serving some of the best is Aji-Ichiban in Virginia Beach, under the watchful eye of owner Jing Below, one of the few female sushi chefs around. After you're done in the sushi bar, settle in to enjoy tempura, teriyaki, yakitori, tonkasu and hot pots, washed down with either a Sapporo, the well-known Japanese beer, or sake. If you do happen to be a sushi fanatic, don't miss the Saturday night all-you-dare-to-eat sushi buffet.

KYUSHU

400 Newtown Rd.
$$ 499-6292

Fresh, beautifully presented sushi and sashimi platters are the standard at this award-winning sushi bar. Watching chef Ebigasko deftly layer a touch of wasabi (horseradish root) and a slender slice of yellowtail on an oval of rice is true culinary theater. Of note here is the "kiss roll" of seaweed and rice filled with garlic, a very different taste for the bored palate.

MATSURI KOREA HOUSE

4768 Shore Dr.
$$ 460-0000

Another popular sushi bar serving traditional Japanese seafood dishes, Matsuri has been around since 1986, and owner Chong Kim sees to it that his restaurant offers not only some of the tastiest sushi in town, but also the most elegantly presented. Tuna, salmon and yellowtail are the favorite ingredients here, but vegetable sushi is offered to those who can't, or won't, eat raw fish. A restaurant with a split personality, the Japanese dining room shares the spotlight with the Korean section, serving a full menu of authentic Korean dishes like Kal Bee, slices of bone-in beef ribs and Sewoo Bok Kum, stir-fried shrimp with vegetables and rice in a brown sauce. No matter which dining area and international flavor you choose, the kimono-clad servers are delightful, right down to the warm cloth for after din-din hand cleansing.

SHOGUN

313 Hilltop Shopping Center
$$ 422-5150

You just know you're in for something extraordinary when you first spot those chefs wearing tall, brilliant red chef's hats and neck scarves and bearing mega-sized knives sharp enough to split a human hair. You have entered the Shogun zone, and you are going to have the most entertaining meal of the year — a full seven courses prepared with the speed of lightning right before your very eyes. The food, especially the tempura, is excellent, and watching the skilled preparation is an event. Don't miss it.

Mexican

Norfolk

COLLEY CANTINA

1316 Colley Ave.
$ 622-0033

We can't quite figure out whether it's the food or the fun that keeps this place in Ghent jammed every night. As Mexican food goes, this is all your favorite basics . . . lots of it for a reasonable price. But toss in a phenomenal Margarita and perhaps you've unlocked the secret to this popular place's success. It's especially nice in spring through fall, with outdoor seating where you and your taco can watch the Colley Avenue cruising.

EL RODEO

5834 Virginia Beach Blvd. at Janaf   466-9077
6209 Providence Rd.   474-2698
$

Direct from Guadalajara in the state of Jalisco, Mexico, comes the Lopez clan, opening their 14th restaurant in the Mid-Atlantic region. El Rodeo at Janaf joins its sister on Providence Road in Virginia Beach in serving dishes that represent the various sections of Mexico, from the hot and spicy beef steak à la Tampiquena to combo dinners like a pair of tacos, enchilada and chile con queso. Whether you like your Mexican spicy or mild, there's a dish to please the palate and the pocketbook.

Virginia Beach

AMIGOS MARGARITA GRILLE
2272 Great Neck Rd.
$$ 481-3133

Under the watchful eye of manager Rick Maggard, here's a Mexican restaurant that's on the border . . . Southwest that is. Along with the popular Cantina for a custom Margarita, the restaurant offers more than just the standard Mexican fare, tossing in some real tasty items like fish grilled with citrus. Upbeat and spunky, it's a terrific place to go when only a fajita will soothe your nerves.

SAN ANTONIO SAM'S
604 Norfolk Ave.   491-0263
1501 Colley Ave., Norfolk   623-0233
$

It's Tex-Mex and more in this jumping place packed with Lone Star memorabilia and roadhouse-style tunes on tape. A hint to the creative touches is their wonderful way with enchiladas. Try the crab and avocado or enchiladas del mar, stuffed with crab, scallops and shrimp. Find San Antonio Sams, the sequel, on Colley Avenue in Ghent with a casually Western showplace atmosphere. Sway to the classic '60s and '70s tunes on the house soundtrack while you chomp on state-of-the-art Tex-Mex revisionist cuisine like crab and avocado enchiladas and quesadillas with turkey chili. You can even take home their signature salsa and barbecue sauces, bottled for retail by owners Ben Rogers and Dave Marine.

MI CASITA
Rosemont and Bonney Rds.
$ 463-3819

Arguably the area's most authentic Mexican eatery, this place is so packed with pinatas dangling from the ceiling and draped on shelves that you have to blink to make sure you haven't been whisked to a sidestreet in Tijuana. All your favorites are here, as well as some superb homemade guacamole and chips to wash down with a bottle of Tecate, but we'd advise staying clear of the cactus that's stir-fried with tomatoes and onions. They make a mean Margarita, and the huevos rancheros they serve only at lunchtime are muy bueno.

Photo: Phil Ruckle

Many restaurants offer excellent views to enjoy while dining.

EL AZTECA
First Colonial and Laskin Rds.
$ 437-1890

If you're longing for a Mexican feast that's more like authentic Mexican than Tex-Mex, here's the place. Sit inside or out under the umbrella-covered tables on the walled patio and enjoy our favorite, a chicken enchilada topped with sauce mole. The salsa is fresh and spicy, and even the chips are great. Bring amigos and give it a try.

Portsmouth

LA TOLTECA
6031 High St.
$ 484-8043

If you can pronounce camarones al mojo de ajo, order it. It's shrimp sauteed in garlic and butter and it's to die for. Or, be dull and go for the familiar fajitas or tacos. . . they're exceptionally good here too. And, if you're watching your fat intake, Chef Jose Baragas uses a more healthful vegetable oil, rather than the standard lard, for frying. So, go ahead and indulge.

New Southern

Norfolk

BIENVILLE GRILL
723 W. 21st St.
$$ 625-5427

You'll find Louisiana-style cuisine with a kick, with Cajun and Creole dishes that can't be matched in Hampton Roads at this great spot. Chef Mike Hall was instrumental in introducing Cajun to our area, bless his little Andouille sausage. A Louisiana native, he's brought a bit of the French Quarter to Ghent, along with some pretty mean live jazz on weekends

and, as Mike says, "killer catfish." The restaurant has won so many *Port Folio* Golden Fork awards, it's enshrined in its Hall of Fame.

CAJUN CAFE
The Waterside
$ 626-3711

Bienville Grill's Mike Hall opened this Waterside eatery in 1992 to spice up the food court with some hearty Cajun cooking. For a cheap price, diners get a jumbo plate of red or black beans and rice or shrimp creole. All come with a hunk of homemade French bread. Beef brisket and grilled chicken sandwiches also are served. Open daily.

THE DUMBWAITER
117 Tazewell St.
$$ 623-3663

It is absolutely impossible to describe Dumbwaiter owner Sydney Meers and keep a straight face. The man is a trip, and so is his popular restaurant.

The place is a whimsical madhouse, crammed with happy people munching on regional dishes with a down-home Southern flair. You've never had real grits, sweet potatoes or meat loaf until you've tasted Sydney's. If you're close to Downtown Norfolk, you'd be missing something special if you don't stop in. At lunchtime, a must-order is the grilled chicken breast on black-eyed peas with blue cheese dressing. And, try not to laugh when you see "Dumbketchup" and "Dumbmustard" on the table.

In 1994 the Dumbwaiter moved to Tazewell Street from its original location a block away. The move added a bar and more room to dine. The decor can best be described as "avant garde urban chic" so go see it. Look for live jazz, folk and blues music on Saturday nights. The restaurant has made it into *Port Folio* magazine's Hall of Fame for earning a multitude of Golden Fork awards.

Virginia Beach

RAGIN' CAJUN
3108 Atlantic Ave.
$$ 491-8267

The name says it all at this friendly place where the menu changes daily. Expect to be tempted by blackened shrimp, spicy wings or other Cajun delicacies. Red beans and rice is irresistible. Last year the restaurant moved to bigger quarters at the EconoLodge at 3108 Atlantic. It serves dinner year round and cooks up breakfast and lunch during summer.

PUNGO PLACE
LIGHTHOUSE RESTAURANT
1824 Princess Anne Rd.
$$ 426-2670

Cajun food is the specialty of this restaurant founded in 1987. Since Pungo Place is in the heart of Pungo — one of Virginia Beach's rural areas — its menu often features seasonal produce grown right down the road. Seafood, steaks, pork and chicken are restaurant staples, with a blackened fish of the day and a blackened prime rib always on the menu. Wednesday is Cajun night with creole, jambalaya and other Louisiana favorites. Alligator is a popular appetizer as is a puff pastry stuffed with andouille sausage, shrimp and crab. Homemade fruit cobblers and cheesecakes are available. Ice cream comes from two local sources — Bergey's Dairy Farm and Uncle Harry's Cones and Cream. Pungo Place closes on Tuesdays and also Mondays during summer. It accepts reservations.

Nouvelle American

Norfolk

BISTRO 210
210 York St.
$$ 622-3210

There have been almost as many rave reviews of this eatery in downtown Norfolk as there have been patrons. That said, we too would follow owner/chef Todd Jurich anywhere he chooses to hang his ladle. An upstart and innovator when it comes to combining tastes and textures, Jurich has whipped up some unusual — and unusually delightful — surprises. Try the carpaccio of pastramied lamb or the salmon glazed with molasses, cayenne and cinnamon. It may sound a bit off the deep end of the griddle, but those and so many other weird menu concoctions that change with seasonal availability are fantastic. A *Port Folio* Golden Fork award winner, they've started accepting reservations to assure you a table.

CAFE 21
742G W. 21st St.
$$ 625-4218

A real neighborhood bistro, Cafe 21 features ethnic and American cuisine. Enjoy their risottos, curries and couscous, along with a mean pasta Alfredo. The fresh-baked desserts are tempting and delicious, and an order from the Espresso Bar makes a savory after-dinner finale. Cafe 21's eclectic, world-ranging, healthful fare and cosmopolitan atmosphere have just earned it a loyal following.

CRACKERS
821 W. 21st St.
$$ 640-0200

If you drive by too fast, you'll miss it. Cracker's may be small in stature, but it's a giant in the eyes of those who know a great meal when they're served one. Inch for inch, it might just be the best little restaurant in Norfolk. Everything is prepared from scratch daily, and nightly specials are the whim of the wizard chef/owner David Blackstock, who writes them down on a chalkboard for your selection. The neoclassical cuisine changes with the season and Blackstock's mood du jour, but you can count on the consistency of excellence. If you plan to dine on Thursday through Saturday, make certain to reserve one of the few tables in advance.

PALETTES CAFE AT THE CHRYSLER MUSEUM
245 W. Olney Rd.
$ 622-1211

Insiders adore this delightful restaurant located on the first floor of The Chrysler Museum. With its dark walls and crisp tablecloths, it is an elegant little bistro offering a seasonal variety of salads, like Thai chicken and fresh tuna Nicoise, as well as sandwiches served on dark Bavarian bread and in pita. Tempting soups and a few selected entrees are available too, and it's a wonderfully peaceful oasis for a quiet and intimate lunch.

Virginia Beach

THE BIG TOMATO
Second and Atlantic
$$ 437-0155

Cioppino with lobster tail, corn flake-fried crab cakes and silk tomatoes dangling from the ceiling . . . got your interest? The Big Tomato is the newest brainchild of chef Chuck Sass who carries on his American regional theme with a twist and a sense of humor. While the crab cakes are an Insiders' favorite, why not give the Cajun "martini" of bronzed

shrimp in a long-stemmed glass a whirl. You'll also find a 27-seat covered outdoor cafe where you can soak up the beautiful ocean views while you nibble on quail and rattlesnake sausage. Go on, try it.

BLUE WATER CAFE
3301 Atlantic Ave., Four Seasons Resort
$$ 491-0188

Killians' Red beer-battered shrimp with orange chipotle sauce. Got the idea? This is a true gem of an oceanfront cafe, with wall-to-wall windows that spill in natural sunlight by day and that transforms into a cozy, intimate rendezvous in the evening. Marvy salads, stellar entrees and sumptuous desserts fight for star billing . . . you'll be pleasantly surprised no matter what your menu or chalkboard choice. Pleasant summer evenings demand you dine alfresco on the large, covered patio. Parking is free, right around the corner on Pacific and 32nd Street.

COASTAL GRILL
1427 N. Great Neck Rd.
$$ 496-3348

From the minute you land a table at this intimate bistro, you start right off into the wonderful world of food. A waiting basket of sourdough bread with crocks of unsalted butter may tempt you, but save that appetite for the superb entrees, including beautifully prepared and presented lamb, duck, rabbit and fresh seafood. If you think you'll have room, order the spinach salad, topped with a surprising garnish of chicken livers.

FIVE 01 CITY GRILL
501 Birdneck Rd.
$$ 425-7195

Be advised that this is one of the hottest meal tickets in town. It's just smokin' with its cool clientele, big, casual bar and devastatingly delicious menu. Host Mike Atkinson and chef Corey Beisel have a winner by serving some of the tastiest treats in town. Veal chop grilled with goat cheese is perfect to follow a starter of charred tuna sashimi with spicy kim chee or the house's signature Michelob shrimp. To top it off, sample the sweet bread pudding drowning in Jack Daniels. What a way to go . . . and you should.

LUCKY STAR
1608 Pleasure House Rd.
$$$ 363-8410

When chef supreme Amy Brandt puts the pedal to the kettle, wonderful things happen. Here in the sparkling white interior, sprinkled with the works of local artists, Amy and partner Butch Butt lay out one magnificent spread after another. Combinations are innovative and seasonal, influenced by the Pacific rim. Crawfish spring rolls, spicy corn cakes and Thai chicken salad are among our favorites, but when it's apple season, there's no telling what wonderful aromatic delights will greet you at the Lucky Star.

MONROE'S
8180 Shore Dr.
$$ 588-0100

Wherever master chef Monroe Duncan goes, flocks of gourmands are sure to follow. Namesake Monroe's is no different than any other fine eatery where magician Monroe has hung his culinary shingle. Be prepared for an overwhelming menu with hidden delights like curried conch fritters for starters and Trinidadian shrimp curry with papaya chutney for the main course, then fight over the last morsel of fluffy blueberry cheesecake or sweet potato pecan pie. It simply amazes us how Monroe dreams up some of his offerings (roasted banana halves with zucchini?), but judging from

the repeat patronage at this wonderful eatery, where you can watch sailboats bobbing outside the window, he's dreamed up a whimsical winner.

PHIL'S GRILL
205 11th St.
$ 491-7674

The bartender's too busy to chat, the volume of music and voices is high and your wait for a table is probably a beer and a half. That's okay, because while you wait, you can get those taste buds into a frenzy watching Phil Haushalter in the open kitchen throwing plates around at blazing speed. Then, before you know it, your dinner of stir-fried chicken in ginger-scented sauce or sauteed shrimp and linguine in a rich, parmesan-dusted cream has landed on your table with shriek velocity from the hands of a baseball cap-clad server. This is not just a restaurant, it's a happening only enhanced by Phil's "shut-up and eat" philosophy. But then, with super-generous portions that average under seven bucks, who's gonna complain. Not a soul.

TANDOM'S PINE TREE INN
2932 Virginia Beach Blvd.
$$ 340-3661

Since 1927, an evening at Tandom's Pine Tree Inn has been a treat for the entire family. Starting with the award-winning 60-item salad, hors d'oeuvres and raw bar, you can settle in a comfy chair and watch the parade of Black Angus beef, pasta, seafood and Cajun dishes go by. We're prejudiced about Tandom's superbly prepared veal and chicken entrees, presented by some of the most knowledgeable and personable servers in town. Tandom's has brought its reputation to Norfolk with a spin-off operation called Tandom's Madison Grill in the Downtown Ramada Hotel, 627-2222.

SWAN TERRACE

The Founders' Inn and Conference Center
$$$ 366-5777

Putting a spin on Colonial cookery, the Swan Terrace literally sparkles from the beautifully appointed dining room to the individual tables set to Miss Manners' smug satisfaction. Seasonal entrees vary, but not the policies that prohibit smoking or the consumption of alcoholic beverages.

Seafood

Norfolk

BLUE CRAB BAR & GRILLE

4521 Pretty Lake Ave.
$$ 362-5620

With its location overlooking the waters of Little Creek, this is a scenic spot to dine — complete with boats tied up at a neighboring marina. Blue Crab opened in 1989 with a menu that features a lot of seafood prepared in Caribbean and Cajun styles. Salmon, tuna, catfish and crabs are menu staples, with seasonal fish offered when available. Blue Crab closes on Monday but serves lunch and dinner the other days. Brunch is offered on Sunday. Reservations are recommended on the weekend.

LOCKHART'S SEAFOOD RESTAURANT

8440 Tidewater Dr.
$$ 588-0405

Since 1959 the Lockhart family has prided itself on its seafood. Don't expect anything trendy here. Instead, you'll find excellent renditions of old favorites like crab Norfolk, deviled crab and fried fish. Lockhart's is open for lunch and dinner and closed on Mondays.

O'SULLIVAN'S WHARF

4300 Colley Ave.
$$ 423-3753

This is a popular spot near Old Dominion University for dining or relaxing with a beer. It sits on scenic Knitting Mill Creek with boats anchored outside. In warm weather O'Sullivan's deck is a popular gathering spot. Menu offerings include crab cakes and seafood combinations. There also is a variety of sandwiches, soups and salads. The restaurant is open for lunch and dinner daily and frequently has live entertainment. Reservations are accepted.

PHILLIPS' WATERSIDE

333 Waterside Dr.
$$ 627-6600

This is one of the anchors for The Waterside festival marketplace. Its view of the Elizabeth River is unbeatable, and on warm days you can dine on an open-air patio. Phillips' is a spin-off of Phillips' Crab House, which opened in Ocean City, Maryland, in 1956. Menu offerings include a wide variety of seafood, including crab cooked any way you can imagine. There also are some steaks on the menu as well as a raw bar. The restaurant is open daily for lunch and dinner. You may want to call for reservations, particularly on weekend evenings.

SHIPS CABIN

4110 E. Ocean View Ave.
$$$ 362-4659

A Norfolk dining landmark since 1967, the Ships Cabin has been in the Hoggard family for two generations. Owner Joe Hoggard is one of the region's best-known restaurateurs. His lovely restaurant has a terrific view of the Chesapeake Bay and a seafood menu to go with it.

Menus frequently change — especially now that star chef Bobby Huber is manning the stove — but there are some staples that local diners have come to expect. Servers continually make the rounds with a variety of great bread, including blueberry, raisin, honey wheat and Bavarian wheat. Oysters Bingo (named after a local attorney) are oysters sauteed with shallots, butter and wine. Crab soup and crab cakes are other menu mainstays. Other offerings include a variety of shrimp, crab and fresh fish as well as steaks. Regulars know to save room for the whiskey pudding after dinner.

The restaurant is open for dinner daily and takes reservations. The Ships Cabin has a AAA Four-Diamond rating and is a consistent winner of *Port Folio* magazine's Golden Fork awards

SKIPJACKS RAW BAR & GRILL
112 College Place
$$ 626-3505

Fusion cuisine is the house specialty at this downtown restaurant that was the longtime home of the now-defunct Le Charlieu. The lobby is dominated by a raw bar. Seafood is prepared with a touch that draws from the Philippines, Italy and other exotic locales. While heavy on seafood, the menu also finds room for chicken, pasta and sandwiches. Skipjacks is open for lunch and dinner.

Virginia Beach

ALEXANDER'S ON THE BAY
4536 Oceanview Ave.
$$$ 464-4999

Devastated by a 1993 fire, Alexander's was rebuilt and reopened last year. The elegant restaurant is a standout for its terrific view and fine dining. It's a romantic restaurant where diners can eat on an open deck overlooking the Chesapeake Bay. Since Alexander's originally opened in 1985, one of its signature appetizers has been Oysters Alexander — sauteed herb-coated oysters served with a white wine and shallot sauce. Entrees range from seafood to steak and veal. Popular entrees are seafood Madagascar — shrimp, scallops and lobsters cooked in a creamy peppercorn sauce — and a mariner's platter loaded with five types of seafood. Favorite desserts are homemade cheesecakes. Dinner is served daily, and reservations are recommended.

ANCHOR INN
1716 Pleasure House Rd.
$$ 363-1885

In 1993 this new location replaced two former Anchor Inns. This has long been a locals-only place highly recommended by seafood lovers. The fish is fresh, and menu offerings include a three-fish platter and crab cakes. For appetizers try fried calamari or crab-stuffed mushrooms. Homemade desserts include chocolate mousse pie and Key lime pie. The Virginia Beach inn has been in business since 1983 and is open for dinner daily and lunch everyday but Saturday.

ANGELO'S
37th and Oceanfront
$$ 425-0347

Right next to Howard Johnson's sits a jewel of a restaurant, a Beach favorite for more than 20 years. While Angelo and brother George will be pleased to put a 16-ounce Black Angus New York strip in front of you, we have to suggest the wonderful seafood pastas, like shrimp over a steaming bed of linguine or our favorite pasta dish with lobster, scallops, mussels and shrimp. If you can't decide between the two, order the famous Land and Sea

Platter with a fork tender filet and delightfully seasoned New England lobster tail. Don't let the homemade desserts overwhelm you, especially the chocolate Chambord cake.

BLUE PETE'S
1400 N. Muddy Creek Rd.
$$ 426-2005

This is the ultimate off-the-beaten-path restaurant. But once diners find Blue Pete's, they're glad they made the trek. This rustic restaurant, founded in 1973, is known for its variety of fresh seafood. It recently expanded its menu to include all-natural Colorado beef. The house specialty is sweet potato biscuits, and the restaurant cheerfully hands out the recipe for this treat. Blue Pete's typically closes during the winter, but from spring through fall it is open for dinner Monday through Saturday. Call for directions and reservations. Driving to Blue Pete's will take you on a jaunt through rural Virginia Beach. The restaurant has been a recent People's Choice winner in *Port Folio* magazine's Golden Fork awards.

BLUE WATER CAFE
33rd and Atlantic
$$ 491-0188

This innovative restaurant has some of the best food at the Beach. Its location in the Four Sails Hotel also gives it a front-row view of the ocean, which makes for a pleasant outing. Expect the unexpected here, such as salmon with wild mushrooms baked in parchment. Be sure to save room for homemade Key lime pie, rum cake and other divine desserts. During summer the outdoor dining area is a wonderful place to while away an evening. The Blue Water serves breakfast, lunch and dinner. Reservations are recommended in the evenings.

CAPTAIN GEORGE'S
1956 Laskin Rd.   428-3494
2262 Pungo Ferry Rd.   721-3463
$$$

These restaurants originated the gorge-till-you-burst concept in the region. They offer an amazing variety of seafood, salads, side dishes, soups and desserts for one price. For landlubbers, there is a good selection of other foods. The steamed crab legs and shrimp are irresistible to most diners, especially since they can fill their plates as often as they like. The restaurants do a big volume of business, so fresh batches of food are continually being hauled from the kitchen. Captain George's opens daily for dinner.

CAPTAIN JOHN'S SEAFOOD COMPANY
4616 Virginia Beach Blvd.
$$$ 499-7755

If you're really starved, head for this all-you-can-chow-down seafood buffet. It seems to stretch for a mile with a gargantuan array of crabs, clams, fish and shrimp prepared in endless ways. You'll also enjoy all kinds of other entrees, salads, side dishes and scrumptious desserts. You'll find Captain John's anchored next to Pembroke Mall and serving lunch and dinner daily.

CHARLIE'S SEAFOOD RESTAURANT
3139 Shore Dr.
$$ 481-9863

Charlie's is a homey seafood place near the Chesapeake Bay with a 1950s aura. It was started in 1946 and six years later moved across the street to this location. Little has changed since then in this utilitarian restaurant. It remains in the Rehpelz family, with the founder's grandsons now at the helm.

The menu of flounder, fried oysters, steamed clams and seafood platters is still intact. Home-cooked side dishes include squash, collards and black-eyed peas. One standout is the she-crab soup. It's so good we've even heard strangers in Pennsylvania describing how sublime it is. Desserts usually feature Key lime, lemon meringue and chocolate banana pies.

On most nights there is an all-you-can-eat steamed shrimp special. Snow crab legs are discounted on Monday and Wednesdays nights. Charlie's is open for dinner daily and serves lunch every day but Monday. Reservations are accepted.

CHICK'S OYSTER BAR
2143 Vista Circle
$$ 481-5757

This casual restaurant on the Lynnhaven River is a local hangout with a deck overlooking the Lynnhaven Inlet. Fresh fish is the backbone of the menu that features the best of what is currently available. Chick's is one of the few restaurants that serves deviled crab. Steamed mussels and shrimp also are big sellers. You can dine inside or eat outside on the deck and watch the boats. Chick's has won a Popular Choice award as part of *Port Folio* magazine's Golden Fork awards.

DUCK-IN & GAZEBO
3324 Shore Dr.
$$ 481-0201

The Duck-In has an ideal location right on the Chesapeake Bay with a beach and gazebo in its back yard. Diners can eat inside or on a deck under a striped canopy overlooking the bay. The restaurant is renowned for its crab cakes, hushpuppies and fisherman's chowder. It's been in business since 1952 when it was converted from a bait shop into a restaurant.

Although its regular menu of seafood platters, crab and shrimp is good, the Duck-In has gained a following for its

buffets. The all-you-can-eat buffet is offered nightly during the summer and on Friday and Saturday during off-season. It usually is loaded with snow crab legs, shrimp creole and other seafood dishes. Popular desserts include bread pudding with pecan glaze and the volcano — a brownie and ice cream with all the fixings. The Duck-In serves lunch and dinner daily and has breakfast on weekends. Reservations are accepted.

GUS' MARINER RESTAURANT
57th St. and Atlantic Ave.
$$$ 425-5699

With its ocean view and excellent cooking, Gus' has earned a permanent positive reputation with area diners. It has been in the Ramada Oceanside Tower since 1981. There are usually at least five types of fresh fish on the menu. Hushpuppies are hard to resist. Specialty desserts include Belgium whisky pudding made with pound cake and raspberry sauce. Gus' serves breakfast, lunch and dinner daily with a brunch on Sundays. After winning countless Golden Fork awards, *Port Folio* magazine has enshrined Gus' in its Hall of Fame.

HARPOON LARRY'S OYSTER BAR
216 24th St.
$$ 422-6000

Fresh seafood served in a casual atmosphere is the draw at Harpoon Larry's. The restaurant opened near the beachfront in 1990 as a spin-off of a Hampton restaurant. The menu is heavy on shrimp, crab legs and seafood platters. There are lots of appetizers, including chicken wings. Harpoon Larry's has a raw bar. It is open for dinner daily. Lunch is served daily during spring and summer and on weekends the rest of the year.

HENRY'S RAW BAR & SEA GRILLE
3319 Shore Dr.
$$ *481-7300*

Located on the Lynnhaven River near the Chesapeake Bay, Henry's is a big, busy restaurant founded in 1938. It changed hands in 1986 and underwent a major renovation and expansion. One claim to fame is having the world's largest cylindrical aquarium in its lobby.

Menu standouts include jumbo fried shrimp, pure crab cakes made with no filler and Turtle Creek salmon — broiled fish topped with shrimp, mushrooms, crab and Dijon mustard. Henry's also is known for she-crab soup and its blackened scallops. The restaurant is open Monday through Saturday for dinner and for a Sunday brunch buffet. During weekends there is usually entertainment on the deck overlooking the river. Reservations are needed during the summer, especially on weekends.

HOT TUNA BAR & GRILL
2817 Shore Dr.
$$ *481-2888*

As Hot Tuna's name suggests, you'll find tuna fixed in some adventuresome ways — Oriental style, blackened and in fajitas. The menu is much broader than that, however. Hot Tuna also serves barbecue ribs, crab cakes, steaks and pasta. Although this lively restaurant leans toward heart-healthy cooking, it also prides itself on its fried calamari. Hot Tuna is open for lunch and dinner daily. There are daily early bird dinner specials. Reservations are accepted. Hot Tuna has won a Popular Choice award from *Port Folio* magazine.

KING OF THE SEA
27th and Atlantic
$$ *428-7983*

This venerable seafood restaurant has been at the same location since 1965 and was remodeled in 1993. It draws crowds with its nightly all-you-can-eat crab leg and shrimp specials. The family-run restaurant is known for broiled seafood platters and blackened fish as well as steaks. King of the Sea is open for lunch and dinner daily. Reservations are accepted.

LAVERNE'S SEAFOOD RESTAURANT AND CHIX CAFE
Seventh & Oceanfront
$$ *428-6836*

There are lots of early bird specials to tempt diners at Laverne's and sister restaurant, Chix Cafe. Both are in the Hilton Inn in Virginia Beach. The restaurants have been cooking fresh seafood since 1981 and have identical menus. Specialties include build-your-own-seafood platters as well as a prime rib and seafood combination. The restaurants are open daily for breakfast, lunch and dinner.

THE LIGHTHOUSE OCEANFRONT
First St. and Atlantic Ave.
$$$ *428-7974*

Located on the Atlantic Ocean at Rudee Inlet, this airy restaurant has a terrific view. To make it even better, outdoor seating is available in summer. The Lighthouse is a special-occasion restaurant that has been in business since 1963. House specialties are she-crab soup, steamed shrimp and crabs and a variety of broiled fish. Lobster tails are flown in from New England while shellfish come from the Eastern Shore. Steaks brought from the Midwest and trimmed on-site also are popular menu items. Dinner is served daily, with lunch offered on Saturdays and brunch on Sunday. There usually are early-bird specials for dinner. Reservations are accepted.

LYNNHAVEN FISH HOUSE

2350 Starfish Rd.
$$$ 481-0003

This popular restaurant is on the Lynnhaven Fishing Pier right on the Chesapeake Bay and just off Shore Drive. Since 1979 it has prided itself on having an atmosphere similar to San Francisco's Fisherman's Wharf. Noted menu items include she-crab soup, Mediterranean salad and at least five types of fresh fish. Crab cakes, oysters on the half shell and surf-and-turf-platters are menu staples. Dessert features Belgium whiskey pudding and a variety of cakes. The fish house is open for lunch and dinner daily. Reservations are accepted. This is a Popular Choice winner in *Port Folio's* Golden Fork Awards.

NICK'S HOSPITALITY RESTAURANT

508 Laskin Rd.
$$ 428-7891

Founded in 1952, this is a mostly-locals restaurant, partly because Nick's location next to a laundry doesn't seem too exciting. Inside, the menu is another story. Nick's serves fresh seafood in a comfortable atmosphere that's changed little since the '50s. The menu features whatever is in season with bargain-priced daily specials such as lobster tails and all-you-can-eat flounder. This is one of the few places where you can get crack-'em-and-eat-'em steamed crabs. They're usually in season May through October. The menu sometimes has surprises like blackened alligator and other Cajun dishes. Nick's serves breakfast, lunch and dinner daily. One best-seller at breakfast is the crab omelette. Maybe it's just as well that we locals keep this one secret. . .

ROCKAFELLER'S

308 Mediterranean Ave.
$$ 422-5654

This restaurant and raw bar opened in 1990 on the scenic Rudee Inlet. Its specialties include Oysters Rockefeller and Clams Casino. While seafood is a big part of the menu, Rockafeller's entrees also include pasta, chicken and seafood. Lunch and dinner are served daily, with brunch offered on Sunday.

RUDEE'S ON THE INLET

227 Mediterranean Ave.
$$ 425-1777

This casual Rudee Inlet restaurant is known for its raw bar and steamed-shrimp specials. Steaks, crab, scallop and lobster round out the menu, which also includes sandwiches. There is a wide variety of seafood appetizers. Desserts range from Key lime pie to carrot cake. Rudee's, which was started in 1983, serves dinner daily and is open for lunch Monday through Saturday, with brunch served on Sunday. Reservations are accepted.

SANDBRIDGE RESTAURANT & RAW BAR

205 Sandbridge Rd.
$$ 426-2193

Open only from March through December, the Sandbridge Restaurant has been around since the early '60s and is one of the few restaurants in the Sandbridge beach area. Fresh seafood and prime rib are the house specialties. Baby-back ribs also are big sellers. Dinner is served nightly, lunch on Saturday and brunch on Sunday.

SEA CREST RESTAURANT

1776 Princess Anne Rd.
$$ 426-7804

Located in Pungo, the Sea Crest prides itself on its she-crab soup, broiled seafood platter and prime rib. Its noted dessert is rice pudding. The Sea Crest is open Tuesday through Sunday for dinner but closes during the winter.

STEINHILBER'S THALIA ACRES INN
653 Thalia Rd.
$$$ 340-1156

Steinhilber's is one of Virginia Beach's oldest restaurants, and you can count on it for good food served in an elegant environment. One Pennsylvanian we know who travels the East Cost for a living calls Steinhilber's his all-time favorite restaurant. His top pick: the delicate tempura-fried shrimp. Steaks are a close runner-up. Fresh seafood grilled over a mesquite fire is also a delicacy. Steinhilber's is open Tuesday through Saturday for dinner and is a winner of *Port Folio* magazine's Popular Choice award. Reservations are a must. (See our sidebar in this chapter for more information on Steinhilber's.)

SURF RIDER
605 Virginia Beach Blvd.   422-3568
4501 Haygood Rd.   464-5992
723 Newtown Rd., Norfolk   461-6488
$$

Started in 1979, the Surf Rider on Virginia Beach Boulevard has spawned two popular offshoots. The casual Surf Riders have a loyal following who like their crab cakes and other fresh seafood. Everything is homemade, including cream of broccoli soup with crab, clam chowder and a variety of pies. The Virginia Beach Boulevard location is open daily for lunch and dinner. The other two restaurants close on Sunday.

Chesapeake

LOCK'S POINTE AT GREAT BRIDGE
136 Battlefield Blvd.
$$ 547-9618, 436-0845

Overlooking the Atlantic Intracoastal Waterway, Lock's Pointe lets diners watch boats plying the waters. The restaurant opened in 1984 and has never wavered from its emphasis on seafood. Specialties include baked salmon stuffed with prosciutto and Gouda and topped with a crab sauce. A veal, crab and artichoke pasta also is a crowd pleaser. Meals often start with Oysters Rockefeller or she-crab soup. There are at least six homemade desserts on the menu. Lunch is served on weekdays and dinner every day. There is a Sunday brunch. Reservations are recommended.

THE OYSTERETTE
3916 Portsmouth Blvd.
$$ 465-3336

The Oysterette opened in 1992 to give some dining diversity to the Western Branch area of Chesapeake. This small, casual raw bar is in Stonebridge Center at the foot of the Hodges Ferry Bridge. Its menu includes crab cakes, stuffed flounder and a variety of other fresh seafood. There is a large assortment of appetizers, and each weekday night a different entree is highlighted with a bargain price. The Oysterette serves dinner daily and also lunch on weekends. It stays open late for night owls.

Portsmouth

AMORY'S SEAFOOD
5909 High St.
$$ 483-1518

If anyone knows fresh seafood it's George Amory, owner of Amory's Seafood. His family has been in the seafood business for more than 100 years and at one time was the East Coast's largest seafood distributor. Amory opened his restaurant in 1976 in the Churchland area of Portsmouth. The menu offers many shrimp, scallop, crab and fish dinners. Some are made from old family recipes, including crab Maryland and flounder supreme. Popular items include she-crab soup, a New England clambake and homemade marinara sauce for pasta. There is a raw bar, and Amory's oysters come from the family's oyster beds. On weekday nights there are bargain-priced specials on the menu. Lunch and dinner are served daily. Reservations are accepted.

AMORY'S WHARF
10 Crawford Pkwy.
$$ *399-0991*

An Amory's Seafood spin-off, this waterfront restaurant opened in late 1992. Its owner is David Amory, a Culinary Institute of America graduate whose father runs the other Amory's. Both restaurants share many of the same seafood dishes. However, the Wharf puts its own spin on the menu with some upscale, trendy dishes such as a mozzarella appetizer wrapped in romaine and prosciutto, grilled with garlic and served with a fresh tomato vinaigrette. Besides seafood, there are pastas, steaks, sandwiches and salads on the menu. The Wharf is in downtown Portsmouth at the end of a marina. It is a compact restaurant overlooking the Elizabeth River and Downtown Norfolk across the water. It has a small parking lot inside the marina fence, and in the summer it offers valet parking to a nearby parking deck. In December this is one of the best spots for viewing the 10 miles of holiday lights in downtown Norfolk.

THE CIRCLE
3010 High St.
$$ *397-8196*

Since its opening in 1947, The Circle has been a Portsmouth dining landmark. It retains the same round, diner look it had back in the days when it had car hops and was a Chicken in the Rough franchise. On one wall are caricatures of Hollywood celebrities whose heydays have long passed. Ambiance aside, The Circle is known for its seafood and steaks. Menu standouts include crab cakes, lobster tails and seafood platters. There also is a raw bar and a solid list of reasonably priced entrees such as ribs, ham steak and a broiled chicken breast. Side dishes include cabbage, yams, black-eyed peas and collards.

The Circle is open for three meals a day, including a big breakfast buffet. On Sunday there is a popular buffet that includes all-you-can-eat crab and prime rib at night. Reservations are accepted and definitely needed on weekends. Children who clean their plates are rewarded with free ice cream.

LOBSCOUSER
337 High St.
$$ *397-2728*

This downtown restaurant bears the nickname for the chef on a ship. Its menu leans toward fresh seafood with some beef and chicken included for balance. There are usually four soups on the menu, and homemade desserts often include bread pudding and strawberry shortcake made with sweet biscuits. Lobscouser is open for lunch and dinner daily. Reservations are accepted. Lobscouser is a People's Choice winner in *Port Folio's* Golden Fork awards.

SCALE O' DE WHALE
3515 Shipwright St.
$$$ *483-2772*

Since the opening of the Western Freeway in 1992, this obscure seafood restaurant on the Western Branch of the Elizabeth River has been a little more accessible. It is located in a ship permanently moored in a marina and has a varied menu that features seafood, beef and chicken. Noted entrees are the Neptune feast — a dinner for two that includes

Photo: Richmond Newspapers

Many seafood delights like Caribbean shrimp and black bean salad can be found in the many gourmet restaurants.

lobsters, filet mignon and stuffed shrimp — and kebabs laced with shrimp, scallops and filet mignon. The she-crab soup is excellent. Homemade desserts include apple cobbler and bread pudding with lemon custard. Dinner is served daily with lunch offered on weekdays. Reservations are accepted. Be sure to call for directions to the restaurant.

Brunch

One of our most favorite, and caloric, Sunday pastimes is the long-standing tradition of brunch, prepared, naturally, by someone else. Along with the obligatory eggs and trimmings, many local restaurants go out on a limb to create the most savory offerings you've ever tasted. You must start with a mimosa, then barrel ahead to such delectables as the steak Benedict at Tandom's Pine Tree Inn, seafood Benedict at Ellliot's in Ghent, and make-and-top-your-own donuts at Tradewinds in the Virginia Beach Resort and Conference Center.

Here's a quick rundown of some of our favorite places to head with the Sunday paper and your partner to waste away a lazy afternoon with a brimming plate of delicious cuisine and attentive service:

NORFOLK
Blue Crab Bar & Grill, 4521 Pretty Lake Avenue, Ocean View
Chesapeake Cafe, Howard Johnson Hotel-Norfolk
Elliot's, 1421 Colley Avenue, Ghent
Freemason Abbey, 209 West Freemason, Downtown Norfolk
Harbor Grill, The Waterside
Omni Hotel Riverwalk, Downtown Waterfront
The Promenade, Norfolk Airport Hilton

VIRGINIA BEACH
Tandom's Pine Tree Inn, 2932 Virginia Beach Boulevard
Rockafeller's, 308 Mediterranean Avenue
Blue Pete's Seafood Restaurant, 1400 N. Muddy Creek Road
Henry's Seafood Restaurant, 3319 Shore Drive
Tradewinds, Virginia Beach Resort and Conference Center
Lighthouse, First Street and Atlantic Avenue
Jewish Mother, 3108 Pacific Avenue
The Bistro & Rotisserie, 324 North Great Neck Road

CHESAPEAKE
Cara's, 123 N. Battlefield Boulevard
Cheers Cafe and Tavern, 1405 Greenbrier Parkway
Lock's Pointe, 136 N. Battlefield Boulevard
Ruby Tuesday, Crossways Shopping Center and Chesapeake Square Mall

PORTSMOUTH
The Max, 435 Water Street
Vic Zodda's Harborside, Holiday Inn, Portsmouth Waterfront

Inside
Accommodations

Pull right up . . . your room's waiting! If you're traveling for pleasure, it's a pretty sure bet that you're headed for one of our ocean- or bayfront hotels. Travelers with business on their minds are drawn to the hotels circling our major business districts, like Downtown Norfolk or the Newtown Road corridor in Virginia Beach. And, if you're in town to visit family or friends lacking in a guest room, you're likely to unpack in a comfortable, moderately priced suburban motel right around the corner.

If you're pillow-counting, there are more than 20,000 hotel and motel rooms to lay a weary head in Hampton Roads. Virginia Beach alone boasts 11,000-plus and counting! The range of accommodations is nearly as great, from econoboxes to luxury high-rises, mega conference centers to a charming bed and breakfasts. Only your particular destination in our area will dictate which of the many brand-name or independent alternatives you're able to target.

Pick your destination, pick your price. Because of the area's ownership of miles of beautiful beaches along the Chesapeake Bay and Atlantic Ocean, demand for beachfront accommodations is heaviest during the summer season, with rates adjusted upward accordingly. On average, however, rates throughout the area take the big swing from a low of about $30 per night all the way to $300 for a drop-dead luxury suite. Your pocketbook, and your need to be pampered, will be your deciding factor, especially if you're planning an extended holiday.

As in any other part of the country, if you are planning a peak resort-time or holiday visit, advance reservations with

Many high-rise hotels are located on Virginia Beach's oceanfront.

Photo: Virginia Beach Convention and Visitor Development

deposit are definitely a must. On summer weekends and holidays, many hotels require a two- or three-day minimum stay for confirmed reservations, so plan accordingly. Payment with plastic is the general rule, since it is a rare establishment that will accept a personal check (including restaurants). So pack heavy with credit cards, cash or traveler's checks.

If your plans should change, make certain that you are aware of your chosen hotel's cancellation policy. Some require at least a 72-hour notice for a change in reservation dates, and up to seven-day's notice for complete cancellation. Ask about specific rules and refund policies when making your initial reservations.

While it's impossible to list every accommodation alternative in the area, we'll highlight those hotels and motels that are not only local favorites for out-of-town visitors, but generally applauded by the business community for both amenities and consistency of guest service.

Accommodations will be listed in various categories by city, along with from one to five dollar signs ($) based on the typical daily rates for a standard room with two double beds. Keep in mind that, come resort or holiday time, these rates may take a considerable hike, so be sure to confirm prior to making any firm reservation commitments.

Also note the weekly rental possibilities in cities where beach properties are available for extended family vacations. These are often privately owned, fully furnished and appointed homes, ready to move into for a week or two of beachy relaxation.

Less than $30	$
$31 to $50	$$
$50 to $75	$$$
$76 to $90	$$$$
$91 and more	$$$$$

For assistance in selecting the hotel/motel property that best suits your visiting needs, you can call the following for advice, availability and specific rate information:

Virginia Beach   (800) VA-BEACH
Norfolk   (800) 843-8030

Norfolk

Norfolk definitely has a split personality when it comes to accommodations. Downtown is home to our convention hotels, all within walking distance of The Waterside festival marketplace with its restaurants and shopping. Ocean View offers rooms for sandy feet overlooking the Chesapeake Bay, where bathers, anglers and sun-worshippers happily commingle. Undergoing a dramatic rejuvenation, the Ocean View area is regaining its popularity among vacationers, lost during its decline of the '60s and '70s. Today, with new bayfront parks and well-lifeguarded beaches, it is once again becoming a favorite for families with small children because of calm, warm waters. Folks headed to the vicinity of Old Dominion University, the airport/Military Circle hub or elsewhere in the city will find a suburban motel perfect for their overnight needs.

Downtown

BED AND BREAKFAST AT THE PAGE HOUSE INN
323 Fairfax Ave.
$$$ **625-5033**

You'll enjoy this award-winning bed and breakfast in the heart of Downtown Norfolk's lovely historic neighborhood. Elegant accommodations are available in this Georgian Revival (c. 1899) inn, meticulously restored in 1991 by owners Stephanie and Ezio DiBelardino to the

tune of $600,000. Six absolutely charming rooms are here, and the daily tariff includes a homemade, delicious, gourmet breakfast spread. All rooms are furnished with period antiques and canopied beds, and three of the rooms have fireplaces. There are even two suites that incorporate a touch of today — whirlpool baths. No major credit cards are accepted, except to make advance reservations, so be prepared with either cash or check.

NORFOLK WATERSIDE MARRIOTT HOTEL

235 E. Main St.   627-4200
$$$$ (800) 228-9290

A jewel in the crown of Downtown Norfolk, this glamorous facility welcomes you with the most elegant lobby in the area, just a taste of the good life that awaits you during your stay. A favorite of conventioneers, the hotel offers 405 guest rooms, including eight suites and three concierge levels. From health club and rooftop indoor pool to The Dining Room, The Piano Lounge, Stormy's Pub and Sidewalk Cafe, The Marriott is like a plush mini-city you might never want to leave. There's more than 15,000 square feet of flexible conference space, with a ballroom that can accommodate a banquet for 720. Most of the standard guest rooms are small, however, but you can make up for the size by requesting a room with a view of the Elizabeth River.

OMNI INTERNATIONAL HOTEL/NORFOLK

777 Waterside Dr.
$$$$ 622-6664

Having undergone a massive multi-million-dollar renovation to match the elegance of its Marriott neighbor, The Omni has new management committed to pampering you in 446 deluxe rooms including 20 executive suites with spectacular views from balconies overlooking the Elizabeth River. Adjacent to The Waterside festival marketplace, you can take advantage of the hotel's fine dining facilities: The Riverwalk Cafe with outdoor veranda seating on the river and The Lobby Bar, a favorite and comfortable place for an aperitif. The International Ballroom can accommodate 1,200, along with 14 banquet rooms. Extra perks are the indoor/outdoor pool and access to the superb health club located next door in Dominion Tower.

HOWARD JOHNSON NORFOLK
700 Monticello Ave.
$$$ 627-5555

Adjacent to Scope Convention Center and Chrysler Hall, this 344-room hotel began life in the '60s as the Golden Triangle, the largest and most elegant hotel of its time. It has gone through many renovations, and names, since those early popular days and seems at last to have found a renewed life under the Howard Johnson's banner. The facility includes Harvey's Lounge and the Chesapeake Room restaurant, an Olympic-size outdoor pool and lobby shops. This is a reasonably priced alternative for the Downtown visitor.

RAMADA NORFOLK HOTEL
Granby and Freemason Sts. 622-6682
$$ (800) 522-0976

A landmark hotel in the heart of the original Downtown shopping district, The Ramada features one-, two- and three-room suites along with two restaurants, an attractive lounge and complimentary health club and racquetball facilities at the Downtown Athletic Club across the street. There are five meeting rooms with more than 5,000 square feet, and banquet facilities can serve 275 guests. Some of Downtown's most popular restaurants are within one block's walking area, and The Waterside is about five blocks to the south, although we do not suggest you attempt the short hike after dark if you're all alone.

COMFORT INN TOWN POINT
Virginia Beach Blvd. at Tidewater Dr.
$$ 623-5700

This is a comfortable place to stay if you want a more relaxed atmosphere

that's a stone's throw from the Downtown financial district. The newly remodeled, 167-room motel has an on-premise health club, sauna and whirlpool, plus an outdoor pool surrounded by a charming, well-tended courtyard. Continental breakfast is included in your tab, and a courtesy van is available for airport transportation. Note: This is not in a neighborhood where you should wander at night.

Suburban Norfolk

QUALITY INN LAKE WRIGHT
6280 Northampton Blvd. 461-6251
$$ (800) 228-5157

A quick zip to the interstate and airport, this 304-room resort and conference center has an easygoing attitude. For specifics, there are eight suites and meeting rooms covering over 22,000 square feet of flexible space, plus a fine restaurant and cocktail lounge. It also boasts a great neighbor: the very popular 18-hole golf course and driving range. A swimming pool and tennis courts are also on the premises.

COMFORT INN AIRPORT
6360 Newtown Rd. 461-1081
$$ (800) 221-2222

Near Koger Executive Park, the 138-room Comfort Inn offers one suite and more than 5,676 square feet of meeting space. Just off the Norfolk-Virginia Beach Expressway, I-44/264, there's a courtyard pool, fitness center and the very popular Adams' night club. Especially nice touches for guests are the in-room coffee makers and free washer-dryer, with microwaves and refrigerators available.

DOUBLETREE CLUB HOTEL
Military Hwy. and Virginia Beach Blvd.
$$ 461-9192

If you were born to shop, stash your traveling bags here. An "anchor" of Mili-

tary Circle Center Mall, you can spill right out of your room into over 150 great stores, shops, restaurants and movie theaters. The 208 recently renovated rooms are quite comfortable, and you'll be smack dab in the center of Hampton Roads and near the interstate for a quick getaway.

HAMPTON INN

1450 Military Hwy.   466-7474
$$ (800) 489-1000

Just a skip from the airport to the north and Military Circle to the south, this is a lifesaver for the budget-conscious traveler who wants a lot for the overnight dollar. While there's no restaurant on the premises, there is an outdoor pool and complimentary continental breakfast served each morning. Offered are 129 comfortably sized rooms, with free local phone and the obligatory cable/HBO.

HILTON HOTEL-AIRPORT

1500 Military Hwy.
$$$ 466-8000

A real architectural mystery to many Insiders, this deluxe 250-room hotel is as close to the airport as you want to be and also close to the USAA regional headquarters complex. A decorator's vision of contemporary with Oriental overtones, the lobby is impressive with its piano bar accented by polished brass accessories and teak and marble floor. Dining, both casual and elegant, is here too, along with a super popular nightclub that rocks to the wee hours. (If you're intent on getting a sound night's sleep, request a room in the back!) A high-tech fitness center with Jacuzzi and sauna plus a swimming pool and tennis courts round out the amenities. For getting down to business, there are nine salons, parlors and conference rooms, along with the grand ballroom with foyer and a garden. A nice feature of the guest rooms is the in-room mini-bars.

OLD DOMINION INN

4111 Hampton Blvd.
$$ 440-5100

This inn is a relatively new facility and a welcome one for visitors to both Old Dominion University and the major medical complex a short hop down Hampton Boulevard. Sixty guest rooms are surprisingly spacious and well appointed, and restaurants and shops that serve the University are right across the street.

HAMPTON INN-NAVAL BASE

8501 Hampton Blvd.
$ 489-1000

Minutes from the main gate at Naval Station Norfolk, the Hampton Inn offer 119 rooms with free continental breakfast and local phone calls. There's an indoor pool plus whirlpool, and the rooms have kitchenettes plus modem jacks for those who must stay in touch even when they're on vacation.

COMFORT INN-NAVAL BASE

8051 Hampton Blvd.
$ 451-0000

A few blocks from the Hampton Inn, this 120-room motel also welcomes guests to Naval Station Norfolk. An indoor swimming pool and on-site laundromat plus refrigerators in every room and free local phone calls make this a popular place to stay.

Ocean View

ECONO LODGE

9601 Fourth View St.
$$$ summer, $$ winter   480-9611

While not directly on the Bay, this motel with 70 rooms and 22 efficiencies offers clean, comfortable accommodations, worth the easy walk across the street to access the beach. Also close to the popular Harrison's Boat House and Fishing Pier, you'll find a hot tub and sauna along with a guest laundry room and cable TV.

HOLIDAY INN
1010 W. Ocean View Ave.
$$$ summer, $$ winter   587-8761

Find traditional Holiday Inn hospitality in this 120-room oceanfront hotel. It's a comfortable place to hang the family's wet bathing suits in summer and a nice place for business travelers to watch ships and fishing boats any time of year. You have access to swimming and kiddie pools, a cocktail lounge and restaurant, and banquet facilities too.

RAMADA INN-OCEAN VIEW
719 E. Ocean View Ave.
$$$ all seasons   583-5211

Always with a diverse guest list of business people, vacationing families and military guests, this 101-room inn sits directly across from a popular family beach, with next-door tennis courts and the Ocean View Golf Course just a few blocks away. On-site is a swimming pool, restaurant and popular night spot.

Virginia Beach

Now you're talking hotel rooms. From the ocean to the bay, central business district to the suburbs, Virginia Beach uses more hotel-issue bed linens than any city in Hampton Roads. To help you decipher between the 122 choices, we'll divide the city into hotel-heavy areas, like oceanfront, Chesapeake Bay and out there in the Suburbs.

All of these properties offer free in-room cable TV, refrigerators and microwaves, but you should confirm availability early, especially in peak resort or holiday season. Every on-premise restaurant features a pendulum swing of choices, all

constantly changing. Most of the properties along the Boardwalk area are within a short stroll of gourmet, casual and convenience dining, with fresh seafood the predominant bill of fare year round. When you're shellfished-out, you'll find excellent alternatives for beef, Italian, Caribbean, Mexican and good old Southern food just another step away.

Ocean Area

(While not noted, count on a $$$$$ rating during the resort season.)

RAMADA OCEANSIDE TOWER RESORT & CONFERENCE CENTER
57th St. and Oceanfront   428-7025
$$$ (800) 365-3032

We'll start just off the Boardwalk path with this fine facility that's nestled on North Virginia Beach's "Gold Coast" and that puts you in the midst of the prime residential oceanfront community. The 215 rooms, including three suites, are so nice they helped the property win a recent Best Ramada Inn in the Country. Conference facilities include 12 meeting rooms and banquet facilities for 400. You'll love the swim-up bar in the heated indoor/outdoor swimming pool, and there's also an exercise room and excellent restaurant on premises.

HOLIDAY INN ON THE OCEAN
39th and Oceanfront
$$$ 428-1711, (800) 94BEACH

Everyone is renovating, and this 266-room Holiday Inn is no exception. There's new life to the expanded outdoor pool, a new indoor pool complex with two whirlpools, improvements to the banquet facilities that can serve up to 400, and over 9,000 square feet of meeting space on the top floor overlooking the ocean. It's right on the Boardwalk, so that means if you decide to pass on their excellent restaurant, you've got oodles of dining choices just a short walk away.

THE CAVALIER HOTELS
42nd and Oceanfront and 42nd On The Hill
$$$ *425-8555,   (800) 446-8199*

For sheer Southern hospitality in a seaside manner, nothing comes close to the Cavalier on the Hill, a landmark in the Beach community, and its newer, slicker sister along the oceanfront. This 18-acre seaside resort offers more than 400 guest rooms and eight suites overlooking the 600-foot private beach along the Atlantic Ocean. Boasting the largest hotel ballroom in the Commonwealth of Virginia, you can throw an intimate dinner for 1,400 with no problem. With its AAA four-diamond rating, there are also three restaurants, two lounges, tennis courts, indoor and outdoor swimming pools and a health club. Other amenities include jogging tracks and facilities for racquetball.

THE DIPLOMAT RESORT HOTEL
Oceanfront at 33rd St.   *428-8811*
$$$ *(800) 752-1424*

From secluded oceanfront balconies to heated outdoor pool, The Diplomat stands tall along one of the most popular sections of "The Strip." With spacious guest rooms and oversized efficiencies that are 100 percent oceanfront, it offers the ever-popular (and scarce) free parking and is a quick walk from restaurants and shopping.

SHERATON INN
36th and Oceanfront   *425-9000*
$$$ *(800) 325-3535*

Rising above the Boardwalk, this 203-room hotel also has eight luxury suites, along with nine meeting rooms that cover 12,000 square feet, two ballrooms and banquet facilities for 600. Along with glorious ocean views, the Sheraton offers a heated, outdoor swimming pool, exercise room, dining room and lounge.

OCEAN HOLIDAY
25th and Oceanfront   *425-6920*
$$$ *(800) 345-SAND*

With 105 rooms, each with a private balcony that hangs over the beach, Ocean Holiday boasts an indoor oceanfront pool and complimentary morning coffee in the lobby. Don't forget to slide through the gift shop for some tanning lotion before heading to the sundeck to catch those rays. If you want to go all out, call early to reserve one of their specialty rooms that comes with a full-size Jacuzzi tub and VCR. You can even bring along your favorite pet who will be as welcome as you are.

OCEAN KEY RESORT
424 Atlantic Ave.   *425-2200*
$$$ *(800) 955-9300*

This is a great place for a longer visit because each of the 150 rooms is actually a two-room suite. Along with 1,500 square feet of meeting space and banquet facilities for 150, the Park Inn has an indoor swimming pool, fitness center,

---

Insiders' Tips

When you get too much sun, one of the best cures is to wrap the crispy areas in cold, wet towels. Any product with "aloe" listed in the ingredients is also a great soother.

Waterside Convention Center and the adjacent Marriott hotel in Norfolk accommodate numerous conventions every year.

Photo: Norfolk Convention and Visitors Bureau

restaurant, lounge and, of course, the beautiful beaches of the Atlantic.

CLARION RESORT & CONFERENCE CENTER

Fifth and Oceanfront   422-3186
$$$$ *(800) 345-3186*

Insiders love this part of Virginia Beach, down near Rudee Inlet where all the city's charter boat fleets congregate. The Clarion has 168 rooms, swimming pool, whirlpool, sauna, tennis courts and a health club.

RADISSON HOTEL VIRGINIA BEACH

1900 Pavilion Dr.   422-8900
$$$ *(800) 333-3333*

At the foot of the Norfolk-Virginia Beach Expressway, adjacent to the Pavilion Convention Center, the Radisson offers 296 lovely rooms along with 14 luxury suites. Banquet facilities for up to 450 and 12,000 square feet of meeting space make it a convention favorite. Although it is a few blocks to the oceanfront, it does have an indoor swimming pool, jogging track, tennis courts, popular restaurant and lounge and a cozy library too.

THE VIKING

2700 Atlantic Ave.   428-7116
$$ *(800) 828-3063*

How much room do you need? At The Viking, you can pick from single or double rooms up to one- and two-room efficiencies with separate bedrooms, equipped kitchens and dining area. Whichever you unpack in, you'll have the second-floor swimming pool with a unique see-through window along with the great restaurants and shopping just a step away. The beach is just a hop across Atlantic Avenue.

Family-Oriented/Ocean Area

For accommodations that cater to families on the run from the real world, without that "conference center" feeling, check out these friendly beachfront and beachside hotels:

ANGIE'S GUEST COTTAGE

302 24th St.
$$$ 428-4690

Whether you opt for the Bed & Breakfast, Lacy Duplex or American Youth Hostel, there's no doubt that Angie's is unique in this sweep of high-rise towers and glitzy motels. Built in the 1900s, the original house was used to accommodate the families of surfmen stationed at the U.S. Coast Guard Station, now the Life-Saving Museum of Virginia. Both Barbara Yates and mom, Garnette, answer to the name "Angie" and roll out a warm welcome in rooms scented with fresh flowers and breakfast of breads, fruit and cheeses served on the cozy front porch. The Hostel, affiliated with Hostelling International-American Youth Hostels, offers five dormitory rooms. Strict rules on no alcoholic beverages and "quiet period" — read curfew — apply.

THE ATRIUM RESORT HOTEL

315 21st St.   491-1400
$$ (800) 96-SUITE

You'll run right into The Atrium as you shoot down 21st Street off the Norfolk-Virginia Beach Expressway. There's no bad room in the 90-room house, because every one is actually a two-room suite with fully equipped kitchen, perfect for whipping up a hearty breakfast on a family vacation. Someone with a lot of class dreamed up the indoor pool and Jacuzzi, as evidenced by the comfy sofas in a true atrium where you can linger to watch the splashing swimmers. What's really neat is their tanning room, so you can go home glowing even if the weather's not in a cooperative mood.

BOARDWALK INN

2604 Atlantic Ave.   425-5871
$$ (800) 777-6070

While not perched over the ocean, the Boardwalk Inn can boast amazingly spacious rooms and efficiencies, with thick, squishy carpet that welcomes bare feet. Each of the 106 rooms is cable connected and has balconies to check out the sun-worshipers who lounge around the center court pool. There's easy access to on-site washers and dryers and plenty of parking too, so you can go about your vacation business without a care.

THE BREAKERS RESORT INN

16th and Oceanfront   428-1821
$$$ (800) 237-7532

There's not a room in this house that doesn't look out over the blue Atlantic, and every room comes equipped with a coffee maker and a fridge to chill that post-beach beverage. If you want to go first class here, ask for the deluxe king room with Jacuzzi, a two-room efficiency or, what the heck, the bridal suite, and have a beach blast. You'll have to come out of your room sometime, so if you're weary of the lifeguarded beach with umbrella and chair rentals, request a free bicycle and pedal through the strip.

CERCA DEL MAR

410 21st St.
$$ 428-6511

If you're packing the kiddies, the Cerca Del Mar is a great place to head. Fifty-five two-room efficiencies provide more space for the beach toys than a regular size hotel room, plus the rates are perfect for a family budget. There's an outdoor pool, plus a kiddie pool, and children younger than 18 can splash and snooze for free.

COLONIAL INN MOTEL

29th and Oceanfront   428-5370
$$ *(800) 344-3342*

Ah heck, just go for the king suite with Jacuzzi . . . it's your vacation after all. Even if you're more practical and opt for a regular double-bed oceanfront room, you'll still get a refrigerator, private balcony hanging over the beach and TV with cable and HBO.

The indoor heated pool is kind of nifty, with bright flags hanging from the rafters. But on a glorious sunny day, you'll probably want to go for the outdoor pool and sundeck. If you're too lazy to go somewhere else to eat, Cary's Restaurant and Boardwalk Cafe will treat you just fine for breakfast, lunch or dinner.

DAYS INN OCEANFRONT

32nd and Oceanfront   428-7233
$$$ *(800) 292-3297*

This is a handsome hotel, where every oceanfront room comes equipped with a private balcony. Each of the 120 rooms is surprisingly spacious, and you can zip down the hallway to the laundry when your favorite beach outfit gets pooped. There's an indoor pool, too, for those afternoons when you're not quite in the mood for the beach crunch. And the '50s diner and lounge called Happy Days is a swell place to wind up a sun-filled day.

DUNES LODGE/DUNES MOTOR INN

Ninth and 10th and Oceanfront   460-2205
$$/$$$ *(800) 634-0709*

You can squeeze out a lot of Coppertone on the 425 feet of oceanfront

that stretch out in front of the Dunes. It's right on the boardwalk with a broad-grassed ocean terrace enveloping a super outdoor pool. For more privacy, you can head up to the third and fourth levels and plant your bod on the tanning deck with whirlpool spa standing by to soothe. When you're burnt to a crisp, rent a bike or head indoors to their oceanfront game room sporting two pool tables, a ping-pong table and even more tables for a heated game of bridge or gin rummy. For the hungries, there's the Snack Shop or the Pancake House — serving from morning 'til night.

NEWCASTLE MOTEL

12th and Oceanfront   428-3981
$$ *(800) 346-3176*

You know you're going to like this place when you first pull up. Every one of the 83 rooms has an oceanfront vista from a private balcony, along with refrigerator, microwave and whirlpool tub. If you opt for a two-room suite, you'll get a full kitchen as well as a large master bedroom with a king-size bed, a super option for a longer stay. Start out on the ocean view sundeck or indoor heated pool, then warm those lazy muscles with a free bicycle and pedal down the boardwalk to check out the action.

OCEANFRONT INN

29th and Oceanfront   422-0445
$$$ *(800) 548-3879*

Sprawling along primo beachfront, the Oceanfront Inn is just that . . . oceanfront. From your private balcony, you can eavesdrop on all the beach activity and then maybe dog-paddle a few lazy laps in the heated indoor or outdoor pools. There's the nifty canopied Beachfront Cafe for a leisurely lunch, and a lounge and restaurant too. Sideview and west side rooms are less expensive, but as long as you're on vacation, why not go for a king-size oceanfront job. We would.

PRINCESS ANNE INN

25th and Oceanfront	*428-5611*
$$$$	*(800) 468-1111*

One of the long-standing beachtime favorites along the resort strip, the Princess Anne Inn is smack in the middle of all the hot night action. That means you can check in, check your car and then not worry about any transportation other than your own two feet to get you to all the best that Virginia Beach nightlife has to offer. Each of the 60 rooms here has an enclosed balcony, and you'll mix and mingle with fellow guests at the indoor/outdoor pool and Jacuzzi. A lounge and coffee shop are here too, just in case you don't want to venture beyond the Princess Anne's territory.

WINDJAMMER HOTEL

19th and Oceanfront	*428--0060*
$$	*(800) 695-0035*

Early morning beach joggers can just roll out of bed into their Nikes and hit the sand running. Choose from regular or deluxe variety accommodations, or maybe go for an efficiency fully equipped with dishes, utensils and cookware. You'll enjoy great benefits like private balconies, L-shaped oceanfront outdoor pool, guest laundry and cable TV with HBO. Since it's on the boardwalk, you can slide out of your room and into the beach's night action with no trouble at all.

Chesapeake Bay

VIRGINIA BEACH RESORT HOTEL & TENNIS CLUB

2800 Shore Dr.	*481-9000*
$$$	*(800) 468-2722*

Rising dramatically over the Chesapeake Bay, each of the 295 luxuriously appointed two-room suites overlooks the private beach from its own balcony. Relax in the indoor/outdoor swimming pool, try out the health club, or dine in the two restaurants. Affiliation with the nearby tennis club brings you 30 outdoor and six indoor tennis courts. There are banquet facilities for up to 300, and more than 14,000 square feet of meeting space.

Suburban

THE CLARION HOTEL

4453 Bonney Rd.	
$$	*473-1700*

Just off the Norfolk-Virginia Beach Expressway, midway between Norfolk and the Beach in the Pembroke business and shopping corridor, is this popular eight-story hotel with 149 guest rooms, health club, indoor pool and restaurant.

HOLIDAY INN EXECUTIVE CENTER

5655 Greenwich Rd.	*499-4400*
$$	*(800) HOLIDAY*

The "anchor" of the Newtown Road corridor hotel cluster, you can't miss its six-story green roof from the Norfolk-Virginia Beach Expressway. It's pretty much green inside too, with its miles of green carpeting and lavish indoor plantings. The 336 rooms are quite comfortable, and most come with hair dryers in the bathrooms, a nice touch. If you travel heavy, you'll appreciate their seven parlor/meeting suites, which include two parlor suites with adjoining king bedrooms. You'll also find both indoor and outdoor pools, whirlpool, sauna and health club, along with the popular Ashley's restaurant that's always busy with local business people for breakfast, lunch and after-work drinks.

Convention Facilities

Both Norfolk and Virginia Beach have city-owned convention facilities. Norfolk has Scope and the Waterside Convention Center. Scope has 83,630 square feet of space and is six blocks from the downtown waterfront. It is where the Ringling Bros. Barnum & Bailey Circus performs, the Hampton Roads Admirals play ice hockey and college basketball teams have their games, 441-2764.

The Waterside Convention Center opened downtown in 1991. It is connected to the Marriott Hotel and is across the street from the Waterside festival marketplace. It has more than 36,000 square feet of function space, 628-6501.

Virginia Beach's Pavilion Convention Center is six blocks from the ocean and has 57,000 square feet of space. Call 428-8000.

Throughout the region there also are numerous hotels with conference space.

COURTYARD BY MARRIOTT

5700 Greenwich Rd.   490-2002
$$ (800) 321-2211

What appears to be a charming apartment complex is really a 146-room hotel that sprawls across four acres. Most of the rooms face a beautifully landscaped courtyard with swimming pool and garden gazebo plus an exercise room and a Jacuzzi. Business travelers in town for several days really love this place that accommodates them with large desks. There is a restaurant on the premises, but we hear that taking food back to the room from the pick-up counter is a favorite choice for the bone-tired executive.

DAYS INN

4564 Bonney Rd.
$$ 497-4488

Convenient to the Pembroke area of Virginia Beach, which we call "the central business district," this 144-room inn is a popular stopover that's close to office complexes and shopping. There is a swimming pool and cable TV with movies, as well as a restaurant for a quick bite for breakfast.

THE FOUNDERS INN AND CONFERENCE CENTER

5641 Indian River Rd.   424-5811
$$$ (800) 926-4466

Still sporting its original shine, this gorgeous facility, tastefully furnished in the Colonial manner, is located close to the Christian Broadcasting Network (CBN) and Regent University. Overlooking English gardens surrounding a small lake where swans swim, the Inn offers 249 beautifully appointed rooms, with common and sitting areas that have a true resort feeling. Amenities include a fitness center, tennis and racquetball courts, indoor and outdoor swimming pools, sand volleyball court and playground. Award-winning chefs serve sumptuous gourmet specialties in the Swan Terrace Restaurant, and banquet facilities for 1,000 are available. Meeting space covers over 22,000 square feet and includes a 132-seat amphitheater. No alcoholic beverages are served, and smoking is prohibited throughout the complex.

Portsmouth

It's not that visitors don't want to stay in Portsmouth, it's just that the competition from neighboring city beaches and business centers preclude many overnight options in this city. Here's where Insiders would stay if they were to overnight in Portsmouth.

HOLIDAY INN-
PORTSMOUTH WATERFRONT
9 Crawford Pkwy.
$$ *393-2573*

This is the place to stay. Two hundred and seventy rooms and suites on the waterfront in Olde Towne are just the beginning, because you're not only just across the river from Norfolk's Waterside but also adjacent to Tidewater Yacht Agency marina, one of the area's busiest, as well as Portside. Vic Zodda's Harborside Restaurant overlooking the Elizabeth River has been a local favorite for years, and Madeline's Peppermint Lounge stays busy with its '50s- and '60s-themed atmosphere. Rooms are comfortable and spacious, but be sure to request one that has a view of the river to catch the harbor activity and spectacular sunsets.

ECONO LODGE-OLDE TOWNE
1031 London Blvd.
$ *399-4414*

The overnight choice for those with business at the Portsmouth Naval Hospital or Portsmouth General Hospital,

you're only five minutes by ferry to Waterside in Downtown Norfolk. Sixty-one rooms are offered, with fast food restaurants within walking distance in the local neighborhood.

Chesapeake

One city that should be suffering from growing pains, there's always a new hub of activity that seems to spring up out of nowhere in the blink of an eye. For most visitors to Chesapeake, however, the Greenbrier corridor seems to be the most logical overnight destination choice since it puts you smack dab in the hustle-bustle for primo shopping and good food, as well as being a quick hop to the interstate.

HOLIDAY INN CHESAPEAKE
725 Woodlake Dr. at Greenbrier Pkwy.
$$ *523-1500*

Here's a real beauty, packed with frills to thrill the overnight guest. There are 190 rooms and suites in seven stories of Holiday Inn at its finest. Our favorite room is the King Executive, with a king-size bed in spread-out comfort, plus a queen-size pullout sofa and nifty wet bar. There's also an indoor swimming pool, whirlpool, sauna and fully equipped exercise room. The Key West Restaurant and Lounge is an especially popular spot with its nightly entertainment, and generous banquet facilities can accommodate up to 700 people with ease. Complimentary airport transportation is available on

---

Insiders' Tips

Be your own tour guide with "Tales of Tidewater, Virginia, and Tour of Virginia Beach, Virginia." It's a 78-minute audio cassette that takes you on a self-directed driving tour of historic and modern Virginia Beach. Snag one at the Virginia Beach Visitors Information Center at the foot of the Expressway for $8.95, including a map.

Private cottages rise from the semi-isolated shore in Sandbridge, located south of Virginia Beach's main resort district.

request, and you're just 15 minutes from the airport, Downtown Norfolk and the Virginia Beach oceanfront.

COMFORT SUITES OF GREENBRIER
1550 Crossways Blvd.
$$ **420-1600**

One hundred twenty-three all-suite rooms complete with refrigerators, microwaves, cable TV/HBO and VCRs are the offering at this Comfort Suites. An outdoor swimming pool, fitness center with steam room and sauna, and a wide variety of restaurants, shopping and entertainment just around the corner at Greenbrier Mall make it a convenient choice.

DAYS INN
701A Woodlake Dr.
$ **420-1550**

Just off I-64 and a short distance to restaurants and shopping, the Days Inn offers 119 rooms with free cable/HBO and complimentary continental breakfast. The outdoor swimming pool is open in season.

RED ROOF INN
724 Woodlake Dr.
$$$ **523-0123**

Sitting practically on top of the Holiday Inn is the alternative to budget-watching travelers who just want a clean and pleasant place to stay, hold the frills. To eat or shop, you'll have to drive just a few miles down the road, but there is complimentary coffee and a newspaper waiting for you in the lobby each morning.

ECONO LODGE-CHESAPEAKE
3244 Western Branch Blvd.
$ **484-6143**

This is our pick for an overnight other than in the Greenbrier area. This small and down-home friendly, 48-room motel can offer you a clean, comfortable room and morning coffee in the lobby, but no amenities like a restaurant or swimming pool. Its big advantage is its location in the Western Branch section of the city, an older, established neighborhood with nearby shopping and fast food.

WELLESLEY INN

1750 Sara Dr. at Woodlake   366-0100
$$ (800) 444-8880

Like a corporate bed and breakfast, The Wellesley Inn is a favorite of both business people on the road and visiting families. With 106 rooms, plus an outdoor heated pool, you can hop just a half-mile down the street to full health club facilities. The king and queen suites here are especially plush, with coffee maker, refrigerator, microwave and wet bar. A laundry facility is available to all guests, along with a free continental breakfast served daily.

Resort Rentals

For a home away from home for a family vacation, it's hard to beat the many condominium and cottage rentals available in Virginia Beach. All are fully furnished and appointed with all the right appliances and kitchen gadgets, although some may require packing your own bed linens and towels. For a week or two, even a month, all you need to do is to slide your bathing suits and shorts in a duffle and hit the road.

As with hotel and motel reservations, plan early for a summer or holiday stay, and remember that cash, credit cards and traveler's checks (not personal checks) are the accepted currency. When making reservations, make certain you request the specific cancellation, early/late checkout and refund policies, as they do vary from property to property.

Condominiums

You'll literally be living high on the hog when you check into one of Virginia Beach's condominium rentals, as most are of the high-rise flavor. As a general rule, you can expect a swimming pool outside and full kitchens inside, along with balconies and beachfront either at your door or a few short blocks away. Most are two-bedroom/two-bath units that sleep two to 10 adults. Do check specifics, especially the availability of linens, when making reservations. Summer rates run from $500 to $1500 weekly, depending on the amenities, size and location of the property.

Beach Breeze Condos, 208 57th Street, 422-0579. Three 2BR/2BA, one block to ocean.

Colony Condominiums, 13th and Oceanfront, 425-8689. Thirty-eight 2BR/2BA, on the ocean.

Dolphin Run Condominium, 3rd and Oceanfront, 425-6166. One hundred and ten 1-, 2-, and 3BR/2BA, on the ocean.

Edgewater Condominium, 37th and Oceanfront, 425-6261.. Thirty-five 2BR/2BA, on the ocean.

Mai Kai Condo Resort Apts, 56/57th and Atlantic, 428-1096. Thirty-eight studio, 1- and 2BR/2BA, on the ocean.

Oceans II Studio Condominiums, 40th and Oceanfront, (800) 845-4786. Forty-two studio units, on the ocean.

Oceanfront Rentals, 2408 Artic Avenue, 428-7473. 2 BR/1 BA, two blocks to the ocean.

Seacrest Condominiums, 21st and Artic, 428-4441. Eight 2BR, two blocks to the ocean.

The Seasons, 109-111 52nd Street, 428-4441. Four 4BR/3½BA units, a few steps from the ocean.

Cottages

For one of the beachiest vacations you'll ever have, head to the southernmost part of Virginia Beach and hit lands' end at Sandbridge. You won't find any glitz, glamour or hopping nightlife in this secluded community, just the pleasure of rolling dunes, clean beaches and the salt-water surf of the Atlantic Ocean. If it's a getaway to total peace and lazy relaxation you're after, this is the place to come. But not to worry about those creature comforts you can't live without. There's a well-stocked grocery (Ben & Jerry's, anyone?), gas station and a few great boutiques for that wayward cloudy day.

Architecture of the Sandbridge rentals varies wildly, from ye olde cottage to high-tech contemporary . . . with rental rates that are in sync with the luxury offered. Most owners have named their homes, and for natives the moniker is a better handle on location than the actual address. All sleep at least six quite comfortably and come with everything you need but bed linens and towels. In summer months, expect to pay from about $900 to $2,500 for a week of the pleasure of sleeping in a real live house rather than a hotel room.

And, should you forget something critical, like a cooler, crib or boogie board, there are several reputable "you need it — we got it for rent" places that will even deliver the required goods to your door. Check with your rental service for the equipment rental firm they recommend.

Those who know what's available, when and for how much, are very helpful in matching your particular family and budget to a rental property in Sandbridge. One quick call will win you a brochure with photos of all possibilities and their particulars.

Siebert Realty-Sandbridge Beach, 601 Sandbridge Road, (800) 231-3037.

Affordable Properties, 613 21st Street, 428-0432, (800) 639-0432.

Atkinson Realty, 5307 Atlantic Avenue, 428-4441.

Hudgins Real Estate, 3701 Pacific Avenue, 422-6741, (800) 553-7089.

Properties are also available for rent in the heart of the resort action, with a wide swing in style, proximity to the ocean and rental rates. Any of the above real estate companies can provide detailed information on cottages in the main resort area.

Campgrounds

For those whose pulses race at the mere thought of sleeping among the bugs under the stars, the backwoods and campgrounds of Hampton Roads have a patch of shaded dirt ready for the thrill. Since most the Insiders we know consider serious camping out an overnight at a Holiday Inn, it's hard to understand the attraction of any accommodation with a three-foot high ceiling and a bathroom with trees rather than white ceramic tile and fluorescent lights. But, if camping is your thing, we feel it's our duty to point your canoe in the right direction.

You'll find overnight camping sites clustered primarily in rural Virginia Beach, the Hampton Roads city that still has pioneer spaces to accommodate L.L. Bean types. Lest you think we're totally primitive, most facilities do offer comfort zone amenities like swimming pools, restrooms and showers, playgrounds and camp stores for those basic necessities.

Rates vary with the season and the hookup requested (water, electrical, sewage, etc.), and reservations are recommended to secure your spot. Most also allow pets on leash, so don't keep Rover away from all the fun.

Virginia Beach

BEST HOLIDAY TRAV-L-PARK

1075 General Booth Blvd. (800) 548-0223

Convenient to Croatan Beach, this 1,100-site park welcomes tents, recreational vehicles and pets on leash. Pools, laundry facilities, bathhouses, stores and restaurant are on-site or nearby. Cabins are also available.

KOA CAMPGROUND

1240 General Booth Blvd. 428-1444

This popular spot is open March through November with 165 sites plus cabins. Pools, bathhouses and a store are added attractions.

NORTH BAY SHORE CAMPGROUND

3257 Colechester Rd. 426-7911

This Sandbridge campground offers 165 sites with a pool, bathhouse and store. Its open April 15 through October 1.

SEASHORE STATE PARK

2500 Shore Dr. 490-3939

This is our most popular camping destination, so even with 235 sites, you'd best reserve early through Virginia State Parks or Ticketmaster. There's no water or electricity, but there are bathhouses and a store. Cabins are also available. They're open March 30 through November.

SENECA CAMPGROUND

144 S. Princess Anne Rd. 426-6241

There are 230 sites here plus cabins, with a pool, bathhouses, boat ramp and store to add to your good time.

SURFSIDE AT SANDBRIDGE

3665 Sandpiper Rd. (800) 568-7873

Directly on North Bay, one block from the ocean, there are 175 sites with access to bathhouses, a game room and general store. Surfside is open April 1 through October 31.

Chesapeake

NORTHWEST RIVER PARK

Indian River Rd. 421-7151

Nestled in the center of this 763-acre park are campsites serviced by a camp store and bathhouses. The park itself offers a wealth of goodies for the outdoors person, including extensive hiking trails, boat and canoe rentals, an equestrian center and a gorgeous lake that stretches almost the entire length of the park.

Portsmouth

SLEEPY HOLE PARK

Sleepy Hole Rd. 393-5056

Overlooking the Nansemond River in Suffolk, this Portsmouth-operated park plays host to 50 campsites with your pick of provided utilities. Also available: bathhouses, laundry, fire rings and sports fields with recreation equipment checkout.

Inside
Nightlife

We have come to the conclusion that there must be something in the water in Hampton Roads that gives us the stamina to stay up all night and boogie. And, judging from the sheer numbers of hot places where you can exercise your right to pop, rock, bluegrass and jazz yourself into a wee-hours frenzy, we must be drinking from that well every night of the week.

Which brings us to a word on drinking. The legal age to enjoy alcoholic beverages in the Commonwealth of Virginia is 21 — no ifs, buts or fake IDs. Patrons who are at least 18 may be allowed into most nighttime hot spots, but are usually burdened with a hand stamp that indicates their money's no good at the bar. Bouncers and bartenders alike find no joke in any underage shenanigans. After all, their jobs and reputations are at stake.

So, while taking teenagers to dinner in our region is encouraged and appreciated, please park them in a safe place before taking off to a night of festivities at any local night spot.

Now that we have the attention of all you adults in the audience, let's crowd in the car and take a trip to some of the area's most lively late night happenings. Most revolve around the music du jour, so we've chosen to separate your destination choices by "the beat." Whether your rhythm of choice is pop, beach, jazz, acoustic or just plain loud, you won't have far to go to find night owls who share your tastes. Since it's not humanly possible for your Insiders' hosts to have frequented every hot spot in town, we'll give you our best shot at those we know are the places to see — and be seen — on

Photo: Virginia Beach Convention and Visitor Development

The Beach Boys entertain music fans and beach goers at just one of the many music fests held every summer.

tips from wired friends and associates who require minimal sleep.

The social architecture of the area is such that many places that rate highest marks for the evening meal are also transformed into the hottest nightspots in town. This is especially true for the primo eateries at the Beach, like the River House and Five 01 City Grill, where a preplanned linger after dessert can mean entry into a whole new tidal wave of late night party-people and fantastic entertainment. If you're just out for a delectable dinner, hang around. You never know what's going to happen when the ten o'clock curtain rises.

Pop/Rock

Norfolk

KING'S HEAD INN
4220 Hampton Blvd.   489-3224

A university hot spot, the King's Head packs them in for pop, rock, funk and rap. The crowd is real young, the music's real loud and the beer is ice cold. Parking to get here, or to Friar Tuck's down the street for similar stimulation with the college crowd, is pretty tight, so plan on walking a block or two. Name-brand headliners require a cover charge, usually around five bucks.

O'SULLIVAN'S WHARF
43rd and Colley Ave.   423-3753

What first appears to be a couple of weather-worn shacks tossed together by some sarcastic hurricane is actually the home of some of the tastiest food and entertainment on Norfolk's west side. After a fantastic meal of crab cakes, Alaskan crab claws or tempura shrimp, you can settle in for the nightly acoustic entertainment.

Open when weather permits is a great deck that juts out over a branch of the Elizabeth River, which always seems to catch a great breeze. The crowd's a mix of ODU students, professors and just plain locals . . . you'll fit right in.

THE VAMPIRE ROOM
853 E. Little Creek Rd.   480-2222

OK. So we're not too sure about The Vampire Room, what they're calling a rock club for the '90s. Indeed, the interior has been described as strip-mall Transylvanian, with faux brick walls smothered by climbing ivy, brooding vampire portraits and a black-lit psychedelic nook near the back. The music is '90's-style heavy alternative rock, but, hey, maybe a Bloody Mary or "Blood Du Jour" drink special will perk you up.

WATERSIDE LIVE!
The Waterside, Downtown Norfolk 625-LIVE

Waterside Live! may be the reason you never want to go home at 5 o'clock again. Having taken over the Waterside extension along the waterfront, it's a 40,000-square-foot dining and entertainment complex with a flavor to meet any taste. Try Legends, a glitzy kind of place dominated by two large bars and wraparound windows, with its big-city-style dance club feeling. Then mosey on to check out the All-Star Bar and Grill, Il Porto, Schooners Harbor Grill and the yet-to-be-named faux Hard Rock Cafe due to open soon.

Virginia Beach

ABBEY ROAD
203 22nd St.   425-6330

Celebrating more than 10 years in the entertainment game, Abbey Road has been the magnet for some of the finest acoustic action in town. The oceanfront night club has built a reputation on its excellent menu too. Usually packed tight with happy patrons, there's live entertainment seven nights a week in the summer, six in the off-season. Along with a kitchen that's open from 11 AM until 1 AM, you can drink your way around the world from the largest collection of imported beers in the area. There's ample on-premise parking, too, a real benefit for the seasonal gridlock we've come to expect during summer evenings at the Beach.

THE ABYSS
19th St.   422-0480

You've got to have the strength of youth to make it big at The Abyss, a techo club with DJ music on Wednesday nights and weekends. Ages 18 and older spill onto (and into) the sunken-pit dance floor, and the bravest make it up to the rear gangway that doubles as a dance stage, as they make their bodies move to the techo and alternative rock music. If you hit it on the right night, you'll have first peek at up-and-coming college rock bands who perform on a national basis. This place can get really, really crowded, even at the pool tables. But, if you're into blinding strobes, synchronized Intellibeam lights and a booming sound system, go for it.

THE BAYOU
Radisson Hotel, 19th St.   422-8900

Squeeze on into one of the new up-start hot spots in town, where the young and the hip hit the small dance floor in the Big Easy spirit. We're talking New Orleans themearama, from the Spanish moss hanging from the ceiling to the gas lamp-topped signposts. There is a cover charge on most nights to get into the

Bourbon Street beat, but maybe you can win back the entry fee at the pool tables.

HOT TUNA
2817 Shore Dr.   481-2888

Yuppie is as yuppie does, and the youngest and the most beautiful are to be found at Hot Tuna. Great food and a beautiful place to hang out, weekends play host to "unplugged" style bands. If you're hankering to meet a Fly Boy or Seal, here's where you'll most likely find one.

OCEAN EDDIE'S
14th and Oceanfront, Fishing Pier   425-7742

Literally plopped out on the fishing pier is the loudest, most crowded and most absolutely fun place to hang out after the sun goes down. A generally more mature crowd — say thirtysomething plus — squeezes into Ocean Eddie's every night of the week. It's blistering hot in the summer, and that's both in popularity and sheer physical heat from the crowd. If you can find the elbow room to eat, try their superb crab cakes. There is a cover charge, but it varies from night to night, and is well worth every penny.

RIVER HOUSE
530 Winston-Salem Ave.
Rudee Inlet   425-8188

When you hear "valet parking," you know this is a place you could love. And you will. Upstairs is a fine window-walled dining room serving one of the tastiest lobsters in the area. Downstairs, you can stay inside in the comfy glass-front casual dining lounge and bar, or stroll outside to the huge deck that catches the cool evening breezes off Rudee Inlet. Music-wise, find acoustic upstairs and pop down . . . plus lots of happy patrons no matter on which level you land. They even offer a V.I.P. card for locals that bestows privileges, like no cover charge and invitations to private parties. This rates as one of our all-time favorite places for a Beach evening out.

South Beach Grill

Norfolk Ave. and Birdneck Rd.   428-0820

If you've graduated from alternative rock, head to South Beach Grill for some bluesy, classic good-time rock from house band The Snard Brothers and other local legends. South Beach attracts an older locals crowd, and very casual is the standard attire.

Sunset Grille

2973 Shore Dr.
Lynnhaven Colony Shoppes   481-9815

Head on to Chesapeake Beach and take in the action at Sunset Grille. This is music like it should be . . . good old '50s and '60s rock 'n' roll from popular local bands like Snuff and the Barflys. Don't plan on sitting in your comfy chair to nibble on those 10¢ wings or shrimp . . . the music will have you swaying on the dance floor and enjoying every minute of it.

Worrell Brothers

19th and Atlantic Ave.   422-6382

Chill out on the deck at Worrell Brothers, especially during Friday and Saturday afternoon happy hour. There's a DJ most nights, and occasionally a classic rock cover band, to compete with your conversations. A little older crowd hangs

out here, which means that the decibel level is bearable.

Chesapeake

Winston's Cafe

1412 Greenbrier Pkwy.   420-1751

It's got that Jewish Mother kind of atmosphere, what with all the local lounge lizards that stream in to Winston's, especially on Friday and Saturday nights when they roll back the carpets for the crowds of pasta-hungry patrons. There's live entertainment on Thursday and Saturday nights, but the casual come-as-you-are (or want-to-be) feeling prevails all week long, from 11 AM until 2 AM every day except Sunday.

Portsmouth

Towne Point Pub

3558 Towne Point Rd.   483-2500

This is a Western Branch destination for hordes of regulars, who pop in for one of the Pub's enormous club sandwiches. Live bands grab the mikes on Wednesday, Friday and Saturday nights, and the rock 'n' roll gets even the shyest guest out on the dance floor. This is a real friendly, neighborhood place where there's not a stranger in the crowd.

Bogies

975 Hodges Ferry Rd.   488-1195

There are two sides to Bogies in Portsmouth. Their restaurant, On the Green, makes one of the most wicked racks of lamb in a fine dining atmosphere. On the other hand, there's the nightclub that's shoulder-to-shoulder practically every night of the week, both seated and on the crowded dance floor. If the waitress can hear you above the DJ, you can order a hefty sandwich and a brew. Tuesdays here are especially boisterous, with the featured "Battle of the Bands."

Jazz

Norfolk

BIENVILLE GRILL
723 W. 21st St.   625-5427

Late night at the Grill has some wicked tunes coming your way, thanks to the live jazz every Friday and Saturday nights from 9 PM until 12:30 AM. For more about this divine gem of a restaurant, see the Restaurants chapter for all the info.

PIZAZZ RESTAURANT AND LOUNGE
Granby and Tazewell Sts.   627-2569

The sultry strains of live jazz at last return to Downtown Norfolk at the new Pizazz Restaurant and Lounge, just about a block from the Wells Theater. The first level, newly renovated with high ceilings, chandeliers and windows opening to Granby Street, is the dining area. Walk up the stairs, or ride the elevator to the second floor, and you've got yourself an evening of jazz, highlighting local acts like Connie Parker on Wednesday, Friday and Saturday evenings, with a DJ spinning on the other nights of the week. Reflecting the upscale atmosphere, a dress code will be strictly enforced after 9 PM on weekends and cover charges range from $3 to $5.

Virginia Beach

THE JEWISH MOTHER
3108 Pacific Ave.   422-5430

Self-billed as the premier blues club in town, the Jewish Mother tops its corned beef with a blues jam every Wednesday night, with live blues performers every other night of the week. It's a pretty popular stopover on an all-night Beach hop, especially if you get the hungries. Their excellent food and generous portions are legendary, and you can even slide into Mom's Deli Section and brown bag some fresh-sliced meats, cheeses and sinful desserts.

HOUSE OF JAZZ
314-A Constitution Ave.
Pembroke East Shopping Center   456-0884

Anyplace called the House of Jazz better be! And it is. Jazz fans pack the place Thursday through Sunday nights (Thursday is Ladies Night, and there's an 8:30 PM jam session every Sunday). There is a $10 minimum, but locals who are members of the Tidewater Jazz Society can sneak in free. If you're a newcomer who would like to find out all you can about jazz in the area, call the Society at 499-3157.

Country/Bluegrass

Norfolk

THE BANQUE
1849 E. Little Creek Rd.   480-3600

I'm in a Garth Brooks kind of mood. Take me to The Banque for the cure. We are now talking country . . . real country . . . and you'd better know your Achy Breaky before you put your boots on the dance floor. Proclaimed Club of the Year by the Virginia Country Music Association for the third year in a row, it seats 500 people (most of whom are on the huge dance floor). The Banque has live toe-tapping music, super food and you can even get free dance lessons five nights a week. If you get country fever, you can do a little late night shopping at Belle's Dry Goods located inside. Open Tuesday through Sunday from 6 PM until 2 AM.

THE LIDO INN

839 E. Little Creek Rd.   *480-1953*

A lot of people we know go to The Lido just for the steamed shrimp, some of the best in the region. Many of these people are the same folks who don't admit to hanging around to get into the country rhythm frenzy that picks up when the live entertainment begins. But, plenty of patrons are known to leave half-finished plates to hit the dance floor. It's really a fun place, with the broadest range of guests, older and younger, and they're truly kind in teaching you how to line dance around the dance floor without looking too much like city folk. There's no cover, so give it a try for a real good time.

Virginia Beach

THE COUNTY LINE

717 S. Military Hwy.
The Executive Inn   *420-2120*

We've got your dinner specials, your door prizes, your dance lessons every Sunday night. We've got a ride to the County Line, and we've got country music loud and clear. Monday's there's no cover, Tuesdays are Ladies Nights, and Thursdays there's a talent contest for the bravest among us. Country-western is the County Line, and if you want to hear the best twangs and see the most proficient two-steppers in town, here's the place to show up seven nights a week.

SUSI'S NASHVILLE EAST

1724 Potters Rd.   *491-9950*

How would you like your Loretta Lynn served tonight? Nashville East books all the must-hear country bands and gets you moving without too much of a shove. Music's loud, food's OK, but the friendly folks who call this place "home away from home" can make you feel mighty dog-gone comfortable. If you don't know the latest dance step (we hear Horse'n Around is the latest 32-count craze), this is the place to come. Wear your boots and your ten-gallon, or at least fake it.

DESPERADO'S

315 17th St.   *425-5566*

"We're not snooty . . . we're rooty tooty." That's what they say, so we guess that's what they mean. Home to the only mechanical bull in the area, and perhaps the state, Desperado's rocks with country seven nights a week. Food's pretty good too — Tex-Mex style with some pretty mean jumbo nachos and a taco plate that will set you on fire on Saturday nights.

Teenology at Night

Say you're in your teens, ages 13 to 17 — pretty grown up, but with no place to go but to a movie and Taco Bell. Whatcha gonna do to put a little night music into those dreary evenings? In Hampton Roads, while there aren't too many places for teens to hang after dark, there are a few nightspots that do throw out the welcome mat for the almost-adult crowd. Be warned, however, that not all of them have a phone, some are open a few nights a week and their stability is much like the patrons they serve . . . here one day, out in the ozone the next.

As of this writing, here are the hottest teen clubs in town.

THE FIRE ESCAPE

17th and Pacific Ave.
Virginia Beach   459-5724

It's painted pond scum green with a black and white checkerboard floor. The dance floor is tiny and the music, from acoustic to hard core, is deafening. Parking is almost impossible and snacks at the mock bar are mediocre. Sure sounds like your kind of place. Really, though, the place is kept very clean, and concerts start around 8:30 PM. Cover charges range from nada to $10, depending on the performers.

THE BOATHOUSE

119 Bessie's Pl., Behind Waterside
Norfolk   622-6395

Don't plan on sitting down in this cement-floored warehouse that showcases live bands as they drift through town. You'll probably need to purchase tickets in advance (they range from $5 to $18), and the beer garden is strictly off limits to anyone younger than 21. Word of mouth is the best way to hear who's playing at any given time.

KINGS HEAD INN

4220 Hampton Blvd.
Across from ODU   489-3224

Most every teen loves to hang around with the older, college crowd, and the Kings Head is the best place to do it. The live bands aren't always that great, but the noise and crowds make up for it. Be warned about the cover charge . . . you'll pay more if you're under 21, up to as much as $10.

JEWISH MOTHER

3108 Pacific Ave.
Virginia Beach   422-5430

Check out the Mother on Wednesday nights, when this popular restaurant turns to blues heaven. Rumored as a great date place, teens can order a milk shake or soda and enjoy the live music along with the rest of the crowd, paying around $4 for the privilege. You'll likely find gaggles of teenlings gathered here prior to wheeling off to a show.

Our spies tell us that the jam session on Sunday from 8 PM until midnight is a hoot. Better check it out, with or without us.

COUNTRY LEGEND
BILLIARDS & RESTAURANT
1479 General Booth Blvd.   *428-0139*

This country kid on the block is coming on strong. Opened just a couple of years ago, the 10,000-square-foot building has a split personality: dance club and restaurant for the left brain and billiards room and bar for the right. Tuesday is Men's Nite, and Wednesday is reserved for the ladies. Tuesday through Saturday, Bubba Blackwell will get you two-steppin' in no time at all, backed up by DJ Mark Evans. There's live music Thursday through Saturday, and sports lovers can belly up to the bar for an eyeful of cable TV.

Portsmouth

BILLY BOB'S
3960 Turnpike Rd.   *397-4681*

When you start with a 70-foot bar, you can only go uphill. So here we are at Billy Bob's with the largest dance floor in town and ever-patient Greg and Tracy are trying to teach the Down and Dirty to a couple who are almost as behind the corral as we are. But somehow the music and the good-old-folks who have packed in have that encouraging look in their eyes. You stake out a dark corner of the floor and go for it. You're moving with the beat and, hey, it's not as hard as you thought it was! Doesn't matter that you're not doing it like a pro . . . you're having a blast. And, that's what Billy Bob's is all about. Even if you're a country-western want-to-be, this is the place to put your toes in the water. The staff and regular patrons are very forgiving.

Chesapeake

BLAKELYS
414 Battlefield Blvd.   *482-2121*

Self-billed as the only one of its kind on the East Coast, Blakelys is becoming Chesapeake's premier night club, and, in fact, was nominated for the Country Music Club of the Year award. Get two-steppin' through two floors of fun, and slap your boots on the dance floor for your free line dancing lesson every Wednesday through Saturday from 7:30 to 8:30 PM. DJ's and live bands take the stage each night, and, if the hungries should hit, you can order up some of their world famous BBQ, steak or seafood. They're open Wednesday through Saturday only, from 6 PM until closing at 2 AM.

And, there's more???

Two categories for after sundown entertainment that we haven't covered are comedy clubs and movies. The former has deep roots in two local spots, **The Comedy Club** at the Thoroughgood Inn in Pembroke Meadows Shopping Center and **The Comedy Zone** at Magoo's in the Day's Inn Airport, both in Virginia Beach. Here you can catch some national talent on the rise on Friday and Saturday nights.

When it comes to movie theaters, we've got them playing first-run flicks from one end of the region to the other. As Insiders, however, we feel it's our duty to point out three of the many theaters that have as much personality as the reels they run up in the projector room.

The Naro Expanded Cinema in Norfolk's Ghent is an old-fashioned, big 70MM screen armed with Dolby stereo and comfy seats, with the added benefit of baklava and Quibel for sale in the lobby.

Along with current hits, you'll likely find those Academy Award winners you missed during the first run, along with some arty, off-the-wall offerings. If the movie is a dud, pop out to the concession counter for brownies or a giant cookie.

The Commodore in Portsmouth is what a movie theater experience is all about. A grand art deco theater with a huge 42-foot screen, squishy carpet, murals and chandeliers, you plop in a stuffed chair at your own private table. Got a hunger twinge? Just pick up the phone on your table and order in some carrot cake or hot chocolate with tiny floating marshmallows. Even with the super THX sound system, the homelike atmosphere gives you that kick-your-shoes-off and enjoy the movie feeling.

In Virginia Beach, there's the **Cinema Café**, where you also are assigned a table with comfortable chairs for the feature film. This is one theater where you can go straight from the office (or the beach) because the menu includes heftier fare, like a pretty good chicken sandwich, fries and an ice cold beer.

As long as we're on the night prowl, we would be negligent if we didn't mention the Hampton Roads' craze that just won't die, even if we think it's a little close to the edge. It's the current club fad called "karaoke." In brief, this means that a mildly intoxicated patron takes the stage of the nightclub, grabs a microphone and tries desperately to sing the lyrics (in tune) to a popular song played in the background. This in front of the entire evening's crowd . . . and they tell us it's really fun. If you're an exhibitionist, you can give this Japanese-inspired trend a shot nightly with The Comedy Zone's "Singing Machine." More power and rhythm to ya.

And, lastly, another debatable fad that's strictly for the young and strong of heart is the hyper-beat techno-rave that we hate to say is taking hold of young night owls in Hampton Roads. It started with the Tidal Rave held a while back at the old seaside amusement park from 10 PM until 6 AM . . . yes, 6 AM. Now other nightspots are trying to become dance-til-dawn spots with a similar theme like the Kings Head Inn near Old Dominion University that goes semi-techno on Monday nights for dancers 18 years of age and older who, for only one buck, can stay awake through the whole ecstatic line dancing thing. Jumping on this '90s version of disco fever is PRAHA gallery in the old Virginia Stage Company rehearsal and shop space in Downtown Norfolk. Their "Planet Rave" doesn't occur every Saturday night, but upcoming all-nighters are well publicized. We Insiders would have definitely gone to personally check out this latest techno/electro-rave, but our skintight day-glo polyester jump suits were at the cleaners. Darn it.

The Portside marketplace features more than 11 open-air restaurants on the Portsmouth waterfront.

Inside
Shopping

Some of us were born to shop. Others were born to drive us from mall to mall. That's the undeniable truth of life, and one burden (of shopping bags and boxes) we must somehow learn to bear.

The one really good thing about Hampton Roads is that we missed that lecture preaching that conspicuous consumption was out . . . just try to find a parking place close to any mall entrance on a rainy day. Indeed, it is a sign of today's new perspective on accumulation that we must all carefully study the most advanced extracurricular activity of shopping and hone our expertise on field trips taken weekly to meticulously examine all the stuff we couldn't afford even if we did have loads of money.

If you're a visitor to our fair land of outlet malls and outrageous boutiques, we'll not keep those precious little plastic cards bottled up for long. You owe it to yourself, your country and our local economy to arm yourself with padded Air-Nikes and shop, shop, shop. We Insiders would give almost anything to go along with each and every one of you for a personally guided tour, but we know full well that we would be the first to succumb to the world of temptation that lies just behind those glass double-doors. Therefore, we accept the responsibility, and the duty, to point you in the direction of our favorite shopping haunts, and hope you leave the really-marked-down size eight's behind for us.

Other than knowing where the major malls and specialty shopping places are, there are no magical skills or creative insights that we can share with you. Because we know how much it can hurt to go home empty-handed, we've taken great care to aim you at places where you're certain to fall madly and inseparably in love with something that your conscious brain won't admit you don't really need. Not to thank us now. It's only your complete customer satisfaction that we strive for.

Let's shop!

Da Malls

Norfolk

THE WATERSIDE
Waterside Dr., Downtown Norfolk

Is it a mall? Is it a restaurant place? Is it a night spot? Yes to all the above and more. With more than 120 shops, kiosks and pushcarts, six international restaurants and over 25 specialty food shops, The Waterside is one of our favorite places to waste a lazy afternoon. There's always activity, and very often live entertainment, on the lower level where most of the fast food-type restaurants are located. Upstairs, there's the broadest spectrum of shops like **Barr-ee Station Catalogue Outlet** where you'll not be able to resist bargains from J. Crew, Clifford & Willis and, on occasion, Polo. **Queen Anne's**

Lace has drop-dead lingerie and lovely gifts; **The Lodge** has a great collection of industrial strength Gap-style casual wear; and **The Flag Stand** waves with flags of every nation, plus some adorable seasonal house flags. **In Your Image** is packed to the rafters with art prints, figurines, books, cards and jewelry. And you must pop in for a quick check of the bargains at **Lillian Vernon**, thumb through the tomes at **Waldenbooks**, discover all things Virginia at **The Virginia Shop**, and check out the wonderful handmade crafts at **Annabarbara**.

For restaurants, there's the seafood adventure at **Phillips Waterside**, a bit of Brit at **Reggie's British Pub**, golden chopsticks at **Shine Shine Palace** and northern Italian specialities at **Il Porto**, that we swear uses more garlic than allowed by law. Sporting a magnificent copper and brass grill is **Harbor Grill**, where you'll be served some of the best BBQ ribs, chicken and steak in town. Weather permitting, most restaurants offer outdoor dining, overlooking the busy Elizabeth River.

Waterside comes alive at night in the 40,000-square-foot entertainment and dining complex called **Waterside Live!** See the Nightlife chapter for all the goings-on.

As far as parking, there's the huge city lot directly across the street that you access by a pedestrian bridge over Waterside Drive. Take your parking ticket inside for validation with purchase . . . it will save you in parking fees.

SELDEN ARCADE

212 East Main St., Downtown Norfolk

Thanks to the rebirth of our downtown waterfront, this charming antique has been restored to its former glory and is a popular spot for workers in the financial district. **Beecroft & Bull, Ltd.** is the ultimate for men's clothing and accessories, **Goldman's Salon Shoes** carries all those designer brands you'd never wear in the rain, and both **Facets** and **etceteras** are great for browsing singular jewelry and gifts. Food wise, **JP's SmokeHouse Restaurant** is the place for a hearty helping of good old American favorites. Another tempting Arcade eatery is **Yorgo's Bageldashery** with umpteen kinds of bagels and sandwiches. For a marvelous selection of fine books with a cup of your favorite java on the side, slide into **Prince Books and Coffeehouse,** just across the street from the Arcade on Main Street.

GHENT SHOPPING

Colley Ave. and 21st St., Ghent

While not really a mall, the time you can spend sauntering in and out of the many shops and restaurants in Ghent puts it in the park-and-shop category. If you're a parallel parking pro, you can whip into **Bouillabaisse**, the ultimate chef's shop for kitchen goodies, **Gale Goss Country French Antiques** for absolutely divine furnishings, china and accessories, and **Harbor Gallery** for original art by local artists. If you need a card or gift for someone you've left at home, try **The Entertainers**. Around the bend on 21st Street, you can browse through **Turn The Page Book Shop, Decorum** for exquisitely affordable home furnishings, and then pop into **Lili's of Ghent** for that must-have ensemble. Tucked away farther down 21st Street is an all-hands-alert shop-stop . . . **Foxglove Ltd.** While they claim it's a place for gifts for home and garden, it's a homey place full of all kinds of European-flavored accessories and au courant knickknacks you just can't resist. New to the eclectic mix of shops and eateries are

Papa John's Pizza, Subway Sandwiches & Salads, Peter's Ten Top and **Supercuts**.

Throw those bags over your shoulder and head a bit farther down the road to more great shopping finds like **NYFO Boutique** for designer clothing like nothing in your closet. Besides these wonderful places, there are restaurants galore, antiques shops and even the **Naro**, a good old-fashioned movie theater.

MILITARY CIRCLE
Military Hwy. at Virginia Beach Blvd.

One of the original mall experiences in the area, Military Circle has undergone some major renovation in the past years. So now it looks like every other mega-mall around and houses basically the same kind of mall-flavored shops. Of course, we're partial to **The Limited** and **Waldenbooks**, but for department-store atmosphere, **Hecht's** and **Leggett** certainly hold their own as anchors. **JCPenney's** here, too, along with six movie theaters and a plethora of shoe stores and clothing shops. For the younger crowd, **Legends** is a favorite, with all the right name-brand sports shoes and sports gear.

JANAF SHOPPING CENTER
Military Hwy. at Virginia Beach Blvd.

Ok, so this isn't a "real" mall. But if you're out to bargain shop, don't drive past without a quick swing through. You pop into **TJ Maxx** or **Marshalls** while Dad and Junior swoon over the latest in audio-video at **Circuit City**. (For the Circuit City of flea collars, check out **Petstuff**, with more than 7,000 pet supplies we're sure Rover's been asking for.) Teenagers find **A&N** a magnet for sweats and tennies; seamstresses and craftswomen can touch all the new bolts and patterns at **Piece Goods Shop**; and **The Sports Authority** offers up more sports stuff than humankind could ever play with in a lifetime. If kids are in tow, a stop at the **Discovery Zone** should wear them out for that afternoon nap.

If you need a reality shock, stroll through **Portfolio**, the JCPenny furnishings showcase. You'll see absolutely top-rate furniture and accessories that will make you go home and rip up every room in the house. (Track your expenses with supplies from the nearby **Office Max**!) Floating out on the perimeter of Janaf is **Montgomery Ward**, connected at the hip to a brand new **HQ Super Store**, and **Hooters**, a restaurant known for their great Buffalo wings and skimpily clad servers. Navy newcomers will appreciate the handy Navy Information Center in Janaf. There's also a post office as well as a city library in this shopping center, and **Comp USA**, the computer superstore, is right across the street just in case you need your daily computer game fix.

Virginia Beach

PEMBROKE MALL
Virginia Beach Blvd. at Independence

Right in the hub of what is called Virginia Beach's Central Business District, Pembroke Mall has sprawled larger and larger to accommodate both new stores and stalwart shoppers. The tool department at **Sears** is where we usually park our menfolk while we head straight to Pembroke's newest shopping experience, **Proffitt's**. Here you'll find all the latest apparel for every member of the family, plus a grand shoe and accessory department, all temptingly displayed. **S&K**, one of the best menswear discounters, along with **Stein Mart** and **Upton's**, is here, too, plus **Waldenbooks** and **Hit or Miss**.

Sports-minded kids head for the **Athlete's Foot** and **Foot Locker** and, when you need a break, you can cruise over to the cinema for a new release. Across from the movies, there's **Boardwalk Golf & Games**, boasting an indoor miniature golf course, plus all the popular arcade games.

And nearby . . .

Just when you get comfortable with a broad expanse of emptiness, along comes a very sharp developer who knows just what you've been missing. **Columbus Village**, just across the Boulevard from Pembroke Mall, has risen out of nowhere to a hub of activity where parking spaces are scarce. There's an enormous **Barnes and Noble**, complete with an oh-so-chic coffeehouse, and Columbus Movies, 12 screens of the newest releases.

And then there's...

Music lover alert! **Planet Music** has been sighted! No ordinary extraterrestrial music store, Planet Music has a population of 100,000 CDs and tapes spread over 30,000 square feet of space. To make contact with the music, just stop at one of the 100 listening stations to check out foreign titles before you buy. And, if the name of that song or artist is lost in cyberspace, four touchscreen database kiosks called Muze systems need only a key word to investigate. To ensure a safe return to earth, you can sign up for The Star Club and save 20 percent on anything, anytime you buy.

LYNNHAVEN MALL
Lynnhaven Pkwy.

Many of us go to Lynnhaven just to take a "trip out of town." While it isn't very far away in miles, once inside, you can leave your worries in the parking lot and drift aimlessly inside all day long.

Two major book stores, endless women's and men's apparel (including the **Gap**, **Shulman's**, a gorgeous **Lerner's** and cosmopolitan-sized **Limited**), jewelry stores and an out-of-this world **Disney Store** await. On the upper level is a food court to soothe whatever taste you have, from burgers to Chinese to pizza. Two separate **Hecht's** (one for men and home furnishings, the other for women and children), **JCPenney**, **Montgomery Ward** and **Leggett** are the big anchors, but some of our favorite shops are of the smallish variety, like **The Bombay Company**, **Crabtree & Evelyn**, **Victoria's Secret** and **Deck the Walls** (great posters!). For movie buffs, there are eleven theaters. A special note to newcomers: Inside the mall is a Division of Motor Vehicles office (DMV Express) which is a blessing for simple registrations and driver's license renewals.

COUNTRYSIDE SHOPS
Landstown Rd.

This is an absolutely darling place, and just 10 minutes from the oceanfront next to the Farmer's Market. The Coun-

One of the neatest things about living here is that you can still get fresh milk delivered to your door in glass bottles. This little perk makes us feel like we're living in an Ozzie and Harriet family. Both Bergey's Dairy Farm, 482-4711, and Yoder Dairies, 497-3518, have home delivery to many neighborhoods.

Insiders' Tips

tryside Shops are weathered and purposely worn-looking on the outside, but inside is a hallway of boutiques with many one-of-a-kind collectibles. **Heart & Hand Gallery** offers antiques, pottery and jewelry; **The Gardenia Boutique** is Barbie doll dress heaven, and **The Spotted Cow** has a charming hodgepodge of moo cow collectibles and gifts. We especially like **Mrs. Claus' Country Closet** with its St. Nick collectibles and ornaments and **Just Imagine**, with its doll houses and miniatures. The **Countryside Deli** has wonderful homemade soups and desserts, with great overstuffed sandwiches and Virginia BBQ for your middle course.

CRAFTERS MALL

4740 Baxter Rd., one block off Independence Blvd.

If you're in a crafty kind of mood, this is the only place that will satisfy your hobby hunger. The Crafters Mall in the Baxter Run Shopping Center is 10,000 square feet of handmade art, dolls, pottery, jewelry, floral designs and wood crafts. There are more bunnies, bears, kittens and cows, in painted, stuffed and patchworked varieties, than you can even imagine. Plus some pretty interesting Southwestern art and country crafts from more than 300 talented crafters, selling direct to you. If you want to snag a delightful, one-of-a-kind gift, this is definitely one place you won't leave empty handed.

THE GREAT AMERICAN OUTLET MALL

3750 Virginia Beach Blvd.

OshKosh B'Gosh, you can find a lot of neat stuff at neat discount prices at the Great American Outlet Mall! Once you survive the kamikze parking lot, you can hoof through stores galore like **Famous Footwear**, **Spiegel Outlet**, **Dress Barn**, **Drug Emporium**, **Westpoint Pepperell**

Bed, Bath & Linens and **Bugle Boy** . . . all outlets with savings up to 70 percent off retail. Country and western folk will go ga-ga in the **Boot Village**, and you can snag a sexy slip or nightie at **Bare Necessities**. Connected to the Mall is **B.J.'s Wholesale Club**, packed to the unadorned rafters with everything from toys to computers, books to power tools and lots of food in between. While you do have to be a member to get the very best lowest price, guests can get a pass to wheel a cart through the aisles, and pay just 5 percent over the marked price.

HILLTOP SHOPPING CENTER

Laskin and First Colonial Rds.

Covering the compass points, there's Hilltop East, North, West and South. Each is a fine collection of stores, restaurants and specialty shops that cater to the Beach's picky residents and our many resort guests. Not to pass by places include **Dan Ryan's for Men**, **Barnett's Lighting and Gifts**, and **Lily's Fashions**. **Blue Ridge Mountain Sports** is a great place for rugged outdoor wear, and **Baker's Crust** along with **The Real Bread Company** are guaranteed to add those delicious pounds by just taking a sniff. Along with popular **Shoney's** and **Morrison's Cafeteria**, try out **Bella Monte** and **Taste Unlimited** on the food trail. Just across the street is the place for all you **Kmart** shoppers, along with grocery stores and drug chains. Also, a sure-to-shop is the new **Leggett's Outlet Center**, a clearinghouse for this major department store with tempting bargains for ladies, men, kids and the home.

LA PROMENADE

1860 Laskin Rd.

This is one center of distinctive shops where the shoppers look as rich as the merchandise offered. From the exquisite linens at **Arcana** to designer fashions at **Madison** (Anne Klein, Donna Karan, Michael Kors, DKNY and others), you can pop from one boutique to another just swooning over the lushness of it all. There's **NYFO** and **Dakota** for exceptional women's clothing, **Suzanne Jacobson Stationery** for fine writing papers, along with **Facets Jewelry, Kids Kids Kids, Victorian Charm, My Doll House** and **Talbots.** Don't pass up a trip through the racks at **Jos. A. Bank** or slip into some new dancing shoes at **Pappagallo.** For sophisticated dining that matches the upscale taste of the center, slip into **Aldo's Ristorante** for some designer pasta.

REGENCY HILLTOP
1900 Laskin Rd.

If you have any pennies left over from La Promenade, head a short hop down the road to the bargain shopping at Regency Hilltop. Here's off-price heaven, with **Burlington Coat Factory, Michael's Arts and Crafts, Only One Dollar, Phar-Mor, Blockbuster Music** and **Rack Room Shoes.** Satisfy the hungries in the popu-

lar **Old Country Buffet** or at **Sal's Italian Restaurant.** Computer addicts should check out **Software Hogs.** Here, you can "rent" your favorite software title, business or entertainment . . . a great way to test-drive very expensive software before you buy.

LOEHMANN'S PLAZA
4000 Virginia Beach Blvd.

World famous Loehmann's is center stage at this plaza that also tempts you with two **Lillian Vernon Outlet Stores, Linens & Things, Marc Lance Mens,** the **Baby Superstore** and the mega **Herman's World of Sporting Goods. Egghead Software** is also here for you computer nerds, and home decorators will go zonkers in **Calico Corners** with their huge selection of decorator fabrics and trims. Not to go hungry, slide into a booth at **Applebee's** or at **Chili's,** both right across the street.

Chesapeake

GREENBRIER MALL
Greenbrier Pkwy.

Rising like a modern monument on a huge berm is Greenbrier Mall, where

Chesapeake shoppers travel to spend their paychecks. Run amuck through two levels of temptation, including the fabulous **Earth Friendly Company**, with popular anchors **Sears** and **Leggett**, plus the new **Proffitt's**. On the top level of the mall is a particularly inviting food court, with your choice of pizza, Chinese or good old American hamburger.

CROSSWAYS SHOPPING CENTER
Greenbrier Pkwy.

Right across the street is Crossways Shopping Center, bursting at the sidewalks with great places to shop. Along with a plethora of specialty boutiques, there's **Marshall's**, **Upton's**, **S&K Menswear**, **Rack Room Shoes** and **Dress Barn** waiting to spiff up your wardrobe, **Best** and **Montgomery Ward** for household stuff and **Drug Emporium** and a huge **Builder's Square** for every need in between. In the good eats department, there's **Old Country Buffet** in the center itself, the **Black Eyed Pea** and **Lone Star Steakhouse** floating on the perimeter and **Cheer's** (waiting your arrival with an ice-cold brewsky) right across the parkway.

CHESAPEAKE SQUARE
Portsmouth Blvd. and Taylor Rd.

One of our newest malls, Chesapeake Square grew out of a faraway pasture, and suddenly traffic was ferocious. Sparkling new, modern and spit-polished, it's a replay of your favorite places, like anchors **Proffitt's**, **Leggett**, **Sears**, **Montgomery Ward** and **JCPenney**. Inside are the book stores you expect to find, plus some special places like **Tuerkes Luggage**, **American Eagle Outfitters**, **Sea Dream Leather** and **Ingle's Nook** (super kitchen stuff). If you're feeling a little frisky, there's a **Frederick's of Hollywood**, and to pull you back home to earth, there's **Country**

Seat, home of the Levis. A brand new **Limited** and **Limited Express** cover a zillion square feet. There's little way you won't find everything you like here, but if not, pop across the street to The Crossroads and run amuck in **TJ Maxx**, **Circuit City** and **Wal-Mart**.

Portsmouth

TOWER MALL
Airline Blvd.

This is an older mall that's holding its own, especially with Portsmouth residents. It's a friendly sort of place that's usually pretty quiet except on payday weekends, so if you seriously need to have a mall fix, it's a recommended destination. Quite a few stores have come and gone since it's inception, but still going strong are **Montgomery Ward** outlet store, **Waldenbooks** and **World Bazaar**, a hodgepodge of imported wicker and inexpensive china. The movies are here, too, and that brings a lot of folks out just before and after showtime.

Suffolk

Suffolk maintains a traditional downtown whose ongoing Main Street revitalization program is giving a facelift to the city's storefronts.

There is plenty of metered parking along downtown streets so get out of your car and go for a stroll. There are several upscale clothing and shoe stores downtown. **Denison's** at 177 N. Main specializes in women's clothing. **Holmes Ltd.** at 139 N. Main sells both women's clothing and shoes while **The Shoetique** at 147 N. Main is strictly a shoe store. **G.S. Hobbs Ltd.** at 126 N. Main specializes in men's clothing.

Virginia-Grown Gifts

If you want to take home typical Virginia souvenirs, try some of the Commonwealth's highly acclaimed food products. Peanuts, wine, jams, pound cakes and hams are the logical choices. You'll also find well-done cookbooks and the Blue Crab Bay Co. line of seafood-related products from the Eastern Shore.

For one of the biggest selection of all kinds of Virginia products stop by the Virginia Shop in The Waterside in Downtown Norfolk, 623-4547.

In Suffolk there are two choice for peanuts. The Planters Peanut Center at 308 W. Washington Street, 539-4411, sells Planters' products, many of them made in the company's Suffolk plant. Store employees create a wonderful aroma by cooking peanuts in an antique roaster. The Nutcracker Peanut and Gift Shop, also in Suffolk, is inside the Producers Peanut Co. peanut butter plant at 337 Moore Avenue, 539-7496. It sells peanut products in gift packages and has a mail-order business.

For hams try the Old Virginia Ham Shop, 217 E. Little Creek Road, Norfolk, 583-0014. This shop looks like a red barn and is in the Wards Corner area. In Suffolk the Pruden Packing Co. at 1201 N. Main Street, 539-6261, has a retail shop that sells hams cured in the plant.

Another delightful place is Rowena's at 758 W. 22nd Street in Norfolk, 627-8699. This Ghent business has gained international acclaim for its homemade pound cakes — especially when topped with Rowena's lemon curd sauce. Rowena's sells an innovative line of jams, sauces and other tasty food products. The business is run by its founder Rowena Fullinwider, and her products are made right here. For many locals Rowena's is their first stop for out-of-town holiday presents.

Another culinary treat is coffee from the First Colony Coffee House at 2000-1 Colonial Avenue in Norfolk and 1550 Laskin Road in Virginia Beach. All types of gourmet coffee are roasted in a Norfolk plant built in 1902.

If you're ready for a coffee break you'll find a busy soda fountain at **Nansemond Drug Co.** at 115 N. Main that turns out old-fashioned milk shakes, lemonades and grilled cheese sandwiches. You may also want to pick up some peanuts fresh from the antique roaster at the **Planters Peanut Center** at 308 W. Washington.

There are no malls in Suffolk but there are several shopping centers with grocery stores, discount stores and smaller businesses. You'll find them on **Holland Road, Constance Road** and on **N. Main Street**.

Specialty Shops

While you'll find a good variety in the region's malls and shopping centers, there are plenty of other jewels waiting to be discovered on side streets and specialty shops. We love to wander through antique stores, used book shops and out-of-the-way spots when we visit other cities. We've included some tidbits about some of our favorite places here at home. Have fun exploring them.

Antiques

There are numerous small shops to tempt you if you're interested in antique furniture, glassware and bric-a-brac. In fact, there are more than 125 dealers in the region and several flea markets or antique malls with multiple vendors.

Shops range from those filled with rare antiques to the ones selling the Mrs. Butterworth bottle you unloaded at your last garage sale. The thrill of antiquing is in the hunt for that perfect oak filing cabinet or piece of Depression glass, so grab your checkbook and start prowling.

Since we can't cover all the shops, we'll steer you in the direction of areas that have a concentration of stores. That way you can hit a bunch of shops on the same trip. For other suggestions check the Yellow Pages. The *Virginian-Pilot/Ledger-Stars*' classified sections are the place to watch if you are interested in auctions and estate sales. For household goods, baby furniture, antiques and just about anything else you want, buy a copy of the *Trading Post*. The shopper is published each week and is filled with merchandise for sale by private owners.

In Norfolk one must-see area for antiques is along **21st Street** between Manteo and Granby and in the 2600 block of **Granby Street**. There are about 25 antique shops in Norfolk, and the bulk of them are along these two streets. You'll need to drive from 21st Street to Granby Street since its antique district is across the railroad tracks. The merchants have produced a brochure on antique shops in Norfolk so try to pick up a copy to guide you.

Some shops you may want to check out are the **Norfolk Antique Company** at 537 W. 21st Street and the **Palace Antiques Gallery** at 21st and Lewellyn. Both have several dealers in them. For '50s and '60s kitsch, wander into **Metropolis** at 3824 Granby Street.

There also are dealers on Colonial Avenue. **Nero's Antiques & Appraisals** at 1101 Colonial Avenue bills itself as Ghent's oldest antique shop.

In Chesapeake, you'll want to hit the shops along **South Military Highway** at Canal Drive. For one stop along the way try **Eddie's Antique Mall** at 632 S. Military Highway, which has a huge stash of furniture and frequent auctions. By the time you cross over the Gilmerton Bridge you'll be convinced you're hopelessly lost. Keep going and you'll find shop after shop that has been doing business for years. One place to stop is **Strick's Auction Center** at 917 Canal Drive, which has a small antique mall with about 10 dealers.

In Virginia Beach, there are several large dealers. **British-European Antique Importers Ltd.** is near the oceanfront at 606 Norfolk Avenue. It has a 10,000-square-foot warehouse. **Shomiers** at 3205 Virginia Beach Boulevard has an interesting mix of antiques and reproductions.

Suffolk has one of our favorite places to buy antiques — one we like so much we hesitate to tell you about. This is the **Village Auction Barn** at 101 Philhower Drive. It is on the outskirts of Suffolk as you drive into town, but it's easy to miss, so call for directions, 539-6296. The barn holds an auction every Saturday night that draws dealers as well as regular folks. Some weeks feature estate sales, but about twice a month veteran auctioneer Dewey Howell hauls in a load of furniture and goods from England. These English nights are the prime time to be at the auction barn, especially if you're in the market for oak furniture. Check the

SHOPPING

Waterside marketplace in Norfolk provides a wide variety of shops and boutiques.

classifieds in the newspaper for specifics. Prepare to spend the evening at the barn and eat a sandwich and homemade dessert from the cafe. Out front is a small antique mall.

There are several dealers scattered throughout Suffolk. One place to start is downtown at **The Attic Trunk** at 167 S. Main. **Nansemond Antique Shop** at 3537 Pruden Boulevard on the outskirts of town is another possibility.

In Portsmouth **Prison Square Antiques** is a well-stocked, eclectic store at 440 High Street. It specializes in American and English collectibles.

Used Bookstores

Part of the joy in shopping in these stores is never knowing what you'll find — a cherished book from your childhood, a rare volume of poetry or a spellbinding novel for the beach. Here are some of the used bookstores we frequent:

The Bibliopath Bookshop & Bindery, 251 W. Bute Street, Norfolk. Owners H.L. and Linda Wilson maintain one of the region's best-stocked stores. Their inventory runs from the classics to military history and paperback westerns. Besides used and out-of-print books they also sell records, CDs and tapes and do bookbinding and appraisals. Be sure to look for Wallaby and the Great Catsby, the resident cats, when you visit this Freemason area store. The Wilsons have been in this location since 1988 and previously ran another Norfolk book shop. Around town the Bibliopath is known for its New Year's Day party — a must-do event for regular customers.

Octavo Books, 1645 Laskin Road, Virginia Beach. You'll find the general classics and much more in this store in the Hilltop area.

Great Bridge Books, 404 Woodford Drive, Chesapeake. Located in an old house in the Great Bridge area since 1975, this shop features a good selection of Virginiana, literature and children's books.

Pfeiffer' Books and Cards, 432 High Street in Portsmouth, opened in 1993 in the heart of downtown. It offers a variety of used books as well as some new ones. The store has a sideline of selling candles

• *113*

and calendars decorated with wizards. It also rents books on tape.

Beacon Books of Ghent, 824 W. 21st Street in Norfolk, has all kinds of used books crammed into a cozy store.

New Bookstores

In addition to the usual national chains, there are local stores with great selections run by people who adore books. Two of the largest general book stores are **Prince Books and Coffeehouse** at 109 Main Street in downtown Norfolk and **Turn the Page** at 331 W. 21st Street in Norfolk. Prince Books relocated from across the street last year and added a small coffeehouse that's one of our favorite downtown lunch spots.

The best variety of children's books is at **Once Upon a Time** in The Willis Wayside shopping center at 4220 Virginia Beach Boulevard. In Virginia Beach, **Riverbend Books'** eclectic selection appeals to public radio fans as well as children and other readers. The shop is in the Great Neck Village Shopping Center on Great Neck Road. For religious books try **Dolphin Tales** at 2955 Virginia Beach Boulevard or **Dudley's Christian Books**. Dudley's has two locations: 7501 Granby Street in Norfolk and 4314 Virginia Beach Boulevard in Virginia Beach.

One nice new wrinkle in the book business is **Echo Audio Books**, with two locations — one at 525 N. Birdneck Road and the other in the Fairfield Shopping Center, both in Virginia Beach. Here you can rent or buy audio books and hardcover editions (only at the Birdneck location). They have the largest selection of books on tape we've seen. We wouldn't even think of going on a long road trip anymore without a good book to listen to. Try it! You'll be to your destination before you know it.

The biggest book selection is at the giant **Barnes & Noble** bookstore that

Your Gift Dollars Help

Many of the region's museums and some of its churches have gift shops that sell unusual items. Spending your money at these nonprofit organizations lets you help them while checking off your gift list. The shops with the widest variety include those at The Chrysler Museum, the Norfolk Botanical Garden, Nauticus, and the Virginia Zoo in Norfolk, the Virginia Marine Science Museum and the Virginia Beach Center for the Arts in Virginia Beach, Riddick's Folly in Suffolk and the Children's Museum of Virginia in Portsmouth.

Churches with interesting gift shops include The Church of the Good Shepherd, 1520 N. Shore Road, 423-3230, Christ & St. Luke's Church, Olney Road and Stockley Gardens, 627-5665 and St. Andrews Episcopal Church, 1004 Graydon Avenue, 622-5530. All are in Norfolk.

The Norfolk Senior Center, 924 W. 21st Street, Norfolk, 625-5857, runs a gift shop with mostly handmade items. For a hostess or housewarming gift, there's nowhere we'd rather shop than the Sugar Plum Bakery at 1353 Laskin Road in Virginia Beach, 422-3913. This nonprofit bakery trains and hires disabled workers. A box of Sugar Plum's cookies or pastries is a real treat.

opened in Virginia Beach last year. The bookstore is across from Pembroke Mall at the intersection of Virginia Beach Boulevard and Constitution Drive adjacent to **Planet Music**, which opened in late 1993. For a relaxing visit, sip some cappuccino at the bookstore's coffee bar while making your selection.

Gourmet and Wine Shops

All-purpose gourmet shops let you pick up unusual spices, grab a sandwich and select a special wine. Stores to visit include **Grape & Grain, The West Side Wine Shop** and **Taste Unlimited**. Grape & Grain is at 2973 Shore Drive in Virginia Beach. West Side Wine is at 4702 Hampton Boulevard in Norfolk. There are four Taste Unlimiteds. The Norfolk location is in Ghent at 1619 Colley Avenue. Virginia Beach shops are at 638 Hilltop West, 36th & Pacific and 4097 Shore Drive.

Although you'll find plenty of wines and beers in grocery stores, for a more adventuresome selection check out the stock in specialty shops. Be sure to sample some of the Virginia wines that are gaining national acclaim. **East of Napa**, 2224 Virginia Beach Boulevard, specializes in domestic wines. Other good selections are at **Reisner's Delicatessen** in the Janaf Shopping Center in Norfolk and in Virginia Beach at **P.J.'s Java Cafe**, a gourmet sandwich, coffee and wine shop at 960 Laskin Road and at **Bella Monte Gourmet Italian Marketplace & Cafe**, 134 Hilltop East.

Health Foods

If you long for tofu, organic tomatoes and fresh cilantro, you'll find several health food stores. The largest in Norfolk is the **Whole Foods Co-Op** at 119 W. 21st Street in Ghent. The co-op, which has more than 400 members, started in 1973. You don't have to be a member to shop there, but you'll get a discount if you join.

There is a good selection of bulk grains, nuts and seeds. You'll also find olive oil and tahini for Mediterranean cooking. There are more than 200 fresh spices and herbs and many foods for diabetics and others needing special diets.

The biggest shop in Virginia Beach is **Heritage Health Food Store** at 314 Laskin Road. It has been in business since the late '70s. There is a big selection of organic and health foods. The store has the region's only organic deli, which features all wheat-free and sugar-free products. Affiliated businesses include a bookstore and holistic health services.

For kosher products try **The Kosher Place Meats & More** at 738 W. 22nd Street in Norfolk.

Consignment Stores

Since becoming a parent, used-clothing stores have become our favorite haunt. Besides snaring some terrific duds for our fast-growing child, we've also picked up some designer labels for ourself. To get the bargains, you need to frequent the shops, be open-minded about what you're looking for and have an eye for quality. There are plenty of wealthy people in the region with expensive castoffs that have hardly been worn. These shops are the perfect places to snare special-occasion clothes. Here are some of our best shopping spots.

The White Rabbitt, 310 W. 21st Street, Norfolk, has all kinds of children's clothes. Its women's and maternity sections also are worth checking out. This Ghent shop is a great place to buy gifts since it features jewelry and crafts created by local artists.

Banbury Cross, 738 W. 22nd Street, Norfolk, has both new and gently used children's clothes. You'll find some delightful smocked outfits among the new clothes.

Act II, 816 A 21st Street, Norfolk and 3411 Virginia Beach Boulevard, Virginia Beach. These shops are run by the Organization Through Rehabilitation and Training (ORT). Act II specializes in women's clothes, has a big selection of party clothes and often sells new clothes donated by local stores.

Sand Bucket, 3006 Arctic Avenue, Virginia Beach, specializes in quality children's clothes and accessories.

Elephants Galore, 3900 Bonney Road, Virginia Beach, is a two-story store with a little bit of everything — baby items, furniture and lots of clothes for the entire family.

2nd Time Around, 3772 Virginia Beach Boulevard, Virginia Beach, has clothes for adults and children as well as a good selection of jewelry. There's usually a variety of party clothes.

Things Unlimited, 501 Virginia Beach Boulevard, Virginia Beach, is a big store with all kinds of clothes and household goods. It has a wonderful costume department that is a mainstay for Halloween. Proceeds benefit the Virginia Beach Friends School.

Encore, 3636 Virginia Beach Boulevard, Virginia Beach. This two-story shop has men's and women's clothes, jewelry, furniture, books and household goods.

Echoes of Time, 320B Laskin Road, Virginia Beach, is a huge vintage clothing store with garments and jewelry from

the 1800s to the 1950s. It's a fun place to browse.

The Velveteen Rabbit, 3115 Western Branch Boulevard, in Portsmouth is in the Churchland Place Shopping Center. It has a mix of both new and used children's clothes.

Consigning Women & Kids, 1920 Centerville Turnpike, Suite 115 in the Woods Corner Shopping Center in Virginia Beach, carries mostly clothes as well as some accessories, bags and shoes.

That Baby Place, 2354 E. Little Creek Road in Norfolk, is filled with clothing, cribs, high chairs and other paraphernalia for babies and toddlers.

Baby Express, 1485 General Booth Boulevard in Virginia Beach, has high-quality clothes for newborns through size 8.

Discovery Shop, 1556 Laskin Rd. in the Hilltop East Shopping Center in Virginia Beach, features women's clothing, accessories and housewares, many of them new. Proceeds benefit the American Cancer Society.

In addition to these shops, you can find bargains among goods donated to local charities that operate thrift shops. Many organizations have loyal supporters who would rather give away their old stuff than sell it. There are five **Childrens Hospital of The Kings Daughters Thrift Stores**, five **Goodwill** stores, three **Salvation Army** stores, three **Union Mission** stores, two **Hope House Foundation** shops, one Disabled American Veteran store and one **Trinity Mission** shop.

Collectible Shops

We have friends always on the prowl for that special baseball card, comic book or old record. Here are a few suggestions for them.

Baseball card and comic book collectors will find about 40 shops listed in the Yellow Pages. Some places to check out include:

Trilogy Comics, 857 Lynnhaven Road and 5773 Princess Anne Road, Virginia Beach, 700 E. Little Creek Drive, Norfolk and 3916 Portsmouth Boulevard, Chesapeake. Besides comics, Trilogy sells baseball cards, games and science fiction merchandise.

Comics & Things, Holland Plaza Shopping Center, Virginia Beach, sells new and collectible comics, collector cards, *Star Trek* items and related paraphernalia.

D&D Sports Cards, 5660 D Portsmouth Boulevard, Portsmouth, sells new and used cards.

Home Run Sports Cards, 2148 Great Neck Square Shopping Center and 981 Providence Square Shopping Center, Virginia Beach, has a large selection of all types of sports cards.

For collectible records, rummage through the oldies but goodies at **Skinnies Records & Tapes** at 814 W. 21st Street in Norfolk's Ghent area.

You'll find more than 30 shops specializing in new compact discs and tapes. The largest is **Planet Music**, which opened in late 1993 in Virginia Beach. It is at the intersection of Virginia Beach Boulevard and Constitution Drive and has an unbeatable selection of CDs and tapes. Before buying, shoppers also can take a listen at one of dozens of listening spots.

The most prolific record shop is **Blockbuster Music** (formerly Tracks Record Bar) with seven locations, including Lynnhaven Mall, Greenbrier Mall and the outskirts of Military Circle Mall. For jazz try **Birdland Records Tapes & Compact Discs** at 957 Providence Road, Virginia Beach.

Quilt Shops

This is a big interest of ours, and we love to search these shops for the perfect fabric to add to our stash at home. There are some well-respected shops here. All are well stocked, offer excellent classes and have helpful staffs.

What's Your Stitch 'n Stuff at 5350 Kempsville Drive in Virginia Beach, is our favorite place for fabric and supplies. It recently moved from Norfolk to the Kempsville area and is behind Kempsriver Crossing Shopping Center near CBN.

Sis 'n Me, 5941 Churchland Boulevard in Portsmouth, is just off High Street. However, you may get turned around trying to find this cozy shop so call for directions, 484-2647. It sells fabric and all types of supplies.

Fabric Hut, 3520 N. Military Highway, Norfolk, has the region's best selection of all kinds of fabric — from wools to bridal satin. It maintains a fully stocked quilting department.

Just for Children

Although you'll find several **Toys R Us** and **Kids R Us** outlets here, you may want to shop at some specialty toy and children's clothing stores.

Other fun toy stores include the **Teachers & Parents Store** in Loehmann's Plaza and Kemps River Crossing Shopping Center in Virginia Beach. There's also a store in the Greenbrier South shopping center. The biggest selection of stuffed animals is at the **Embraceable Zoo** in The Waterside in Norfolk, while the best toy train selection is at **Mike's Trainland** at 5661 Shoulder Hill Road in Suffolk. Lynnhaven Mall has become a hot spot since it recently added a **Disney**

Store. For children's books try **Once Upon A Time** in the Willis Wayside shops at 4220 Virginia Beach Boulevard in Virginia Beach.

Our child's dream merchants are the dollar stores where his buck from Grandma will buy anything from earrings for mom's birthday to a bag of plastic cowboys and Indians. There are two different dollar store chains in area malls and shopping centers — **Everything's A Dollar** and **Dollar Tree**. Both have gone national after getting their start in Hampton Roads.

There are more than 20 specialty clothing shops for children. Some to check out are: **The Zoo** at 1900 Colley Avenue in Norfolk, **Kids Kids Kids** at 222 W. 21st Street in Norfolk and 1860 Laskin Road in Virginia Beach, **Honey Tree for Children** at 4218 Virginia Beach Boulevard and 1043 Independence Boulevard in Virginia Beach, and **Evelyn's Small World** in the Suffolk Shopping Center. Of area department stores, **Upton's** has the best-stocked children's department. **Kids R Us** carries a huge variety of clothes and shoes. Its store is at 2701 N. Mall Drive in Virginia Beach.

For shoes for growing feet, we rely on **Hirschler's Shoe Stores**, which have been around since the '40s. Stores are at 7534 Granby Street in Norfolk and Providence Square Shopping Center in Virginia Beach.

Unusual Stores

Two unusual stores we've never seen anywhere else are Grande Junquetion and Wine & Cake Hobbies. Both are fun to wander through and are the favorite places for many hobbyists.

Grande Junquetion, 100 S. Lynn Shores Drive in Virginia Beach, is the kind of place that defies description. People who like to tinker with projects love this surplus store crammed with all kinds of gadgets, tools and electronic equipment. The merchandise is unpredictable and comes mostly from military surplus and bankrupt businesses. The store is just off Virginia Beach Boulevard.

We're still amazed that wine-making and cake decorating are big enough hobbies to justify this huge store. But it's a busy place stocked with every type of cake pan and decorating paraphernalia as well as everything you need to make wine. There's also a large party supply department. **Wine & Cake Hobbies** is at 6527 Tidewater Drive in Norfolk. The road curves around a viaduct at this point so call for directions, 857-0245.

One local retailing legend is **Norfolk Wholesale Floral Corp.**, founded more than 60 years ago. Besides selling wholesale, this cavernous business at 601 E. Brambleton Avenue in Norfolk does a brisk retail trade. Two huge buildings are crammed with plants, cut flowers, floral arrangements, wicker baskets and party supplies. Prices are reasonable and the selection unbeatable.

Inside
Attractions

There is so much to do in Hampton Roads that you can live here for years and never get to everything. But there are three good ways to get motivated to take in all the varied attractions:

·Be a tourist determined to make the most of your visit.

·Be a new resident eager to explore your adopted environs.

·Have out-of-town visitors.

We're long past relying on the first two excuses, so we're always grateful to have guests come and get us out of our rut. If you need a stash of brochures about area attractions there are several places to check. The Hampton Roads Chamber of Commerce, which has offices in each city, has some pamphlets. But for the best selections, contact city convention and visitor bureaus.

For information on Norfolk call the Norfolk Convention & Visitors Bureau and order a visitor's guide. Call (800) 368-3097. For hotel reservations call (800) 843-8030. Once in town, there are several places to pick up information:

•Norfolk's Convention & Visitor's Bureau is downtown at 236 E. Plume Street. It is open from 8:30 AM to 5 PM Monday through Friday (441-5266).

•The Bureau operates a Visitor Information Center just off Interstate 64 (Exit 273) in the Ocean View area near the Hampton Roads Bridge-Tunnel. It is open from 9 AM to 5 PM daily, 441-1852. The center is stocked with brochures and has a helpful staff to answer questions and assist with hotel reservations.

•There also is an information center downtown in The Waterside festival mar-

The Chrysler Museum in Norfolk is considered one of the best art museums in the country.

ketplace that has maps, brochures, tickets to some area attractions and a fascinating short film on the city's history that runs every half-hour during the day.

To learn more about Virginia Beach call (800) 822-3224 and order a visitor's packet of information. You may call (800) VABEACH to make hotel reservations. If you're in the city and want immediate information, stop by the Visitor Information Center at 2100 Parks Avenue, 437-4888. You can't miss it if you are entering the city on the Virginia Beach-Norfolk Expressway (I 44/264), since the center sits in the middle of the divided road. The center, operated by the city's Department of Convention and Visitor Development, opened in 1990 as a gateway to the resort. It is open 9 AM to 5 PM daily with longer hours during the summer. Besides having a staff to answer questions and hundreds of brochures, the center has a short video to watch. It also can help with hotel reservations.

For information on Portsmouth call the Portsmouth Convention and Visitors Bureau at (800) PORTSVA or 393-5327. To pick up brochures check the Portside Visitor Center on the banks of the Elizabeth River in downtown. It is operated by the tourism bureau at the corner of Water Street and North Street and is open

from 9 AM to 5 PM daily, 393-5111. Information also is available weekdays from 8:30 AM to 5 PM at the city tourism bureau in the city hall complex at 801 Crawford Street, third floor.

Neither Suffolk nor Chesapeake has tourism bureaus. Your best bets are the local Hampton Roads Chamber of Commerce offices. They are at 1001 W. Washington Street in Suffolk, 539-2111, and 400 Volvo Parkway in Chesapeake, 547-2118.

Museums

Norfolk

THE CHRYSLER MUSEUM

245 W. Olney Rd.   664-6200
Hours: Tuesday-Saturday, 10 AM-4 PM; Sunday, 1-5 PM
Admission: Free with $3 donation suggested, $2 for children

This is the region's premier art museum. With more than 30,000 pieces from every time period, this massive museum is considered one of the best art museums in the country. The Chrysler's 8,000-piece glass collection is one of the world's largest. Holdings include works by Renoir, Matisse and Gauguin. To hear a recorded rundown on current exhibitions

Photo: Norfolk Convention and Visitors Bureau

The Moses Myers House in Norfolk is the home of the first Jewish residents to come to this region.

call 622-ARTS. For detailed information see the Arts chapter.

HAMPTON ROADS NAVAL MUSEUM

Inside the National Maritime Center (Nauticus)
One Waterside Dr. 444-8971
Hours: Summer, 9 AM-9 PM daily; other times: 9 AM-4 PM daily
Admission: Free

The museum is on the second floor of Nauticus. It relocated there in late 1994 after many years on the Norfolk Naval Base. Exhibits include naval artifacts and a collection of prints and artwork. Displays focus on regional warship construction from the frigate *Chesapeake* in 1799 to today's aircraft carriers. They also focus on major naval actions and events, including the duel between the *Monitor* and the CSS *Virginia* (*Merrimac*) during the Civil War, the departure of the great White Fleet and the first flight from a ship. The naval museum is open even on Mondays during off-season when the rest of Nauticus typically is closed. To see just the naval museum, enter Nauticus' guest relations door. (For more details see the Nauticus entry in this section.)

THE DOUGLAS MACARTHUR MEMORIAL

MacArthur Square 441-2965
Hours: 10 AM -5 PM Monday-Saturday; 11 AM-5 PM Sunday
Admission: Free

This is the burial spot for Gen. Douglas MacArthur, whose main link with Norfolk was that the city was his mother's childhood home. Since 1964 the museum's extensive holdings have detailed the life of the famous general. It is in Downtown Norfolk on the corner of Bank Street and City Hall Avenue. The main building, a Virginia Historic Landmark, was Norfolk's 19th-century courthouse and has recently received a facelift. Inside the exhibits were revamped in 1994 and several new ones were added, including ones on female war prisoners during World War II and segregated military forces. There are three other buildings on the grounds, including a library, gift shop and theater.

To begin your visit, stop in the theater building for a 24-minute film on MacArthur that features newsreel footage. Inside the main building, the first thing you will see is MacArthur's final resting spot in the rotunda. There are nine galleries on two floors that take MacArthur's life from boyhood to his glory years as General of the Army. One display includes his desk, uniform, medals and signature corncob pipe. Don't miss the gift shop outside; that's where MacArthur's gleaming 1950 Chrysler Imperial limousine is displayed. Out front of the memorial is a bronze statue of the general that is a popular photo spot.

THE NATIONAL MARITIME CENTER (NAUTICUS)

One Waterside Dr.   *664-1000*
10 AM-7 PM daily May through September, 10 AM-5 PM everyday but Monday the rest of the year.
Admission: Adults, $7.50; Children, $5 older than 6; seniors and military personnel, $6.50. A Nauticus explorer package that includes tickets to three major attractions costs $14 for adults, $8.50 for youths and $13 for seniors and military personnel.

The newest attraction in Hampton Roads takes visitors on high-tech thrill rides while educating them about maritime technology. After nearly three years of construction, this $52 million attraction opened in 1994.

This 120,000-square-foot hybrid museum/science center/attraction anchors the western edge of the Downtown Norfolk waterfront. With its location adjacent to Town Point Park and near The Waterside festival marketplace, Nauticus helps make the Norfolk waterfront as lively as Baltimore's Inner Harbor.

Plan to spend about four hours in Nauticus. Paid parking is available in city garages across Waterside Drive. Once you've ditched the car, follow the wooden gangplank to the Nauticus entrance where a reflecting pool blends with the Elizabeth River to make the whole building look like it's floating. Look up to see the A-4 Navy jet parked on the roof and painted like a Blue Angels flying machine. Three gangways lead to the main lobby where you can quiz the staff at the guest relations desk Also on this floor is a well-stocked gift shop and a restaurant.

Then step on the world's longest inclined people mover, whose design ripples like waves. In 90 seconds you're on the third floor ready to start your tour. For the less adventuresome, old-fashioned stairs and elevators also will whisk you skyward. Once on the third floor, you can use telescopes to check out the view. Among the highlights are the world's largest floating drydock, historic Portsmouth and the buoy that marks Mile 0 on the Atlantic Intracoastal Waterway.

The third floor houses Nauticus' 350-seat wide-screen theater. *The Living Sea* is an underwater adventure created just for Nauticus. There's a $2.50 charge to see the film unless you purchased the explorer package. Since the theater exits onto the second floor, be sure to check out all the third-floor attractions before watching the film. The third floor houses the bulk of Nauticus' major displays in more than a dozen themed areas. Among the best are a ship's bridge complete with captain's chair and all kinds of mind-boggling instruments, a working submarine periscope that goes right through the roof and a hands-on marine exploration area for younger children.

Also on the third floor are interactive exhibits where you can hunt for submarines with Sonar, design a ship, land a fighter jet on an aircraft carrier and navigate a tanker. There are also small theaters devoted to shipbuilding and the Port of Hampton Roads. Another video wall shows the Blue Angels flying team in action. One major attraction is the Aegis Theater, which costs an extra $2.50

(again, it's included in the explorer package). In a Universal Studios' twist, actors, film and computers meld together for a 15-minute adventure. About 40 visitors enter what looks exactly like the command center of a Navy destroyer. They pretend to be part of a routine briefing and even have computer monitors to use. Then all hell breaks lose as the ship comes under attack. Seats rock, alarms blare, and the thrill is on.

For the environmentally inclined, both Old Dominion University and Norfolk State University operate working labs on this floor. ODU monitors water quality in the Chesapeake Bay while NSU runs a cell biology lab. There is an aquarium nearby as well as a touch tank with crabs and other hardy creatures in it. The National Oceanic and Atmospheric Administration (NOAA) has an exhibit on weather. Next door is a TV studio where you can do your best Willard Scott impression and make a video as you give a weather report.

Highlights of the second floor include a virtual reality room where visitors board submarines, don 3-D glasses and take a wild ride that's different every time. (This costs an extra $2.50, and by now you know for sure you should have sprung for the explorer pass!) Next door is the Hampton Roads Naval Museum, which moved from the Norfolk Naval Base to Nauticus and is operated by the Navy. The museum's ship models, uniforms and treasure trove of other artifacts chronicle 200 years of Navy history. With its move to Nauticus, the museum has doubled its space and brought many artifacts out of storage. You can easily spend an hour wandering through here. The naval museum also has jazzed up its displays to correspond with Nauticus' high-tech touch.

If you're weary after all this action, take a break in Nauticus' first-floor restaurant. Outside is the relaxing Celebration Pavilion, a 40,000-square-foot covered deck with comfortable seating. Adjacent to it is a pier where there frequently will be a Navy or other ship to tour.

Hint: If you only want to see the naval museum, you can be admitted to this part for free, since it is operated by the U.S. Navy. It is open daily. Enter through the guest relations door. Call 444-8971. (See entry above for more details.)

The first floor of Nauticus, which includes a gift shop and restaurant, also is open to the public so you don't need a ticket to peek inside. To fully experience Nauticus buy the explorer package, which includes a ticket to the three big attractions. If you want to enjoy them again, $2.50 tickets are available inside for each attraction.

Virginia Beach

LIFE-SAVING MUSEUM OF VIRGINIA

24th St. and Oceanfront   422-1587
Hours: Tuesday-Saturday, 10 AM-5 PM; Sunday,
noon-5 PM. Open Mondays during the summer
with longer daily hours
Admission: $2.50, $1 for children older than 5

The museum is housed in a former U.S. Life-Saving/Coast Guard Station built in 1903. The simple clapboard structure along the Virginia Beach boardwalk gives a hint of simpler pre-condo days at the oceanfront. Two galleries highlight the history of those who risked their lives to save others during shipwrecks. A permanent display focuses on the impact of World Wars I and II on Virginia Beach.

ROYAL LONDON WAX MUSEUM

1606 Atlantic Ave.   425-3823
Hours: Open daily in summer and on weekends
in fall and spring
Admission: $3.95, $2.95 for children

This museum has been around for about a decade but has recently spruced up its displays. The museum's 100 wax figures range from the Beatles and Pinocchio to Dr. Martin Luther King Jr. and Joan of Arc. There also is a chamber of horrors that is easy to avoid if you're squeamish or have children with you.

VIRGINIA MARINE SCIENCE MUSEUM

717 General Booth Blvd.   437-4949
For recorded information   425-FISH
Hours: 9 AM-5 PM off season; longer hours
during summer
Admission: $4.95, $4.25 for children, $4.50 for
senior citizens

This is one of the most popular museums in Virginia, and its ever-changing exhibits keep local residents coming back. The native fish swimming in the museum's 50,000-gallon aquarium mesmerize all ages. There are 60 hands-on exhibits exploring Virginia marine life

that let visitors tong for oysters or create waves. Children especially like the touch-tank where they can get their hands on crabs, turtles and starfish with the help of museum docents. The museum frequently features a decoy carver and other demonstrations. Outside, a boardwalk takes you on a peaceful walk through the Owls Creek salt marsh.

Educational boat trips are featured occasionally, and reservations fill up fast. Each year the museum takes thousands of nature lovers on outings off the coast to view whales and dolphins. In the winter of 1995, a whopping 23,000 people braved winter seas to spot whales. Popular in-museum activities include SCUBA demonstrations at 11 AM on Saturdays, Sundays and holidays, fish feedings at 10 AM and 3 PM and an interpreted marsh walk at 11:30 AM daily.

In fall 1994 the museum embarked on an ambitious $33 million expansion that will triple its space and make it one of the country's best marine museums.

Portsmouth

CHILDREN'S MUSEUM OF VIRGINIA

221 High St.   393-8393
Hours: 10 AM-5 PM daily, until 9 PM on Fridays
Summers, 9 AM-9 PM daily
Admission: $3; a $5 pass allows you to also visit
three other nearby Portsmouth museums. Free
for children younger than 2.

This is the liveliest place in the region and is a must-see for anyone with children. The city-owned museum is fun for all ages — from toddlers, who can safely roam the "quiet room" stocked with simple toys, to even the most jaded teenager.

For nearly 15 years the downtown museum thrived in Portsmouth's historic 1846 Courthouse on High Street. Even with only 3,000 square feet of space and three major displays, the museum drew 60,000 visitors a year. With its move in December 1994 down the street to a revamped former department store, the museum has mushroomed into the largest children's museum in Virginia.

The response to the $3 million-plus expansion has been overwhelming, so watch out for weekends and holidays when as many as 2,000 people a day try to crowd in for hours of fun. If time is critical, go early or late in the day on a weekend or on a weekday when all you're likely to face are school or summer camp groups.

Even with heavy attendance, the 27,000-square-foot museum has plenty of room to spread out. Fans of the old museum will feel at home with bigger and better versions of their old favorites — the room full of bubbles to play with, the thousands of Legos to challenge creativity, and the city room with its grocery store and mail-carrier's equipment to stretch the imagination.

The museum has 14 major displays, ranging from a crane that hoists white foam beams to activities that focus in a fun way on flexibility, balance and reflexes. All exhibits allow hands-on entertainment. Our favorites are:

• The rock-climbing wall strong enough to support even adventuresome adults.

• Art Moves, a darkened alcove where colored laser lights project your image on screen as you dance to music.

• The city room with its 1960 Mack fire engine and real police motorcycle.

• The Science Circus where you can race rolling hockey pucks and pound a rubber air cannon all in the name of testing scientific principles.

• The art room lined with old Frigidaire doors where kids can post with magnets their favorite masterpieces.

The museum includes a 64-seat planetarium with frequent shows. Admission is included in your $3 museum fee. Be sure to ask for a ticket at the museum entrance to hold you a seat for a specific show. Get there early to make sure your family can sit together.

Plan on spending several hours in the museum. There is a large gift shop but no food or drink available other than water. Be sure to feed the kids before you come and have drinks in the car for when your tired, thirsty bunch leaves. Immediately behind the museum on County Street is a large, city-owned parking garage where you can park for free on nights, weekends and holidays.

Still to come in 1997 are a second-floor expansion that will include a real light from a lighthouse as well as the Lancaster Train and Toy Museum now housed at Mike's Trainland in Suffolk. The toy train display is the largest on the East Coast and is valued at nearly $1 million. It was donated to the museum in late 1994 by a local resident and longtime train collector.

Buying a $5 museum pass also gets you admission to three other nearby city-owned museums — the Lightship Museum, the Portsmouth Naval Shipyard Museum and the Arts Center of the Portsmouth Museums, which is housed in the 1846 Courthouse. You must visit all the museums on the same day to take advantage of the pass.

LIGHTSHIP MUSEUM

Water St. and London Blvd.   393-8741
Hours: 10 AM-5 PM Tuesday-Saturday;
1-5 PM Sunday
Admission: $1; a $5 pass includes admission to three other city museums

This is a restored lightship that was

commissioned in 1915 to help mariners navigate through treacherous waters. It was once anchored at strategic locations to guide ships. Today it's a tourist attraction on the banks of the Elizabeth River. In 1989 the lightship became a National Historic Landmark. The bright red ship has been restored to its early 20th-century appearance and includes the captain's quarters, officer's head and officer's mess. Pass holders also can visit the Portsmouth Naval Shipyard Museum, the Arts Center of the Portsmouth Museums and the Children's Museum of Virginia on the same day with no extra charge.

PORTSMOUTH NAVAL SHIPYARD MUSEUM

2 High St.   393-8591
Hours: 10 AM-5 PM Tuesday-Saturday;
1-5 PM Sunday
Admission: $1; a $5 pass includes three other museums

Housed in an old machine shop for the Portsmouth-Norfolk ferry, the museum pays tribute to the Norfolk Naval Shipyard. The government-owned shipyard, which is in Portsmouth, is the oldest shipyard in the country. The museum displays models of ships constructed at the yard as well as uniforms, swords, cannon balls and other memorabilia. The museum, which was founded in 1949, also has a piece of the USS *Virginia* (the *Merrimac*), which was built at the yard and had its historic battle with the *Moni-*

tor in nearby waters. Pass holders also can visit the Children's Museum of Virginia, the Lightship Museum and the Arts Center of the Portsmouth Museums.

Suffolk

LANCASTER TRAIN AND TOY MUSEUM

5661 Shoulder Hill Rd.   484-4224
Hours: 10 AM-6 PM daily; 10 AM-9 PM
November-December 24
Admission: Donation

This museum is part of Mike's Trainland, one of Virginia's biggest model railroad stores. Mike's opened in 1983 and bills itself as the largest combined museum and train shop between Pennsylvania and Florida. The museum showcases the collection of A.J. Lancaster, an area nursery owner and train buff. It includes the mid-Atlantic's largest indoor Gauge 1 layout. It also features Lionel, LGB and other trains in various gauges. Both children and adults are fascinated by the elaborate train displays as well as numerous Buddy L trucks and antique tin mechanical toys. Be sure to keep a few quarters in your pocket to activate the train displays.

Outside is a new short-line railroad to ride for $1. The museum is in the country on the outskirts of Suffolk and is close to Portsmouth. Just follow High Street out of town. To be sure where you're going, call for directions. Note: By 1997 the train museum is scheduled to move to the Children's Museum of Virginia in Portsmouth.

THE SUFFOLK MUSEUM

118 Bosley Ave.   *925-6311*
Hours: 10 AM-5 PM Tuesday-Saturday;
1-5 PM Sunday
Admission: Free

The city-owned museum is housed in a former library near downtown. It opened in 1986 to emphasize art and features changing exhibits. Some are created by regional artists; others are traveling exhibits from the Virginia Museum of Fine Arts in Richmond. The museum also has periodic arts and crafts, theatrical and children's programs. It is home to the Suffolk Art League.

Historic Houses and Sites

Norfolk

FORT NORFOLK

810 Front St., Norfolk
Hours: Usually open Sunday afternoons
Admission: Free

You may have trouble finding Fort Norfolk, but it is worth the hunt. The fort along the Elizabeth River near downtown was authorized by President George Washington in 1794 to protect the Norfolk harbor. Most of the buildings date from 1810. Since then the fort has hardly changed. Its arched gateway, double oak doors, gunpowder magazine, guardhouse and other buildings remain. Surrounding the fort are a wall and ramparts built to protect against British invasion.

Today the fort is property of the U.S. Army Corps of Engineers, whose glassy regional headquarters dwarfs this historic site. After being closed to the public for years, the fort is gradually being renovated with the help of the Norfolk Historical Society. The society has its head-quarters in the fort. To get there, take Brambleton Avenue to Colley Avenue and head south. Go a few blocks until the road dead ends at Front Street. You will think you've made a mistake since you appear to be in a warehouse district. But, go right on Front Street and the road will end at the fort. For an extra treat, visit the fort during one of its special events when local military re-enactment troupes are camped there. One fun re-enactment takes place on the weekend before Halloween and has a ghostly feel to it.

HERMITAGE FOUNDATION MUSEUM

7637 North Shore Rd.   *423-2052*
Hours: 10 AM-5 PM Monday-Saturday;
1-5 PM Sunday
Admission $4, $1 for ages 6-18

This English Tudor-style home is in Lochaven, one of Norfolk's loveliest neighborhoods. It was built in 1908 on 12 acres along the Lafayette River as a summer home for art patrons William and Florence Sloane. They established the Hermitage Foundation in 1937 to promote the arts. Today both the house and its contents are a treat to see. The house features intricate woodcarving, while its holdings range from paintings, glass and textiles to carvings and other art works.

The Hermitage grounds are a terrific spot for picnics or strolling. There is no charge to enter the yard, which has picnic tables. In front of the house is a large, shady playground.

HUNTER HOUSE VICTORIAN MUSEUM

240 W. Freemason St.   *623-9814*
Hours: Wednesday-Saturday, 10 AM-3:30 PM;
Sunday, noon-3:30 PM. Closed in winter.
Admission: $3, $1 for children

Built in 1894, this is a Victorian jewel that showcases the furnishings and household goods of the James Wilson Hunter family — whose children never married and appear to have never thrown anything away. The house is in Norfolk's oldest neighborhood, the cobblestoned Freemason district near downtown. During 1994 the museum celebrated its centennial with all kinds of special events.

The three-story home is in the Richardsonian Romanesque style and has gorgeous stained-glass windows. Inside are a nursery filled with delightful toys, a bed covered with a crazy quilt and all kinds of Victorian bric-a-brac and furniture. One room preserves the medical office of one son who was a physician. Tours begin on the hour and half-hour. The museum often has special events such as teas and storytelling that make it even more interesting to tour.

Although this is a narrow house filled with breakable items, the museum welcomes children and has a children's membership for ages 4 to 8. On some Saturdays the museum sponsors a Victorian children's hour with crafts, games and other activities.

MOSES MYERS HOUSE

323 E. Bank St.   627-2737, 664-6200
Hours: 10-5 PM Tuesday-Saturday; noon-5 PM Sunday. Closed Sunday and Monday from January through March; opens at noon on Tuesday-Saturday during winter.
Admission: $2, $1 for children older than 6; $4 combination ticket available for three homes. Free for active duty military.

This is one of three historic homes operated by The Chrysler Museum. It was the home of the Moses Myers family, the region's first Jewish residents. Myers was a merchant who moved to Norfolk in 1787, ran a successful import-export business and served on the city council. He also was known as the last man in Norfolk to continue wearing a Colonial-style ponytail. The Myers family raised nine

children in the Georgian townhouse built in 1792. The home stayed in the family for six generations. Seventy-five percent of the home's current furnishings and artifacts belonged to the Myers' family. The historic house is in Downtown Norfolk and is the only one in the country to feature programs on Jewish practices in Colonial times.

ST. PAUL'S CHURCH

201 St. Paul's Blvd.   627-4353
Hours: 10 AM-4 PM Tuesday-Friday; Sunday during worship services
Admission: Donation

This was the only building to survive the burning of Norfolk that started on New Year's Day 1776 by the British. Its war wounds include a British cannonball stuck in its southeastern wall. The building features a Tiffany window and its original box pews. Outside is a traditional burial ground that is undergoing a historic restoration. See the Worship chapter for more details.

WILLOUGHBY-BAYLOR HOUSE

601 E. Freemason St.   664-6200
Hours: Open by appointment only; $2; $4 includes admission to three other historic homes

This 18th-century home is one of three operated by The Chrysler Museum, which is transforming it into a period educational center. In the meantime, the house is usually open for a daily 2 PM tour. Guests must make an appointment in advance.

The house was built in 1794 by Capt. William Willoughby, and its style is a blend of Georgian and Federal. Period furnishings reflect the inventory made in 1800 when Willoughby died. The grounds of this Downtown Norfolk home include a lovely garden. Plans call for the house to be made into an education center focusing on 18th-century life in Norfolk.

Virginia Beach

ADAM THOROUGHGOOD HOUSE

1636 Parish Rd.   460-0007
Hours: 10 AM-5 PM Tuesday-Saturday; noon-
5 PM Sunday. Closed Sunday and Monday from
January through March; opens at noon on
Tuesday-Saturday during winter.
Admission: $2, $1 for children older than 6; $4
combination ticket available for three homes.
Free for active duty military.

Operated by The Chrysler Museum, this home bears the name of Adam Thoroughgood who came to Virginia in 1621 as an indentured servant. He performed the first survey of the region and started the first ferry service across the Elizabeth River. King Charles I rewarded Thoroughgood with 5,350 acres. The home was built by a Thoroughgood descendant around 1680. About three acres of the original grounds remain with the home, one of the oldest brick houses in the country. Its style resembles an English cottage. Outside are herb and flower gardens.

BATTLE OFF THE CAPES MONUMENT

Fort Story

A monument, overlook and plaques help visitors understand the important Revolutionary War battle that took place near this spot. In 1781 the French victory over the British at this spot helped pave the way for the British surrender at Yorktown. This site is in Fort Story near the Old Cape Henry Lighthouse and First Landing Cross.

FIRST LANDING CROSS

Fort Story

This large cross marks the spot where it's believed some of America's early English settlers landed upon arriving in the New World in 1607. It is in Fort Story near Old Cape Henry Lighthouse and an overlook where the Battle off the Capes took place.

FRANCIS LAND HOUSE HISTORIC SITE

3131 Virginia Beach Blvd.   340-1732
Hours: 9 AM-5 PM Tuesday-Saturday;
noon-5 PM Sunday
Admission: $2.50, $1 for children older than 6

This home was built around 1732 for one of the first settlers in Princess Anne County. It was home to four generations of the Land family and later was an exclusive dress shop. Today the house is sandwiched among a busy strip of stopping centers. The City of Virginia Beach saved it from demolition by buying it and the surrounding 35 acres of land in 1975. The house is in the midst of ongoing restoration but remains open for tours. It features a Dutch gambrel roof and period furnishings. Docents in period costumes lead the tours. Outside the grounds include authentic plantings, such as flax.

LYNNHAVEN HOUSE

4405 Wishart Rd.   460-1688
Hours: noon-4 PM Tuesday-Sunday from June
through September; open weekends in May and
October; closed otherwise
Admission: $2.50, $1 for children

Built around 1725 by the Thellaball family, this is one of the best-preserved

18th-century buildings in the country. It is owned by the Association for the Preservation of Virginia Antiquities. The brick house features period furnishing and frequently has cooking and crafts programs that showcase the lifestyle of 18th-century residents. Costumed docents lead tours.

OLD CAPE HENRY LIGHTHOUSE

Fort Story   *422-9421*
Hours: 10 AM-5 PM daily mid-March through October
Admission: $2, $1 for students

Completed in 1791, the lighthouse guided mariners until it was replaced in 1881. Its construction was authorized by President George Washington, making the lighthouse the first federal public works project. The stone used in the structure came from the same Virginia quarry that supplied the White House, Capitol and Mount Vernon. Construction of the lighthouse cost $17,500.

Since 1930 the lighthouse has been owned by the Association for the Preservation of Virginia Antiquities. Kids particularly like climbing to the top of the 75-foot tower and peering out the windows. The lighthouse is the official symbol of Virginia Beach.

Even when the lighthouse isn't open, you can drive onto Fort Story, usually by showing a driver's license, and look at it from outside. Nearby is the newer lighthouse as well as the First Landing Cross and the site of the Battle Off the Capes.

Portsmouth

HILL HOUSE

221 North St.   *393-0241*
Hours: 1-5 PM Wednesday, Saturday and Sunday from April through December
Admission: $2, 50¢ for children

This circa 1825 home is headquarters for the Portsmouth Historical Association. It is in the heart of the Olde Towne His-

Children like visiting the Virginia Marine Science Museum to gaze at the multitude of native fish in its 50,000-gallon aquarium.

Photo: Virginia Beach Convention and Visitor Development

toric District and is the only residence there open to the public. The home was given to the association in 1961 by the last of the six Hill children, none of whom ever married. The four-story English basement home is furnished entirely with Hill family furnishings.

While in the neighborhood be sure to allow time to stroll through Olde Towne, which has the largest collection of Virginia homes on the National Historic Register.

Suffolk

RIDDICK'S FOLLY
510 N. Main St.   934-1390
Hours: 10 AM-5 PM Tuesday-Friday;
1-5 PM Sunday
Admission: Free

This is a massive Greek Revival home with 21 rooms, 16 fireplaces and four floors. It was built in 1837 by Mills Riddick, who had 14 children, and is dubbed his folly because the house is so big. In 1967 the city of Suffolk purchased the home to save it from demolition. It had a major restoration in 1988, and work is continuing on the top floor. There is only one original piece of Riddick furniture — a butler's desk. But other period furnishings show off the graceful lines of the house, which has elaborate plaster moldings and ceiling medallions. On the third floor are penciled messages from the family who fled the Union occupation during the War Between the States. Riddick's Folly was used as a hospital during the war, and the walls also bear messages from recuperating Union soldiers.

The house features a gallery with changing exhibits. Permanent exhibits are on the manufacturing of Planters peanuts, which started in Suffolk, and native son former Gov. Mills Godwin.

Military Bases

Norfolk

NORFOLK NAVAL BASE
9809 Hampton Blvd.   444-7955
Hours: Daily tours; weekend ship visitation
Admission: Free except for guided tours

The world's largest Navy base is a big draw for area visitors. Even people not normally interested in military affairs are intrigued by the sight of mammoth aircraft carriers and stealthy submarines. The base encompasses thousands of acres and includes some charming buildings from the 1907 Jamestown Exposition.

There are several ways to get on the base: through a guided tour, by riding in a car with a Department of Defense sticker on it or by obtaining a visitor's pass. Unless your host is a real Navy insider, you'll learn the most by taking the guided tour offered through Tidewater Regional Transit (TRT). Tickets and transportation are available at The Waterside in downtown Norfolk and at the Naval Base Tour Office at 9079 Hampton Boulevard. Tours cost $4.50, $2.25 for children. Note: In January and February, tours originate only at the Naval Base Tour Office.

During the summer naval base tours depart hourly from 10 AM to 2 PM from Waterside and every half-hour from 9:30 AM to 2:30 PM from the Naval Base Tour Office. Their schedules vary during other times of the year with six daily tours offered in September, four a day in early winter, one a day in January and February and six a day in spring. Tours last about an hour. For times and details consult a TRT trolley and tours brochure. But to be sure you don't miss the bus, call the Naval Base Tour Office, 444-7955, or TRT, 640-6300.

Naval base tours take passengers past the piers where they can see ships and submarines, the Naval Air Station and the historic homes of the Jamestown Exposition.

A guide boards the bus at the Tour and Information Center and conducts the entire tour from the bus.

On Saturdays and Sundays from 1 to 4:30 PM, except Christmas day and New Year's day, there is at least one Navy ship open for visitation. Check with the Naval Base Pass Office on Hampton Boulevard to see if you need a pass. Children especially like to clamber up and down ladders and check out the captain's bridge. You'll find the sailors on board eager to answer your questions. In the summer, arm yourself with hats, sunscreen and snacks for children. The wait to get on board can be long, and you'll swelter standing on the hot tarmac. Touring the ships is free.

If you're in the area during December, it's worth driving onto the base at night to see the lighted ships.

Virginia Beach

FORT STORY
Atlantic Ave.   422-7164

This World War I-era Army base is at the extreme north end of Atlantic Avenue. There also is an entrance off Shore Drive to the Fort, which is affiliated with Newport News' Fort Eustis, a major Army

transportation center. Fort Story's white-washed buildings give it an appealing look, and it has a great beach that is open to the public on weekends during late spring and summer. There are also several historical sites on the base — First Landing Cross, the Old Cape Henry Lighthouse and the Revolutionary War site of the Battle Off the Capes. To get on base either show your driver's license to the guard on duty or have a Department of Defense sticker on your car.

NAVAL AMPHIBIOUS BASE LITTLE CREEK
Shore Dr.   464-7923

This is the Navy's major amphibious base. It's where the elite Navy SEALS do their training. It is open to the public on weekends for ship visitation and during December to see holiday lights; you do not need a pass to enter then. Drivers with a Department of Defense sticker on their car are allowed on base at other times.

OCEANA NAVAL AIR STATION
Oceana Blvd.   433-3131

This is one of the Navy's four master jet bases, and you can see traces of it as F-15 Tomcats and A-6 Intruders streak across the sky. It's one of the busiest airfields in the world, with a plane landing or taking off every few seconds. Oceana is home to 22 aviation squadrons. It is not normally open to the public, but drivers with Department of Defense stickers

---

Insiders' Tips

From Memorial Day through Labor Day there are several special ways to tour Olde Towne Portsmouth, which dates to 1752. Options include horse-drawn carriages or 20-passenger trolleys pulled by horses. Motorized trolleys also make the rounds. On Tuesday nights a guide in period costume leads lantern tours. For details call 393-5111 or 393-5327.

on their cars can enter. However, in the summer there usually are Saturday morning bus tours. To find out about them call the Virginia Beach Visitor Center at 437-4700.

Miscellaneous Attractions

Some of the region's major attractions are unique and defy easy categorization. But they are definitely worth seeing while you're in town or if you live here and haven't made it out to them yet.

Norfolk

D'ART CENTER

125 College Pl.   *625-4211*
Hours: Tuesday-Saturday, 10 AM-6 PM;
Sunday, noon-5 PM
Admission: Free

This is a fun place to wander because you never know what you will find. It's a cooperative center for about 30 area artists who have their studios here. You'll find sculptors, jewelry makers and painters at work. If you find something to your liking, the artist will be happy to sell it to you. The center opened in the late 1980s in Downtown Norfolk and is renovating its building.

NORFOLK BOTANICAL GARDEN

Azalea Garden and Airport Rds.   *640-6879*
Hours: 8:30 AM-sunset daily
Admission: $2.50

The 155-acre garden has more than 12 miles of pathways and is a wonderful oasis in the middle of Norfolk. With its location adjacent to Norfolk International Airport, it gives airport arrivals an impressive first look at the city.

The botanical garden was started in 1938 as a Works Project Administration grant. Since then it has gained status as one of the country's top-10 gardens and is renowned for its rose garden. The botanical garden is in the midst of a $10 million improvement plan that will include a new visitors center and education building.

Although spring is the peak time to see the garden when thousands of azaleas are in bloom, it's a treat any time of year. Among the highlights are the Renaissance Garden, the Japanese Garden and a pathway lined with statues. Climbing the NATO Tower gives a vista of the garden, while another overlook lets visitors watch planes land at the neighboring airport. Despite all the aviation activity, the botanical garden remains a secluded spot.

To get a better view of the gardens, take either a relaxing tram or boat ride (available only in warm-weather months). Each lasts about 30 minutes and costs $2, with young children riding for free. If you have time, enjoy a picnic overlooking Lake Whitehurst or bring along a pole (and the appropriate license) for fishing.

THE VIRGINIA ZOO

3500 Granby St.   *441-2706*
Hours: 10 AM-5 PM daily
Admission: $2, $1 for children

The 42-acre zoo is a favorite spot for all ages, but children particularly get a kick out of it. Although you won't find any giant pandas, lions or gorillas, the zoo has a charm of its own. In recent years it has reduced the number of animals to ensure that it has the proper environment for those in its care. One popular exhibit features two elephants who amuse visitors by getting baths from zookeepers or splashing each other with water. Other zoo favorites: the llamas, ostriches and primates. (Be sure to look for Lefty the friendly black gibbon with only one hand.)

New in 1992 were two Siberian tiger cubs confiscated from a private owner. They were housed temporarily in the zoo and won the hearts of local residents who started a fund-raising campaign to build an area for them. The cubs quickly became the zoo's star attractions. This spring they moved into a new tiger habitat designed just for them.

While in the zoo be sure to take a walk through the barn yard, the reptile and small mammal house, the gazebo where injured birds recuperate, and the turn-of-the-century botanical conservatory. Kids love getting a handful of food from a dispenser to feed ducks in the pond. They also like stopping by The Beastro restaurant and eating a reasonably priced lunch that comes in a box decorated with animals. Outside the zoo

Photo: Nauticus

The "Bio-Accumulation Machine" at Nauticus shows how toxins travel through the food chain.

grounds are a playground and picnic area in Lafayette Park.

The zoo is at the start of a $15 million improvement plan created by the designer of the renowned Audubon Zoo in New Orleans. Plans call for a Dismal Swamp walkway, butterfly house and African Plains exhibit.

THE WATERSIDE

333 Waterside Dr.   627-3300
Hours: Monday-Saturday, 10 AM-9 PM; Sunday,
noon-6 PM. Longer hours during summer.
Admission: Free

This is Norfolk's festival marketplace — the city's version of Boston's Fanueil Hall. It has a lively mix of shops, restaurants and entertainment and is on the "must-do list" of most visitors. The Waterside opened in the mid-1980s to revitalize the Downtown Norfolk waterfront along the Elizabeth River. Waterside has had one expansion that brought the total number of shops and dining spots to 120.

Waterside includes a food court with vendors offering tasty treats from Greece, Japan and Mexico as well as typically American fare. There are also several full-service restaurants. Shops feature gifts, clothing and souvenirs. There frequently are musicians performing on the stage in the food court.

The top outdoor attraction is the never-ending parade of tugs, sailboats and Navy ships moving along the Elizabeth River. A boardwalk takes visitors past some huge yachts anchored at a marina.

There are numerous benches for relaxing. Neighboring Town Point Park is the site of festivals on most weekends.

Waterside is also the place to catch the ferry to Portsmouth, embark on a harbor tour or take a trolley tour of the city. There is a city-owned parking deck across the street.

Virginia Beach

ARTISTS AT WORK:
GALLERY AND STUDIO

2407 Pacific Ave.   425-6671
Hours: 10 AM-5 PM Tuesday-Saturday
Admission: Free

This is a cooperative of 30 area artists that opened in 1991. About 10 artists have their studios here while the rest rent walls to display their works. All art is for sale. Artists working on site include marble sculptors as well as painters and weavers.

ASSOCIATION FOR RESEARCH
AND ENLIGHTENMENT (A.R.E.)

67th St. and Atlantic Ave.   428-3588
Hours: 9 AM-8 PM Monday-Saturday;
11 AM-8 PM Sunday
Admission: Free

The A.R.E. is one of Virginia Beach's more intriguing attractions. This organization is dedicated to Edgar Cayce, a psychic who resided in Virginia Beach and was known worldwide for falling into a trance and being able to diagnose and prescribe treatment for medical ailments. Cayce, who died in 1945, built the Edgar

Cruising

The best way to get a feel for this coastal region is to take a look at it from the water. While you're here, try a leisurely sightseeing cruise so you can check out the largest natural harbor in the world. You have a variety of inexpensive ways to set sail.

Spirit Cruises operates the *Spirit of Norfolk*, which has lunch, brunch, dinner and moonlight cruises. Spirit Cruises is a Norfolk-based company that initiated the idea of local dinner cruises and now operates in Boston, New York and other major cities. The *Spirit*, which was completed in 1992 and resembles a cruise ship, has room for 450 guests and runs year round. The ship leaves from The Waterside and cruises along the Elizabeth River from Downtown Norfolk to the Norfolk Naval Base. Cruises last two to three hours and cost from $19.90 at lunch to $34.45 at dinner, with weekend rates slightly higher. The price includes a buffet, bands and a musical revue starring a talented wait staff. Discounts are available for children, retired people, military personnel and groups. Call 627-7771.

The *Carrie B* is a replica of a 19th-century riverboat that has been plying the Hampton Roads harbor since 1959. The *Carrie B* offers 90-minute cruises and takes in the downtown harbor and Norfolk Naval Shipyard. The boat holds 275 and runs from April through October, with up to three trips a day during summer. There are also 2½-hour cruises that take visitors to the Norfolk Naval Base and site of the *Monitor* and *Merrimac* battle during the War Between the States. The *Carrie B* picks up passengers both at The Waterside in Norfolk and Portside in Portsmouth. Reservations aren't necessary. The cost is $12 for the shorter cruise, $14 for the longer one, with children older than 16 half-price. Group rates are available. Hamburgers, hot dogs and drinks are sold on board. Call 393-4735.

Photo: Portsmouth Convention and Visitors Bureau

The Carrie B *is a replica of a 19th-century riverboat that has been plying the Hampton Roads harbor since 1959.*

Rainy Day Guide

Don't Let A Rainy
Day Keep You
From Having Fun...

Here Are Some Places
To Go And Have A
Good Time...
RAIN OR SHINE!

D1505042

THE CHRYSLER MUSEUM *of* ART

Recognized by *The Wall Street Journal* as "one of the nation's top twenty art museums," The Chrysler Museum of Art houses a world-renowned glass collection, works of art from African, Asian, Egyptian, Pre-Colombian and Islamic cultures, sculpture, decorative arts, and a magnificent array of European and American paintings — from the classic to the contemporary.

Our restaurant, *Palettes*, offers great dining and the perfect ambience for lunch or an afternoon refreshment, and The Museum Shop is the perfect place to find gifts and collectibles. Our three Historic Houses interpret the lifestyles of the seventeenth- and eighteenth-centuries, providing a unique view of living history.

Come discover the treasures of The Chrysler Museum of Art. Call (804) 622-ARTS for information on current exhibitions and events.

245 West Olney Road · Norfolk, Virginia · 23510-1587

The *American Rover* bills itself as the "largest three-masted topsail passenger schooner under U.S. Flag." The 135-foot ship was designed and built by a local naval architect in the 1980s and resembles a 19th-century tall ship. When the *Rover's* massive sails are at full mast, it is a breathtaking sight. The *Rover* sails through the Hampton Roads harbor from late April through October up to four times a day. Cruises last two or three hours and leave from The Waterside in Downtown Norfolk. Costs range from $12.50 for the shorter trips to $16. Children younger than 12 sail for $6 or $8. Group rates are available. Snacks, sandwiches and drinks are sold on board.

The Elizabeth River ferry offers the quickest and cheapest way to take in the downtown harbor. It is a paddlewheel boat that regularly runs from The Waterside in Norfolk to Portside in Portsmouth. It makes an occasional extra stop at High Street near Portsmouth's museums. The ride lasts about five minutes and costs 75¢ each way; 50¢ for children. The ferry is operated by Tidewater Regional Transit, the area bus company. Call 640-6300.

Discovery Cruises offers a different water view. Its yacht takes passengers through the secluded bays and inlets of Virginia Beach. The sights include luxury homes costing up to several million dollars as well as marinas for both pleasure craft and commercial fishing boats. Both lunch and dinner cruises are available from May through October. Lunch lasts about 1½ hours; dinner cruises go for 2½ hours. The cost is $16.50 for lunch, $28 for dinner. The yacht, which seats 92, leaves from 600 Laskin Road in Virginia Beach, 422-2900.

For another option, check with the Virginia Science Museum, 473-4949, to see if it is running any boat tours. The museum periodically sponsors interesting programs that take participants out on the water. Popular outings include whale and dolphin watching trips.

If you are interested in seeing the Great Dismal Swamp, the *Carrie B* makes a few one-day excursions down the swamp's canal to Elizabeth City, North Carolina, in the spring and fall. Call 393-4735 for details.

Cayce Hospital in Virginia Beach in the late 1920s. The hospital, which focused on holistic healing, failed to survive the Great Depression and closed in 1931.

Today the white frame former hospital is headquarters for A.R.E., whose conferences draw participants from around the world. Adjacent to it are the A.R.E. Visitor and Conference Center. Stop by and you can view videotapes about Cayce's life, hear free lectures and see exhibits on Cayce's work. You can also enjoy a meditation room overlooking the ocean and a well-stocked bookstore. Outside is a serene Japanese-style garden. In the summer there are guided tours of the Cayce headquarters at 11:15 AM and 2 PM.

Try to sit in on the group ESP testing if you can. Visiting relatives of ours who attended a session proclaimed it to be one of the most fun things they did on their vacation. During the testing, a leader asks volunteers to send messages to each other by using an electric box that flashes shapes at one person. Another volunteer and the audience try to pick up on the vibes from the sender. The leader also administers other ESP tests and answers questions about psychic phenomena.

THE CHRISTIAN BROADCASTING NETWORK

1000 Centerville Tnpk. 523-7123, 424-7777
Hours: Daytime, Monday-Friday
Admission: Free

Virginia Beach is headquarters for The Christian Broadcasting Network and its affiliated Family Channel, one of the fastest-growing cable TV channels. CBN's 685-acre complex features attractive Georgian-style buildings, including the home of founder Rev. M.G. "Pat" Robertson.

Tours are available Monday through Friday during the day. You can take your chances that you'll be there at the right time for a tour, but it's best to call ahead. Guided tours take visitors behind the scenes of this international TV network and its ministry. If you want to sit in on a television show, call ahead and get reservations for the "700 Club." The "700 Club" is CBN's flagship program featuring Robertson as host. It is usually produced five mornings a week. Try to call at least a day or two in advance for reservations.

OCEAN BREEZE

849 General Booth Blvd.   422-0718
Hours: 10 AM-10 PM daily Memorial Day-Labor Day; open weekends in spring and fall
Admission: $16 for WildWater Rapids or $11 for children under 42 inches tall; free for ages 3 and younger; $6 for 18 holes at Shipwreck Golf; $2 for ride tickets at Motor World; $2 for 15 pitches at Strike Zone.

This amusement park is less than two miles from the oceanfront. It has four components: WildWater Rapids, Motor World, Shipwreck Golf and Strike Zone. Guests can choose to spend a day and take in all attractions or concentrate on one or two parts.

WildWater Rapids is the only water park in south Hampton Roads. Its six acres include eight slides, a half-acre wave pool and a big activity pool. Young children can ride down slides and get in the pools with their parents. Once you've paid the WildWater admission, you are issued a wrist band, which gets you discounts at the other attractions.

Motor World has nine acres of mini-race tracks. The most popular is the Grand Prix track with 3/4-size race cars. Drivers race against a clock and hit speeds up to 35 m.p.h. as they loop around a track. The cost is $2 a lap. There are four other race tracks, bumper boats and an activity area for younger children.

Shipwreck Golf is a 36-hole miniature golf course that challenges golfers with sunken ships, caves and other special effects.

Strike Zone has nine batting cages that cater to all ages. Batters can choose to hit either softballs or baseballs. Pitches can go from slow to lightning fast.

The more adventuresome may want to check out the 130-foot bungee tower run by an outside company. In 1994 a single jump cost $30.

TIDEWATER VETERANS MEMORIAL

1000 19th St.

Unveiled in 1988, this memorial is dedicated to military veterans from the area who served in all wars from the Revolutionary War to more current ones. The memorial's concept came from area students and was carried out by a local architect. The symbolic structure includes a waterfall, flags and a series of split spheres. The project was built with both city and private support.

VIRGINIA BEACH
CENTER FOR THE ARTS

2200 Parks Ave.   425-0000
*Hours: 10 AM-4 PM Tuesday-Saturday;
noon-4 PM Sunday
Admission: Free, donation suggested*

This is the only arts center in the region to focus on 20th-century art. It was formed in 1952, and in 1989 completed a new center whose highly acclaimed architecture touches on Oriental and Southern styles. The center is near Virginia Beach's Visitor Center and is one of the most attractive buildings in the city. Featured are changing exhibits as well as classes and programs for all ages. The center sponsors the popular Boardwalk Art Show each June.

VIRGINIA BEACH FARMER'S MARKET

1989 Landstown Rd.   427-4395
*Hours: Open daily, weather permitting
Admission: Free*

This is a fun place to wander. The market is in the rural part of Virginia Beach so it's best to call for directions and hours. It has 17,000 square feet of rough-hewn stalls that house about 19 permanent vendors. Produce is seasonal, making this a great place to pick up a pumpkin or buy peaches, apples or whatever is in season. Some vendors specialize in meats, baked goods, dairy products, plants and outdoor furniture. Some weekends you may catch a flea market, craft show or other special event. There is a restaurant here serving good country cooking as well as a shop selling Bergey's homemade ice cream.

Portsmouth

PORTSIDE

6 Crawford Pkwy.   393-5111
The festive blue-and-white-striped tent that covers Portside gives a distinct look to the Portsmouth waterfront. The Portside Visitor Information Center is open year round. Portside is a docking point for the Portsmouth-Norfolk Ferry. From April through the fall it also has six restaurants dishing out crabcakes, sandwiches and other casual foods. There also are several places to buy frozen yogurt or ice cream. During warmer months Portside frequently has weekend entertainment.

VIRGINIA SPORTS HALL OF FAME

420 High St.   393-8031
*Hours: 10 AM-5 PM Tuesday-Saturday;
1-5 PM Sunday
Admission: Free*

Organized in 1966 the Hall of Fame honors Virginia sports heroes, including basketball player Cy Young, golfer Sam Snead and tennis star Arthur Ashe. Inductees include well-known names in football, basketball, golf, baseball, auto racing, horseback riding, speedboat racing, wrestling, bowling, swimming, sail boat racing, track, tennis and coaching. Displays include uniforms, photos and other memorabilia.

Chesapeake

CHESAPEAKE PLANETARIUM

300 Cedar Rd.   547-0153
*Hours: 8 PM Thursdays
Admission: Free*

The planetarium opened in 1963 and was the first in Virginia to be built by a school district. The Chesapeake School District continues to operate the planetarium, which attracts 40,000 visitors a year. Program topics change monthly and recently have included the summer sky, falling stars and the Christmas star. Reservations are needed. Programs last about an hour with a telescope available afterward for star gazing on clear nights.

Photo: Virginia Beach Convention and Visitors Development

Kids like nothing more than a day of playing in the ocean.

Inside
Kidstuff

While thumbing through this book you'll find dozens of ideas for entertaining your children. But just in case you miss them — or we couldn't find the right category to place them — here are 30 suggestions to keep kids of all ages on the go:

1. If you do nothing else, go to the Children's Museum of Virginia in downtown Portsmouth, 393-8393. This 27,000-square-foot wonderland hit a big growth spurt in December 1994 when it moved from cramped quarters in a historic downtown Portsmouth building to a former department store just down High Street. The $3 million expansion and renovation has made the museum the coolest place to be for kids of all ages.

Fourteen major displays range from a room filled with soap bubble experiments to a real fire truck in the city section. There are dozens of computer challenges and hands-on games to challenge both the mind and body. The museum also includes a planetarium with daily shows. Our family favorites are the rock-climbing wall and Art Moves, a laser-light room where images of your body in motion are projected on a colored screen. Still to come in an upstairs expansion are the East Coast's largest toy train display and a real light from a lighthouse.

Admission is a bargain at $3. Be forewarned, kids *never* want to leave this fun place.

2. Make the kids think they've been to sea by taking a jaunt on the Norfolk-Portsmouth Ferry. The trip lasts only about five minutes, but it's neat to breeze across the Elizabeth River on a paddlewheeler. The cost each way is 75¢ for adults, 50¢ for children 12 and younger. Catch the ferry at The Waterside festival marketplace in Norfolk or at Portside in Portsmouth. You can wander around at either end and explore the shops. Once an hour the ferry stops at the foot of High Street in Portsmouth where it's a quick walk to see three Portsmouth museums, including the children's museum. You can also walk to the museums from Portside.

3. Check out the National Maritime Center (Nauticus), 664-1000. This $52 million museum/attraction opened in June 1994 on the downtown Norfolk waterfront. While geared toward adults and older children, even preschoolers will find plenty to amuse them inside. Nauticus takes a high-tech, energetic look at the Navy and maritime industry. It's a hands-on place with lots of computer-interaction exhibits. Favorites include Virtual Realities, a simulated trek to retrieve the Loch Ness monster's eggs, and the tank full of sharks to pet.

4. Go camping at Northwest River Park in Chesapeake — or at least spend

the day there. This terrific park is nearby but makes you feel like you've truly escaped city life. The 763-acre park has a 29-acre lake, numerous trails and 72 well-maintained campsites. It also features Charlie, the resident peacock, and hungry ducks and geese to feed. There are canoes and paddleboats to rent and miniature golf. Friendly park rangers are ready to answer questions or lead programs on snakes or other woodland creatures. The park is at 1733 Indian Creek Road. Call 421-3145 or 421-7151 for directions and camping reservations.

Another great camping spot is Seashore State Park in Virginia Beach with campsites near a pristine beach along the Chesapeake Bay. Call 490-3939 for reservations.

5. Visit Bergey's Dairy Farm at 2221 Mount Pleasant Road in Chesapeake. It's a pleasant country drive to this working dairy farm, known for its residential milk deliveries and scrumptious homemade ice cream. Be sure to call for directions, 482-4711. The kids can see cows and horses and pet some Guernsey calves. Best of all, you can go in Bergey's store for an ice cream cone. During one spring weekend, the farm sponsors back-to-the-farm days with hayrides and other entertainment. But otherwise you can visit any day but Sunday.

6. Head to Pungo to pick whatever's in season in this rural section of Virginia Beach. If it's summer you'll find strawberries, blueberries and blackberries. If it's fall you can pull a pumpkin out of the patch. To keep up with what's in season look in *The Virginian-Pilot/Ledger Star* classifieds under the section called "Good Things to Eat." Be sure to call and get directions. Once you're in Pungo, you

may want to keep going a few miles to Knotts Island, North Carolina. If it's late summer there is a peach orchard just ripe for the picking.

7. Go to the Virginia Marine Science Museum, 717 General Booth Boulevard in Virginia Beach, 437-4949. One Virginia Beach grandfather marvels that his visiting grandkids never tire of this museum. It's a hands-on place that lets kids touch turtles and crabs and other hardy sea creatures. They can watch a woodcarver create duck decoys, and they can tong for oysters. A 50,000-gallon fish tank will amaze them. Outside is a meandering walkway along a saltwater marsh. The museum is in the midst of an expansion that will triple its size. Admission costs $4.75 for adults, $4.25 for children. Those younger than 4 are admitted for free.

8. Visit The Virginia Zoo, 3500 Granby Street, Norfolk, 624-9938. The zoo has wide-open spaces for kids to run around, and many of their favorite animals live here. To get to know the zoo better, sign up preschoolers for the Zoo Tot or Early Bloomers programs. These are held on Saturday mornings to give children and parents a behind-the-scenes look at the zoo. They meet animals up close or work with plants. Sessions include crafts, games and songs. Students who have finished kindergarten can participate in summer zoo camps. There also are occasional weekend camp-outs in the zoo for kids and parents. The zoo recently started a major expansion.

Admission costs $2 for adults, $1 for children older than 2.

9. Plan an outing to Kids Cove at Mount Trashmore Park in Virginia

Beach. This is the crown jewel of the region's playgrounds. Built by 3,000 volunteers in 1993 and paid for with everything from school kids' pennies to corporate donations, Kids Cove is a 22,000-square-foot wooden wonderland. There are lots of nooks and crannies to explore as well as a mini-trampoline, slide, swings, swinging bridges and much more. Kids Cove is handicapped accessible, and there are plenty of benches and picnic tables for parents. It's always crowded but is so big that it doesn't matter. Look for similar parks to be built in 1995 by volunteers at Chesapeake's City Park and Norfolk's Northside Park.

10. Take a day trip and go to Fort Fun in Newport News. Slightly smaller than Kids Cove, this terrific playground was built by volunteers in 1992 in Huntington Park off Warwick Boulevard (near Mercury Boulevard). Children can play in the fort for hours, and there are comfortable benches overlooking the James River for weary parents. The playground has lookout towers, mazes and traditional swings and slides. There are also picnic tables.

11. Check out Discovery Zone in the Hilltop North shopping center in Virginia Beach and the Janaf shopping center in Norfolk. These high-energy indoor playgrounds are for kids 12 and younger. For $5.99 on weekdays ($6.99 on weekends) children can play for as many hours as they want in a gigantic rumpus room. There's a trapeze to propel kids into a pit of colorful balls, ropes for climbing, slides and tunnels for crawling. Parents, who get in free, can join in the fun or park themselves on nearby benches or the snack bar. Be sure to bring extra cash for the arcade games in the back, and watch out for rainy days or weekend afternoons in winter — the crowds are overwhelming. Call 491-5000 in Virginia Beach or 459-8020 in Norfolk.

12. Ride the Pokey Smokey in Portsmouth's City Park. This is a real coal-fired miniature train that puffs through a lovely 93-acre park along the

Photo: Virginia Beach Convention and Visitors Development

Children love playing on the new beach sculptures on the Boardwalk in Virginia Beach.

Elizabeth River from April through November. Rides are daily during the summer and on the weekends otherwise. They cost $1. Nearby is a nifty playground. Call 465-2937.

13. Explore the Norfolk Botanical Garden, 855-7460. Kids can run around and look at whatever is in bloom. Be sure to leave time for either a tram ride or a boat ride (boats run only in the spring through early fall). Either one costs $2, with young children riding for free. Kids will love the rides, and you get to see parts of the gardens you didn't know were there. Pack a picnic lunch because there is a playground with tables on the shores of Lake Whitehurst. If your kids aren't into nature, they may like the overlook that lets them watch planes take off from neighboring Norfolk International Airport. On Sunday afternoons there usually are free, themed nature walks at 2 PM geared for the whole family. The garden is midway through a $10 million expansion. Admission costs $2.

14. Visit Mike's Trainland at 5661 Shoulder Hill Road in Suffolk, 484-4224. It bills itself as the largest combined train shop and museum between Pennsylvania and Florida. This is out in the country on the edge of Suffolk and Portsmouth, and it's a great place for a weekend outing. The front part is an excellent train store. In the back is the Lancaster Train & Toy Museum filled with tiny trains racing around the tracks and other antique toys. (The train display is destined for the Children's Museum of Virginia in 1996. In the meantime it remains at Mike's.) Admission is free, with a donation requested. The Santa Fe, an outdoor short-line railroad, was added in 1993. Train fans can hitch a ride for $1.

15. Attend a Family Fun Day activity at the Chrysler Museum, 245 W. Olney Road, Norfolk, 622-1211, Ext. 268. These are usually held twice a month on Sunday afternoons. The free events are designed to get families into the art museum, and they truly are fun. Most events have a theme. Sometimes it ties in with an exhibition or a holiday. The series has included storytellers, bands, crafts, scavenger hunts, plays and even a family circus.

16. Head to the beach for a day. It's hard for out-of-town friends to imagine living this close to the beach and not going there all the time. But that's what tends to happen. So drag out all the paraphernalia, pack a picnic lunch and head on down for some fun. Insiders are particularly fond of the beach during the spring and fall when it's less crowded. In the summer, going in early morning or late afternoon will help you avoid throngs of people.

17. If you're a mother looking for companionship for you and your children, sign up for a mother's group or start your own. The busiest organization is The Moms Group organized by some stay-at-home mothers of preschoolers in Virginia Beach. Members now come from all area cities. The $15 annual membership gets you a monthly newsletter whose calendar is crammed with outings and play groups. There also are such spin-offs as a craft club, mom's dinner club and gourmet club for member couples. For information call 479-4216.

Another option is the Mother's Center run by the YWCA of South Hampton Roads. Call 625-4248. One morning a week the Young Moms Church Group gathers at the chapel of Little Creek Naval Base in Norfolk. For details call or 363-8178.

18. If it's warm weather, spend an afternoon at Ocean Breeze. This amusement park has Wild Water Rapids with eight giant slides, Motor World with its race tracks for mini-cars, Shipwreck Golf for miniature golf and Strike Zone with nine batting cages. It is open weekends in spring and fall and open daily during the summer There is an admission fee; call 422-4444.

19. Take your children to some spectator sports. Both Old Dominion University and Norfolk State University field some fine teams. Kids love Norfolk Tides baseball games in the summer and Hampton Roads Admirals hockey games in the winter. The region also boasts a professional soccer team, the Mariners.

20. Go see some performances geared toward children. The Hurrah Players troupe features talented children in its productions, 627-5437. Willett Hall sponsors the Portsmouth Storybook Theater Children's Series, which brings traveling productions to town, 393-5144. In 1994 the Virginia Symphony created a family concert series, 623-8590. There are several puppet troupes that regularly perform in the area, including the Wappadoodle Puppets, 481-6658, Spectrum Puppets, 491-2873, and Fuzz & Stuffing Puppets, 480-2991. Each December the Old Dominion University Ballet produces *The Nutcracker*, a treat for children of all ages, 683-4486. In 1994 even the Virginia Stage Company, the region's professional theater, got in the act with a sold-out production of *Peter Pan*. Look for the Stage Company to work a family production into its calendar each year.

21. Go to some of the free weekly story hours sponsored by area libraries. Besides reading stories, innovative librarians often have seasonal crafts and other activities to occupy children.

22. If it's December, check out the holiday lights in Norfolk. Since 1985 the city has strung its downtown office buildings with thousands of white lights. With more than 10 miles of lights, from a distance downtown Norfolk looks like a giant gingerbread village. For a different perspective, go to downtown Portsmouth and gaze across the river. To kick off the season, the city of Norfolk sponsors a wonderful lighted Christmas parade, usually on the Saturday evening before Thanksgiving. There is a whole roster of Holidays in the City activities that goes along with the lights.

The ships at the Norfolk Naval Base and the Naval Amphibious Base in Virginia Beach also are lighted at this time of the year. For one of the best displays of gaudy but great Christmas lights, head to Commodore Park in Norfolk. This neighborhood is just off Granby Street across from Northside Junior High. Just follow the line of cars, and you'll be amazed at how each neighbor tries to outdo the other with elaborate Christmas scenes and lights.

New in 1994 were elaborate lighted displays at Norfolk Botanical Garden and the Virginia Zoo. The botanical garden's extravaganza was a drive-through event ($6 a carload), while the zoo featured a lighted night walk with entertainment ($3 a person). Both should be bigger and better in 1995.

23. Another December must is a trip to Coleman Nursery at 4934 High Street in Portsmouth, 484-3426. Since 1966 the

Kids and Eating Out

If you're dining with children, you'll find your family welcome almost anywhere. Although there are many familiar fast-food restaurants here, branch out and try some local spots. Even if your children detest seafood, they'll usually find chicken fingers or hamburgers on the menu. The only restaurants where you might hesitate to take the young ones are to some of the romantic Continental or French restaurants and the trendy Nouvelle American or New Southern bistros.

Once the lack of a babysitter forced us to take our 3-year-old son on our anniversary dinner to a candlelit restaurant by the bay. We went early and were treated graciously by the staff. However, if you aren't sure whether a restaurant welcomes children, call ahead and ask.

At most restaurants you'll find children's menus, booster seats and a staff quick to supply a basket of crackers while you wait for food. At places where there is no children's menu (like most Chinese restaurants), we find an appetizer that will work or just share our dinners if portions are large enough. No one seems to mind.

There are numerous restaurants that hand out crayons and menus to amuse children. The following are some that go the extra mile to make young customers feel welcome.

***Billy Bob's Pizza**, Lynnhaven Parkway and Lishelle Place in Virginia Beach (formerly Chuck E Cheese), is the ultimate kids' place. Pizza is the mainstay along with an animated musical show and lots of games and rides that require you to buy tokens. There is a big play area bursting with colored balls. This is a popular place for birthday parties and reaches the pandemonium level on weekends and rainy days.

***Doumar's**, 20th and Monticello in Norfolk, has car hops, burgers, shakes and other kid fare. The owners often handmake ice cream cones on a vintage machine.

***Elliot's Restaurant**, 1421 Colley Avenue in Norfolk, puts its children's menu in a coloring book and provides the colors. Budding artists can tack their masterpieces on the wall. The varied menu includes a peanut butter snack plate. A funhouse mirror is in the restaurant foyer.

***Fuddrucker's Restaurant**, 4625 Virginia Beach Boulevard in Virginia Beach, lets children eat free Monday through Thursday in the evenings. Be sure to ask for one of the paper Fuddrucker's hats like the ones the workers wear. Other amusements include video games and an outdoor playground.

***The Jewish Mother**, 3108 Pacific Avenue in Virginia Beach, serves children's sandwiches on a Frisbee they can take home.

***The Lighthouse**, First Street and Atlantic Avenue in Virginia Beach, provides a relaxing upscale outing for parents in a kid-friendly atmosphere. Children can chow down on a lobster tail dinner for $7.95 or get all-you-can-eat crab legs for under $5. Popular diversions include kids' cocktails and junior-sized sundaes.

***Lynnhaven Fish House**, 2350 Starfish Road in Virginia Beach, is a treat for parents and perfect for kids. They can peek at lobster tanks and the fish-cutting rooms. Look for the seahorse on the menu to find half-price children's portions.

***Phillips Waterside**, 333 Waterside Drive in Norfolk, has a great view of the busy Norfolk harbor. Dine outside in warm weather. Children get their menu in a coloring book that also makes a captain's hat. They eat free on Sundays.

***Spaghetti Warehouse**, 1900 Monticello Avenue in Norfolk, offers dining in a trolley or brass bed. The kids' menu is packed with activities. Picky eaters can choose from 12 pasta sauces. Balloon artists and magicians often entertain on weekends.

plant nursery has played Christmas to the hilt with its Christmas Wonderland. Two buildings showcase dozens of animated Christmas scenes of animals, Santa and elves, and even a circus. For many area families, visiting Coleman's is a holiday ritual. Admission costs 25¢ for children and 50¢ for adults. Arm your kids with handfuls of pennies to toss at the elaborate displays. All donations go to charity. There also are well-stocked shops selling candy, Christmas decorations, plants and Virginia food products.

24. To get in the holiday spirit, spend a few hours at the annual Holly Festival. The location varies but it is always held in downtown Norfolk on the first weekend in December and is sponsored by The Children's Hospital of The Kings Daughters. In recent years the festival has been at The Waterside. The festival typically has the area's best Santa, a kindly gentleman with a real beard and a jaunty candy-striped cane. If you buy tickets ahead of time, children can have breakfast with Mr. and Mrs. Santa. Even if you miss breakfast, there are plenty of other things to occupy children — a gigantic gingerbread house display, pint-sized entertainment and Christmas crafts.

Another holiday option is to check out the December gingerbread display sponsored by the Virginia Beach Visitor Information Center. Started in 1992, the display has mushroomed and moved to bigger quarters in the Pavilion Convention Center. It usually runs the first couple of weeks in December. Call 437-4888 for information.

Let your kids chat with Santa or Mrs. Claus on the Hillhaven Ho Ho Hotline. It operates in December with the help of residents of area Hillhaven nursing centers. Children can call and talk to either Santa or Mrs. Claus, 623-HOHO, 481-HOHO, 463-1707. If you live in Norfolk, the city Parks and Recreation Department sponsors Santa calls early in December. For information call 441-2149. If children prefer to write Santa, local elves help Santa answer all letters addressed to him, stamped and dropped in mailboxes.

25. Buy your child a membership to the Hunter House Victorian Museum, 240 W. Freemason Street, Norfolk, 623-9814. It costs $7 and is for ages 4 through 8. This entitles them to a newsletter that includes games and stories. They also get a gift and discounts on monthly programs

The bubble room is a favorite spot at the Children's Museum of Virginia.

scheduled for April through December. On the second Saturday of the month the Victorian Children's Hour offers programs ranging from croquet or tea parties on the lawn to turn-of-the-century crafts.

26. Plan some day trips to Williamsburg, Yorktown, Jamestown, Hampton and Newport News to soak up history that spans from the settling of the country right to the Space Age (see the Daytrips chapter.)

27. While on the Peninsula, see some of its other attractions that children love, such as the Virginia Air and Space Center and the restored carousel next door in Hampton or the Virginia Living Museum and Mariners Museum in Newport News. Anyone enamored with the Civil War will like Fort Monroe in Hampton. Another possibility is the petting zoo and menagerie of exotic animals maintained by the Newport News SPCA. Scenic Newport News Park is one of the largest city parks in the country.

28. On the weekend before Halloween take the annual Ghost Walk in Portsmouth to learn about ghosts and other spooky legends of historic Olde Towne. Reservations are a must for this sellout event. For information call the Portsmouth Convention and Visitors Bureau at 393-8481. One other holiday event to check out is a ghostly re-enactment at Fort Norfolk. Typically held on the weekend before Christmas, this tour of the early 19th-century fort teaches history in a fun way. Call 625-1720 for details.

29. Attend the Virginia Children's Festival in October at Town Point Park in Norfolk. This popular weekend extravaganza is sponsored by The Children's Hospital of The Kings Daughters. There are countless activities, a parade and booths designed for children of all ages. The festival generally brings in national performers for concerts. If you miss this festival, there are plenty of other weekend fests going on throughout the year that your family will enjoy. Another favorite for kids is Blackbeard's Pirate

Kids Love Ice Cream

For some wonderfully rich ice cream that's made locally there are two places to go: Uncle Harry's Cones & Cream and Bergey's Dairy Stores.

Uncle Harry's has four locations in Virginia Beach and Chesapeake. Each features a dozen flavors of the day, such as chocolate amaretto and raspberry truffle. A house speciality is putting the ice cream on a marble slab and mixing in toppings such as M&Ms, Oreos or candy. The first Uncle Harry's opened in the late 1980s, and the local chain has beeen going strong evern since. Stores are at !412 Greenbrier Parkway in Chesapeake and at 606 Hilltop West Shopping Center, Loehman's Plaza (4000) Virginia Beach Boulevard) and 3623 Pacific Avenue in Virginia Beach. Uncle Harry's is open daily.

Bergey's Dairy Farm has three locations that feature its ice cream as well as sandwiches served on homemade bread. Bergey's makes 27 flavors from its own fresh milk. Flavors range from apple cinnamon to mint chocolate Chip. The first Bergey's store opened on the family farm in rural Chesapeake in 1978. It is at 2221 Mt. Pleasant Road and While there you can visit the Holsteins to thank them for their milk. Call 482-4711 for directions. Other stores are at 1128 N. Battlefield Boulevard in Chesapeake and 1989 Landstown Road at the Virginia Beach Farmer's Market. All feature sandwiches in addition to ice cream. The stores close on Sunday. The farmers' market shop also closes on Monday.

Jamboree at Town Point Park in August. A fun Virginia Beach festival is Discovery Days held in the summer at Mount Trashmore Park.

30. To keep up with children's activities pick up a copy of *Tidewater Parent*, which is published monthly and distributed for free at grocery stores, child-care facilities, fitness centers and many other locations. Each issue of this tabloid newspaper features a comprehensive calendar of events with many ideas to entertain the family, 426-2595. Reading the weekly *Port Folio* and *The Virginia-Pilot/Ledger-Star's* Friday "Daily Break" section also help keep you on top of fun family events.

Photo: Portsmouth Convention and Visitors Bureau

Hailed as one of the biggest sailing celebrations on the eastern seaboard, the annual Cock Island Race is held every July.

Inside
Annual Events and Festivals

Deep inside every mild-mannered citizen of Hampton Roads beats the soul of a party animal. And, on any given weekend in any given month, there's a celebration to feed that passion. From mega-blasts like Norfolk's Harborfest, to food-fetes like the Pungo Strawberry Festival, to social soirees like Norfolk's Holly Festival, there's a party going on . . . and you're invited!

The region literally rocks with activity from March through December, setting the most hectic pace for fanfare and pageantry. Plus, along with the following calendar of annual events and festivals, there are hundreds of smaller community-generated events, including Chamber of Commerce outings, juried art shows and various organization's fund-raising galas. For sports lovers, we've included the highlights of major runs and tournaments in the sports section of the guide. Our media is pretty responsive to all events, regardless of size, so you're sure to have advance warning of any upcoming party that is open to the public.

Before you become a card-carrying Hampton Roads party-goer, you should know the rules. First, come hungry. Food vendors literally come out of the back kitchen with the best finger-lickins for every taste. While prices are normally a bit higher than at your local fast food drive-through, the thrill of eating a steaming hot pit-cooked barbecue sandwich while juggling an ice cold beer is an adventure not to be missed.

Second, if you want quiet, stay home. Practically all events feature live entertainment super-enhanced by gargantuan speakers. The decibel level is something previously considered unattainable by mortal man but actually adds to the ambiance of reckless abandon that a REAL party should exhibit.

And, lastly, all the real biggie events have instituted a transportation system to help ease traffic congestion. So don't even think about driving to the heart of Harborfest, the Chesapeake Jubilee or the Neptune Festival at the Beach. From convenient pickup locations, you can be zipped to partyland for a very reasonable charge and with very little gridlock.

One special note for newcomers to our great region. Every event listed here is the brainchild of a volunteer group and executed by scores of equally dedicated, unpaid, overworked volunteers. If you're new to the area and want to meet some fine people, offering to jump into the party-making spirit will gain you not only the opportunity to have a hands-on experience (and a VIP parking pass!), but also the chance to work with business people and community leaders whom you might otherwise not have the good fortune to meet.

Make a note too that the nearby Eastern Shore area is the scene for other very popular annual events — like the Chincoteague Seafood Festival in May or the Eastern Shore Harvest Fest in October — so put on your traveling shoes

Indulge in food, festivities and fireworks at Norfolk's annual Harborfest, held every June.

every once in a while. See our Eastern Shore chapter for details.

Major sponsoring organizations are listed following the events calendar. Unless otherwise noted, all events listed are free and open to the public. So, get the spirit. Get involved and go have some fun!

Springtime Revelry

March

ST. PATRICK'S DAY CELEBRATION

'Tis a fine party under the Big Top Tent in Norfolk's Ghent neighborhood. Green beer and Irish specialties are the order of the evening. Expect live music, zany contests and a bit of jiggin' for the big day for wearing o' the green.

ST. PATRICK'S DAY PARADE

A family favorite in the area's largest "Irish" stronghold, the shamrock shenanigans wind their way through Ocean View on the weekend before St. Patrick's Day.

A real treat for the little leprechauns in your family. 597-3548. Norfolk.

CRAWFORD BAY CREW CLASSIC

Rowing teams from water-worthy colleges and universities converge on the Elizabeth River to row to victory. 393-9933. Portsmouth.

April

DOWNTOWN DOO DAH PARADE

No one can claim that Hampton Roads residents don't have one heck of a sense of humor! This April Fools Day folly of a parade turns high powered business people, charitable organizations and clubs of distinction into out-of-sync units that march to a different drummer through the streets of downtown Norfolk. 441-2345.

ANNUAL EASTER SUNRISE SERVICE

With the Elizabeth River as the background, join all denominations for this annual outdoor Easter Sunrise Service in

Town Point Park on the Downtown Norfolk waterfront. 441-2345.

ANNUAL CHILDREN'S EASTER EGG-STRAVAGANZA

Scramble the kids together for one of the largest Easter egg hunts in Hampton Roads. A full day for fun, games and kid's crafts at Town Point Park in Downtown Norfolk. 441-2345.

INTERNATIONAL AZALEA FESTIVAL

Paying tribute to the North Atlantic Treaty Organization (NATO), the Supreme Allied Command Atlantic (SACLANT), and the military community of Hampton Roads, this, the oldest ongoing festival in the region, is the only festival in the country to honor the international command. NATO countries from all over the world select one young woman to represent their country in the Festival's court, with the candidate of the Most Honored Nation serving as Queen. Packed with pomp and circumstance, highlights include the flag raising at SACLANT headquarters, Saturday's Grand Parade through Downtown Norfolk, coronation of the Queen and her court in Norfolk's beautiful Botanical Gardens and the City of Norfolk Azalea Ball on Saturday evening. Complementing these events is a weekend of entertainment at Town Point Park and a super spectacular Air Show held Saturday and Sunday at the Naval Air Station Norfolk. Cosponsored by the City of Norfolk and Chamber of Commerce. 622-2312.

HISTORIC GARDEN WEEK

Peek into the homes of the rich and famous during this week when both historic homes and exquisite private residences are open for touring. Initiated in April of 1929, this annual event attracts thousands of visitors to the meticulously maintained homes and gardens that reach their peak beauty during this spring month. Proceeds from the event make possible the restoration of gardens throughout the Commonwealth of Virginia. To receive a guidebook for all homes included in this year's Garden Tour, contact Historic Garden Week Headquarters, 12 E. Franklin Street, Richmond, Virginia 23219.

May

T.G.I.F. AND RIVER ROCKS CONCERTS

May signals the annual kickoff for the T.G.I.F. After Work Concerts in Downtown Norfolk's Town Point Park. T.G.I.F. and River Rocks (which feature bigger name performers) are the place to see and be seen for workaholics of every age each Friday evening during the season. Each event, with hot music and cold beer, benefits a local charity . . . and is definitely the place to start your weekend!

OCEAN VIEW BEACH FESTIVAL

Celebrate along the shores of the Chesapeake Bay with food, entertainment and arts and crafts. Hosted by the residents of Ocean View and Willoughby Spit, this three-day event is the first official beach blast of the year. 583-0000. Norfolk.

THE GREEK FESTIVAL

Talk about good things to eat! Every year this annual celebration of the rich heritage of our Greek community draws throngs of Hampton Roaders who set aside their diet-for-summer plans just to smell and sample the divine dishes prepared by some of our community's best cooks. After you're full, roll out to see works of Greek artists and many hand-made arts and crafts. At the Greek Orthodox Church on Granby Street in Norfolk. 440-0500.

THE GHENT ART SHOW

Contemporary oils to photographs, ceramics to watercolors — if it's art, it's here at the annual Ghent Arts Festival, celebrating over 20 years of success. More than 200 artists are on hand displaying their work, with food and entertainment right alongside at Town Point Park in Norfolk. 441-2345.

VIRGINIA RENAISSANCE FAIRE

Take a step back in time and experience a 16th-century English village during their celebration of spring. Celebrate the pageantry, bawdiness, grand feasting, royal shenanigans, amusing antics and merrymaking of a Renaissance village. 441-2345.

AFR'AM FEST

An African marketplace, foods and music bring out thousands to celebrate African-American heritage. At Town Point Park in Norfolk. 456-1743.

MEMORIAL DAY WEEKEND CELEBRATION

Hit the Beach for one of the biggest parties in town! There's a volleyball tournament, food and hot entertainment for filling the long vacation weekend. 437-4800.

MAY MUSIC FESTIVAL

Shag til you drop . . . it's the May Music Festival at Virginia Beach! Crowd on in to hear national beach music stars take the stage for this annual three-day event. 463-1940.

SEAWALL ART SHOW

Here's the perfect weekend to snap up an original piece of art while enjoying a stroll through the lovely Veteran's Riverfront park in Portsmouth. Every year, more professional and amateur artists join the respected list of artists on hand to discuss their work with show visitors. 393-8481.

SALTWATER FISHING TOURNAMENT

Not many get away from these anglers who come from all over the country to compete in this annual tournament, held in Virginia Beach. 491-5160.

PUNGO STRAWBERRY FESTIVAL

Be tickled pink with the variety of strawberry cuisine offered in this rural Virginia Beach harvest celebration. Live entertainment is always on hand so you can dance away the calories. 721-6001.

THE CHESAPEAKE JUBILEE

Not to be outdone by neighboring cities, Chesapeake pulls out all the stops for this annual free-for-all in Chesapeake Park. Top-name entertainment, carnival rides, food of every description and more is the order of the weekend. This is one event to check into shuttle service to the festival site. Sponsored by The City of Chesapeake and Chamber of Commerce. 547-2118.

Summer Spectaculars

June

HARBORFEST

If most of Hampton Roads' festivals are whirlwinds of activity, Harborfest is a tornado. The star of the East Coast annual waterfront spectaculars, Harborfest is a nonstop flurry of live entertainment, sailing ships, water and air shows, more food than you could possibly sample in a weekend and capped by the most singular display of fireworks you'll witness all year. Visitors number in the trillions, so use the efficient shuttle service available from a multitude of convenient locations. 627-5329. Norfolk.

SEAWALL FESTIVAL

To mirror the activity on Norfolk's waterfront during Harborfest, Portsmouth answers with its own festival. Live entertainment, food galore and a children's park compete for your attention just across the Elizabeth River. 393-9933.

BAYOU BOOGALOO AND CAJUN FOOD FESTIVAL

This one is hot . . . literally! Spicy foods and equally spicy music by nationally known entertainers is found here. If zydeco music and New Orleans flair get you swaying, move on in to this one. 441-2345. Norfolk.

BOARDWALK ART SHOW

The granddaddy of local art shows, this juried one, sponsored by The Virginia Beach Center for the Arts, draws artists of every medium from all over the country to set up their masterpieces on the boardwalk in Virginia Beach along the Atlantic Ocean. From paintings to photography to pottery, this is your chance to stroll through the area's largest outdoor art gallery. 425-0000.

July

TOWN POINT AIR SHOW AND FOURTH OF JULY CELEBRATION

Aeronautic displays and exhibits, children's activities, live music plus daring aerobatics, stunts, sky divers and wing walkers over the Elizabeth River celebrate the Fourth of July. There's down-home food plus, of course, an all-American fireworks display. 441-2345.

DECLARATION CELEBRATION

Ditto food, entertainment and fireworks to celebrate the Fourth. At Portsmouth's Veterans Riverfront Park. 393-8481.

BLACKBEARD PIRATE JAMBOREE

Revelry for the rogue in you! Pirate's garb is the norm for this annual scalawag of an affair, featuring a parade of sail, children's events, costume contests and the Pirate's Ball. Bring all your little scoundrels to Norfolk's Town Point Park for this one. 441-2345.

August

TOWN POINT JAZZ FESTIVAL

You get to see the hottest jazz artists around for free! It's a hot, jazzy weekend on Norfolk's downtown Waterfront. At last count, more than 60,000 jazz lovers traveled to Norfolk to get in tune with world-class jazz acts. 441-2345.

Fall Festivities

September

THE NEPTUNE FESTIVAL

Virginia Beach's premier festival, this five-day family affair includes activities that range from the Sand Castle Classic to a spectacular Air Show. Not to mention tons of fresh seafood and top-billed entertainment. King Neptune, chosen from the city's business and civic leaders, leads his court of young outstanding

Photo: Virginia Beach Convention and Visitor Development

Virginia Beach's popular Neptune Festival attracts thousands every September.

women through the festivities, right up to the royal fireworks display. King Neptune's Ball, a formal affair, is one of the highlights of the Beach's social season. 498-0215.

ELIZABETH RIVER BLUES FESTIVAL

You can get the blues nonstop from the best regional and national blues performers. At Norfolk's Town Point Park. 441-2345.

RIVER RIB FEST

A fierce bar-b-q cook-off accompanies foot-tapping music all weekend long. Great fun for the entire family, especially the ever-popular SPAM carving contest at Norfolk's Town Point Park! 441-2345.

October

VIRGINIA CHILDREN'S FESTIVAL

If anyone under four feet tall lives in your home, get them to Town Point Park in Norfolk for this magical day! Kids on Parade, costumed characters, nationally known children's entertainers, giant pup-

pets and more attract kids of all ages for this all day event. 441-2345.

VIRGINIA TOWN POINT WINE FESTIVAL

Whether you fancy a cabernet sauvignon blanc from the heart of the Shenandoah or a rich burgundy from Williamsburg, this palate-pleasing event is for you. Sample products from almost 20 premium wineries throughout the Commonwealth along with the most gourmet of foods. It's one of the largest outdoor wine festivals in the state, and it's right here at Norfolk's Town Point Park. 441-2345.

CHESAPEAKE BAY MARITIME FESTIVAL AND CLASSIC BOAT SHOW

Celebrating the fine old crafts of the Chesapeake Bay, the featured attractions of this two-day event are the classic and antique wooden boats. Interactive exhibits, the Chesapeake Bay Maritime Art Show, a seafood pavilion and, of course, live music, make this a super magnet for landlocked seamen. 441-2345.

OLDE TOWNE GHOST WALK

Be spooked out of your trick or treat as actors dressed for the ghoulish occasion tell tales of ghosts and goblins while you tour through Portsmouth's historic district. 399-5487.

PEANUT FESTIVAL

It's really worth the drive to the area's "nuttiest" festival, held at Suffolk's Municipal Airport. There's entertainment, a parade, the phenomenal Shrimp Feast and so much more . . . all to celebrate the area's top crop. 539-2111.

Winter Wonders

November

HOLIDAYS IN THE CITY

Miles of tiny white lights outline the skyline of Norfolk's downtown as a beacon to the holiday season. A month-long celebration, there are parades on land and sea, fireworks, plus a multitude of family events that run through the end of December. 627-1757.

December

HOLLY FESTIVAL

This annual Norfolk event to benefit The Children's Hospital of The Kings Daughters brings out the very best of the season, from the Festival of Trees to a plethora of handmade goodies and gifts. For an Insider's look at very special private residences, there's the Holly Homes Tour; for all-out glitz and glamour, there's the Holly Ball. 628-7070.

HOLIDAY FESTIVITIES

Grand illuminations, yuletide carols and good cheer can be found in every city in Hampton Roads. Yule logs are stoked to the max by the spirit of the season. For those who prefer their holiday with 18th-century ambiance, Colonial Williamsburg's Grand Illumination is really a spectacular, and humbling, experience. Watch local papers for specific dates and times for all these special events.

NEW YEAR'S EVE PARTY

Make merry under the heated tent as Town Point Park in Norfolk becomes the biggest party in town. The fireworks at the stroke of midnight are spectacular! 441-2345.

Who's Putting On The Show?

For more details and schedules of the events listed here, you may contact:

NORFOLK

Festevents, 120 West Main Street, Norfolk, Virginia 23510, 441-2345

PORTSMOUTH

PortsEvents, 355 Crawford Street, Portsmouth, Virginia 23704, 393-9933

VIRGINIA BEACH

Virginia Beach Special Events and Film Office, 1000 19th Street, Virginia Beach, Virginia 23451, 437-4800.

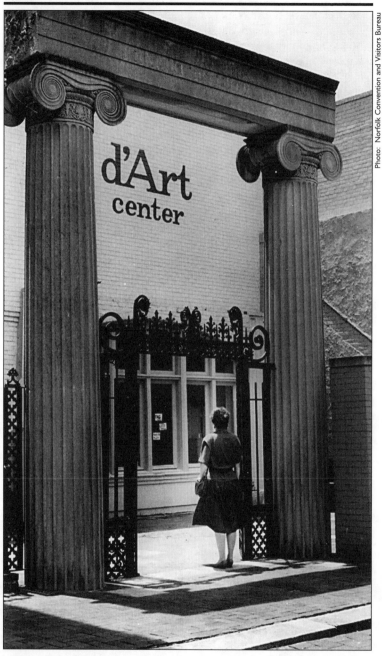

Photo: Norfolk Convention and Visitors Bureau

The d'Art Center is the ideal place to witness the creation of art.

Inside
The Arts

If you're from New York, Boston or some other metropolis, you may not expect Hampton Roads to have much to offer in the way of arts. But open your eyes, ears and mind, and you will be pleasantly surprised.

Arts aficionados will find their calendars crammed from October through May with operas, ballets, concerts, lectures and exhibits. Even during summer, there are plenty of performances and shows to entertain all ages.

South Hampton Roads has nearly 100 arts groups that regularly perform and exhibit here. Since it's a major metropolitan area only three hours from Washington, D.C., the region is a regular stop on the traveling circuit that buses in talent ranging from the Bolshoi Ballet to the Sesame Street characters. Local arts groups include large, professional organizations as well as shoestring operations glued together by enthusiastic volunteers. Norfolk has traditionally been the region's cultural hub, but in recent years arts groups have sprung up in area cities. The symphony and other performing artists frequently alternate performances between Norfolk and Virginia Beach.

For performing arts the main stages in Norfolk are Chrysler Hall, the Wells Theatre and the Harrison Opera House. Chrysler Hall, with 2,043 seats, is adjacent to the Scope arena. It is Norfolk's all-purpose hall used for everything from the symphony to ballets and lectures. The Wells Theatre, with 677 seats, is home to the Virginia Stage Company but also welcomes other groups. The Harrison Opera House (formerly the Center Theater) is home base for the Virginia Opera but shares its stage with other organizations. The city-owned theater reopened in 1993 after a $10 million facelift. It has 1,680 seats and a history that dates to World War II. Norfolk also has a 300-seat auditorium in The Chrysler Museum.

Concerts in Portsmouth frequently are at 2,000-seat Willett Hall, which sponsors a season of traveling Broadway shows and children's plays. Virginia Beach has the 1,000-seat Pavilion Theater in the Pavilion Convention Center. Across the street, the Virginia Beach Center for the Arts has a 262-seat auditorium. Performing groups also frequent stages at area colleges and schools.

Keeping tabs on all the arts groups can be a tough job. Each September both *The Virginian-Pilot/Ledger-Star* and *Port Folio* magazine publish annual arts calendars. These comprehensive listings are worth saving since they detail the entire season for most arts groups. To stay current on arts events, check the daily papers' "Friday" and Sunday "Daily Break" sections and the weekly *Port Folio*. The publications do a good job of profiling arts groups and upcoming performances. The Cultural Alliance of Greater Hampton Roads publishes an annual resource directory called *Sketches* that gives details on most arts groups. It costs $10 but is available in most area libraries. To obtain a copy of the directory call 440-6628 or write the Cultural Alliance at 5200 Hampton Boulevard, Norfolk 23508.

Once you get a feel for the arts, you may want to hook up with one or more organizations. Since volunteers are the lifeblood of these groups, they will be happy to see you. Most of the larger groups sell memberships or season tickets. These usually entitle you to newsletters, invitations to special events and gift shop discounts. Many groups have guilds that let you do hands-on work.

If you're between 22 and 45 years old you can join an affiliated organization for young adults. Membership fees are very reasonable, and this can be a great way to meet people and learn more about the arts. The Virginia Beach Center for the Arts sponsors Art & Co. The Chrysler Museum has For Art's Sake. The Virginia Symphony has Bravo. The Virginia Opera recently started the Phantoms of the Opera. These popular groups give an inside look at the arts. They serve educational, fund-raising and social functions and get members invited to posh members-only previews and parties.

While all performing arts groups sell season tickets, feel free to sample their offerings by purchasing tickets to single performances. Most groups have two-for-one tickets in the annual Entertainment coupon books that are sold each December by various charities.

The Big Four

There are four dominant arts organizations in the region: The Chrysler Museum, the Virginia Opera, the Virginia Stage Company and the Virginia Symphony. All are large professional organizations with long histories and reputations that extend far beyond the region.

THE CHRYSLER MUSEUM

Olney Rd. and Mowbray Arch
Norfolk 664-6200
Hours: 10 AM-4 PM Tuesday-Saturday;
1-4 PM Sunday
Admission free; $3 donation suggested

This is one of our favorite spots. There is so much to see that you can go time after time and not feel like you're peering at the same art works. Founded in 1933 as the Norfolk Museum of Arts and Sciences, the museum changed its name in 1971 to honor the late Walter P. Chrysler, Jr. Chrysler, the automobile heir and avid art collector, married a Norfolk native and made his home in the city. Many of the 30,000 pieces in the museum are from Chrysler's vast collection.

The museum has one of the largest art collections south of Washington, D.C., and is considered one of the best art museums in the country. Its art library is the largest in the southeastern United States. In 1989 the museum completed an expansion and renovation of its building, which overlooks The Hague in the historic Ghent area.

The museum's permanent collection is an eclectic one, with pieces dating from 2700 B.C. to the present. The museum is renowned for its glass collection, whose 8,000 pieces include the works of Tiffany, Lalique and other masters. The Chrysler has the second-largest collection of Tiffany glass and a special room to house it. The museum is known for its French and Italian paintings as well as its photography collection. It also displays the Norfolk Mace, the silver symbol of the city created in 1753 (see sidebar in History section). Besides the permanent collection, there are always special exhibitions that stay for several months. An elegant cafe, Palettes, is located within the museum and serves lunch daily and Sunday brunch.

Photo: The Chrysler Museum

The Chrysler Museum is a first-class resource for the Hampton Roads community.

With its solemn guards and subdued lighting, the museum seems like an adults-only place. However, it does welcome children, and on many Sunday afternoons it goes all out with free family activities that range from scavenger hunts to crafts and storytellers. The museum also operates three historic houses: the Adam Thoroughgood House in Virginia Beach and the Moses Myers House and Willoughby-Baylor House in Norfolk.

THE VIRGINIA OPERA
Harrison Opera House
160 Virginia Beach Blvd.
Norfolk   627-9545, 623-1223

This is a professional opera company that has national acclaim and has taken some of its performances on the road to South America. The Norfolk-based company was formed in 1975 and performs regular series in Norfolk, Richmond and Northern Virginia. It is led by founding director Peter Mark. During a typical season it produces four major operas that star professional New York and regional singers. In 1994-95 the Virginia Opera presented *La Traviata, Salome, Simon*

Bolivar and *La Boheme*. In the past, the opera has premiered three Thea Musgrave works: *A Woman Called Moses, A Christmas Carol* and *Mary Queen of Scots*. *Simon Bolivar* also was a world premiere that received international acclaim.

The opera's home theater is a former World War I-era USO hall. As part of its fabulous 1993 restoration, the old Center Theater was renamed for two local residents — the late Stanley Harrison and his wife Edythe, the opera's founding board president.

VIRGINIA STAGE COMPANY
Wells Theatre
Monticello & Tazewell Sts.
Norfolk   627-6988, 627-2310

Founded in 1978, this is a professional, nonprofit regional theater company. It puts on a dynamite season with the help of actors drawn primarily from New York and Los Angeles. When the stage company nearly folded in 1991 because of financial problems, 8,000 area residents came to its rescue by purchasing season tickets. Since then the company has been on solid footing. Its 1994-

95 season included *Dirt, Peter Pan, Sea Marks, A Perfect Ganesh, Lady Day at Emerson's Bar & Grill* and *Blithe Spirit*.

It's worth a trip to the theater just to see its home, the venerable Wells Theatre. This elaborate Beaux-Arts structure was built in 1912 and is a National Historic Landmark. A 1985 renovation returned the 677-seat auditorium to its original splendor and erased any signs of its stint as an X-rated movie theater in the 1960s.

VIRGINIA SYMPHONY

P.O. Box 26
Norfolk 23514   623-8590, 623-2310

This is one of the busiest performing arts groups around with more than 100 concerts a year. The symphony, which was founded in 1919, has a core group of 50 professional musicians and about 40 others who play as needed. It is led by JoAnn Falletta, one of America's most promising young conductors. The orchestra performs at Chrysler Hall, the Pavilion Theatre in Virginia Beach, Ogdon Hall in Hampton and Phi Beta Kappa Hall in Williamsburg.

Besides its classical series, the symphony produces pops, dance, Mozart and family concert series. You can also catch its players at free outdoor concerts at some area festivals.

Both the classical and pops series feature prominent guest artists. In 1994-95 they included trumpeter Doc Severinsen and singer Crystal Gayle.

Other Organizations

Other arts groups may not be as large as the four listed above, but they have plenty to offer in the way of talent and diversity. The following is a sampling of area arts organizations.

Dance

OLD DOMINION BALLET
683-4486

Offers classes in various dance styles and has several annual performances. Each December it produces *The Nutcracker*.

VIRGINIA BALLET THEATER
622-4822

This is a semiprofessional company that performs regularly and offers a variety of classes.

VIRGINIA BEACH BALLET
495-0989

This amateur ballet organization offers productions featuring classical ballet and modern dance.

Insiders' Tips

Several arts programs are targeted toward youthful audiences. The Hurrah Players and Willett Hall's Storybook Theater Children's Series present excellent theatrical productions. The Virginia Symphony has a family concert series. The Virginia Beach Center for the Arts offers occasional crafts programs, while The Chrysler Museum has frequent Sunday afternoon family programs. There are several area puppet troupes that perform: Wappadoodle Puppets, 481-6658, Spectrum Puppets, 491-2873, and Fuzz & Stuffing Puppets, 480-2991.

Lectures

THE NORFOLK FORUM
627-8672

This popular Chrysler Hall series always sells out early and has recently brought such notable speakers as retired Gen. Colin Powell and political powerhouses Mary Matalin and James Carville.

OLD DOMINION UNIVERSITY PRESIDENT'S LECTURE SERIES
683-3115

This free series started in 1992 to bring diverse speakers to campus. Recent lecturers include Pulitzer Prize-winning journalist Susan Faludi and former deputy C.I.A. director Bobby R. Inman.

TIDEWATER JEWISH FORUM
489-1371

Sponsored by the Jewish Community Center, this series brings a variety of interesting speakers. Recently they've included comic David Brenner and Michael Berenbaum, director of the U.S. Holocaust Research Institute.

VIRGINIA WESLEYAN COLLEGE SERIES
455-3200

This series covers a variety of topics from story telling to poetry and current events.

Music

BAY YOUTH ORCHESTRAS OF VIRGINIA
461-8834

Sponsors youth concerts throughout the region and also has a string group.

CANTATA CHORUS
627-5665

This amateur chorus specializes in sacred works during concerts at Christ and St. Luke's Episcopal church in Norfolk.

CAPRIOLE
1-220-1248

This professional Williamsburg-based group has several performances in South Hampton Roads. It is a vocal and instrumental ensemble specializing in 17th-century music.

CHESAPEAKE CIVIC CHORUS
421-9784

The CCC is an amateur chorus that presents a variety of music during annual concerts.

EASTERN VIRGINIA BRASS QUINTET
340-6406

This quintet performs chamber music featuring trumpet, trombone, horn and tuba.

FELDMAN CHAMBER MUSIC SOCIETY
498-9396

The Society sponsors concerts by outstanding chamber musicians.

GOVERNOR'S SCHOOL FOR THE ARTS
683-5549

Concerts feature talented high school musicians attending the regional arts school.

HARDWICK CHAMBER ENSEMBLE
424-4277

The Ensemble's concert series focuses on chamber music.

I. SHERMAN GREENE CHORALE
467-8971

This African-American community chorus in its 23rd year performs traditional music as well as the works of contemporary composers.

McCULLOUGH CHORALE
627-8375

Formerly Virginia Pro Musica, this 23-member chorus presents a broad

Photo: Portsmouth Convention and Visitors Bureau

Arts Center of the Portsmouth museums.

repertoire of chorus music ranging from Renaissance to 20th-century songs.

NORFOLK CHAMBER CONSORT
440-1803 or 622-4542

This chamber music group in its 26th year features winds, strings, keyboard instruments and vocalists.

OLD DOMINION UNIVERSITY CONCERT SERIES
683-3120

Free concerts feature up-and-coming national musicians as well as performances by local artists.

TIDEWATER CLASSICAL GUITAR SOCIETY
625-2411

The talented people in this group bring internationally known and regional guitarists to the area for concerts and workshops.

TIDEWATER WINDS
464-9290

This concert band performs in the Sousa band tradition.

VIRGINIA BEACH CHORALE
486-1464

These vocalists present a variety of music during two concerts a year and at benefit performances throughout the year.

VIRGINIA BEACH SYMPHONY ORCHESTRA
426-2225

This community group has a series of concerts with featured soloists.

VIRGINIA CHILDREN'S CHORUS
397-0779

The chorus features youths age 6 to 16.

VIRGINIA SYMPHONIC CHORUS
427-2288

A 60-voice choir performs several concerts a year of classical music.

VIRGINIA WESLEYAN COLLEGE CONCERT SERIES
455-3200

The college's "Familiar-faces" series sponsors performances by local professional musicians.

Theater

THE ACTOR'S THEATRE
557-0397, 425-6575

This amateur company performs at the Virginia Beach Center for the Arts.

BROADWAY AT CHRYSLER HALL
622-0288

The series brings traveling Broadway productions of such musicals as *A Chorus Line* and *Jesus Christ Superstar*.

COMMONWEALTH MUSICAL STAGE
340-5446

This professional theater company uses regional talent to produce musicals.

ENCORE PLAYERS
460-5152 or 436-9512

The Encore Players features actors who are in the military.

FOUNDERS INN DINNER THEATER
366-5749

This theater uses local actors in such productions as *Shenandoah* and *The Gifts of the Magi*.

GENERIC THEATER
441-2160

The innovative theater produces works not previously seen in the region. Long a part of the Norfolk Department of Parks and Recreation, it recently became an independent, professional organization.

GOVERNOR'S SCHOOL FOR THE ARTS
441-2905

Productions feature talented high school students attending the regional magnet school.

THE HURRAH PLAYERS
623-7418 or 627-KIDS

Elaborate musicals feature highly trained local children in productions geared toward families.

LITTLE THEATRE OF NORFOLK
627-8551

This is the country's oldest continuously active little theater. It was founded in 1926 and specializes in light comedies and musicals.

LITTLE THEATRE OF VIRGINIA BEACH
428-9233

This amateur theater produces a variety of plays. Recent performances were *Shirley Valentine* and *Damn Yankees*.

NORFOLK MUSICAL THEATER
588-1072

The NMT is an amateur company that specializes in light musicals. Recent productions include *The Sound of Music* and *She Loves Me*.

Norfolk Savoyards
484-6920

This group specializes in the works of Gilbert and Sullivan.

Norfolk State University Players
683-8341

Productions showcase talent from the university. Recent ones include *Blues in the Night* and *Rapunzel*.

Old Dominion University Players
683-5305

Productions feature ODU students. Recent productions include *Romeo and Juliet* and *Azaleas*.

Virginia Wesleyan College
455-3200

Productions star Virginia Wesleyan students. Recents ones were *The Three Penny Opera* and *Trifles*.

Willett Hall
393-5144

Touring groups bring Broadway musicals and children's performances to this Portsmouth hall.

Mixed Series

Portsmouth Community Concerts
393-5144

Subscription-only concerts and performances at Willett Hall bring professional artists to the region.

Tidewater Performing Arts Society
627-2314

The Society provides some of the most innovative programs in the region by bringing nationally known dance groups, singers and other artists.

Visual Art Museums

Arts Center of the Portsmouth Museums
393-8393

This is part of the city-operated Portsmouth Museums and is housed in the 1846 Courthouse. It brings traveling exhibits ranging from quilts to paintings.

Hermitage Foundation Museum
423-2052

The Norfolk museum features exhibits by local artists.

Insiders' Tips

When driving east on Waterside Drive in Norfolk, take time to admire the whaling wall at the intersection of Waterside and St. Paul's Boulevard. Until 1993, this was a bland parking garage wall. Then Wyland, the California whale muralist who uses no first name, and a 14-member crew spent a weekend transforming the wall into a tribute to the humpback whale. Norfolk's whaling wall was Wyland's 47th mural and one of his largest. It is 260 feet long with the biggest whales averaging 50 feet in length. Most of the mural was painted with a spray gun.

LIFE-SAVING MUSEUM OF VIRGINIA
422-1587

This Virginia Beach museum features traveling displays of maritime art.

RIDDICK'S FOLLY
934-1390

This Suffolk museum features displays related to local history.

THE SUFFOLK MUSEUM
925-6311

A city-run arts center, the Suffolk Museum presents a variety of art exhibits.

VIRGINIA BEACH CENTER FOR THE ARTS
425-0000

The regional arts center showcases 20th-century art with changing exhibits.

Galleries

Artists at Work: Gallery and Studios, 2407 Pacific Avenue, Virginia Beach, 425-6671

Alive Art Studio, 737 Granby Street, Norfolk, 622-7645

Cape Henry Collegiate School, 1320 Mill Road, Virginia Beach, 481-2446

Commons Gallery, Church of the Ascension, 4853 Princess Anne Road, Virginia Beach, 425-6671

Crestar Bank Gallery, 500 Main Street, Norfolk, 583-3586

d'Art Center, 125 College Place, Norfolk, 625-4211

Eastern Virginia Medical School Galleries, Lewis Hall, 700 Olney Road, Norfolk, 446-6050

Jewish Community Center's Lobby Art Gallery, 7300 Newport Avenue, Norfolk, 489-1371

Old Dominion University Gallery, 765 Granby Street, Norfolk, 683-2843, 683-4047

Regent University Library Lobby, Regent University, Virginia Beach, 523-7487

Virginia Natural Gas Gallery, 5100 E. Virginia Beach Boulevard, 466-5439

Virginia Wesleyan College Hofheimer Library, 1584 Wesleyan Drive, Norfolk/Virginia Beach, 455-3222

Visual Arts Center: Tidewater Community College at Olde Towne, 340 High Street, Portsmouth, 396-6999

WHRO Fine Arts Gallery, 5200 Hampton Boulevard, Norfolk, 489-9476, 425-6671

Photo: Virginia Beach Convention and Visitor Development

Rollerbladers hit the Boardwalk for recreation and sun.

Inside
Recreation

On any sunny day, no less than half the residents of Hampton Roads pack up their bikes, bats, balls and boats and head off to one of the numerous parks and recreation meccas scattered throughout the region. And, because we are also known to have perfected the art of vicarious pleasure, the other half packs up beach chairs and picnics to tag along and watch the fun.

Couch potatoes don't get much applause around these parts. With hundreds of public tennis courts, umpteen golf courses, the Chesapeake Bay and Atlantic Ocean and their fine beaches, the fishing, biking, hiking, windsurfing and sailing . . . it's hard to say "no" to the call of the great outdoors. What you'll soon discover, whether you are a visitor or a newcomer, is that neither our fabulously maintained recreational facilities nor our year-round temperate climate will give you much opportunity for just hanging around on the sofa.

While each of the Hampton Roads cities is proud to boast of its own public and private facilities, we've decided to group by specific activity rather than by city. After all, we know that if you're a golfer, you want to find all the courses in one place. Likewise for you nature lovers who want to compare all the possibilities for park pleasure-seeking, or tennis buffs who are itching to round robin from one end of the region to the other.

Whatever your pastime passion, you're sure to find it here. So much of it, in fact, that it would be impossible to list every recreational opportunity in this huge network of community facilities. For more in-depth information about specific cities, a quick call to the following will get you detailed brochures and newsletters listing all the scoop on facilities, leisure classes and athletic programs for all ages:

Norfolk Parks and Recreation
   Department   441-2149
Virginia Beach Department
   of Parks and Recreation   471-5884
Chesapeake Parks and
   Recreation Department   547-6411
Portsmouth Department of
   Parks and Recreation   393-8481

Parks

Norfolk

LAFAYETTE PARK
25th and Granby Sts.   441-2149

One of Norfolk's oldest parks, Lafayette Park boasts two outdoor basketball courts, four tennis courts, an amphitheater, picnic shelters, boat ramp, well-maintained fields for softball and rugby and a grand playground, including special play equipment for the disabled. The scenic pathways that wind through the mature flora and fauna are especially appealing, and you can stop for a soft drink or snack at the nearby concession stand. What we call "City Park" sits next to the 55-acre Virginia Zoo, so plan to spend a full day to take in all this park has to offer.

TOWN POINT PARK
Waterside Drive at Boush St.   441-2149

It's simply amazing to those of us who were raised in Hampton Roads that this wonderful park sits in the very location that we were never allowed to enter after dark while we were growing up. But just look at it today! Just a footstep from Norfolk's primary downtown business district, adjacent to the Waterside festival marketplace, Town Point Park is indeed the visible tribute to Downtown Norfolk's revitalization spirit. With its meandering walkways, gay nineties street lamps, London Plane trees and comfy benches set between large expanses of incredibly lush green lawn, it is a wonderful place for a quiet stroll or to sit and watch ships gliding down the Elizabeth River.

Come any given weekend, however, this sleeping giant really roars. Norfolk Festevents, the city's premier party-thrower, engineers events and festivals that fill even the most insatiable desire for activity, from the weekly T.G.I.F. celebrations to Harborfest to festivals in honor of countries, kids and cultures of every kind.

You'll find public parking at nearby lots and ramps, and you can even take a short ferry ride across the Elizabeth River to Portsmouth for a nominal fee. The Waterside Marina is adjacent to the park, and a favorite Sunday excursion is to walk up and down the docks checking out the visiting vessels and their ports of call. There are also frequent visits from foreign ships that dock at Otter Berth, home port to *The Spirit of Norfolk*, and the public is often invited to come aboard for tours.

OCEAN VIEW BEACH PARK
Ocean View   441-2345

The jewel of Ocean View and a landmark in this close-knit community's rejuvenation efforts, this unique 6.5-acre park is Norfolk's newest addition to its park portfolio. Located on the site of the old Ocean View Amusement Park, it features a large gazebo for presentations and dancing, a beach that's lifeguarded during summer months, boardwalk, beach handicap access ramp and lovely lawns. It plays host to the summer season's free Big Bands on the Bay series, held Sunday nights from 7 PM until 9 PM, and to the popular Chesapeake Bay Crab Feast held each July.

NORFOLK BOTANICAL GARDEN
Airport Rd. off Azalea Garden Rd.   441-5830

Botanical splendor for the viewing along 12 miles of lush pathways awaits every day of the year in this 155 acre floral wonderland. (For more information, please see the Attractions section.)

NORTHSIDE PARK
8400 Tidewater Dr.

Here's where many softball and tennis champs meet to defend their titles. With two lighted softball diamonds, seven tennis courts, outdoor basketball court, BMX bicycle course, skateboard ramp plus playground and picnic shelters, this

Insiders' Tips

January is the month to spot real live humpback whales off the Virginia Beach shoreline. For a closer look, jump aboard a charter sponsored by the Virginia Marine Science Museum.

place is always popping with activity of one sort or another. Especially popular is the year-round indoor pool and sun patio, staffed by certified lifeguards who offer aquatic games and classes for all ages. Seasonal tennis instruction by a part-time tennis pro is also available. There's no direct phone, so to get more information, contact the Recreation Bureau at 441-2149.

LAKEWOOD PARK
1612 Willow Wood Dr.   *441-5833*

Headquarters to the Bureau of Recreation's Athletic and Dance/Music divisions, Lakewood Park sits in the heart of Lakewood, an exceptionally lovely residential neighborhood. Featuring nine tennis courts, two lighted softball/baseball/football/soccer fields, picnic shelters, playground, restrooms and plenty of free parking. Moms who drop off their kids for league play have been known to slip right across the street to the Lafayette Library for a little peace and quiet.

BARRAUD PARK
Off Tidewater Dr. on Vista Dr.   *441-2149*

From June to September, this large, newly renovated community park is staffed to organize activities and sign out equipment. You'll find lighted softball and football/soccer fields, six tennis courts, a playground, picnic shelter and amphitheater, with ample free parking. Summer months offer organized playground games for ages 6 to 12, as well as a summer food program.

TARRALTON PARK
Tarralton Dr. and Millard St.   *441-1765*

The most recent addition to the network of parks maintained by the Rec Bureau, Tarralton features over 70 acres with three family-size picnic shelters, colorful play area and tot lot, lighted tennis courts, lighted basketball court, three soccer fields and a BMX bicycle trail. There's also a Little League complex and softball field.

NEIGHBORHOOD PARKS AND SCHOOL GROUNDS

Throughout the city of Norfolk, you'll find "mini parks," beautiful little pockets of well-manicured common grounds and landscaping. In addition to the 112 such areas maintained by the Norfolk Bureau of Recreation (often located on school grounds), there are many other neighborhood quiet spots, like Stockley Gardens in Ghent. Take a look around . . . there's more than likely a playground or park right around the corner!

Virginia Beach

SEASHORE STATE PARK
Shore Dr.   *481-4836*

Designated a Registered National Landmark in 1965, Seashore State Park is an environmental magnet for visitors and residents alike. Entering this 2,770-acre sanctuary is like stepping out of the hustle-bustle of civilization into a far away world. Much of the park is preserved as a natural area, with sights that run the gamut from semitropical forest to giant sand dunes. In just one day's visit, you're sure to catch a glimpse of a number of the 336 species of trees and plants, ranging from cypress draped with Spanish moss to hardy Yucca trees.

Daytime visitors will find a picnic area, hiking trails, a self-guided nature trail and a Visitors Center with exhibits and book sales. Nine trails, including one for handicapped visitors, cover 17 miles and are part of the National Scenic Trails System. Bikers will find their own 5-mile trail, which connects to the city's bike trails.

The Shore Drive side of the park borders on the Chesapeake Bay where you'll find an overnight camping section with 215 sites and 20 group sites, along with a camp store, mile-long beach reserved for campers, restrooms, showers and amphitheater for interpretive programs. Twenty cabins are also available in this area, but you must reserve early. Call 481-2131.

From 64th Street, you can access the east end of the park, where there's a boat ramp that slides you into Broad Bay leading to Lynnhaven Inlet and then out to the Chesapeake Bay. Near this boat ramp is a favorite place for a lover's picnic . . . a hill that offers a scenic view high above the water. For guided tour information, just stop in at the Visitors Center. Admission to the park is free, but there is a nominal parking fee.

BACK BAY NATIONAL
WILDLIFE REFUGE

4005 Sandpiper Rd.   *721-2412*

If you follow the thousands of migrating geese, ducks and swans, you'll find yourself in the natural habitat of the marshy islands of shallow Back Bay. Here, on 5,000 acres of virtually untouched natural beauty, you can be witness to the splendor of beach, dunes, marsh and woodlands along with resident waterfowl, deer and other animals.

To preserve the integrity of the park, strict rules are enforced. First, the park is only open during daylight hours, from sunrise to sunset. Parking is permitted only in designated areas during open hours, and only those with special permits are allowed motorized vehicle access to beaches and unpaved dirt roads. Other no-no's: unleashed pets, guns, horses or open fires. Likewise, the fragile

dunes are off-limits to visitors, but that still leaves the beach shore and nature trails for hiking.

The Seaside Trail and Dune Trail guides you from the parking lot to the stunning beach. The north mile of the beach is closed to protect shore birds there, but the south beach is open, although swimming, sunbathing and surfing is prohibited. Just consider Back Bay to be the perfect place to bring your binoculars, a canteen of water, camera, picnic lunch and a big can of bug spray.

FALSE CAPE STATE PARK

4001 Sandpiper Rd.   *426-7128*

Five miles south of the Back Bay Refuge sits the home to migratory waterfowl, wildlife and protected marshlands. False Cape State Park is a 6-mile stretch of undisturbed beach along a barrier spit that divides the ocean from Back Bay and is accessible only by foot, bicycle or boat. If you choose to walk, you'll have to hike through 5 miles of Back Bay Refuge to reach the boundaries of the park. You really must have a pioneer camping spirit to overnight here, because other than pit toilets, there are absolutely no amenities, and open fires are not permitted. You'll also have to lug in your own water and anything else you might need to create an overnight comfort zone.

If you're interested in learning all about the park's diverse ecosystem, the Wash Woods Environmental Education Center, housed in a converted hunting lodge near the southern end of the park, is the place to turn. For small groups, comfortable overnight accommodations can be arranged to allow time for more intensive study of the area's natural resources.

For a day visit during peak visiting periods, any questions can be answered

Photo: Richmond Newspapers

Surfing is king in Virginia Beach.

at the park's ranger station located just about a mile south of the northern entrance.

MOUNT TRASHMORE

Edwin Dr.   *473-5251*

Boasting one of the city's highest elevations — 68 feet — Mount Trashmore comes by its name honestly. A brilliantly conceived solid waste management project, what was once a huge hill of 750,000 tons of trash was transformed in 1973 into what is now a beautifully landscaped hub of activity, and one of Virginia Beach's most popular parks.

When you're done flying kites or model airplanes from its peak, you can peer down on the action at the skateboard bowl and ramp and get a bird's eye view of the ramp used annually for the area's Soap Box Derby. Then you can climb down to one of two well-stocked lakes where you can paddleboat away your worries or fish with bait from the on-site tackle shop. Feeling lazy? Just lie back and toss bread crumbs to the resident ducks, geese and coots that have no problem marching right over to you for a handout.

Also part of the complex are several playgrounds, picnic shelters, basketball and tennis courts as well as volleyball nets where pick-up games are the norm. Windsurfers are welcome, and plentiful, during peak summer months, and jon boats can be rented to row alongside.

In the shadow of the mount is one of the region's largest, most ambitious and innovative playground, a 25,000-square-foot park designed for, and by, children called Kids Cove. This colossal wooden playground incorporates slides, mazes, ramps and bridges all built around a nautical theme, and was constructed and funded through an all-volunteer effort that equally matched its project in magnitude. A five-day "barn-raising" in 1993 made this children's fantasyland a reality.

PRINCESS ANNE PARK

Princess Anne Rd.   *427-6020*

Eighty acres of a sports lover's paradise sit right next to the popular Virginia Beach Farmer's Market. Along with plenty of wide open space, Princess Anne Park can be proud of its outstanding facilities, including four playgrounds, a number of baseball and softball fields, plus equipment for basketball, volleyball, croquet and horseshoes. Really special is the horse arena for horse shows and rodeos, as well as a children's garden and popular wooded picnic area.

BAYVILLE PARK

First Court Rd.   460-7569

Bayville has the city's only disc golf course for Frisbee players, an 18-hole challenge that is considered by experts to be one of the toughest in the nation. The tree-shaded 66-acre park has features designed for the handicapped, along with facilities for basketball, shuffleboard, softball, volleyball, handball, badminton and horseshoes alongside a comfortable picnic area. For kiddies, Bayville is a veritable Garden of Eden with one of the neatest playgrounds in town. Just watch their smiles as they come face to face with giant futuristic structures to climb, wood and metal towers, swinging tires and rocking metal disks.

RED WING PARK

General Booth Blvd. and
Poor Farm Rd.   437-4847

Because of its proximity to some of the Beach's favorite attractions, including Croatan Beach, WildWater Rapids and the Virginia Marine Science Museum, Red Wing Park is a super stop-off for a picnic lunch. Once here, you can't leave before you stroll through the beautiful gardens — the lovely Japanese garden and aromatic fragrance garden — along with a look at the prisoner of war memorial.

Activity-wise, Red Wing has a skateboard ramp, fitness course, playground, three ball fields plus facilities for tennis, volleyball, badminton, basketball and horseshoes. And, like most Virginia Beach parks, all you need is a valid I.D. to borrow any sports equipment you forgot at home.

LITTLE ISLAND PARK

Sandpiper Rd.   426-7200

Almost a secret treasure of a park, Little Island takes full advantage of its location on Sandbridge Beach as well as Back Bay, and its fishing pier makes it especially attractive for anglers.

The broad beach is lifeguarded during summer months from 9:30 AM to 6 PM, and after a swim you can move on to the playground, tennis courts, basketball or volleyball courts. A snack bar and shaded picnic area are also here at Little Island.

MUNDEN POINT PARK

Munden Point Rd. off
Princess Anne Rd.   426-5296

Getting to Munden Park is an excursion in itself . . . a long ride through the rural areas of Virginia Beach to the North Landing River. Once here, the 100 scenic acres offer a multitude of choices for boaters and landlubbers alike. Since the North Landing River is a link to the Intracoastal Waterway system, you can either watch

---

Insiders' Tips

Wobbly kneed Insiders try a go at Rollerblading by renting in-line (and roller) skates . . . along with knee and elbow pads . . . at Beach Blades at 31st and Oceanfront at the Beach.

Photo: Virginia Division of Tourism

A family greets the morning sun with a walk through the surf and sand at Virginia Beach.

the fancy vessels powering out, rent a canoe or paddleboat or launch your own boat from the boat ramp for a small usage fee.

Landside, there are softball, basketball, volleyball and horseshoes, along with a playground and picnic area. Noteworthy, too, is a Parcourse Fitness Circuit.

BEACH GARDEN PARK

Holly Rd.   *471-4884*

A quiet retreat from the busy oceanfront scene, this delightful park features a playground, fitness trail and picnic tables.

Chesapeake

CHESAPEAKE CITY PARK

500 Greenbrier Pkwy.   *547-6411*

This 75-acre site features rows of reforested pine trees bordering 45 acres of open space. The open space is naturally divided by roadways into segments that can be rented for corporate or private events according to the space needed, with a network of electricity and water service

in place for support. For regular daytime visitors, there's a fitness trail, play equipment, basketball courts and picnic shelter. New in the spring of 1995 was a gigantic volunteer-built playground.

NORTHWEST RIVER PARK

1733 Indian River Rd.   *421-7151*

This 763-acre park has been developed as a natural recreation area incorporating camping, an extensive trail system, picnic shelters, play areas, an equestrian area, miniature golf and plenty of wide open spaces. Located in the southeastern section of Chesapeake, water abounds, including the lake that stretches almost to the southern activity area that runs along the banks of the Northwest River where canoes and boats can be rented. Of special note is the fragrance trail created for the visually handicapped, along with a ropes and initiative course, 103 campsites with camp store, two modern bathhouses, laundry, picnic tables and fire rings. It's also a favorite place for horseback riding and hikes along the 6-mile nature trail system.

DEEP CREEK LOCK PARK

300 Luray   487-8841

This is a 25-acre site named for the Corps of Engineers' lock that separates the salt water of Deep Creek from the fresh water of the historic Dismal Swamp Canal. The heavily wooded park includes several overlook towers, picnic shelters, play areas, a fitness trail, indoor restrooms and a combination pedestrian bridge and elevated walkway system to traverse a tidal inlet and marsh area. Diverse foot trails wind through the woods, and a canoe launch along with fishing and crabbing are favorite Deep Creek activities.

GREAT BRIDGE LOCK PARK

Lock Rd.   547-6292

Located at the transition from the Southern Branch of the Elizabeth River to the Albemarle and Chesapeake Canal along the Intracoastal Waterway, this 19-acre park features a two-lane boat ramp, picnic shelters and a foot trail along the northern shoreline and through the western portion of the park. There's also a large play area and extensive fishing and crabbing areas from the bulkheaded banks. Because one of the area's favorite activities is boat-watching, bleachers have been erected for glimpsing the many yachts that transit the lock southbound in the fall and northbound in the spring.

INDIAN RIVER PARK

Military Hwy.   424-4238

While the City of Norfolk actually owns the 100-acre tract known as Indian River Park, the City of Chesapeake uses 35 acres of the northern section for activities including basketball, baseball, picnicking and a playground. Discussions on joint development of the southern section, like undeveloped trail opportunities, are still under way.

WESTERN BRANCH PARK

4437 Portsmouth Blvd.   465-0211

The first phase of planned development has been completed for this 80-acre park, with the first of the picnic areas and playgrounds already being enjoyed by Western Branch residents. As a prelude to future development, the city has constructed the park access road and one parking lot, and scouts have marked a rudimentary nature trail, while volunteers have planted thousands of wild flowers. On the boards now are softball fields, tennis and basketball courts, with additional picnic and playground areas.

LAKESIDE PARK

Byrd and Holey Aves.
South Norfolk   543-5721

Large lawn areas, a wooded section, picnic shelters with grills, play areas and walkways highlight this 6½-acre park. Popular here is the fishing along the bulkheaded lake.

GREENBRIER SPORTS PARK

Greenbrier Pkwy.   547-6400

When you come here, get ready to play! A 12-acre site, this sports park lives up to its name with eight tournament-quality lighted tennis courts and two tournament-quality softball fields. For spectators, there's also a picnic shelter and play equipment.

Portsmouth

CITY PARK

City Hall Ave.   393-5162

Tucked behind the tombstones of the Olive Branch Cemetery are 93 gorgeous acres of well-maintained golf course, six lighted tennis courts, boat docks, duck ponds, gardens and playgrounds. Voted best park in the state in 1989 by the Vir-

Attention Birdwatchers

With a strategic East Coast location, Virginia's Chesapeake Bay region is a birding hotspot that draws birdwatchers from many states. The fall is a great time for viewing since the region is part of the flyway leading to warmer climates. But no matter the time of year, you'll see a variety of birds ranging from terns to migrating songbirds and eagles.

Bring out the binoculars and head to the following locations for some excellent viewing.

• In Virginia Beach: Back Bay National Wildlife Refuge, Fort Story and Seashore State Park.

• In Norfolk: The Hermitage in the Lochaven neighborhood, Norfolk Botanical Garden and Weyanoke Sanctuary in the West Ghent section of the city.

• In Chesapeake: Northwest River Park.

• In Suffolk: Dismal Swamp National Wildlife Refuge.

• In Portsmouth: Craney Island.

• On the Eastern Shore: Kiptopeke State Park, Eastern Shore National Wildlife Refuge, the Chincoteague National Wildlife Refuge and the Assateague National Seashore.

• In Newport News: The Mariners' Museum grounds and Newport News City Park.

For more birding tips call one of the two local Audubon chapters at 481-2538 or 588-8410.

ginia Parks and Recreation Association, City Park borders the western branch of the Elizabeth River and Baines Creek. The highlight for little ones is the real live mini-train, a coal-fired engine called Pokey Smokey with open seating behind, that whistles its way through a tunnel and around a pond . . . a real treat of an attraction that was overhauled a year or so ago along with the rest of the park. This is an absolutely delightful place to spend a lazy day — with or without children.

SLEEPY HOLE PARK

Sleepy Hole Rd.   393-5056

Once the plantation of Amadeo Obici, the Italian immigrant who founded the Planters Peanut Company, Sleepy Hole Park was purchased by the city of Portsmouth in 1972 and has since developed into a premier playground for area residents. Along with the popular Sleepy Hole Golf Course, the park boasts a well-stocked lake for fishing, nature trails through the tidal marsh that surrounds the park (including one trail especially constructed so that the handicapped can use it with ease), picnic shelters and playgrounds. A camper's favorite spot, there are 50 camping sites available under the tall oaks — 28 tent sites with water, tables and grills and another 22 with electric and water hookups. Campers also have access to modern rest room facilities with hot showers and a laundry area.

CHURCHLAND PARK

Cedar Ln.   393-8481

This open space, 38-acre community park is home to six soccer fields, two softball fields, a BMX bicycle track, playgrounds and picnic shelters equipped with grills. There are also trails for biking, jogging and leisurely nature walks.

RIVERFRONT PARK

At the Foot of High St.   393-8481

A delightful little park that runs along the banks of the Elizabeth River, Riverfront is the place to relax and just watch the ships glide by. Nearby, you'll find the Lightship Museum, Naval Shipyard Museum, Portside and the Elizabeth River Ferry.

Recreation and Community Centers

Got an urge to learn to tap dance? Weave an Appalachian basket? Strum a guitar? Master your swimming skills? Hampton Roads not only has the talented teachers but the easy-to-get-to facilities where you can take classes on the cheap . . . and have a fantastic time while you're at it!

Special programs, classes and activities are scheduled year round in each of the area's cities, and held at their respective recreation facilities. Because programs change seasonally, we won't be able to be more specific than to say that whatever you've got the urge to do, you'll likely find it coming up in the next class session. In most cases, the following centers are open daily from 10 AM until 6 PM, with some offering various night time hours that change from winter to summer. A call to check on your nearest center's hours is recommended.

Norfolk

To use any of Norfolk's 25 recreation centers, you must obtain a facility use card. Cost of the card is $5 for youths ages 5 to 17 and $10 for adults ages 18 to 64. The cards are available at two sites:

Sherwood Recreation Center, 4537 Little John Road, 441-5824

Huntersville Recreation Center, 830 Goff Street, 441-1545

You will not need a card if you attend a fee-based class or attend a special event or meeting at any of the facilities, and both "good grade" and family discounts are available. You can also get a tempo-

Fox Run Tr. ●
Long Creek Tr. ◉

Photo: Virginia Beach Convention and Visitor Development

Seashore State Park offers numerous trails for recreation and fun.

rary three-day pass to give you an opportunity to check out the facility before you purchase a card.

RECREATION CENTERS

Bayview, 1434 Bayview Boulevard, 441-1768

Berkley, 89 Liberty Street, 543-1230

Southside (Seniors), 500 South Main Street, 441-1911

Bolling Green, 1319 Godfrey Avenue, 441-2746

Crossroads, 8044 Tidewater Drive, 441-1769

Diggs Town, 1401 Melon Street, 441-1975

East Ocean View, 9520 20th Bay Street, 441-1785

Fairlawn, 1132 Wade Street, 441-5670

Grandy Village, 3017 Kimball Terrace, 441-2856

Huntersville, 830 Goff Street, 441-1545

Ingleside, 940 Ingleside Road, 441-5675

Lakewood (Dance/Music), 1612 Willow Wood Drive, 441-5833

Larchmont, 1167 Bolling Avenue, 441-5411

Merrimac Landing, 8809 Monitor Way, 441-1783

Northside Pool, 8400 Tidewater Drive, 441-1760

Norview, 6800 Sewells Point Road, 441-5836

Ocean View (Seniors), 600 East Ocean View Avenue, 441-1767

Park Place, 620 W. 29th Street, 441-1346

Sewells Point, 7928 Hampton Boulevard, 441-5393

Sherwood, 4537 Little John Drive, 441-5824

Tarrallton, 2100 Tarrallton Drive, 441-1765

Theater Arts, 912 21st Street, 441-2160

Therapeutic Recreation, 180 East Evans Street, 441-1764

Titustown Center for Arts & Recreation, 7545 Diven Street, 441-5394

Young Terrace, 804 Cumberland Street, 441-2754

For information concerning specific activities:

Athletics	*441-2149*
Senior Citizens	*441-2109*
Special Events	*441-2140*

THERAPEUTIC RECREATION

The City of Norfolk sponsors a complete year-round program for children and adults with disabilities, from clinics and workshops, sports classes (swimming, golf, tennis, horseback riding and more) to field trips. The Therapeutic Recreation Unit at 180 East Evans Street in Bayview Park boasts a kitchen with lower countertops and work areas that are wheelchair accessible, plus a fresh new look throughout workshops and game rooms. Special events are free and open to the public; class fees range from $6 to $25. For a full schedule and details, call 441-1764 (V/TDD). Note: If you are hearing impaired, press your space bar so that the staff will know you are calling on TDD.

COMMUNITY CENTERS

JEWISH COMMUNITY CENTER
7300 Newport Ave.   *489-1371*

Here you can backstroke any day of the year, thanks to an indoor heated pool protected by a huge domed skylight roof. The gymnasium is almost always a noisy place, thanks to the pickup basketball games you'll find on almost any given day. Ditto for the well-equipped exercise room. The center offers a wide variety of programs for all ages, and membership fees are very reasonable for the beautiful facilities. You need not be Jewish to join.

BOYS & GIRLS CLUBS OF
SOUTH HAMPTON ROADS
W. W. HOUSTON MEMORIAL CLUB
3401 Azalea Garden Rd.   855-8908

Swimming, cheerleading, football, wrestling, cooking and crafts . . . all this and more is offered to kids 6 to 17 years. The large pool is the central focus year round, from lifeguard training to classes designed for babies. Annual membership is $15, with additional fees for special classes and training.

DOWNTOWN NORFOLK YMCA
312 Bute St.   622-9622

It's definitely "the thing" to belong to this outstanding facility located in the heart of Downtown Norfolk in the historic Freemason district. Businessmen and women trade in their suits for jogging shorts and hit the newly expanded cardio-fitness room or one of a zillion aerobics classes before work, at lunch or at the end of the day. Swim laps in the new indoor aquatic center, play racquetball, basketball or volleyball . . . it's all here, and there's always someone to play and strain with. Extra perks are babysitting services available for some classes, along with a super summer camp program and fitness evaluations. Corporate memberships are available.

YWCA
253 West Freemason   625-4248

Right around the corner from "The Y" is a community center dedicated totally to the needs of Hampton Roads women. An exceptional hotline and shelter is offered for battered women, 625-5570, along with timely programs such as "Women in Transition." The staff is small, but thoroughly knowledgeable, sympathetic to problems and applauded by many who have found their services invaluable.

ARMED SERVICES YMCA
500 East Ocean View Ave.   480-3744

One of 50 such facilities in this country and overseas, the purpose of the Armed Services YMCA is to serve as a bridge between the civilian and military communities of our area. The main focus is on recreation for military families, along with spiritual and social programs for all ages. Especially helpful are their special programs for military spouses on subjects ranging from job searching to aerobics to cooking and crafts.

WILLIAM A. HUNTON YMCA
1139 East Charlotte St.   622-7271

The stated purpose of this special YMCA is to "nurture positive self image, develop leadership skills and assist in fostering positive values in our youth." Established to help children and youths who might otherwise be "just hanging out" or a number in the juvenile justice system, the center gears its programs and activities to meet the special needs of these kids, many of whom are from single-parent or low-income families. After school and day care, team sports, youth employment, summer camps and a number of other activities are scheduled year round.

Virginia Beach

Since you can't always go play on the beach, Virginia Beach operates excellent recreation facilities that seem to be jammed with activity almost every day of the year. The program offerings suit practically every taste, from arts and crafts, dance, music, drama and, of course, SPORTS! It almost seems as if no one dares to leave the house without some sort of ball or racquet in their hands. So, if you're a newcomer, the best way to fit right in is to get yourself over to a rec center and learn a sport. You'll meet a lot of nifty people when you do. And, if you're visiting, it's great to have the opportunity to continue your favorite sport while you're away from home.

You'll need a Facility Use Card to use any of the Virginia Beach Rec facilities. For children 6 to 17, the fee is $10; adults 18 to 64, $25. Seniors above age 65 can snag a lifetime membership, the Golden Age Club, for $50. Want to check out the facilities for a day? Get a guest pass for just $3.

RECREATION CENTERS

KEMPSVILLE RECREATION CENTER
800 Monmouth Ln.   474-8492

Here's a huge center serving as headquarters for six popular city programs: Aquatic Services, Athletic Services, Youth Services, the Preschool Program, Adult Services and the Kempsville Playhouse for the performing arts. Highlights include a 25-meter, six-lane indoor pool, a 200-seat theater, youth lounge and game room, two automatic bowling lanes, a gym and exercise room and a number of other rooms that are used for special programs and classes. Outside, there's a lot

more: six lighted tennis courts, six basketball courts, a children's playground, two softball fields, three volleyball courts, two horseshoe pits, picnic area and open spaces for soccer and football. There's also a therapeutic track and field practice course.

BOW CREEK RECREATION CENTER
3427 Clubhouse Rd.   431-3765

A fairly new and attractive center — the lobby even has a fireplace — Bow Creek hosts classes and programs for children, youths, adults and seniors. Especially popular with the kids is a fully equipped game room that's open daily with two billiard tables, table tennis, footsball, bumper pool and other games. For seniors, they can take advantage of a bridge club, ballroom and square dancing, along with lots of special field trips.

OTHER VIRGINIA BEACH RECREATION CENTERS

Bayside Recreation Center, First Court Road, 460-7540

Great Neck Recreation Center, 2521 Shorehaven Drive, 496-6766

Seatack Community Center, 141 South Birdneck Road, 437-4858

Princess Anne Recreation Center, Ferrell Parkway at General Booth Boulevard (opening mid 1994)

THERAPEUTIC RECREATION

A number of programs, many at no fee, are offered for children and adults

If you're headed for a swim in the Chesapeake Bay, pack a jar of meat tenderizer in that beach bag. It's the most effective treatment for soothing the burn of a stinging nettle (jellyfish) sting.

Insiders' Tips

The Great Dismal Swamp

One of the most asked about attractions in Hampton Roads also is one of its most inaccessible. At area convention and visitor's bureaus, the world-renowned Great Dismal Swamp draws frequent inquiries. But unlike many attractions, there are few campgrounds and hiking trails, and many parts of it are accessible only by small boats. Despite its remoteness, the swamp manages to attract more than 10,000 visitors a year.

The 200,000-acre wilderness is much more than pure swamp and is one of the largest natural areas on the East Coast. It is considered one of the most scenic spots in Virginia and North Carolina with lush greenery, cypress trees, calm waters and an incredible variety of wildlife. Among its residents are bears, bobcats, otters, weasels, frogs, 23 fish species, bats and butterflies. More than 200 different kinds of birds have been sighted in the swamp, which is also a haven for swarms of mosquitoes and 21 varieties of snakes. The swamp also has about 1,000 square miles of primeval forest.

Col. William Byrd gave the swamp its gloomy name in 1728. Thirty-five years later George Washington surveyed the swamp and dreamed of draining it and cutting the timber on the 40,000 acres he and several other businessmen owned in the swamp. In 1793 slaves started digging at both ends of a 22-mile canal, which took 12 years to complete. It is still in use today, making it the oldest operating artificial waterway in the United States. The swamp's canal, which has two sets of locks, is an alternate route for the Atlantic Intracoastal Waterway and during spring and fall is lined with yachts headed to and from Florida. It connects the Deep Creek area of Chesapeake with Elizabeth City, North Carolina. The canal is on the National Register of Historic Places and is a National Civil Engineering Landmark.

A second waterway, the Albemarle and Chesapeake Canal was dug through the swamp between 1855 and 1859. It runs from the Great Bridge area of Chesapeake to the Albemarle Sound in North Carolina.

There are several ways to take in the beauty of the swamp, which spreads through Chesapeake and Suffolk as well as northeastern North Carolina:

• In Suffolk there is the Great Dismal Swamp Wildlife Refuge operated by the U.S. Fish and Wildlife Service, 986-3705. The office there is staffed from 7 AM to 3 PM Monday through Friday, and the refuge is open from a half hour before sunrise to a half-hour after sunset. From the refuge you can hike or bike along a 4.5-mile road beside the Washington Ditch, named for George Washington who dug the first spade of dirt to create the canal. The Washington Ditch ends up at Lake Drummond, the largest natural lake in Virginia.

There also is a 7-mile road along the Jericho Ditch that leads to the lake, but it is not maintained as well as the shorter route. For the less hardy or those with small children, there is a half-mile boardwalk. Meandering along it will give you a feel for the swamp.

To get to the refuge take Route 58 to Suffolk, turn left on E. Washington Street (Route 337) and go left on White Marsh Road (Route 642). Look for the refuge signs and turn into the Washington Ditch entrance, which has a parking lot.

• In Chesapeake you can enter a 3.5-mile feeder ditch if you have a small boat or canoe. It is across the Dismal Swamp Canal on Route 17 (George Washington Highway), about 3 miles north of the North Carolina border. There is a city-owned boat ramp and parking lot on Route 17 a mile north of the feeder ditch entrance. You can rent a canoe from the Chesapeake KOA Campground on Route 17, 485-5686. It is about 8 miles north of the feeder ditch entrance. Canoe rental costs $2 an hour or $15 a day.

If you're handy with a paddle, it will take about two hours to maneuver down the ditch to Lake Drummond where the Corps of Engineers maintains a rustic campground. Bathrooms with toilets and sinks are on site but there are no showers or running water. You will find grills, picnic tables, places for campfires and two screened dining areas. No reservations are required, and camping is free. For information call 421-7401. Remember that access to Lake Drummond is only by foot, bicycle or boats weighing less than 1,000 pounds.

To see the swamp, you can also drive to North Carolina down Route 17 S., also known as George Washington Highway, and look at dense woods that border the road. There are several picnic areas along the way.

• Just 3 miles over the state line in South Mills, North Carolina, is the Dismal Swamp Canal Visitor Welcome Center run by the state of North Carolina. It prides itself on being the only visitors center in the country whose clients come by both boat and car. The center provides brochures and maps, has a helpful staff to answer questions and maintains a picnic area. There is a 150-foot dock at the center. Each year about 2,000 boaters tie up there for the night. The center is open Tuesday through Saturday.

• In April 1993 visitors got a new way to absorb the beauty of the swamp. A joint venture between the Portsmouth Department of Tourism and the Elizabeth City Area Chamber of Commerce in North Carolina created cruises along the Great Dismal Swamp Canal. One-day trips in May and October take adventurers from Hampton Roads down the canal on the *Carrie B.* They return by chartered bus the same day. The cost is $79 per person. For details, call Harbor Tours at 393-4735.

who are physically, mentally or emotionally disabled. They include instructional classes and recreational programs to promote independence and are found at the following locations:

Center for Effective Learning, 233 N. Witchduck Road

Main Office, Dept. of Parks and Recreation, 2289 Lynnhaven Parkway

Bow Creek Recreation Center, 3427 Clubhouse Road

Kempsville Recreation Center, 800 Monmouth Lane

For detailed information and program schedules, call 471-5884.

COMMUNITY CENTERS

UNITED WAY FAMILY CENTER
4441 South Blvd.   *499-2311*

If you're traveling on the Norfolk-Virginia Beach Expressway (I-44/264) by Mount Trashmore, you'll spot a sprawling brick building with a parking lot jammed with cars. How that many people can pack the United Way Family Center every day of the year amazes us all, but perhaps it's because the facilities and programs offered are some of the finest in the city. You can swim in the heated pool, learn a little balance beam, play tennis or work out in their fitness center. In summer families love the new outdoor swimming pool. Housed here are a number of charitable organizations, including the YMCA of Virginia Beach, The Boy's and Girl's Clubs of Virginia Beach, Big Brothers/Big Sisters, Family Services and the Retired Senior Volunteer Program. Newcomers should put this top-notch center on one of their first-to-check-out lists.

INDIAN RIVER FAMILY YMCA
5660 Indian River Rd.   *366-0448*

Taking center stage at the University Shoppes across from CBN University is this Y, which looks more like an expensive spa-place. Along with family fitness programs for every level, you'll find a large free weight selection and preschool and before- and after-school care programs.

Chesapeake

It's soccer, basketball and ballet! It's volleyball, quilting and karate! It's more activities, classes, daytrips and workshops than one person can squeeze into a lifetime. But, come on, give it a try. Just hook up with the City of Chesapeake's Parks and Rec facilities and it's bye-bye spare time.

Chesapeake operates six community centers that each feature a full plate of activities and classes. You'll find squeaky-clean gyms and lockers at all, along with weight rooms, kitchens and outdoor sports facilities. Membership and I.D. cards for residents are $5 per year for adults, $2 for kids 9 through 17, free for seniors. One day guest passes are available for $3.

RECREATION CENTERS

Deep Creek Community Center, 2901 Margaret Booker Drive, 487-8841

Great Bridge Community Center, 212 Holt Drive, 547-6292

Indian River Community Center, 2250 Old Greenbrier Road, 547-6292

River Crest Community Center, 1001 Riverwalk Parkway, 436-3100

South Norfolk Community Center, 1217 Godwin Avenue, 543-5721

Western Branch Community Center, 4437 Portsmouth Boulevard, 465-0211

COMMUNITY CENTERS

CHESAPEAKE FAMILY YMCA
1033 Greenbrier Pkwy.   *547-9622*

Adjacent to the city's sports complex, this beautiful, modern facility comes complete with all the sports trappings: a large swimming pool, complete Nautilus center, saunas, showers and locker rooms and large activity room. Take your pick of classes, from scuba diving and gymnastics to aerobics and martial arts. Working moms are particularly fond of the center's Before and After School Fun Club, available for elementary school children and a wonderful, activity-packed program for "latchkey" kids. The Y's summer day camp called Y.E.S. (Youth Experience Summer Program) is especially popular with Chesapeake children.

GREENBRIER NORTH FAMILY YMCA
2100 Old Greenbrier Rd.   *366-9622*

Bring the family to sweat together on this Y's racquetball courts or in the gym. They've just added a new kindergarten program to their excellent before- and after-school programs.

THERAPEUTIC RECREATION

Chesapeake extends a particular welcome for children and adults with disabilities. A full schedule of programs, classes and trips is on the agenda, and many are free. Preschool and after-school programs are also offered. Volunteers are always needed to assist during activities, so if you've got some spare time, this would be a rewarding way to pass an afternoon. For information and assistance, call 547-6639. If you require a TDD, call Chesapeake's main library at 436-8300 to serve as a relay station.

Portsmouth

The game's the same, only the place and people have changed. Any activity, class, workshop or program you can find in other Hampton Roads cities, you can find here at any one of the eight recreation centers operated by the City of Portsmouth. Arts and crafts, games, field trips and the real popular adult softball, basketball and volleyball leagues are par for the frantic pace.

As in other cities, the facilities vary from neighborhood to neighborhood, but all feature gymnasiums and lockers, exercise equipment and activity rooms.

RECREATION CENTERS

Cavalier Manor Recreation Center, 404 Viking Street, 393-8757

Craddock Recreation Center, 45 Afton Parkway, 393-8757

Hi-Landers Recreation Center, 409 McLean Street, 393-8441

Joseph E. Parker Recreation Center, 2430 Turnpike Road, 393-8340

Kingman Heights Recreation Center, 105 Utah Street, 393-8839

Neighborhood Facility, 900 Elm Street, 393-8595

Port Norfolk Recreation Center, 432 Broad Street, 393-8709

COMMUNITY CENTERS

PORTSMOUTH YMCA
527 High St.   *397-3413*

One of the most popular features of the Portsmouth Y is the indoor running track, so you can deliver your laps through wind, rain or snow. Also aboard: pool, gymnasium, basketball, handball and volleyball courts, exercise/weight lifting rooms and sauna, steam room and whirlpool. A variety of classes and fitness evaluations is offered to both regular and corporate members.

EFFINGHAM YMCA
1013 Effingham St.   *398-9348*

You know you're seeing pride and

There's a new, free map available for outdoorsy types who are drawn to the backroads and byways of Virginia. Called A Map of Scenic Roads in Virginia, it offers travel suggestions for more than 2,000 miles of roads that are off the beaten path. Call (800) VA-LOVE or look for one at local travel centers.

Insiders' Tips

practice in motion when you spot the award-winning special drill team from the Effingham Y march in a local parade! This is but one of the outstanding results of the leadership at this Y, which offers a family night program, youth Bible class and a golden age club. Activities include everything from judo and karate to crocheting and ballet, all in a facility that houses a gymnasium, basketball court, pool tables and meeting rooms. A new outdoor pool has been added for cooling off in the summer heat.

ARMED SERVICES YMCA
509 King St. 397-1675

Serving the Portsmouth Naval Shipyard, Portsmouth Naval Hospital and the Coast Guard Support Center, this Y provides recreational and social opportunities to military personnel and their families. It is part of the Armed Services branch of the national YMCA, which began during the Civil War when 5,000 civilian volunteers provided aid to soldiers of both North and South. Today, it serves not only as a complement to programs offered by the military, but offers many dances, parties and social events. Men with a night off from their ships often stay over in comfortable dormitory-type rooms.

NEW GOSPORT FAMILY PROGRAM CENTER
25 Stack St. 396-2047

This fairly new center was opened as a branch of the Armed Services YMCA to provide support for military wives. Along with their very popular support groups, the center offers aerobics and arts and crafts classes, with babysitting available for women attending these programs.

THERAPEUTIC RECREATION

A packed calendar of activities is available for children and adults, each geared to accommodate a specific disability. For full information concerning class offerings, schedules and fees, call 393-8481.

Inside
Golf

From the sting of Honey Bee to the agony of Hell's Point, if you're a golfer, you might as well admit you've come to duffer's paradise. Not only will our average 60 degree temperatures keep your bag parked at the front door almost every day of the year, but our depth of courses will call to you in your dreams. And, because Hampton Roads is such a friendly place, even if you're on your own, you can pick up a foursome at practically any time, although weekends are tougher to access popular tee times unless your golfing buddies are in place.

You'll soon realize you're never alone on any of our courses. According to the National Golf Association, there are 518,000 golfers 12 and older in Virginia, a quarter of whom call Hampton Roads home. That's nearly 10 percent of our population, each and every one of whom has their favorite courses and holes yet to conquer.

Across Hampton Roads, there are beautifully maintained courses — public and private — that will test every club in your bag. Unless you can almost qualify for the PGA tour, those in the know suggest you control your urge to play the bigtime links unless you have stock in the golf ball industry and have more room on your score card to fill in those triple figures. Our area's proud to boast of some of the state's toughest advanced courses, and they got their reputation for good reason. If you're long on ambition but short of temper, it's best to wait until you can confidently break 100 before you consider shelling out greens and cart fees for the most difficult courses. Take it from the pros . . . wide fairways, few sand traps and little or no water hazards will make your 18 a lot more pleasurable if your clubs still have their initial shine.

To that end, we'll list all the play possibilities not only by city, but by ability to

Golfers enjoy a round at Honeybee Golf Course in Virginia Beach.

Photo: Virginia Beach Convention and Visitor Development

really enjoy yourself. We've also included the "Toughest Holes" as defined by some of the area's leading pros.

Fees for play vary as wildly as the complexity of the courses. You can whack at the ball on most of our local basic courses for an average of $10, intermediates for about $20 and killers for around $40. Guess it's a quirk of nature that the more pain you want to inflict on yourself, the more you'll pay. So step up to the white tees, or blue if you dare … and ping your way into one of the most popular sports in Hampton Roads.

The Basic, Beautiful Courses

Virginia Beach

BOW CREEK GOLF COURSE
3425 Club House Rd. 431-3763

Thank goodness, here you'll find wide and forgiving fairways, few man-made hazards and trees. This par 72, 6,800-yard course does have small greens and sharp doglegs along some fairly ominous wooded roughs, so we're not exactly talking cake walk. Even so, it's quite a reasonable course, with greens fees to match. Ask about seniors and juniors special discounts.

KEMPSVILLE GREENS MUNICIPAL GOLF COURSE
4840 Princess Anne Rd. 474-8441

A Russ Breeden-designed 6,200-yard, par 70, this course has the devilish habit of confiscating your ball in one of its three lakes or thick woods. There are some fine greens and an excellent driving range at this city-owned facility. Super senior discounts, too.

Portsmouth

CITY PARK GOLF COURSE
Portsmouth City Park 393-8005

Let's start easy. This nine-hole course is really the easiest to test your clubs on in the area. It's the perfect place for juniors and others just getting their first taste of the golf bug. Matching the ease of the course are the truly affordable fees for both unlimited weekday and 36-hole weekend play.

Norfolk

LAKE WRIGHT GOLF COURSE
6280 Northampton Blvd. 461-6251

Sure, it appears easy enough, what with the practically wide open front nine. But make the turn and you'll find trees and water along the back nine — as well as nasty prevailing winds — and your glorious score may just take a downward spiral. Even so, No. 5, a testy par 3, is a 190-yard nightmare over Lake Wright, and judged the fourth toughest hole to play in the area. If you make it over the lake, you're up against a trap to the left and bunker to the right of the green. Just pray the wind's going in your direction. For extra practice, however, there is one of the best driving ranges in the area, plus a pro shop.

Insiders' Tips

Virginia Beach's popular golf packages include 12 different courses. Call 437-4700 or (800) 882-3224 for details.

OCEAN VIEW GOLF COURSE
9610 Norfolk Ave. 480-2094

Many area golfers describe this course as "flat," but the straight, if narrow, fairways, a few sharp doglegs and trap-lined greens give it a bit of a challenge. During the week you can play this 5,900-yard course with cart for less than $20. Ask about the special two-fer for weekday play.

Intermediate Play

Portsmouth

SLEEPY HOLE GOLF COURSE
Sleepy Hole Rd. 393-5050

Even though it's long and surrounded by water, the secluded Suffolk location of this City of Portsmouth-owned course offers little distraction, or excuses, from city noise and bustle. It boasts the second-toughest hole in the area, the par 4, 423-yard 18th that requires a long, slight draw off the tee to clear the rolling hill and carry down the open fairway to within 180 yards of the green. Don't even think about the marshes of the Nansemond River on the left and Clubhouse and trap on the right as you land on the green. Just lob your second shot short, chip and pray.

BIDE-A-WEE GOLF COURSE
Greenwood Dr. 393-5269

This par 72, 6,308-yard beauty is not only a pretty rough trip for even a fairly good shotmaker, it boasts the number one toughest hole in our area . . . the 405-yard No. 8. If you've got a booming tee shot,

you're looking at a narrow, critical landing area flanked by sentinel oaks. Ahead there's more to outsmart you on this, one of the longer dogleg par 4s in the area . . . an elevated green with water hazard to the left and woods that flank the entire right side of the hole. Just try and break 73, the course record that stood for many years.

Virginia Beach

HONEY BEE GOLF COURSE
5016 S. Independence Blvd. 471-2768

Designed by Rees Jones, Honey Bee is a 6,700-yard challenge, what with its 80 monstrous sand traps, elevated tees and water on 10 holes. Virginia Beach's newest golf course, it's privately owned but open to the public, and is home to the Virginia Beach Golf Academy, an assemblage of four of the finest teaching professionals in the area. Carts are required at peak time on weekends.

OWL'S CREEK GOLF CENTER
415 South Birdneck Rd. 428-2800

Designed by Brook Parker, this is a great course for the golfer who wants to pack 18 into three hours or less. Dubbed "The Little Monster," this executive 4,155-yard, par 62 course, all par 4s and 5s, does offer the opportunity for extra practice on its lighted driving range and super practice putting greens.

RED WING LAKE GOLF COURSE
1080 Prosperity Rd. 437-4845

The greens are large and fairways are

Hampton Roads can boast about its 40 golf courses with more than 1,000 holes. Even so, it's imperative that you call in advance for preferred tee times, especially on weekends.

Hampton Roads offers some of the Virginia's toughest advanced courses.

wide . . . but you'll still have to face water hazards on 10 holes and 84 traps along the fairways and long sloping greens. If you're adept at short iron shots, have at the par 5 No. 18, the ninth-toughest hole in the area. It not only challenges your birdie with the lake in front of the heavily trapped green, but tests accuracy just getting there through a narrowing fairway.

STUMPY LAKE GOLF COURSE

4797 Indian River Rd.   467-6119

This is one to write home about. A Robert Trent Jones-designed 6,757-yard course, Stumpy Lake is surrounded by water on four sides and entered via a bridge. Amateurs and professionals alike fear the par 4, 400-yard No. 5, the 10th-toughest hole in the region. The dogleg right to an elevated, gently trapped green presents a hint of the difficulty that awaits. Your choice at the tee is directly over the trees or a long fade or slice to hold the fairway. And, don't count on the green to hold a flat approach shot. At least you can enjoy the quiet tranquility of the secluded location.

Suffolk

SUFFOLK GOLF COURSE

1227 Highland Rd.   539-6298

With wide fairways on the front nine and narrow ones on the back, Suffolk claims a birdie killer with its par 5, 450-yard No. 18, the 18th-toughest hole in the area. A gambler's hole, it's dominated by a lake that begins on the left side of the fairway and lingers to about 20 yards short of the narrow green. If you make it through the 15-yard wide fairway, look out for the traps to the right, left and rear of the green.

Chesapeake

SEVEN SPRINGS GOLF COURSE

1201 Club House Dr.   436-2512

A relatively mild yet fairly tight course, as of this writing only 10 of 18 holes are open for play, but the management was expecting all holes to be open by June of 1995. Play weekdays for less than 10 bucks and for only $12 on weekends.

Killer Courses

Virginia Beach

HELL'S POINT GOLF CLUB

2700 Atwoodtown Rd.   *721-3400*

Designed by Rees Jones, the 6,900-yard Hell's Point has been rated one of the top 130 courses in the country by the Golf Architects of America. If you survive the three large lakes and 61 sand traps, you'll still have great stories to tell about the snake that fought you for your ball in the dangerous rough. Watch out for the 389-yard No. 2, judged the 11th-toughest hole in the region. It's a long par 4 with a narrow fairway and double-trapped green. For the thrill of defeat, you can reserve a tee-time a week in advance, and carts are required for play.

CYPRESS POINT GOLF & COUNTRY CLUB

5340 Club Head Rd.   *490-8822*

So beautiful, the Bermuda fairways and rough and lush bent grass greens. Ha! Pack your bag heavy for this 6,740-yard, par 72 romp through a killer designed by Tom Clark of Ault Clark Associates. Just step up to the 469-yard, par 4 No. 7, judged the 14th-toughest hole in the area. It's another long tee shot to a dogleg right, bunkered left and right. Be-fore you: a huge, elevated green trapped on three sides. You could be looking at a 100-footer, and putting over a tier. Good luck. On the backside, is the picturesque 17th, a 175-yard, par 3 with water and front and a three-tiered green.

Private Courses

There are several private courses in Hampton Roads worth chumming up to a member to play. This is where well-heeled residents take in 18 to practice their swings . . . all beautiful courses with equally beautiful clubhouses waiting at the end of a round.

Of real excitement to local swingers longing for a new 19th hole, there are a couple of brand new clubs on the horizon. Plans are proceeding for Bayville Golf Club to be built on 200 acres along Pleasure House Creek, with course design by one of the very best: Tom Fazio. Membership will be limited to 350, with the general membership drive now under way. The public sector, not to be caught in the rough, has announced the purchase of 185 acres near the Virginia Beach Municipal Center for construction of a state-of-the-art course to be named West Neck Golf Course. Brassie Golf Corp. of Southport, North Carolina, is now busily at work on course design.

"Driving" ambition is the goal of Golf-O-Rama, the end-all to local driving ranges. There are covered tees on the practice range so you can test that Big Bertha in any kind of weather, plus there are separate greens for both putting and chipping. Try out the challenging 18-hole Seascape Mini-Golf Course, and then turn to the PGA Pro to sign up for lessons. Speed that cart to Golf-O-Rama, 920 South Military Highway, 424-3114.

Insiders' Tips

Portsmouth

ELIZABETH MANOR

1 Ace Parker Dr.   *488-4534*

Area pros agree that Elizabeth Manor's 14th and 15th are the toughest back-to-back holes in Hampton Roads. We'll take you right to No. 14, where long off the tee is the only way to a relatively flat green with bunker and out-of-bounds left and a small knoll to the right. Then cart straight to No. 15, where a long, accurate tee shot of at least 270 or so is a prerequisite to clear the drive bunkers. This hole plays especially sinister a few days before or after the Eastern Amateur in August when the rough is longest and thickest. If you're keeping score, the 14th was judged the 16th-toughest hole; the 15th right up there at the fifth-toughest in the region.

Virginia Beach

CAVALIER GOLF & YACHT CLUB

1052 Cardinal Rd.   *428-6161*

If you crave treacherous closing holes, here's a place you'll find nirvana. Designed to decide tournaments, a thin, carrot-shaped green waits on a hole with water on three sides, not to mention the five bunkers. This, the 18th, serves to destroy any decent score up to this point. If you bail out and hit short, chip up and putt, you might hold par. This is the third-toughest hole in the region, you know.

PRINCESS ANNE COUNTRY CLUB

38th St. & Pacific   *422-3360*

Rambling through primo Gold Coast territory, this luscious course plays host to the rich and famous of Virginia Beach. The most dangerous parts are cart paths that cross roads leading to secluded private residential communities.

BROAD BAY GREENS GOLF COURSE

2120 Lord's Landing   *496-9092*

A beautiful course that winds its way through one of Virginia Beach's newer private residential communities, this Ault and Clark designed 6,135-yard, par 70 features unique elevated tee platforms, numerous mounds and medium-sized, well-bunkered greens. The challenging second hole rated a "toughest hole" honorable mention from area pros. A treat is the handsomely appointed clubhouse, along with a tempting pro shop.

Chesapeake

GREENBRIER COUNTRY CLUB

1301 Volvo Pkwy.   *547-7375*

A course that weaves through an upwardly mobile residential community, the hole that gets attention is the long, twisting par 5 closing hole, a popular favorite among area pros. You really need to bang it here, with bunkers popping up along the fairway and a steeply elevated green. Hit short, pitch and putt on this, the seventh-toughest hole in Hampton Roads. And, look out for big club . . . it's the par 4, 461-yard No. 3 with a green that's large and flat with a two-foot bowl indention in the middle left. It's the 12th-toughest hole in the area.

Inside
Fishing

Oh, to be an angler when spring hits Hampton Roads. You can tell the season is starting because all those funny, fuzzy little lures, rods and reels start taking over shelf space where footballs used to be. Fishing frenzy hits, and the throngs head to the seas . . . each probably looking for the one that got away last season.

The beauty of it all is that you don't have to have a lot of talent or a lot of money to enjoy this sport. The basic prerequisites are patience and a lift to the nearest pier or head boat. Whether you're inshore or offshore, the biting's grand from March through December, thanks in great part to the Chesapeake Bay, considered by some marine biologists to be the country's premier spawning ground for saltwater fish. Each spring, many fish,

like striped bass, herring, shad and sturgeon, migrate to the bay's tributaries to spawn. Others, like speckled trout, flounder, spot, croaker and gray trout, call the bay home for the first stages of their lives.

Beyond the bay, the big bluefish, bluefin and yellowfin tuna, marlin, dolphin and wahoo are a hook away in the Atlantic Ocean. Likewise, there's some of the hottest angling action when the big billfish, amberjack, cobia and black drum start their summer runs.

Whether you cast a line on one of hundreds of freshwater lakes, head off to a quiet cove, drag your tackle to the nearest pier or trawl for big ones on the open ocean, your chances of a big catch are better here than almost anywhere on earth. And, that may or may not be a fish

Photo: Virginia Beach Convention and Visitor Development

Anglers show off their catch of the day.

story depending on your results on any given day.

No fishing license is required to fish in salt water. Freshwater fishing requires licenses for resident anglers 16 years and older, are valid for the calendar year January 1 through December 31, and cost $12. Nonresidents can purchase a five-day license for $6. You can pick one up at numerous places throughout the area, including most bait and tackle shops, marinas and department store sporting goods counters.

For avid anglers, take note of the Annual Virginia Saltwater Fishing Tournament, held April through November. It is a program that maintains state records and honors certain catches with a "citation," a laminated plaque that displays the angler's name, species caught, date, etc. The tournament is open to anyone, with 22 species eligible for citations. If you're interested, call the tournament's headquarters at 491-5160.

If you're a clubby kind of fisherman, there are a few local organizations who'd love to lure you in. Get the angler's angle from:

LITTLE CREEK BASSMASTERS
Chesapeake   548-3784

TIDEWATER'S ANGLER'S CLUB
Virginia Beach   496-3664

VIRGINIA BEACH ANGLER'S CLUB
Virginia Beach   481-5719

Freshwater Fishing
Fishing Piers

Norfolk

HARRISON BOAT HOUSE AND PIER
414 West Ocean View Ave.   587-9630

A Chesapeake Bay landmark on the fishing scene, this is the place to count on the biggest spot and croaker hauls. Granted, these are little league fish, most less than 12 ounces, but their numbers are incredible. Harrison's is the perfect location to be when Virginia's most popular inshore fishing season begins in late July or early August. The season lasts well into September, and even into October if mild weather continues.

WILLOUGHBY BAY MARINA
1651 Bayville St.   588-2663

Even if you're not a fisherman, this is a great place to wander on a summer's day, taking in the sights of sailboats and boaters in the Chesapeake Bay. Count on more spot and croaker than you can catch all summer long.

LAKE SMITH
5381 Shell Rd.   464-4684

One of the largest freshwater lakes in the area, Lake Smith boasts an ample supply of largemouth bass, bluegill, crappie, catfish, stripped bass and carp. Eighty boats are available for rent, or you can just cast off from shore. A fully stocked

These commercial fishing boats indicate the huge economic industry the Chesapeake Bay has.

bait and tackle shop is right there for anything a promising angler might need for a day of heavy fishing.

Portsmouth

SLEEPY HOLE PARK
Sleepy Hole Rd.   *393-5056*

Located in Suffolk, this gorgeous park with its immense mature oak trees shelters a lake well-stocked with panfish, catfish and large mouth bass. Charge is only $1 for a full day of possible frustration.

Virginia Beach

VIRGINIA BEACH FISHING PIER
15th St. and Oceanfront   *428-2333*

Fish, or just watch those who try, 24-hours a day all summer long. You can even rent a rod to try your own luck. Crabbing is also popular from this Atlantic Ocean pier, where crab cages and bait are available. Open April through October, there's a small fee to fish, even smaller fee just to watch.

LYNNHAVEN INLET FISHING PIER
Starfish Rd. off Shore Dr.   *481-7071*

Another 24-hour fish-a-thon happens here along the Chesapeake Bay all summer. Look for spot and croaker early in the season, then cast for flounder, speckled trout and puppy drum. There's a small fee to fish or watch; rod/reels rentals are available.

SEA GULL FISHING PIER
Chesapeake Bay Bridge-Tunnel
South Island   *464-4641*

Perhaps one of the country's most un-

All hail the lovely brook trout, the official state fish of the Commonwealth of Virginia. For you trivia buffs, a mussel shell called "Chesapecten Jeffersonius" is the official state fossil.

Insiders' Tips

A marina off the Chesapeake Bay docks numerous fishing boats.

usual fishing piers, Sea Gull extends 600 feet into the middle of the Chesapeake Bay. Beginning in mid-June, you might reel in a cobia of 40 pounds or more. It's also the best time to catch the biggest gray trout. There's no fee to fish here, but you will have to pay the regular $10 one-way crossing fare.

LITTLE ISLAND FISHING PIER

Sandbridge, Atlantic Ocean   426-7200

It's possible to snag a big bluefish from this pier, along with a plethora of other choppers that come close to the shoreline. A favorite summer hangout for Sandbridge visitors, there's a small fee to park as well as to fish from April through October.

Deep Sea Fishing and Marinas

How about a 1,000-pound blue marlin? Or a 50-pound white marlin? Not to mention bluefin tuna, dolphin, wahoo, false albacore, amberjack and more. They're all out in the blue waters of the Atlantic, and there are almost as many charter boats waiting to make a wake out to where they can be found.

Offshore fishing does have its price, however. Fleets sail from several sites in both Norfolk and Virginia Beach, and you can be aboard for from $300 for a day of bottom-fishing to as much as $1,000 for a jaunt out to the marlin grounds. An alternative is an outing on a headboat, so named because they charge by the person, or the "head." These headboats, which also depart from Norfolk and Virginia Beach, concentrate mainly closer to shore, with rates running from as little as $10 for a four-hour spot fishing trip to $35 for an all-day adventure.

All these charter and headboats are very popular, especially when local angler forecasters raise the checkered flag for a big score. Call well in advance to confirm availability, amenities and fees.

Norfolk

CAR HARBOR CUSTOM CHARTERS
863-3 Little Bay Ave.   587-5645

COBBS MARINA
4524 Dunning Rd.   588-5401

HARRISON BOAT HOUSE
414 West Ocean View Ave.   588-9968

WILLOUGHBY BAY MARINA
1651 Bayville St.   588-2663

Virginia Beach

VIRGINIA BEACH FISHING CENTER
200 Winston-Salem Ave.
Rudee Inlet   422-5700

D&M MARINA
3311 Shore Dr.
Lynnhaven Inlet   481-7211

BUBBA'S MARINA
3323 Shore Dr.
Lynnhaven Inlet   481-3513

INLET STATION MARINA
Foot of Mediterranean Ave.   422-2999

LYNNHAVEN MARINE CENTER
2150 West Great Neck Rd.   481-0700

LYNNHAVEN MUNICIPAL MARINA
Lynnhaven Inlet   481-7137

LYNNHAVEN WATERWAY MARINA
2101 North Great Neck Rd.   481-7517

FISHERMAN'S WHARF MARINA
524 Winston-Salem Ave.
Rudee Inlet   428-2111

Inside
Tennis

You've got the gear, you've got the serve, you've even got the backhand. But do you have a court to call your own? Yes! There are literally hundreds of free courts for the volleying throughout Hampton Roads, and one of them is sure to be lit at night for that after-work workout.

Virginia Beach alone has more than 188 public tennis courts, Norfolk, 150, most of which are lighted and may be played at no charge. The majority of these public courts can be found in the parks and schools maintained by each individual city. Here, we'll give you the locations of the most popular courts in each locale, and highlight those specific ones where classes are offered. Also note the private, indoor facilities listed for each city.

Norfolk

TIDEWATER TENNIS CENTER
1159 Lance Rd.   461-3015

Not only can you play indoors and out here, but you can also be videotaped to reveal every single flaw in your game. Instructors are forgiving and encouraging, however, so it's a great place to winter your game in preparation for the big time.

NORTHSIDE PARK
8400 Tidewater Dr.   441-2149

Headquarters for Norfolk tennis activity is Northside Park, where classes for all levels are offered seasonally by resident pros. Many of the city's tournaments are held here at a facility that offers lighted courts to soothe night-owl lobs.

Other city courts, most of which are lighted:

Azalea Garden Jr. High School, 7721 Azalea Garden Road

Barraud Park, Barraud Avenue

Booker T. Washington High School, 1300 Virginia Beach Boulevard

Granby High School, 7101 Granby Street

Lafayette City Park, 3500 Granby Street

Lake Taylor High School, 1380 Kempsville Road

Larchmont Park, 5210 Hampton Boulevard

Little Creek Elementary School, Tarpin & Little Creek roads

Maury High School, 322 Shirley Avenue

Norview High School, Middleton Place

Ocean View Elementary School, 9501 Mason Creek Road

Ocean View Recreation Center, 600 Ocean View Avenue

St. Helena Elementary School, 903 South Main Street

Virginia Beach

VIRGINIA BEACH TENNIS AND COUNTRY CLUB
1950 Thomas Bishop Ln.   481-7545

If you see a car packed with tennis players in a rare severe cold snap, chances are they're headed here. Of course, you'll have to be a member, but if you're a got-to-play fanatic, this is the place to be. Six indoor courts plus 30 outdoor courts are just an appetizer for what's available, including both group and private lessons from some of the most patient, encouraging pros in the area. The vibes from all the tennis mavericks who wander around only make the experience all the more invigorating — or intimidating, depending on your skill level. Check out the excellent junior academy in the summer, as well as the swimming pool, exercise room, sauna, Jacuzzi and pro shop.

OWL'S CREEK MUNICIPAL TENNIS CENTER
928 South Birdneck Rd.   *437-4804*

Secluded, shady, well-lighted . . . this is just for starters. Named one of the 50 best municipal tennis centers in the country by *Tennis Magazine*, here the grand-slam want-to-be's can find expert instruction from U.S.P.T.A. and U.S.P.T.R. instructors who conduct private and group lessons as well as various clinics. On hand are 12 hard-surface and two tournament courts, with seating for 1,300 spectators. Fees vary, as well as reservation requirements, so do check in advance.

LYNNHAVEN JUNIOR HIGH SCHOOL
1250 Bayne Dr.

This is a super popular place to test the reaction to your new tennis outfit. There are 12 courts here that stay lit until 11 PM, with no fee to play, nor are there reservations taken. If courts are full, you can always get in a practice session at the backboard.

Find other lighted Virginia Beach courts at:

Bayside High School, 4960 Haygood Road

Bayville Farm Park, First Court Road

Center for Effective Learning, 233 North Witchduck Road

Creeds Athletic Park, Morris Neck & Campbell Landing Road

First Colonial High School, 1271 Mill Dam Road

Great Neck Junior High, 1840 North Great Neck Road

Green Run High School, 1700 Dahlia Drive

Kellam High School, 574 Kempsville Road

Kempsville Jr. High School, 860 Churchill Road

Kempsville High School, 574 Kempsville Road

Lynnhaven Park, Bayne Drive

Plaza Junior High School, 3080 South Lynnhaven

Princess Anne Park, Princess Anne Road

Princess Anne High School, 4400 Virginia Beach Boulevard

Chesapeake

The City of Chesapeake sponsors men's and women's team tennis for ages 18 and older for both spring and fall seasons. For more information on team tennis sign-up, call 547-6642.

GREENBRIER SPORTS PARK
Greenbrier   *547-6400*

Take center court on any of eight tournament-quality lighted courts — this is the big time in Chesapeake. Novices bored with ball-chasing can always sneak away to the softball fields or picnic areas.

CHESAPEAKE COUNTRY CLUB
411 Cedar Rd.   *547-9366*

Ten clay and two hard surface courts await you here at the club's new facility. Six of the courts will be lighted for night play, along with a stadium court for exhibition play. And, don't spend too much in the well-stocked pro shop.

Find additional lighted public courts in Chesapeake at:

Crestwood Junior High School, 1420 Great Bridge Road

Deep Creek Junior High School, 2901 Margaret Booker Drive

Deep Creek High School, 1955 Deal Drive

Great Bridge Junior High School, 301 West Hanbury Road

Hickory Elementary School, 2701 South Battlefield Boulevard

Indian River High School, 2301 Dunbarton Drive

Oscar Smith High School, 2500 Rodgers Street

Western Branch High School, 4222 Terry Drive

Portsmouth

Classes for all skill levels and ages are offered during the summer through the Portsmouth Parks and Recreation Department at both Churchland Park and City Park, along with annual Junior and Senior Tournaments. For more information, class schedules and fees, call 393-8481.

Lighted courts available for public play:

Cavalier Manor, 404 Viking Street

Churchland Park, 5601 High Street, West

City Park, City Park Avenue

Craddock High School, 4300 George Washington Highway

I. C. Norcom High School, 2900 Turnpike Road

Manor High School, 1401 Elmhurst Lane

Park View Athletic Complex, 1401 Crawford Parkway

Tidewater Community College, Frederick Campus

Woodrow Wilson High School, 3701 Willett Drive

There are a couple of local tennis organizations that would love to take a swing at signing you up:

Chesapeake Tennis Association   *543-3347*
Norfolk Tennis Patrons   *543-9555*

Inside
The Beautiful
Bay Sail Away

It's 4:30 AM. Dark outside, and all the excitement shared over the plans for the "sail of the century" doesn't seem quite as exhilarating as it did last night over that grand bottle of Cabernet Sauvignon with charts spread out over the kitchen table. But, favorable winds call and sails have been double-checked and properly bagged. We're off with very, very good friends for a cruise up the Chesapeake Bay on our Cal 36 for some lazy, glorious days of sun, warm friendly breezes, lazy starlit evenings and . . . no real live showers. What a kick. Come on along.

It's truly amazing how much stuff is required when you set off with Robinson Crusoe gusto to be one with the sea and the sky. You must have bags and bags of ice for the galley "refrigerator" to maintain the proper temperature of the caviar. Then there's the necessary sustenance foodstuffs, like chips and salsa. Not to mention all the proper accoutrements for a full bar (to be set up punctually at 6 PM as soon as anchor is dropped). Add in linens, reading materials, boom boxes for tunes, every anticipated cooking utensil, baby Weber grill and paper goods. Space is not a great commodity below deck, so planning what you'll need is truly essential. As for wardrobe, no awards for fashion plates here. . . a few pairs of shorts, T-shirts, bathing suits, maybe a sweater if evenings are cool and the all-important rain slicker. Dragging all this aboard and

stowing it away in a somewhat memorable manner takes almost as much concentration and energy as preparing for that motor away from the dock.

Up until this point, traditional genetics are in force. Women to the basic human survival necessities, men to the business of sails, charts and bilge pump checks. But, once those docking ropes are tossed and you head out to open waters, forget that myth about the weaker sex. Everyone works together on equal, if unbalanced, footing to work the sails, the charting and all the million and one things that makes sailing seem to the uninitiated like such a relaxed, leisurely sport.

We at last pull away from Norfolk, our port of call, into the Elizabeth River that will spill us into the Chesapeake Bay. The journey we will describe is not exactly how it was, but how we would have liked it to be, touching on all the favorite places for Bay sailors on the charted course north to the Rappahannock. And, while we will point out some important markers and obstacles along the way, we'd advise you not to use this journal as a guide for your next excursion. For the protection of your vessel and your crew, carefully adhering to current charts, tides and weather advisories is essential when you steer out of the main Bay waters.

We motor out into the Elizabeth River, sticking close to the channel, as proper depth and avoidance of hidden obstacles are imperative. Here, as throughout the Bay waters, what may appear to be open water a half-mile deep may actually have a depth of just a few feet. We pass Lambert's Point, with its coal piers where train cars dump their cargo into the holds of colliers. Then, as sails are raised, we glide past the piers of the Norfolk Naval Base, where aircraft carriers and submarines are tethered in their respite between patrolling of the oceans. We are heading for what is called Norfolk Harbour Reach, our connection northward to the Bay. Along with the two infamous submerged rocks, thankfully marked with white warning boards, it is here where water traffic, including various tugs, barges, motor and sail craft, starts to become heavy. It goes without saying that utmost caution and adherence to the rules of seamanship are critical to avoid a collision course.

We are now in the waters called Hampton Roads, where shipping channels are well-used and, fortunately, very well marked. Pleasure craft try to stay just outside these channels, as waters are sufficiently deep and there are no hazards. Concrete islands mark the almost mile-wide entry into the harbor, and to the east you can see Fort Wool where, in 1862, President Abraham Lincoln stood to watch Union artillery men lob cannon shells at Confederate troops in Norfolk. The Fort is partially restored today, after having been neglected for many years.

The waters of the James River are ahead to port, but our course takes us in a more northerly direction towards Hampton. If we had chosen to travel up the James, we could sail on to Williamsburg, or even all the way to Hopewell and Richmond. As we approach Hampton, waters again get very busy, as this city is one of the most frequented on the Virginia coast.

We can easily spot the Chamberlain Hotel, eight stories of Southern hospitality that has been lovingly restored, and a landmark on the grounds of Fort Monroe. This Fort lays claim to the notoriety of being the prison for Confederate President Jefferson Davis after the Civil War.

The trip hasn't taken all that long, but we're ready for our first stop, at Salt Ponds Marina, halfway between the Hampton Roads Channel and the Back River Channel. We follow the markers on a westerly course to the rock-lined cut that takes us about 100 yards through the dunes, and though traffic is heavy, we're able to throw a line at the marina long enough to stretch our legs with a walk on the boardwalk.

The York River

Before we enter the mouth of the York River, we'll take a quick sidetrip to Chisman Creek that offers many choices for anchorage on the Poquoson River. Careful chart reading is especially important in these waters, as Poquoson Flats have claimed many a craft by parking it with a hard grounding.

Once we pass the vertical clearance of 60' under the swing bridge at Yorktown, we aim for the York River Yacht Haven in Sarah Creek at Gloucester Point, our first night's stopover. As we approach, we can see the refinery and wharves on the south shore of the river and watch the fishermen as they tend their fish traps along the north bank. The York River Yacht Haven offers accommodations for 300 vessels, so we're certainly not alone. Always a popular stopover, today it's particularly busy, and the entrance is narrow to boot. But once safely at our reserved berth, we can all take a much-needed shower in the marina's squeaky-clean, air-conditioned restrooms and waste away the evening sitting at the outdoor deck of the Rivers Inn Restaurant chowing down on the catch of the day.

Back onboard at the dock, we go about the drill of turning daytime benches and forward v-berth into our makeshift beds, pulling out the extra blankets to ward off the evening's chill. After a comatose night's sleep and makeshift breakfast with super-strong instant coffee, we set out to do a little exploring of the York River, where sunken warships from the battles of the Revolution still lie on the river bottom. The river itself is about 35 miles long, straight and fairly wide. Even though the lower areas of the York are often crowded, the upper York can boast great waters for just cruising around, deep enough for even deep-draft vessels. Several creeks off the river's northern waters offer beautiful, tranquil anchorages, and smaller boats than ours can put in to the Poropotank River or check out the York River State Park sitting to the south.

The York River splits at West Point into the Mattaponi and Pamunkey rivers, both unspoiled jewels for small boat explorers, with banks lined with farms and timberland. Tides are brisk, however, and there are few facilities, so planning and care are especially important if you plan to drop the dinghy for a side trip.

Mobjack Bay to Windmill Point

The pristine waters of Mobjack Bay are a favorite for sturdy sailors, who have their choice of cruising the East River, North River, Ware River and Severn River that all sprout like spread fingers from Mobjack's waters. On the south side of the Severn is Guinea Neck, a longtime center for commercial fishing, and, indeed, some of the most skilled watermen in the Bay hail from here. The East River's claim to fame is that it is home to an abandoned tidal water mill once owned by John Lennon, the late Beatle, and his wife, Yoko Ono. Both the North River and Ware River are popular and pleasant places to drop anchor for a peaceful night with only a canopy of stars for your roof.

Needless to say, Mobjack Bay is a bustling place in warm weather, but only on the water. You'll find few facilities and mostly undeveloped shores, so self-sufficiency on your craft is the rule. And, think twice about taking a refreshing dip in the clear waters on a hot day, no matter how inviting it appears to be. Jelly fish and crabs just adore these waters and aren't particularly hospitable to intruders.

From New Point Comfort, marked by the towering but abandoned white silo at the entrance to Mobjack Bay, we steer north to Gwynn's Island, where the current runs fast, often three or four knots. It's also a main route for working watermen, so we post a sharp lookout on the bowsprit. There's a swing bridge here that opens on demand, so we call ahead to the tender on VHF channel 13 for passage. Beyond is Milford Haven, home to a Coast Guard Station, and the waters that separate Gwynn's Island from the mainland.

If we go farther up the Piankatank River, we come to Fishing Bay on the south side of Deltaville. This is time-warp land, where everything but time-honored good manners and Southern hospitality seems to have been frozen in history. On the Broad Creek side is the main harbor of Deltaville, just around the bend from Stingray Point, where we're warmly welcomed at Dozier Marine Center, still called Dozier's Dockyard by the old-timers. Here, we replenish our soda and chip supply at the ship's store and even shop for a new sailing caps for mementos. While charming little Deltaville (human population 2,000, boat population, 3,000) is a long way from anywhere by land, it's a most popular anchorage for both motor and sail boats. It's such a quaint place, we decide to take Dozier's up on their offer of free bicycles to take a loop through town, and we take a cooling splash in the pool before setting sail again.

We're off now directly across the Rappahannock to Windmill Point, a first-class marina that sits along a protected harbor on Fleets Island, and guards the entrance to the Rappahannock River. We'll overnight at Windmill Point Resort, a fantastic place to dock and relax on solid ground with other windburned floaters. Here, there's a white sand beach and two pools, plus tennis courts, croquet and volleyball for the exercise starved. The waterfront restaurant, the Dockside Hearth, is excellent, and we make a note to pick up a few loaves of their freshly baked french bread before setting out in the morning.

The Rappahannock

One of Virginia's biggest and most beautiful waterways, the Rappahannock is the star of the Northern Neck region. Beginning on the eastern slopes of the Blue Ridge Mountains far to the west, it can be very powerful after heavy rains in the piedmont. Depending on the winds and the tide, the entrance to the Rappahannock can be rough as its waters pour into the Chesapeake Bay, so we plan to make our run during a moderate tide.

After passing under the Rappahannock River Bridge, we sail just 2nm (nautical miles) to Carter's Creek and the tiny village of Irvington, best known as the home to the four-diamond Tides Inn and The Tides Lodge, the only resort on the Bay to win the Atlantic Cruising Club's highest award, "Five Bells." We reluctantly pass on pulling into anchor here because the Inn is quite a formal place, and our battered seaman's cutoffs would just not be acceptable. Sadly, we decide that tonight we'll just pretend we're enjoying a highball at The Pub, followed by a sumptuous five-course candlelight supper.

Cruising on to the west, we enter the broad Corrotoman River, a new mecca for out-of-towners who have discovered the stress-reducing qualities of the shoreline and are busily building second getaway homes here. After a picnic lunch on deck (Windmill Point's french bread, summer sausage and cheese), we head to the Rappahannock's south shore for a stopover at Urbanna, protected by a man-made breakwater. Here we dock at Urbanna Sales & Service, chat with the dockmaster and replenish fuel and water supplies.

This is the end, or should we say, midpoint, of our sail on the western shores of the Chesapeake Bay. We'll anchor out tonight, burn some fillets on our baby Weber and heavily toast our luck with the winds and weather. Because tomorrow, we'll turn the bow towards the south and retrace the Bay waters home . . . and maybe even catch a glimpse of Chessie, the Chesapeake-ness monster, who old-timers say stalks the waters near the Bay Bridge. If we do, that's a whole other chapter.

Jibe-ho!

Inside
Participatory and Spectator Sports

Hampton Roaders can create more ways to exercise and compete than you can shake a racquet at. Here, we'll give you a brief rundown of the most reasonable of the area's participation sports and who to contact if you're interested in finding out more. For you really pro-sports fanatics, an excellent reference tool is a special magazine called *Hampton Roads Sports*, produced by the Sports Promotion Task Force of the Hampton Roads Chamber of Commerce. Available at all local visitors centers, it's packed with the inside scoop on all the most popular, and going-to-be-popular, sports along with a complete facilities and organization list.

Local organizations well-respected for their sports savvy:

Norfolk Sports Club, Virginia Beach, 497-9583

Southside Athletic Association, Suffolk, 539-9657

Virginia Beach Sports Club, Virginia Beach, 428-1470

Participatory Sports

Basketball

Each of the Hampton Roads' cities sponsors both adult and youth basketball leagues, with registration beginning in November and play continuing through mid-March. Youth leagues begin at age 10, and you must be 18 before you join

Photo: Hampton Roads Admirals

The Hampton Roads Admirals offer the best of ice hockey in the area.

the adult ranks. For complete information, contact your city's recreation department. All phone numbers are listed at the end of this section. Other contacts for avid slam-dunkers are The Sharks in Virginia Beach, 436-6037, and Virginia Beach Future All-Stars, 468-1820.

For casual hoopers, scads of indoor and outdoor courts are scattered throughout the region: at schools, parks and recreation facilities. You shouldn't have far to go for a quick game of one-on-one.

Baseball/Softball

Again, leave it to the cities to organize highly competitive teams for both adults and kids. Registration normally begins in early March, with the season dragging on from May through the heat and humidity of late July. Teams for males, females and coeds are here for the joining. Call your specific city for exact registration times and locations.

Hampton Roads is home to the Amateur Softball Association, the largest amateur association in the world, that operates in each Hampton Roads city and provides playing opportunities for children and adults. In any given year, you can count as many as 150 different teams in the association, and they can play as many as 200 games on a weekend. Junior Olympic leagues are for girls ages 12 to 18, with play in the fall. Adult leagues, for ages 18 and older, are grouped according to ability, with a season that runs from April to November. For more information, call 427-5219 or 428-0784.

For baseball players 18 years and older, check into the Virginia Adult Baseball League. For information, 487-0824 or (800) 435-3588.

Boxing

Sweet Pea-wanna-be's have it made in Hampton Roads. For starters, Claude Taylor of Norfolk's rec department has been teaching boxing for years at Barraud Park in Norfolk, and Sweet Pea Whittaker, the undisputed Lightweight Champion of the World, was one of his students. In Virginia Beach, Wareing's Gym is as good as you can get for training and a really scary sparring partner.

Cycling

Have bike, will travel. And travel Hampton Roads' cyclers do. Weekend leisure riders will find bike paths throughout Hampton Roads and special trails reserved for bikers in most of our area's parks. Mini-bikers, mountain bikers and BMX aficionados will find their own tracks too. (See the Parks and Recreation chapter for specifics.) Serious peddlers won't want for companionship, with several clubs active in planning special

---

Insiders' Tips

Spot a Troubled Turtle? While you're enjoying the oceanfront, if you should happen to spot a troubled turtle or a whale or dolphin who's lost his way, call for help. The Virginia Marine Science Museum has set up a new service that's the equivalent of our human 911. Call 437-4961 immediately to report any marine wildlife in distress.

events, competitions and field trips. To get the full scoop, contact The Tidewater Bicycle Association (touring and racing), 523-2596; L'team Junque (touring and training), 486-1948; or Colley Off-Road Club (touring and training), 622-0006. To rent a bike on your visit to Virginia Beach, check out Northend Bikes, 425-5120, or Oceanfront Bikes, 428-4235, both along the Boardwalk.

Crew

Crewing is an up-and-coming sport in this region blessed with quiet waters. In fact, just recently, a senior member of the Hampton Roads Rowing Club contributed $65,000 toward the construction of a 5,000-square-foot boathouse for the organization to call home. Novices and experienced oarsmen are welcome to join the club for both recreational and competitive thrills. Call 451-8488.

Fencing

Yes, fencing. The Tidewater Fencing Club is always looking for new targets to sign up for membership in this very active organization. Annual membership is $80, which includes instruction and equipment. Call 460-2975.

Football

Knock 'em, pop 'em, sock 'em. Pack your kids into the pads and get them off to sign up for your city's youth community football league. Registration is in August, with power play for city titles running from September through November. Volunteer coaches are widely respected and known for teaching more than just the principles of the game.

Sportsmanship, leadership and team spirit messages prevail, even if you're on the bench. Contact your city's rec department for exact registration times and locations.

Horseback Riding

Virginia Beach, Suffolk and Chesapeake are the area leaders when it comes to facilities to mount a steed and ride off into the sunset. In the still-rural areas of Virginia Beach, many people still board their own, and there are many private stables where you can rent a ride. In Chesapeake, Northwest River Park offers the city's only designated horse trails, with 3 miles of interconnected loops. Private stables and farms also offer mounts for lessons and rental. Suffolk offers boarding, training and lessons, but no rentals are available. Excellent sources for information to steer you in the right direction are:

Acredale Saddlery	467-3183
Hillcrest Farms Ltd.	471-4646
Indian River Stables	471-9232
Pleasant Ridge Stables	721-3819
Sterling Meadows Farm	471-2133
Royal Meadows Stables	255-0729

Ice Skating

Even in a region of moderate temperatures, ice skating is popular . . . for Olympic want-to-be's as well as for one heck of a great party idea. The center for the activity is Iceland Skating Center at Virginia Beach, 4915 Broad Street, 490-3907, where excellent instruction is available. The most promising students are part of a figure skating team that has traveled as far as Chicago to compete in United States Figure Skating Association events. There's also The Tidewater Fig-

The region's flat terrain makes it ideal for biking.

ure Skating Club that welcomes all skating abilities, 423-5411. If you've got a hankering for the game of ice hockey, check out the Virginia Beach Open Hockey League, 490-3999.

Jet Skiing

If there's a sport, there's a club for it here, with folks who share your passion. If you're into jet skiing, find out about the Tidewater Personal Watercraft Club that meets monthly at Marina Shores in Virginia Beach, 496-2325. To rent a jet ski for a trial run, call the pros at Rudee Inlet Jet Ski Rentals at 428-4614.

Rugby

There are bumper stickers around town that say " Love an Animal . . . Kiss a Rugby Player." Well, maybe *before* one of the games sponsored by the Virginia Beach Rugby Club, that fights it out at Princess Anne Park in Virginia Beach.

Right now, they're looking for new players (makes you wonder what happened to the old ones!). Go ahead, give them a call at 497-2208.

Racquetball

A most civilized racquet sport, you won't find many public facilities to satiate the habit, but there are several membership facilities where you can happily box yourself in. In Norfolk at the Downtown Athletic Club, 625-2222 or at the YMCA, 622-6328, or in Virginia Beach at Gymstrada, 499-9667.

Running, Jogging, Walking

Whatever your speed, you can be in a crowd — or all alone — when you put one foot in front of the other for recreation. Every park in every city has well-marked, well-shaded paths for walking and jogging, and you'll see people of all ages out in neighborhoods, on the Boardwalk at the Beach, around the Hague in Ghent, and even on covered tracks at the YMCA in Downtown Norfolk.

If you're more serious about leaving your footprints in jogging or walking history, you might check out several clubs in the area that sponsor a multitude of competitive and recreational events:

Tidewater Striders	627-RACE
Gator Volksmarching Club	486-0664
Mount Trashmore Walking Club	474-0460
Suffolk Field Trail Club	986-4585
From Start to Finish	482-5932

Sailing

If you don't know the difference between a boom-vang and a spinnaker, you'll miss out on one of the most popular addictions in the area . . . sailing. From baby sunfish to beamy Morgans, there's a vessel just waiting to reach you out into the calm waters of the Chesapeake Bay. One great place to chart your sailing adventure is the Chesapeake Sailing Association, located at Willoughby Harbor in Norfolk. CSA offers ASA-certified sail training, along with super five-day "Learn to Sail" vacation packages. Call them at 588-2022. At the Beach, Chick's Beach Sailing Center, 481-3067, is a beehive of sailing activity, and a great place to take a lesson, rent a boat or just hang around to pick up some sailing lingo.

Skateboarding and In-Line Skating

For those few who haven't traded in their skateboards for in-line skates, you can head to the last remaining bowls and ramps located at the beach at Mount Trashmore, Red Wing Park and Wave Riding Vehicles. At all these facilities, proper safety equipment is required, as well it should be. In-line and roller skaters can wheel with the pack by joining the Beach Skater Club, 422-6105.

Skydiving

Beam me up, Scottie! If leaping for your life into thin air is the kind of thing that turns you on, head out to Suffolk Municipal Airport. Skydive Suffolk, Inc. offers lessons on Saturday mornings by appointment, and you can make your first jump that same day. For the experienced skydiver, an accelerated free-fall program is also offered. For fees and details, call 539-3531.

Soccer

Soccer's hot here, so sign that kid up quick. Every city and practically every neighborhood has its own team, so have

Want a chance to see Olympic hopefuls on their way to the 1996 games in Atlanta? Check out the Bud Light Men's Pro Beach Volleyball League Tournament in Virginia Beach in August. This tour stop is one of the 12-tournament, $1 million purse series of the men's tour and will be nationally televised. To the victors comes the opportunity to be on the very first two-man beach volleyball team playing for medals in the history of the Olympic games.

Insiders' Tips

your child talk to classmates about the best place to put on the cleats.

Youth soccer leagues sprout up so quickly that they can't be counted . . . boys and girls are not only encouraged to join up, but have a great time wearing their uniforms after the games. Contact your city's rec department for full details on spring and fall registration times and locations. In Norfolk, the Norfolk Youth Soccer League, 588-3294, is the place to call.

Adults don't have to miss out, either. Several soccer clubs are active and alive in Hampton Roads. To find out specifics:

Tidewater Soccer Association, at 489-2724, is a men's league and member of the USSF. It's for those experienced enough to play at collegiate level or better.

Southeastern Virginia Women's Soccer Association, 625-2414, is a regional league that's busy all year, with teams divided according to age and play ability.

Southside Soccer League, 423-3147, is for men who play well but not quite at championship speed.

Virginia Beach Soccer Club, 424-8800, has over 7,000 members. This club for both youths and adults has leagues for both neighborhood play and advanced teams. To accommodate, both spring and fall seasons are packed with play.

Surfing

Surf's up! Well, maybe it's not Hawaii, but when a Nor'easter blows, it's get-out-your-wet suit time around the Virginia Beach oceanfront. Even if our waves might not be giant killers, we're still host to the East Coast Surfing Championships every year, with stiff competition from the best in the business.

Needless to say, Virginia Beach lays claim to all surfing rights in the area . . . you'd look ridiculous trying to catch a ripple at Ocean View. There are certain places you can and cannot take your board, however. Surfing areas are restricted to protect your average lazy backstokers and waders, as well as surfers themselves. Leashes are required, and you'll have to pay a $50 fine if caught untethered from your board. If you get the urge to wax a board, call Wave Riding Vehicles at 422-8823 for the local surf report and head to:

Area A: Little Island Park. Stick to the north side of the pier from Memorial Day to Labor Day, 9 AM 'til 5 PM.

Area B: South of Little Island Park. You are allowed to catch a wave off False Cape's beach, but restricted within the boundaries of the Back Bay National Wildlife Refuge.

Area C: Between the southern line of the U.S. Naval Reservation/Dam Neck and the northern line of Little Island Park. Between Memorial Day and Labor Day you can only surf here before 10 AM and after 5 PM. Otherwise, surf's up between sunrise and sunset.

Area D: North of Camp Pendleton to 42nd Street, except for the area 300 feet north and south of the pier. Again, you're beached between 10 AM and 5 PM, May 15th through September 30th. Other times, have at it from sunrise to sunset.

Area E: Fort Story to 42nd Street. No surfing between 10 AM and 5 PM, Memorial Day through Labor Day. Allowed sunrise to sunset at all other times.

Area F: South end of Croatan Beach (600 feet). Except for occasional military maneuvers, you can maneuver on your board from 9:30 AM until 6 PM from Memorial Day through Labor Day.

Area G: Croatan Beach for 800 feet

Harbor Park is the home of the Norfolk Tides.

below the southern jetty of Rudee Inlet. Open and waiting for you from sunrise to sunset.

Area H: North of Rudee Inlet's northern jetty (500 feet). Hang ten sunrise to sunset.

Swimming

Well, of course, swimming. Here we are surrounded by water. In fact, one of the hottest baby presents going is lessons for those not even old enough to walk or even complain about the water being too cold.

It is critical, however, whether you're a newcomer or a visitor, that you not venture out into the ocean or the bay without a basic knowledge of our waters or fundamental swimming skills. Strong currents and rip tides (streams of water running under the surface that can draw you out toward sea in no time flat) that are sometimes hard to spot are an ever-present menace to adults and children alike. And that goes double for rafts and

swimming aides that lull you into the feeling of safety. While experienced lifeguards are on duty at the locations listed below to keep a constant eye on you, lives have been unnecessarily lost because the excitement of white sands and blue waters overshadowed the real danger of unpredictable seas. If you are a newcomer from a dry terrain, we urge you to check into the swimming courses offered at nominal fees through your new city's recreation department and to take extreme safety precautions when you visit any of our wonderful beaches.

NORFOLK

City Beach, East End of Ocean View
Community Beach, 601 East Ocean View Avenue
Sarah Constant Shrine, East Ocean View and Tidewater Drive

VIRGINIA BEACH

The Ocean Front, Atlantic Avenue Resort Strip
Croatan Beach, General Booth Boulevard
Fort Story, 89th Street
Sandbridge Beach Park, Sandbridge
Little Island Park, Sandbridge

Indoor Swimming

Whether you want to learn how to backstroke, or dive into the wet world of competitive free style, there are several options for water babies and adults alike. The Tidewater Swim Team is a great connection for youth swimmers, and the team travels to competitions along the East Coast. For information, call 496-3979. To perfect your stroke, call the Old Dominion Aquatic Club at 683-3403. It offers an excellent development program for novice and intermediate swimmers with an emphasis on stroke mechanics. There's also the Springboard Diving Team, 683-5569, for those not afraid of heights, and the Virginia Community Swim League, 441-1547, for fun competition.

For lessons or laps, here are the pools to check out when it gets a little too brisk for a bikini:

NORFOLK

Huntersville Pool, 830 Geoff Street
Northside Pool, 8400 Tidewater Drive
Maury Pool, 322 Shirley Avenue
YMCA, Bute Street, Downtown Norfolk
Old Dominion University, Hampton Boulevard, Larchmont

VIRGINIA BEACH

Little Creek Pool (For military), Naval Amphibious Base, Little Creek
United Way Family Center, 441 South Boulevard
Kempsville Recreation Center, 800 Monmouth Lane

CHESAPEAKE

YMCA, 1033 Greenbrier Parkway

Volleyball

When you're hot, you're hot. This is one old sport that's enjoying a major renewal across Hampton Roads — as evidenced by the nets strung out along the beaches and parks throughout the area. There are city leagues wherever you live, just waiting for a great spiker like you. When you get the action down pat, why not call the Tidewater Volleyball Association at 498-5052 or the Volleyball Pro Shop at 422-9466 to get the low-down on any upcoming tournaments.

Windsurfing

Looks easy. It's not. But, if you want to put that upper body strength and miracle balance to the test, here's the place to do it. You can start easy, with a smooth glide along the lake at Mount Trashmore, then graduate to the more wicked waters of the Chesapeake Bay. Why not let the experts at Chick's Beach Sailing Center give you a lesson or two before you rush out to invest in a board of your own. If you already know what you're doing, they'll rent you a board. Other great guidance counselors can be found at Wave Riding Vehicles. We're talking Atlantic Ocean now, so be easy on yourself.

Danger Zone Sports

A lot of the Insiders we know consider the new wave of crazy activities to be in the exclusive category of "sports of the brain dead." Gee, who really wants to bungee jump off a 110-foot tower . . . and pay $45 to do it? Just head to Beach Bungee, 422-2700, and check out the lines. And, what about whirly ball — sort of like playing basketball in demolition derby-style bumper cars? (Whirly Ball Center, Chesapeake, 424-2279.) And, how about a first date to climb up, and then presumably down, a 30-foot plastic climbing wall followed by a leap of faith from a 24-foot high rappelling tower? (The Rock Gym, Virginia Beach, 499-8347.) Not only are these the spookiest new trends around, but you also have the distinct pleasure of learning a whole new vocabulary of terms for each sport if you want to be considered part of the looney troop. No thanks.

Who Ya Gonna Call?

For up-to-the-minute info on all sporting activities offered for children and adults through city Parks and Recreation Departments, contact:

Norfolk Athletics	441-2603
Virginia Beach Athletics	471-5884
Chesapeake Athletics	547-6400
Portsmouth Athletics	393-8481

Other local sports-minded organizations:

Virginia Beach Special Olympics	422-4423
Sun Wheelers (a wheelchair sports club)	471-5884

Annual Sporting Competitions

Bulk up on pasta and get ready to rumble. There are a zillion competitions for practically every sport known to humankind in Hampton Roads, and many are not only held annually for competitors who train all year, but bring out scores of spectators. While not every one will lure you to the starting gun, they are indeed annual events that are anticipated by the best in the respective fields, from the Hampton Roads area and well beyond.

SHAMROCK MARATHON & SPORTS FEST
Virginia Beach

An annual March event sponsored by the Tidewater Striders, it's one of Virginia's most popular marathons, averaging 2,000 runners. There's the Open 8K Run, Masters 8K Run, 5K Fitness Walk, Children's Marathon and Sports Trade Show.

BUD LIGHT USTS TRIATHALON
Norfolk

Ouch! An Olympic distance event featuring a 1.5K swim, 40K bike race and 10K run. Starts at the Norfolk Botanical Garden and ends at Town Point Park, hosted by the City of Norfolk.

SANDMAN TRIATHALON
Virginia Beach

Held annually in September as part of the Neptune Festival, it draws the toughest competitors who go neck-to-neck in a 2K swim, 20-mile bike race and 10K run.

THE SENTARA FITNESS FEST
Norfolk

This is by far Hampton Road's largest and most complete athletic and recreational event. It includes the popular

Elizabeth River Run, Southeastern Cycling Classic, volleyball battles and so much more.

VIRGINIA BEACH CHALLENGE VOLLEYBALL TOURNAMENT
Virginia Beach

Madness at the net as the area's hottest spikers volley for the championship!

BUDWEISER FOUR-ON-FOUR MEN'S PRO VOLLEYBALL TOUR
Virginia Beach

Be here to watch the professional men's action on the beach, and maybe to be seen on national TV as the cameras roll to record this exciting event!

IJSBA BUDWEISER JET SKI TOUR
Virginia Beach

This nationally televised event brings out the best in professional personal watercraft competition.

VIRGINIA BEACH EAST COAST SURFING CHAMPIONSHIPS
Virginia Beach

Any local surf shop will be abuzz with the news about this August tournament that attracts the biggest names in surfing. Even if you don't know the first thing about the boards, it's a great excuse to get a lot of sun while watching the competition.

THE CHESAPEAKE CHALLENGE
Virginia Beach

What a sight! It's the annual Hobie/catamaran race that lasts a long, grueling 27 miles.

LOW RENT REGATTA
Chick's Beach

Here's one to jump into — a wild and wacky competition for boardsailing and catamarans. But, beware! There are some competitors that take the title very seriously.

SHODEO
Virginia Beach

For the horsey set, this annual September competition at Princess Anne Park gets big scores for the high level of showmanship.

Spectator and Professional Sports

Baseball

THE NORFOLK TIDES
Harbor Park, Downtown Norfolk   622-2222

The Class AAA farm team of the New York Mets, the Tides are not only the biggest success story of local professional sports, but can boast of some of the big-

Photo: Norfolk Tides

The Norfolk Tides baseball team is a class AAA farm team of the New York Mets.

gest players who started out on the Tide's roster. Primo pitcher Dwight Gooden, super slugger Darryl Strawberry and tough-guy Lew Dystra all started with the Tides before being jettisoned up to the Met's lineup.

The Tides got their start in 1962, competing in the old Sally League at Frank D. Lawrence Stadium. In 1969, they leap-frogged to AAA status, and the following year took up residency at the then brand new Met Park in Norfolk. They swung, they won and they made history as a winning team, and to that end, they have moved their locker gear to another brand new, state-of-the-art facility completed in 1993, along the waterfront in Downtown Norfolk. The new facility, Harbor Park, features plush skyboxes for corporate sponsors, seating for 12,000, a restaurant as accommodating as the old Diamond Club, and a unique walkway constructed from paver stones embedded with the names of anyone and everyone who paid $30 to be a part of history. A visit here to see the Tides, or the many high school football teams that compete during baseball off-season, is a blast. Not only can you get a great chili-laden hot dog or a plate of mean ribs, the park and surrounding parking lots are extremely well-patrolled by Norfolk's finest, giving you the real sense of safety throughout the evening.

Ice Hockey

THE HAMPTON ROADS ADMIRALS
Scope, St. Paul's Blvd. and
Brambleton Ave., Norfolk   *640-1212*

You want winners? You got them! Who would've thought that an ice hockey team in Hampton Roads would not only come out on top of the pack year after year, but would draw sellout crowds to every home game in Norfolk's Scope? In fact, in its five-year history, well over a million screaming, fanatic and intensely loyal fans have packed Scope to cheer on their team. All going to prove that "kinder and gentler" went out a long time ago.

Partners with the Washington Capitals, who have supplied some of the team's leading scorers, the Admirals' season starts in October and face-offs continue through March. You can catch all the action at Scope, but better buy those tickets in advance to ensure you've got a seat to cheer from.

Football

Wrapping up and packing off to a local high school football game has turned into one of the most popular social events of the fall season. Even if you don't have a child in the school, you'll be missing a lot if you don't huddle in blankets on the bleachers to cheer on your neighborhood team. The same spirit prevails for college ball, and following the stats for Norfolk State University and Hampton University, both of whom compete in the highly competitive CIAA, is a local pastime. Old Dominion University's efforts to jump start a football team have failed in the past years, despite substantial local support, both emotional and financial.

For semipro action, **The Tidewater Sharks** take the field each fall in the up-and-coming Mason Dixon football league. Now under new ownership, the team is looking for a knock 'em-sock 'em season as they take the field at the Center for Effective Learning on Witchduck Road in Virginia Beach. Catch the action for just five bucks. For ticket info, call 463-6741.

For another twist on football, take in a game of rugby, played to the fullest by the Norfolk Blues. And, while rugby is still a much understood and unappreciated sport in the region, the sheer ferocity and stamina of this winning team has brought attention, if not small fame, to its stars. To find out all about season play at Layfayette Park, call 445-9037.

Soccer

HAMPTON ROADS MARINERS
ODU or Center for
Effective Learning   *46-GOALS*

Need to put a little kick in your life? Check out Hampton Roads' newest professional team, the Hampton Roads Mariners. The new franchise competes in Atlantic Division of the 72 team United States Interregional Soccer League

(USISL), sanctioned under the U.S. Soccer Federation. The league plays a 20-game schedule, with matches on Friday and Saturday nights from April through August. Watch the local sports sections for announcements of season schedules. Home games are held at either ODU or the Center for Effective Learning (CEL) stadium on Witchduck Road in Virginia Beach.

Basketball

Some of us can remember the old Virginia Squires, with Charlie Scott, George Gervin and Julius "Dr. J" Erving taking center court back in the olden days of the 1970s. The Squires were the first major league sporting franchise in Hampton Roads and died a slow, painful death due to lack of spectator support just before the NBA-ABA merger.

Support is not the problem for the Monarchs of Old Dominion — men and women's teams. Buy your tickets early (or better yet, season's tickets) for games played at Norfolk's Scope for both the Monarchs and Lady Monarchs. Across town, the Spartans and Lady Spartans of Norfolk State University pose an annual threat to the title-grabbing in the CIAA. For schedules and ticket info, call ODU sports at 683-3372 and NSU sports at 455-3303.

There's no cure for hoop fever at the high school level either. Fans pack gymnasiums all over town to cheer on their favorites. We grow them good, too, like Joe Smith of Maury High School, J. R. Reid from Kempsville High School and Alonzo Morning, straight from Chesapeake's Indian River High.

Professional Wrestling

Boy, we really debated whether to include this under "sports" or "theater." Mid-Atlantic Wrestling is a big-time spectator sport for Hampton Roads kids of all ages, just hankering to see that big throw across the turnbuckle. It all happens every year at Norfolk Scope (you can tell when a bout is upcoming from all the screaming TV commercials hawking tickets), and the crowds of seemingly timid, well-dressed patrons turn into vicious, make-him-suffer lunatics. Well, it's not for everyone, but the release of frustrations here can be cheaper than a therapist. Go figure.

Tourists like to visit the Chesapeake Bay for its beauty and tranquility.

Inside
The Chesapeake Bay

When you're in Hampton Roads it's impossible to ignore the Chesapeake Bay, one of the region's most important geographical features. Even when you're not in direct view of the bay, you're near one of the many rivers and creeks that flows into it.

Besides creating some breathtaking scenery, the Chesapeake Bay influences countless aspects of daily life:

· It is the main reason Hampton Roads excels as a port and a popular tourism destination. It is the engine that drives much of the region's industry — from shipbuilding and repair to manufacturing and distribution.

· It provides the livelihood for hundreds of hardy watermen whose families have plied the waters for generations. The crabs and finfish they harvest make Virginia the third-largest seafood producing state.

· The type of fish pulled from the bay has a direct impact on what's on the menu when you go out to eat. If rockfish or softshell crabs are in season, they'll be hot items at area restaurants.

· The bay and the deep Hampton Roads harbor were the main reasons the Navy built its largest installation here.

· The bay enticed the first permanent English settlers in the New World to stay in the area after they landed here in 1607. One of the bay's tributaries led them to Jamestown where they began colonizing this country. The region surrounding the bay gave birth to the New World's first permanent towns and plantations and its initial crops of tobacco and wheat. Today you can see traces of this rich past in a treasure trove of historical sites.

· Because of the bay and its tributaries, getting from here to there can be tricky in this coastal region. Bridges and underwater tunnels are vital links between cities divided by the bay and other waterways.

With its 200-mile length, the Chesapeake Bay is the United States' largest estuary, and Hampton Roads is where it starts its journey northward to Havre de Grace, Maryland.

Huge Watershed

Although the Chesapeake Bay is physically surrounded by only Virginia and Maryland, its watershed stretches as far as Cooperstown, New York, and Pendletown County, West Virginia. In this drainage area nearly 50 rivers and thousands of streams, creeks and ditches empty into the bay, making it vulnerable to any pollutants they carry. The largest tributary is the Susquehanna River in Pennsylvania, which is why that inland state is a key player in keeping the bay healthy. Because of the bay's sprawling watershed, rain that falls on the 64,000 square miles between North Carolina and Vermont ends up in the bay.

For most people, the bay's special meaning comes from watching a glorious sunrise, spending the day pulling flounder or tuna from its waters or strolling along one of its many beaches. Every city in South Hampton Roads is situated on hundreds of miles of coastline along the bay and its tributaries. Portsmouth alone has 185 miles of shoreline, with Norfolk stretching along 140 miles of waterfront.

For environmentalists, the bay is revered as one of the most productive places on the earth. Its waters, marshes and wetlands shelter an incredible variety of life — from clams and flounder to egrets and whistling swans. More than 2,700 species of plants and animals depend on the bay for life — including the succulent crabs the bay is renowned for producing.

The Chesapeake Bay is where salt water from the ocean meets and mingles with fresh river water. Geologists believe it was created at the end of the last Ice Age approximately 12,000 to 18,000 years ago when melting glaciers and rising seas flooded the Susquehanna River. The Indians who were Virginia's first inhabitants called the bay various names that paid tribute to its majesty: "Great Waters," "Mother of Waters" and "Great Shellfish Bay." In the 1600s, British colonists named it "Chesapeake" from the Indian word "Tschiswapeki."

ENVIRONMENTAL CONCERNS

Although the Chesapeake Bay has long been famous for its oysters, crabs and finfish, their population has dropped drastically in the past 100 years. Pollution, overharvesting and the stress put on the bay by development have reduced the oyster population to only 1 percent of what it was in the late 19th century. Rockfish, once one of the bay's most prolific fish, nearly disappeared until a multi-state ban on catching them was implemented in 1986. Its success helped the rockfish rebound, and now anglers can once again harvest regulated quantities of one of the bay's tastiest fish.

After a 1983 Environmental Protection Agency study showed the bay was ailing from too many nutrients, toxic substances and sediment, Virginia, Maryland and Pennsylvania voluntarily united to save the Chesapeake Bay. Their efforts helped create a public awareness that the bay is a fragile resource that must be protected. A ban on phosphate detergents, restrictions on wetland destruction and other coordinated efforts are helping turn the tide for the bay.

You'll still spot blue-and-white "Save the Bay" bumper stickers on cars, but there are hopeful signs that the bay's health is on the mend. One improvement is the growth of underwater grasses, which are vital to filtering pollutants and are one of the best indicators of the bay's health. Grass fields have increased from a low of 35,000 acres in 1984 to more than 75,000 acres today. This is still nowhere near the 300,000 acres that were growing in the early '60s, but it is a step in the right direction.

To get involved in improving the bay, join the **Chesapeake Bay Foundation**. Since its founding in 1966 it has grown to more than 87,000 members. The foundation is headquartered in Annapolis, Maryland, but has a field office in Norfolk at 100 W. Plume Street, 622-1964. The foundation is the country's largest regional environmental organization and a powerful voice for the bay. You can join one of the foundation's local BayWatcher groups whose members dedicate themselves to cleaning streams, planting trees and other environmental endeavors.

Other organizations with an interest in the bay and related areas are the **Southeastern Association for the Virginia Environment**, or SAVE, 426-7501, and the **Back Bay Restoration Foundation**, 427-0685. There is a local chapter of the **Si-**

erra Club, 587-6683, and two Audubon Society chapters, 481-2538 or 588-8410. There also are numerous clubs for anglers. In 1992 the nonprofit Elizabeth River Project was created to restore the Elizabeth River to health. To join its efforts call 625-3648. On the first Saturday of every month the environmental community gathers at the Golden Corral restaurant at 470 Newtown Road in Virginia Beach for an informative breakfast meeting. It starts at 8 AM and often draws more than 100 guests. For information call 427-6606.

Another event that attracts a huge response is the annual Clean the Bay Day on the first Saturday in June. The effort started in this region in 1989 when volunteers joined forces for three hours to clean 52 miles of local waterways. Their reward was the satisfaction of hauling away 30 tons of trash. Since 1989, Clean the Bay Day's momentum has swelled. In 1994 5,000 volunteers combed 212 miles of shoreline and collected more than 100 tons of aluminum cans, old tires and other junk.

As Clean the Bay Day approaches each spring you'll see and hear a barrage of publicity that brings out families (including ours), Scout troops and individuals. But in case you miss the media messages, call 427-6606 or 1-800-SAVEBAY for information (see sidebar in this section).

SEEING THE BAY

With only 2 percent of the Chesapeake Bay's shoreline available to the public, it is sometimes difficult to gaze upon this national treasure.

To truly appreciate the majesty of the Chesapeake Bay, you must get out on the water. There are many fishing boats and tour boats that take groups out daily in Hampton Roads as well as elsewhere along the bay (see our chapter on Fishing and the sidebar on Cruising in the Attractions chapter and on Tangier Island in the Eastern Shore chapter). If you're part of a group you can schedule field trips coordinated by the Chesapeake Bay Foundation. These range from canoeing on creeks to spending a few hours on the foundation's *Baywatcher* boat exploring the Elizabeth and James rivers. Groups can also plan several-day environmental meetings at the foundation's facilities at Port Isobel Island or Fox Island near the Eastern Shore. Both are pristine, uninhabited islands with lodging facilities operated by the Chesapeake Bay Foundation. For information call 622-1964 or 410-268-8816.

To soak up the beauty of the bay there are several places to go in Hampton Roads. Norfolk has its Ocean View beaches, which stretch for miles along the bay's calm waters. You'll find a small boardwalk, gazebo, picnic shelters and restrooms at some parts of the Ocean View beach. The Ship's Cabin, one of Norfolk's oldest and best restaurants, fronts right on the bay in Ocean View and is a romantic spot for twilight dining.

The Cape Henry area inside Fort Story in Virginia Beach has a good stretch of undeveloped beaches open to the public on weekends. Along Shore Drive in Virginia Beach you can dine on the bay at several bayfront restaurants, including the Duck-In, a transformed bait house with a screened gazebo and a private beach. The Virginia Beach Resort and Conference Center also has its own beach as well as a restaurant and rooms that overlook it. Seashore State Park on Shore Drive has a wonderful beach that can only be used by people spending the night.

Photo: Richmond Times-Dispatch

This photo of the Chesapeake Bay Bridge-Tunnel was taken from the Eastern Shore of Virginia, northern terminus of the bridge-tunnel. The mainland of Virginia is the far horizon with the Atlantic Ocean on the left.

Getting one of the 215 campsites and 20 cabins can be a difficult feat, especially in summer. But it's definitely worth the effort. Call 481-2131 for reservations.

You can admire the bay from the Chesapeake Bay Bridge-Tunnel, which connects Virginia Beach with the Eastern Shore and has an overlook on a man-made island. Once on the Eastern Shore, Kiptopeke State Park is probably your best choice (see our Eastern Shore chapter for details). Near the park's beach, the waters are shallow, making this a great spot for families with children. There also is a public beach in downtown Cape Charles. One fun option is to catch a boat to Tangier Island, where you'll find yourself surrounded by the bay.

Across the Hampton Roads Bridge-Tunnel in Hampton, you can see the bay from historic Fort Monroe. Or travel through Phoebus to Buckroe Beach. Be-yond the beach is the Grandview Wilderness Area, which fronts on the bay.

Up The Bay's Western Shore: The Middle Peninsula and The Northern Neck

When the thought of another day of the regular grind gives you palpitations and you start to develop a migraine after just the first paragraph of the business page, the only remedy is a journey to The Land That Time Forgot.

While a million miles away in attitude, it sprawls just north of the Virginia Peninsula, mirroring its sister Eastern Shore, likewise trapped in history by the Chesapeake Bay. The Industrial Revolution took a lunch break when it came to Gloucester and Mathews counties and The Northern Neck . . . it remains to this day a lazy, tranquil network of mini-towns that have retained the charm of yesterday, with little visible intrusion by the scatter-and-panic environment of the urban hubs that surround it.

Unlike Williamsburg, which has purposely, and for a profit, recreated the look and feel of the early days, the Northern Neck comes by it naturally. With picturesque little wharfs where the menfolk still embark every morning to make their livings on the Bay. With tiny, little restaurants serving the same cholesterol-laden suppers as they have for generations. With charming little antique shops and galleries where you might just, by chance, find the proprietor available to let you browse. And with little regard for the pressures of time . . . past, present or future.

From Hampton Roads, one day is just not enough to absorb the full rejuvenating forces of this lovely part of Virginia. There are quite a few warm and welcoming bed and breakfasts, as well as waterfront marinas/motels, where you can stay over relatively inexpensively.

The basic rule is, when heading for the Middle Peninsula or the Northern Neck, whether by auto or by boat, take time to linger, a pastime we bet you've almost forgotten how to do. We guarantee that once you've kicked off your shoes, chatted with a few locals and finished off a dinner of jumbo lump crab cakes, you'll agree. It's like taking a Valium the size of a watermelon.

Gloucester

Tucked into a finger of land bounded by the Piankatank River on the North, Mobjack Bay on the east and the York River on the south, Gloucester County is a picture book of lush green farmlands, yellow carpets of daffodil fields and sparkling blue waters, just the right palette for a lazy-day outing for the action-exhausted.

Named for Henry, Duke of Gloucester, the area proudly claims a rich history back to the early 1600s. In fact, legend has it that it is here that Princess Pocahontas saved the gallant Captain John Smith from a tragic death at the hands of Indians. It was the same Captain John who proclaimed, perhaps in gratitude, "Heaven and earth never framed a better place for man's habitation."

A tobacco producing area in the 1600s and 1700s, many of the original plantation homes and magnificent private homes remain today in remarkably perfect condition. Home to just over 33,000 people, many of whom leave daily from the many seafood wharves to take their livings from surrounding deep tidal waters, Gloucester is at heart an agricultural community of crop and pasture lands. While called the "land of the life worth living" by its residents, insider cityfolk call it the land that time forget. And, that's

Fishing in the Chesapeake Bay is likely to yield plenty of rockfish, spot, perch, hardhead, drum, croaker, whiting and gray trout.

Insiders' Tips

exactly what gives it the charm and the hypnotic personality that draws us to visit.

Getting There

By boat would be our first choice, pulling into any of the numerous marinas that dot the over 100 miles of shoreline. By auto, you'd travel north on Interstate 64, and follow Route 17 across the Coleman Memorial Bridge over the York River to Gloucester County, about 45 miles from Norfolk. It's a leisurely drive, and the only real gridlock might be at the Coleman, often known for traffic tie-ups at the rush hours. Landlubbers will probably want to stick to Route 17 and check out the Courthouse Historic District; old salts will have to pull off the main drag and wind down lesser roads to reach the picturesque sights like **Lands End on the Severn River** or **Windmill Point on the Ware**. Lots of small towns and villages are scattered through Gloucester County, and a stop at any one will surely reap accurate directions to your chosen destination.

Events and Attractions

Let's start with the best, **The Daffodil Festival**, held the first Saturday in April, cleverly coinciding with the time when the daffodils are in full bloom. Sponsored by the Daffodil Festival Committee and the Gloucester Parks and Recreation Department, the festival celebrates the annual daffodil harvest with a parade, arts and crafts show, 5K and 1-mile runs, historical exhibits, live entertainment, food, children's games and rides. Obviously, a very big deal in this sleepy little county that produces one of the world's largest supplies of daffodil bulbs. To check

out the dates of the next scheduled festival, contact the Gloucester County Chamber of Commerce, 693-2425.

Other annual events to consider include **Historic Garden Week**, held Friday and Saturday of the last full week in April, **The Abington Ruritan Seafood Festival** on the third Wednesday evening in May and October (advance reservations required), and the **Annual Christmas Parade and Open House**, at Gloucester Courthouse the first Saturday in December. The Gloucester Chamber can fill you in on specifics, 693-2425.

The **Gloucester Courthouse Square Historic District** on Main Street in Gloucester Court House is like a time-warped version of a movie set, with its immaculately restored Colonial Courthouse, (open weekdays 9 AM to 4 PM), Debtors Prison (now a visitors center open Wednesday and Friday 10 AM to 2 PM), the old jail and many other preserved buildings that envelop a charming walled courtyard landmarked by a Confederate monument unveiled in 1889 to honor the 132 Gloucester men who lost their lives during the War Between the States. South of the Court House, close to Carter's Creek, you might want to explore the **Rosewell Ruins**, the remains of which were called the largest and finest of Colonial mansions. While fire consumed the interior in 1916, the magnificent brick walls, massive chimneys and elaborate doorways framed by superb brickwork survive. It's open Sundays April through October from 2 PM to 5 PM, and voluntary donations for its continued preservation are welcome. Of special note is the **Concert on the Green**, held summer evenings here at the Courthouse Green. Bring a chair or a blanket to enjoy the music and camaraderie.

Chesapeake Bay Facts

* The Chesapeake Bay is the largest and most biologically productive estuary in North America. More seafood is harvested from the bay than from any of the 840 other estuaries in the United States.

* The bay is 200 miles long and averages 15 miles in width. Its depth averages a shallow 21 feet. At its deepest point it is 150 feet.

* If you reduced the Chesapeake Bay to the scale of a football field, its average depth would equal that of three dimes. The bay's shallowness makes it vulnerable to pollution because there is not ample water to absorb toxins.

* Flowing into the bay are 49 rivers with 102 branches and tributaries. They are navigable for 1,750 miles.

* There are more than 15 million people living in the bay's watershed, which includes Virginia, Maryland, West Virginia, Pennsylvania, Delaware and New York.

* The bay is home to more than 2,700 species of plants and animals. The bay's shallow edges help make it one of the most biologically productive places on earth.

* The bay's blue crab harvest annually represents more than half the country's total catch.

* The bay is the winter home for about 500,000 Canada geese and 40,000 whistling swans.

* The bay is the nesting area of choice for 1,600 pairs of ospreys — the largest population in the United States. It also is the nesting area for about 125 pairs of bald eagles — one of the largest populations in the lower 48 states.

* The bay has more than 8,000 miles of shoreline, but only 2 percent of it is accessible to the public. The rest is privately owned.

Source: The Chesapeake Bay Foundation

For true history buffs, a visit to the **Warner Hall Graveyard** may be in order. Located off Route 629 south of Gloucester Court House, you'll see a roadside marker on the right indicating the site of a Colonial family cemetery where ancestors of George Washington, Robert E. Lee and Queen Elizabeth II are buried. Next, at the intersections of routes 616 and 614, is the birthplace of Walter Reed, the conqueror of yellow fever, a small mid-19th-century building, authentically furnished. It's open during Garden Week and the Daffodil Festival only.

Of interest to young and old, is the **Gloucester Point Archaeological District**, just off Route 17 at Gloucester Point. Here you can check out portions of **Tyndall's Point Park**, remnants of Confederate and Union fortifications and the site of colonial Gloucestertown, which is now home to the **Virginia Institute of Marine Science of the College of William and Mary**. Interesting here is **Waterman's Hall**, with its exhibits of colonial artifacts and public aquarium. Waterman's Hall is open to the public 8 AM to 4:30 PM Monday through Friday, 642-7000.

If you need a little exercise after all that site-seeing, pack the family off to **Beaverdam Recreational Park**, which you can enter from either route 616 or 606. Here you'll find boat ramps, canoe rentals, picnic shelters and hiking trails around the Gloucester County Reservoir. Or, you can hit **Gloucester Point Beach Park**, on Route 17. It's a five-acre park right on the York River next to the Coleman Bridge, complete with fishing pier, beach, horseshoe and volleyball courts, along with a concession stand and restrooms.

Food and Accommodations

We'll group these together, because in an area like this, the two often go hand in hand. Standing alone, however, is **Seawell's Ordinary**, in Ordinary on Route 17 just across the York River, 642-3635. A true historical treasure dating back to a 1712 residence, you may just have a glimpse of your former life as you dine by flickering candlelight in the authentic colonial atmosphere of the five dining rooms. Restored by Eleanor and John Evans in 1989, the French-American regional menu, excellent wine list and gracious service have earned contemporary raves from the most critical of Insiders.

The Lighthouse on Route 17 in White Marsh is another favorite for locals and travelers. While you can be certain of an excellent choice if you order an Italian pasta or beef entree, the real pièce de résistance is the fabulous seafood buffet. No ordinary buffet, either. It's spread before your eyes in a monstrous hull of a boat, beached in the center of the restaurant. You might want to show a little restraint before you heap your plate starboard . . . take a few laps around and check out the full selection because there may be one of your favorites, like Alaskan King Crab claws, on a side table. Indulge, but save room for the equally mouth-watering dessert table. Unfortunately, this phenomenal feast isn't offered every day. Call ahead to make certain you don't miss it, 693-5950.

There's only one bed and breakfast in Gloucester County, but it's a real beauty. **The Willows**, on Route 3, just 5 miles from Gloucester Court House, rests on an acre of daffodil fields. It's a large white farm house with a pretty gray slate roof and shady fern and wicker furnished porch. Ted and Angela Kristensen have restored the old house, renovated the general store that dates back to the 1880s, and comfortably furnished the rooms with old family pieces and others collected during their travels. Danish-born Ted and English-born Angela give Southern hospitality an injection of continental spirit, from the chef's Danish country omelette called Aegekage, to afternoon tea on the porch. Each bedroom offers a queen-size bed, private bath and TV, and reservations are highly recommended. Credit cards are not accepted, but personal or traveler's checks and cash will guarantee you a delightful, totally pampered stay. Call 693-4066.

You wouldn't call Gloucester County the mall capital of the world. There aren't any. But when it comes to antiquing, here are a few places we'd suggest. **In The Rough**, Routes 17, 693-9791, buys, sells and trades antiques, along with guns and jewelry. The **Stagecoach Markets and Antique Village**, Route 17, a mile south of Gloucester Courthouse, 693-3951, is an emporium of more than 35 shops selling you-name-it. Open only on Saturday and Sunday, but worth a look-see. Lastly, browse through **Old Thyme Treasures** in Hayes Plaza on Route 17, 642-4264. They also buy, sell and trade antiques and collectibles, and it's the only place you can locate replacement parts for oil lamps. Thought you'd want to know.

Mathews

As you continue your journey up Route 17, you'll come to the smallest of Virginia's counties, Mathews. Mathews is a hot ticket right now, as many Hampton Roads residents have discovered that it's the perfect place to buy a second home. In fact, many of the same people with whom we Insiders used to share a patch of beach in summer or football game in winter now streak out of town to their getaway homes even before the weekend begins.

Separated from Gloucester County by the North River and Mobjack Bay, Mathews County was formed in 1791 and named for Major Thomas Mathews, Speaker of the Virginia House of Delegates who enacted the legislation for its formation. With over 200 miles of shoreline along the inlets and tributaries of the Chesapeake Bay, it's no wonder that the people of Mathews have a deep-seated appreciation for the water, marshlands and forests that comprise the natural environment. Indeed, the water and rich agricultural lands are the mainstay of the economy, with commercial fishing, boat building, field crops and livestock production heading the employment scene. It's an early-to-bed, early-to-rise sort of place, with water sports and just taking time to smell the flowers heading the recreation and relaxation list.

Events and Attractions

Mathews Market Days is the high spot of the year in the county. The Thursday through Saturday big event takes place the weekend after Labor Day at the county's historic Courthouse Green, filled with wares of local craftspeople and artists, along with steaming seafood, music and other entertainment. The Saturday of the festival is definitely the time to make an appearance, especially for the **Governor's Club Blue Crab Derby**, the traditional crab race. Win or lose, you'll want to stay for the evening street dance. Also held at the Courthouse is the **Holiday Parade and Candlelight Open House**, complete with Santa Claus' arrival during the first weekend in December. The Mathews County Chamber of Commerce can provide all the details, 725-9009.

Believe it or not, Mathews is host to Tidewater's capital of country music, **Donk's Theater**, at the intersection of routes 198 and 223. Home to Virginia's "Li'l Ole Opry," hometown and big name

Cleanup Crusader

Back in the 1980s, Robert Dean was a recreational boater who liked to motor on the Chesapeake Bay and its many tributaries. What he noticed on his pleasure trips soon appalled him.

"I saw the garbage everyone was throwing into the waterways," says Dean, who lives in Virginia Beach. "People are using the earth as a trash dump."

Dean got busy. In 1989 he organized the first Clean the Bay Day, an all-volunteer effort to get people out to pick up every can, bottle or plastic container they came across as they walked the shore. That year, about 2,000 people carted away 30 tons of trash from 52 miles of coastline — trash that not only was unsightly but also endangered marine wildlife, especially birds, sea turtles and fish.

After such an auspicious beginning, the cleanup effort continues to grow. Last year, 5,000 volunteers gathered more than 100 tons of coastal debris — everything from microwaves to mopeds — throughout Virginia. With assistance from the Center for Marine Conservation, which operates a field office in Hampton, the cleanup effort has become even more streamlined: Volunteers now are given data cards listing 81 items that might turn up on the beaches along with information on how the card is used to compile an assessment of beach debris.

"Over the last six years, we have picked up just under 1 million pounds," notes Dean. Of that trash, more than 50 percent is plastic. But the No. 1 offender, by far, is cigarette butts. "If you look at our major highway intersections, you'll see hundreds of cigarette butts where people have dumped their ashtrays," says Dean. "When it rains, they get washed into our storm water and eventually reach the bay." And, despite what many people think, it takes six to seven years for a single cigarette filter to break down in the environment, he adds.

It saddens Dean, an avid defender of the environment, to report that there has been little improvement in peoples' habits over the past half-dozen years or so. "We haven't seen any dramatic changes at all," laments Dean, who hopes to someday see the end of Clean the Bay Day, "which would indicate there is no longer a need for a grassroots, all-volunteer organization to clean up the shoreline."

The 1995 Clean the Bay Day will be held Saturday, June 10, from 9 AM to noon. If you're interested in volunteering, call 1-800-SAVE BAY. Or, four weeks or less before the event, you can call the Clean the Bay Day Infoline at 245-5555, ext. 4444.

stars alike show up on the stage every other Saturday night. To get in rhythm with the beat, call 725-7760.

The fourth weekend in June, it's Gwynn's Island's time to shine. The **Gwynn's Island Festival** is a nonstop celebration of food, music, games, balloon rides and an antique show that begins Friday night and ends on Saturday afternoon. While you're on the island, you'll want to stop by the **Gwynn's Island Museum**, where displays of artifacts of Mathews County life from pre-Colonial to modern times can be found. The museum is open May through December, from 1 PM to 4 PM.

For the history buff, your expedition should start at the county's splendid **Courthouse on the Village Green**, a nationally registered landmark in continuous service since it was built in 1792. While you're there, stop into the restored **Tomkins Cottage** (c. 1818) and pick up more information from the Mathews County Historical Society which is headquartered there.

There are many Colonial and Civil War sites to explore, especially **Cricket Hill** which overlooks Gwynn's Island. It was here on July 9, 1776, that Lord Dunsmore, the last of Virginia's Royal Governors, was driven from American shores by Continental sharpshooters. While unused today, you might also want to visit the **New Point Comfort Lighthouse**, guarding the entrance to Mobjack Bay, restored by the county in the 1970s as a National Historic Landmark.

Food and Accommodations

We'll start with **Ravenswood Inn** at Todds Point that sits at the end of Route 613, where hosts Marshall and Linda Warner certainly know how to pamper. From six charming rooms with queen- or king-size beds and private baths, you can stroll to a soothing soak in the hot tub on the outside deck or splurge on a charter on the 30-foot sailboat that waits docked at the end of the pier, ready to sail out the East River and into the Bay. The inn is moderately priced, with complimentary evening cocktails, but no credit cards, children or pets. Call them at 725-7272.

On Gywnn's Island, you'll find the appropriately named **The Islander**, nestled just off the Bay in a sheltered harbor. Here there are 40 waterfront rooms, a swimming pool, sand beach and tennis courts. They do accept MasterCard and Visa; call 725-2151.

For you outdoorsy funseekers, there's the **New Point Campground**, just 7 miles south of the Courthouse on Route 14 E. Open April through October, it's right on the Bay, with a beach, boat rentals, marina, fishing, swimming pool and mini-golf course. For reservations for one of the 300 hookup sites, call Buck Webster at 725-5120.

Like Gloucester, Mathews County is a good place to come for intense treatment for shopping addiction withdrawal. There's the **Mathews Five and Dime**, **Country Casuals** (clothing for men and women) and **Sibley's General Store** where you can find things you never knew you wanted or needed. The best advice from our Insider friends is just to stop by **Fleet's** for a heaping plate of fried chicken and their fabulous potato cakes, swing by **Encore Video** to grab an old movie and keep the pace of total couch potato relaxation at its peak.

The Northern Neck

We move next up to the next skinny finger of land, pointing to the Chesapeake Bay and held by the Rappahannock River to the south and the Potomac to the north. This is the Northern Neck, which has held tightly to its own identity for more than 400 years. Called the Athens of America during the early 18th century, it boasts great plantations and hometowns to presidents, including George Washington and James Monroe. Remaining true to its agricultural heritage, it appears today almost as if no time has past since its earliest days, save for the few gas stations and wine and cheese shops scattered amongst its small, picture-perfect towns. Laced with small rivers and long tidal creeks, it's one of Mother Nature's finest backgrounds for a boater's paradise and, indeed, many Hampton Roads seamen keep their boats in one of the numerous marinas that are here.

In our brief visit, we'll continue to travel north, up the Bay coast, pointing out special places of interest along the way. We won't break everything down town by town, because in this unique community, if you blink, you're in the next town anyway. If, by example, you're planning a peaceful day exploring the Bay, you might pop into the Tri-Star "Social" Grocery in Kilmarnock and then swing over to White Stone to snag a bottle of Chablis from Freddy and Maggie Gilman's Wine and Cheese Shop, then coast back to Irvington to board the boat. All in less than 30 minutes. It's a place that's as intertwined by geography as it is history. And, as you launch over the Rappahannock River Bridge and coast down to its shore, you know it's a place you might never want to leave.

Attractions

As you could probably guess, the main attraction 'round these parts is the water. That means boats, and if you don't have one, you can catch a ride with Captain Gordon Evans who operates **Island & Bay Cruises** out of Reedville, 453-3430, sailing from the KOA Campground and then docking 13 miles off the Virginia Shore at Ewell, the largest of Smith Island's three fishing villages. You're welcome to pack your own picnic lunch or just be served a family-style, all-you-can-eat mega meal at **Smith Island Skipjack Res-**

taurant. You'll need to make reservations for the charter and moonlight sails.

If you've got a bit of fisherman's blood, **Potts Fishing Service**, also in Reedville, can fit the bill. Here, too, you'll need reservations. Call 453-4554 for charters, 453-5327 for headboat. If you'd rather, you can call Captain Bob Warren who operates *The Sunrise*, which can accommodate up to 22 passengers, at 453-4639.

While in Reedville, worth a visit is the **Fishermen s Museum**, 453-5371, open Monday through Friday 3 PM to 5 PM and Sunday from 1 PM til 5 PM, subject to change during the winter months. An original fisherman's cottage, it serves to house artifacts of the industry, especially menhaden fishing. You might arrive by land, but take a peek at visitors who come by water, rowing or motoring in by dinghy to the museum dock. If you've built up a hunger, pop into the **Deli at Smith Seafood**, where scrumptious scallops, shrimp and crab cakes are made daily for you to take out and enjoy.

Just up the road a piece in Heathville, there are a few other fishing boat possibilities. Sailing out of Ingram Bay is Captain Billy's *Liquid Assets*, a 40-footer designed for fishing parties and sightseeing. Best part of this charter is that landlubbers can get personalized fishing and cruising instructions. Call 453-SAIL for reservations. Also in Heathville, you'll find the 1986 Blue Fish Tournament Winner, Captain Danny Crabbe's *Kit II*. Licensed for 26 passengers, make your reserves by calling 453-3251.

From Urbanna, you can weave through Rappahannock River waters on a "Rivah Cruise" aboard the *Bethpager*, a traditional Chesapeake Bay deadrise vessel, beautifully restored for today's passengers. Catering and fishing charters are available; call 758-4349.

While the main evening attraction is the star-laden night sky, if you happen to be in Kilmarnock during the winter months, check for the schedule of events at the **Center for the Arts**, 435-2400. Eight events are held, including children's plays, opera, musicals and other concerts featuring professional and community musicians.

History buffs might want to travel back in time to visit **Hewick Plantation**, a 17th-century Colonial Virginia Landmark, just north of Urbanna off Route 227. The c. 1678 manor house, built for Christopher Robinson, a Burgesses, member of the King's Council and original Trustee of the College of William and Mary, is open for tours from 10 AM to 4 PM. A nominal admission charge will also afford you the opportunity to see the site of William and Mary archaeological department's ongoing dig (active since 1989). A bed and breakfast, **On The Plantation**, is also here, and it's a favorite site for local weddings and receptions. For information, call 758-4214.

Friends have also advised us of the **Annual Carters Creek Boat Parade**, ready to celebrate its third celebration on July 4th. Imitating a small Harborfest, work boats, pleasure craft, mini-tugs and any other floatable devises that happen to pull into the Creek at the appointed hour give a real show as they parade the waters, cheered on by those who line the docks and shoreline.

We saved the best for last. The **Urbanna Oyster Festival**, entering its 37th year and proudly hailed as the Official Oyster Festival of the Commonwealth. Round these parts, and for cities up and down the Eastern Seaboard, it's the place to see and be seen, not to mention getting caught up in the spirit of the Fireman's and Festival Parades, the street sales, carnival, arts and crafts, tall ships and entertainment galore. Held the first full weekend in November, the main attraction is, of course, oysters, served in what seems a hundred different ways . . . raw, roasted, stewed, fried or frittered . . . along with piping hot clam chowder, fritters and cakes, with crabcakes, soft crabs and steamed crabs tossed in for good measure. OK, there's burgers, dogs and ham biscuits too, just in case you needed to know. For a brochure for this year's schedule of events, call the Urbanna Oyster Festival Foundation, 758-0368.

Food and Accommodations

We must start with the place to stay, known worldwide for it's stately, yet casual in a genteel sort of way, atmosphere and primo Southern hospitality, **The Tides Inn** in Irvington, call 800-TIDESIN. It's a quietly elegant pocket of paradise poised on the waters of Carter's Creek and owned and operated by the Stephen's family since 1947. Here, men still don tie and jacket for dinner. Whether it's a round of 18 on the championship **Golden Eagle Golf Course** or the popular **Tartan Course**, a rousing game of bingo or shipboard horse racing in the living room after supper, or a twilight cruise on the *Miss Ann*, a stay here definitely falls into the category of retreat. The three restaurants are equally excellent, too. Our advice: Go for the mouth-watering soft shell crabs, served in season.

A little less expensive, but equally charming is the Tides Inn's sibling, **Tides Lodge**, call 800-248-4337. A AAA 4-Diamond resort and marina, the Lodge is a bit less formal than the Inn without sacrificing any of the attention and lavish service. Even the decor is splendid, as the Lodge is dressed in Campbell plaid to honor Sir Guy Campbell, the famous golf architect. If you choose to dine here, ask for Cynthia to bring you a seafood sampler; it's superb!

If Reedville is your stopover point, there are a few bed and breakfasts worthy of a few nights stay. **Cedar Grove B&B Inn**, 453-3915, operated by hosts Susan and Bob Tipton, is a stately Colonial Revival-style home that overlooks the Chesapeake Bay. From the wicker decorated balcony, you can languish away watching the lighthouse that guards the entrance to the Great Wicomico River and, in winter, spot the Artic swans that make these marshes their home. After a full breakfast prepared by Susan, a former student of the New York Culinary Institute of America, you can bat the ball on the tennis or croquet court, borrow a bicycle for a tour of town or wiggle your toes in the sand of the private beach.

Get acquainted with other visiting guests over a glass of wine at cocktail hour at **Elizabeth House**, 453-7016, an exceptional restoration of a sea captain's home built in 1835. At the foot of Main Street in Reedville, you can borrow the house skiff for a water tour or just stretch out on the dock watching the sailboats glide by. If you elect to stay here, do request the top floor suite that has its own wet bar refrigerator and Jacuzzi. Bring cash, please. No credit cards, children or pets are permitted.

Lastly, in Reedville is another sea captain's home updated for us spoiled guests of the 90s. You can arrive at **The Gables**, 453-5209, by boat to be pampered with a lavish breakfast spread and a long soak in their Victorian footed bathtub with original brass fixtures. (A modern shower is available, too, if you must hurry.) Only two rooms are offered in this fine home that rests just off the Bay on Cockrell's Creek, so do plan ahead. And, just like with the early captain who created this mansion, "plastic" is not recognized.

For a super casual and relaxing stay, we have to recommend **Windmill Point Resort and Conference Center**, 800-552-3743, perched at the end of Route 695 at the tip of the Northern Neck Peninsula where the Rappahannock River flows into the Bay. Wrapped around a 150-slip yacht harbor, the 62-room resort literally spills onto a mile-long sandy beach. If you must get any sort of exercise, you'll find two swimming pools, a golf course, tennis courts, nature trails for hiking and, of course, plenty of boating. When dining at the resort's **Dockside Hearth**, order the delectable crab bisque, and plan ahead for their phenomenal Sunday brunch buffet.

If you "vant to be alone" in a tranquil, wooded setting, try the **Whispering Pines Motel**, 453-1101, on Route 3 just north of White Stone. With just 29 rooms, you can spend quiet evenings and fun-filled days in the pool or with fishing, golf, tennis and restaurants all close by.

If Urbanna is your port of call, there are three particularly charming bed and breakfasts you might consider.

The **Duck Farm Inn**, surrounded by 12 waterfront acres and nestled in the center of 800 acres of lush, rolling fields, is one of the most picturesque places you're ever likely to find. Complete with its own private beach, you can hike in the woods, fish in the river, play board games in the parlor or just lounge on the deck or spacious lawn. The six guest rooms are handsomely furnished, as are the two dining rooms and library/TV room.

In the heart of the historic port town of Urbanna, **Atherson Hall Bed and**

Breakfast, 758-2809, is tastefully decorated with Virginia and Southern antiques, and they even provide bicycles for your ride through the tree-lined streets of this delightful town. Small children and pets are not welcome here, but Phyllis and Winston Hall, the proprietors, will go out of their way to make your visit a very special one. And, besides, you probably need a weekend away from the little ones anyway.

The **Inn at Levelfield**, 435-4887, is another bed and breakfast option. Inside this antebellum house, c. 1857, you'll find lush accommodations, including a private bath and fireplace in every guest room. Lunch and dinner are served Wednesday through Saturday, along with an enormous Sunday brunch and, of course, a complimentary breakfast each daybreak.

If camping in the woods along the water is your idea of a swell time, try the **Bethpage Camp Resort**, 758-4349, in Urbanna. They definitely speak "RV" here. With a lifeguarded swimming pool, swimming lake and beach, restaurant, tennis and basketball courts plus two equipped Recreation Buildings, you'll never want for something to do. And they'll also be pleased to outfit you for crabbing, fishing or cruising on the Rappahannock.

If all this relaxation is making you ravenous, here are a few of the places we've been advised to visit to soothe the hungries and have a good time while you're at it.

In White Stone, give the **Sandpiper** a try. While it doesn't offer the atmosphere of a four-course dinner at the Tides, for less than $20 you can be pampered with great home cooking, generously served. **McPatty's** in Kilmarnock, across from the bowling alley, has been dubbed "the galley in the alley" by the locals. With walls plastered with old pictures, owners Sam and Barbara serve up a great time in a neat atmosphere, along with some pretty tasty menu offerings, mainly seafood of course. On Main Street in Kilmarnock, you might stumble into **Lee's**, with good old home cookin', and then head back to White Stone to the *Annabelle Lee*, an old paddlewheel steamer, permanently docked at the base of the Rappahannock. The bar here is the real hopping nightspot of the area.

Or, if you've got a boat nearby, just pop by the **Tri-Star "Social" Grocery** and grab something fresh from the fryer, a hearty bottle of wine from the **White Stone Wine and Cheese Shop** and head back to the bow for an evening of good friends, good sailing stories and the most glorious night skies in the universe.

For information about the Middle Peninsula and the Northern Neck, contact the **Gloucester County Chamber of Commerce**, 693-2425; the **Mathews County Chamber of Commerce**, 725-9009; or the **Northern Neck Travel Council**, 453-3915 or 800-453-6167.

For those interested in exploring this region by water, the best source of information on publicly owned landings throughout the system is *The Chesapeake Bay & Susquehanna River Public Access Guide*, produced by the Virginia Governor's Council on the Environment under the Interstate Chesapeake Bay Agreement. It's free of charge from the Department of Game and Inland Fisheries, 367-1000.

Inside
Daytrips

No matter how stimulating our great region is, there comes a time when you've just got to get out of dodge . . . to flee the static scenery, to freshen your perspective and boost your mental attitude. These mini-escapes from reality can be made even more fulfilling when you can reach your destination within a few hours and within the comfort of your own sedan. You're the pilot, and you can steer towards a big dose of history, a wild and wonderful shopping excursion, an out-of-this-city dining experience, or just to spread-eagle on an empty plot of sand along some rolling surf with a good pulp paperback.

What we call Daytrips, we might as well call "head trips," because they give us, and you, the primo opportunity to break the everyday pattern and run away with the not-so-rich and famous to renew our spirit while we snoop around in someone else's backyard. Whether you head out over the Chesapeake Bay Bridge-Tunnel to the charming Eastern Shore, don your tri-cornered hat for a stroll through Colonial Williamsburg, or pack up your sand chair and bikini for the broad beaches of the Outer Banks, you can be in what will seem to be a faraway place in no time, all on one tank of gas.

So, fasten your seat belt, please. Come with us on a whirlwind tour of the cities and sights that are right around the corner in miles but galaxies away in explora-tion opportunities for the entire family. Ready? Let's go!

Hampton/Newport News

You've noticed, we're sure, that we constantly refer to our fair community as "southside Hampton Roads." Where, do you ask, is the northside? Well, it's right up there on the other side of the James River and Hampton Roads, and it's called the cities of Hampton and Newport News.

Not that we're competitive, or anything like that, but those folks on the opposite end of the Hampton Roads Bridge-Tunnel insist on having their own newspaper, the *Daily Press*, their own convention dome, the Hampton Coliseum, their own beaches, like the refurbished Buckroe, and even their own superstar attractions. Why, they can even claim the state's largest private employer, Newport News Shipbuilding.

Yet, friendly enemies that we are, we're obliged to give you a quick tour of our northern neighbors. We'll combine our topics for both cities, since they geographically blend from one to the other, and you can choose which places to visit based on your personal preferences.

A quick history lesson is in order too. Hampton was born in 1610 when the first settlers landed on the beach to the utter amazement of the quite content native Kecoughtan Indians. The city lays claim to the beginnings of free education, the downfall of Blackbeard the pirate (though there is, we must admit, a competing claim from Ocracoke Island, North Carolina), and the training of America's first astronauts. If that's not enough, they can also claim a rich military history tracing back to the Civil War.

Newport News got its start in 1607 when the Virginia Company of London gave Captain Christopher Newport the assignment to scope out a nifty spot for a new settlement on the James River. Newport and his crew from the ships *Susan Constant*, the *Godspeed* and the *Discovery* liked the looks of the sandy point at the mouth of the river, set up camp and called their settlement Jamestown. Over the years, as one story goes, because everyone would rush out to the point to spread the word that big boss Newport would be coming in with news from home, by 1619 the name that stuck was Newportes Newes, the oldest English place name of any city in the New World.

Together, Hampton and Newport News are referred to as the Peninsula, and the places to go and things to see will whisk you from the long-ago past to the space age future. We'll give you phone numbers for the attractions you might want to visit, but be advised that calling from southside is a nominal long-distance call.

Getting There

Getting to the Peninsula is a snap, unless you see the flashing light on the Interstate indicating traffic congestion at the Hampton Roads Bridge-Tunnel. If the lights are on hold and you get the all-clear signal, just zip down I-64 W. and in less than 30 minutes you can be inside a museum. An alternate route, an especially wise choice is you're coming from Chesapeake, is the Monitor-Merrimac Bridge-Tunnel (locally referred to as the M&M), accessed through I-664 in Suffolk.

Attractions

Peninsula museums are a visual and rich experience for all ages. Starting in Newport News, you'll want to visit the world-renowned **Mariner's Museum**, 595-0368, which explores our relationship with the sea. You should start with the film *Mariner*, narrated by James Earl Jones, and then set off to examine exquisite miniature ship models, carved figureheads, unbelievable scrimshaw, working steam engines and an Antique Boats Gallery. Alongside the museum is the 550-acre **Mariner's Museum Park** with nature and bike trails as well as boat rentals for fishing on Lake Maury. Open Monday through Saturday from 9 AM to 5 PM and Sundays from noon to 5 PM, there is a nominal admission charge to the museum.

Just across the street from the Mariner's Museum is the **Peninsula Fine Arts Center**, 596-8175, which has tripled its size in the last few years. Changing exhibits by living artists along with contemporary art from museum collections and private sources are on display. The gift shop is a treasure house of gifts, books, cards and unique decorative objects, so while admission to the museum is free, plan on spending a few dollars anyway. Don't try to visit on Mondays, they're closed; but come Tuesday through Saturday, 10 AM to 5 PM and Sundays, noon to 5 PM.

On J. Clyde Morris Boulevard is the museum created for kids of all ages, **The Virginia Living Museum**, 595-1900. Part zoo, part botanical gardens, part observatory and planetarium, there's also an aviary and massive aquarium. Especially popular is the Touch Tank for hands-on learning. Here you can reach out and touch something fishy. Outside there are animals, like skunks and even a bald eagle, that you can observe in their natural wooded habitats. There are nominal admission fees that vary with the parts of the museum you want to explore. We, heavy with children, say go for it all.

Leave terra firma and head to downtown Hampton, to the $30 million **Virginia Air and Space Center**, 727-0800, designated the official NASA Langley Visitor Center. On Settlers Landing Road and open every day of the week, here you'll see aircraft and spacecraft suspended from the center's 94-foot ceiling, a 3 billion-year-old moon rock, a flying machine tested before the Wright Brothers' flyer aircraft, and the Apollo 12 Command Module. Plus, there's the Hampton Roads History Center and the only IMAX theater in Southeastern Virginia. There's an admission charge for the center and the theater. Right next door on the downtown waterfront is the **Hampton Carousel**, built in 1920 and completely restored to its original beauty. For just 50¢, from April through October you can climb aboard history and take a twirl on an original steed or chariot.

Other sightseeing possibilities include **The War Memorial Museum** in Newport News and **Casemate Museum**, **Air Power Park**, **Bluebird Gap Farm** (pet an animal you would never allow in your home) and **Fort Wool/Fort Monroe** in Hampton.

Restaurants

On the Peninsula, you can take your pick of brand-name burger and fast-food places, but here are a few culinary gems

that we favor. **Bon Appetit**, 11710 Jefferson Avenue, 873-0644, is a charmer, with a scrumptious French/Vietnamese menu. Its chefs do wonderful and strange things with chicken, along with some grand stir-fry entrees. **Port Arthur** near the Mariner's Museum, 11137 Warwick Boulevard, 599-6474, is a very popular Chinese place; **Das Waldcafe**, 12529 Warwick Boulevard, 930-1781, is authentic German, with sauerbraten, spatzle and the most divine hazelnut cake. Another eatery on the scene is **Buckroe's Island Grill** at Salt Ponds Marina in Hampton, 850-5757. In the octagonal white dining room you can munch on fresh seafood prepared grilled, blackened or broiled with a multitude of toppings like roasted red pepper sauce, jerk seasonings or salsa. For lighter fare, order a platter of raw or steamed seafood or an appetizer of their delicious crab dip.

A sweetheart of a place is under the green awning at the **Grey Goose**, 723-7978, in Old Hampton across from the Air and Space Museum, with its intimate country ambiance and wonderful homemade soups, Brunswick stew and ham biscuits. It's a shame they're only open for lunch Monday through Saturday. For more of a resort-feel — "I'm out of town so why not go for it" — atmosphere, we recommend **The Restaurants at Kiln Creek Country Club**, 874-2600, off Jefferson Avenue in the delightful Kiln Creek Golf Course Community. Here you can be satisfied according to your hunger, from a wonderful club sandwich to a fine dinner of prime rib.

A relative newcomer to the eatery scene is a wacko place at 12644 Jefferson Avenue, just past the airport. Check out this name: **Oldies Vintage Tin Restaurant and Classic Glass Tavern**, 886-1264. Targeted directly at baby-boomers, you

Christmas in Williamsburg

Christmas in Williamsburg is Christmas in another era, stepping back from the modern shopping lists, wrapping paper and glitzy tinsel into a time more than 200 years past.

For a day or a weekend, nothing will instill the holiday spirit like a visit to Colonial Williamsburg during the holiday season. From the Grand Illumination in early December through Christmas week itself, there are programs, events and exhibitions galore. Not to mention the decorations . . . handmade from fruits, greens, berries and candles . . . one more exquisite than the next. Sing along with the strolling carolers and musicians, delight at the flaming cressets (iron baskets hung from iron poles that burn fat wood) that line the streets for warmth and light, try to count the more than 1,200 candles lit throughout the historic district and simply enjoy the old-fashioned Christmas cheer that's impossible to duplicate anywhere else.

If you do plan to make an overnight stay, reservations should be made as early as possible. For a free Christmas brochure that includes all the programs and events of the holiday season in Colonial Williamsburg, call (800) HISTORY.

can wash your burger down with the nostalgia generated by displays of a bright red 1965 Austin Healey 3000, a 1956 Corvette, a 1951 Ford Country Squire Woody, along with a restored pair of Donald Duck bikes and hundreds of vintage trains. Once you get through the six-page menu, you've got to check out the old-fashioned ice cream parlor, with walls decorated with cap guns, holsters and other cowboy memorabilia from the 1950s TV era. Order a Fuel Injection (an old-timey soda float) or a Tri-Carb (a banana split), go home for a nap, then come back at night for the DJ and band playing '50s and '60s music.

Shopping

A little bit of old, a little bit of new . . . shopping is a mixed-bag on the Peninsula. In Old Hampton, with its quaint brick and tree-lined streets, you'll see some wonderful little shops spotlighted by antique English street lamps. **Harrogate's, Ltd.** is a Peninsula tradition, with its fine china, crystal, Fabergé eggs and pewter collection. If you need to buy a lovely gift for someone that you feel guilty leaving back at home, this is the place to come. **The Old Hampton Bookstore** is filled to the rafters with a phenomenal selection of great tomes; **Kitty & Co.** on Queens Way is a must when you just really must have a fashionable new ensemble or that just-right accessory to complete your power outfit.

For mall lovers, there's **Coliseum Mall** in Hampton, with our favorite **Hecht's** as one anchor, along with your favorites like the **Limited** and so much more. **Patrick Henry Mall** and **Newmarket Mall** are Newport News' shopping haunts with much of the same mall-flavored department stores and specialty shops. The up-and-comers of this area have staked out the Denbigh area of Newport News as the place to build houses and raise kids and pets. Naturally, stores galore have followed the home-steaders, so the area in every compass point from Jefferson Avenue at Denbigh Boulevard has birthed a wide variety of options, like a **Wal-Mart** and **Sam's Club**, **TJ Maxx**, **Bootlegger's Shoes** and a broad stretch of drug stores and home centers.

Accommodations

If you choose to stay overnight, there are two primary hubs we'll point out. One is in Hampton in the Coliseum area off Mercury Boulevard. Because of the proximity to mega-shopping and the convention center, you'll find all the name brands spiffed up to their finest. Our vote goes to the **Radisson Hotel Hampton**, 700 Settlers Landing Road, 727-9700, adjacent to the visitors center and downtown marina. The suites are magnificent, and there's the outdoor dockside eatery, **Oyster Alley**, along with the *Miss Hampton II*, a tour boat that docks just outside the hotel's doors.

In Newport News, the Oyster Point corridor houses not only the nucleus of the city's business brains, but some fine overnight accommodations. The **Omni Newport News**, 1000 Omni Boulevard, 873-6664, is in the heart of the action, along with **Days Inn Oyster Point**, 11829 Fishing Point Drive, 873-6700. Any of these hotels can offer a pleasant night's sleep in clean and comfortable surroundings.

Phoebus

Phoebus is cute. This small pocket of cuteness is actually a tightly-knit Hampton community you can find when you take the Mallory Street exit off I-64 W. (the first exit you come to after the tunnel) and head towards Fort Monroe. Along Mallory are some of the best eats and most unique shopping experiences just waiting to happen, and a stopover there is similar to being whisked back in history to a time when people were friendly, life was slower and love was always in the air.

See what we mean with a browse through the incredible **Benders Books and Cards**, **Phoebus Needleworks and Crafts** and the **Electric Glass Company** where you'll find hand-blown goblets, Tiffany glass and etched glass for your front door. Locals are hard-pressed to reveal the secret that Clyde's serves up the coldest beer and best burger this side of Kansas; **Victorian Station**, in a charming Victorian home, not only offers a silky smooth quiche or chunky chicken salad, but is one of the last remaining places on the face of the earth where you can linger over afternoon tea enjoying with jam-lathered scones, tea cakes and open-faced sandwiches. Even hard-nosed Insiders know that an afternoon in Phoebus is better than a month with a therapist. Don't even think about leaving town until you've been here.

For More Information

As in all Hampton Roads cities, an army of knowledgeable patriots stands ready to swamp you with information about their respective cities. In Hampton, you can reach the **Visitors Center**, 710 Settlers Landing Road, at 727-1102 or (800) 800-2202. In Newport News, the number to call for the **Tourist Information Center**, 13560 Jefferson Avenue, is 886-2737.

Smithfield

Smithfield may be best known for its distinctive, salty-flavored hams. But it's also the perfect destination for a country drive. This is a traditional Virginia town that proudly preserves its historic past.

Smithfield, in Isle of Wight County, has produced its world-famous hams since 1779. By then the town along the Pagan River was a busy port for tobacco and peanuts that flourished in the rich soil. The secret to a Smithfield ham is fattening hogs on native peanuts. The hams also get their flavor from curing over slow hickory fires. To get a Smithfield pedigree, a ham must hail from Smithfield and nowhere else.

Getting There

From Norfolk, Virginia Beach, Chesapeake and Portsmouth, get on Route 17 N. in Portsmouth (High Street) and stay on it until it intersects Route 10. Turn left and follow the signs to downtown Smithfield. The trip will take no more than an hour. From Suffolk, take Route 258 N. and you'll be in Smithfield in about 30 minutes.

Attractions

The town itself is charming and is a National Historic District. Its main street is lined with restored homes, many of them large, ornate Victorians. There are 15 pre-Revolutionary War homes. Many of the back yards run right down to the Pagan River. Smithfield was settled in 1752 by British merchants and sea captains, and for more than 20 years it was a British colony.

To get oriented, stop by the **Old Isle of Wight Courthouse**, which houses the county tourism bureau and chamber of commerce, and pick up brochures and a walking tour map, 357-5182. The courthouse is at Main and Mason streets and is usually open Tuesday through Friday and on weekends in spring and summer.

On your way into town, you'll see a sign for **Saint Luke's Church** on Route 10. Built in 1632, it is the country's only original Gothic church and the oldest church of English foundation in America. This Episcopal church, nicknamed "Old Brick," is still in use and has lovely wooded grounds. Its Jacobean interior features gables, buttresses and traceried windows. St. Luke's, a National Shrine, is open daily except during January, 357-3367. It sits back from the parking lot, so plan on a short, pleasant walk to reach the church. Admission is free.

The **Isle of Wight County Museum**, at Main and Church streets, is housed in a former bank built in 1913 and has archeological displays highlighting county history. Exhibits include a country store and Civil War artifacts. The building itself is worth seeing with its imported marble and tile and impressive Tiffany-style dome skylight, 357-7459. Admission is free.

The Old Isle of Wight Courthouse dates from 1750. Its clerk's office and county jail are restored. The courthouse is owned by the Association for the Preservation of Virginia Antiquities. Call 357-5182.

A walking tour map will lead you by 65 of Smithfield's historic homes and buildings, including **Oak Grove Academy** at 204 Grace Street. It was built in 1836 as a school for young women. The **Keitz-Mannion House** at 344 S. Church Street was constructed in 1876 as a Methodist parsonage and was originally located across the street. For the full tour, allow about an hour plus an extra 15 minutes for a brisk walk to **Windsor Castle** on Jericho Road. This stucco-covered brick home was built in 1750 by Arthur Smith IV, founder of Smithfield.

For a peek inside one of Smithfield's stately houses visit **The Collage and Gallery Studios**, a working studio and gallery in a Victorian home built around the turn of the century. It is at 346 Main Street. Admission is from 10 AM to 3 PM Tuesday to Saturday and 1 to 5 PM Sunday. Many handcrafted items are for sale, 357-7707.

Out in the country is **Fort Boykins State Park** with a fort created in 1623 to protect settlers from Native Americans and raiding Spaniards. The fort on the banks of the James River still has its Civil War-era earthworks and has been involved in every military campaign fought on American soil. There is a gazebo overlooking the river and a picnic area. From the river banks you can see the Navy's "mothball fleet" of retired warships anchored in the James River. The grounds include the second-largest black walnut tree in the state, and you'll always find something blooming in the fort's gardens.

For a real treat, time your visit for Smithfield's popular **Olden Days Festival**. It usually is held on the last weekend in May and starts on a Friday. Free events include an antique car show, street bazaar, fire engine rides, a children's buggy parade and raft races. You can chow down on an all-you-can-eat pancake breakfast or spaghetti dinner or attend an old-fashioned ice cream social.

About 20 minutes outside of town is **Chippokes Plantation State Park** on the James River. The park is on Route 634. From Smithfield take Route 10 west and follow the brown signs. Farming started here in 1619, making this the oldest con-

tinually farmed property in the country. The property includes an antebellum mansion, visitors center, and a farm and forestry museum. There are picnic spots near a beach where fossils poke through the sand. While there's no swimming allowed in the river, a swimming pool is open in warmer months. There is an admission fee. Call 294-3625 or 294-3439. Two fun annual events at the park are a gas- and steam-engine show in June and the **Pork, Peanut and Pine Festival** in July.

Restaurants

For a small town, Smithfield has several good dining choices, from down-home cooking to refined cuisine.

Smithfield Station at 415 S. Church Street, on the banks of the Pagan River, has a regional reputation that draws diners from throughout Hampton Roads. The restaurant serves seafood, pork, pasta and other local favorites during lunch and dinner daily. On Sundays a breakfast buffet includes an omelet bar. Dinner reservations are recommended. After dining, stroll along the boardwalk that links the restaurant to its marina. In warmer months an outdoor raw bar serves crabs and other seafood for casual dining. During summer weekends you may find musicians entertaining here. Call 399-2874 toll-free from Hampton Roads or 357-7700 locally.

Other dining options include **Angelo's Seafood and Steak House**, 1804 S. Church Street, 357-3104, which serves mainly steak and seafood for lunch and dinner. The restaurant is open daily. **Smithfield Confectionery and Ice Cream Parlor**, 208 Main Street, has a menu of sandwiches as well as ice cream. Its classic soda fountain will take you back in time. The restaurant is open daily; call 357-6166. A recent addition to the dining lineup is **Smithfield Gourmet Bakery** at 218 Main Street, 357-0045. The 25-seat cafe will tempt you with a variety of breads, cakes and pastries, including salt-rising loaves. The bakery takes orders for dietetic desserts. Lunch features sandwiches, and in the summer you'll find fresh lemonade on the menu.

We're fond of the **Twins Old Town Inn** at 220 Main Street, a cafe frequented mostly by locals. It is run by twin sisters who whip up good country cooking for breakfast and lunch. The restaurant closes on Sunday and serves only breakfast on Saturday; call 357-3031. Another possibility is **Ken's Bar-B-Q Place** on Highway 258, 357-5601. Fans of North Carolina-style barbecue will find the "que" to their liking. Ribs, pit-cooked steaks and homemade desserts are on the menu during both lunch and dinner.

Accommodations

The **Isle of Wight Inn**, 1607 S. Church Street, 357-3176, has 12 guest rooms, including honeymoon suites with hot tubs and fireplaces. Although it is relatively new, it has a charming historic feel.

Besides being a restaurant (see the above entry), **Smithfield Station** has 15 guest rooms, most of which overlook boats moored at the inn's 61-slip marina. Last fall Smithfield Station added a lighthouse-shaped pavilion that houses elegant suites with panoramic views of the river.

Four Square Plantation recently opened west of Smithfield on Route 620. This bed and breakfast is in an 1807 home surrounded by four landscaped acres that sit in the midst of farm crops. The antique-filled house is on the National Historic Register. It has three guest rooms and serves a full breakfast topped off by Smithfield ham, of course. Call 365-0749 for reservations.

Photo: Paramount's Kings Dominion

Paramount's Kings Dominion, located 20 miles north of Richmond, features the White Water Canyon ride.

Shopping

For antiques try the **Isle of Wight Inn** at 1607 Church Street. Its gift shop has some unusual pieces and is where we go to buy restored antique clocks. **Wharf Hill Antiques**, 218 Main Street, is a general antique store with furniture, glassware and prints. The **Smithfield Antiques Center** has about 25 dealers at 131 Main Street. It is open Wednesday through Sunday. **Smithfield Rare Books**, Main and Underwood, specializes in Virginiana, history and science.

For brass, sterling or porcelain items, visit **Southern Accent's Cards and Gifts**, 913 S. Church Street. If you want a Smithfield souvenir, try **Simpson's Pharmacy**, 221 Main Street. Or for the ultimate Smithfield gift, go to the **Joyner of Smithfield Ham Shop** at 315 Main Street. There you'll find Smithfield and country hams as well as peanuts and gift baskets.

On the way to Smithfield along Highway 10 is the small community of Carrolton where there are several stores specializing in antiques and some reproduction furniture.

Recreation

The **Smithfield Downs Golf Course** is an 18-hole private course open daily to the public. It is on Highway 258 just outside town. Although it is only 5,200 yards long, this course is a challenging one for all golfers. You can reach them at 357-3101.

Williamsburg

If you're seeking the perfect hodge-podge of Colonial ambiance tossed with a little contemporary bargain shopping, turn your cruise control towards mecca . . . to Williamsburg. In fact, you can work up into a full-blown sightseeing/shopping frenzy in the mere 45 minutes on the speedy interstate that it will take you to get there from Hampton Roads.

Because this is intended to be a daytrip guide, we won't even begin to tell you about all the teeth-gritting rides, fabulous architecture and wonderful food that you'll find at Busch Gardens on the fringes of Williamsburg. That alone is a daytrip unto itself. If you're so inclined to stretch your Williamsburg visit into more than one day, there are numerous motels and hotels with open registers, ranging from the sublime Williamsburg Inn to brand name sleep-places like Econo Lodge, Ramada and Holiday Inn. If you plan to stay over during peak summer season or on a holiday, definitely make reservations in advance.

A few notes about conduct in the Historic Area. While touring any restored building, even thinking about fondling the priceless furnishings and accessories is prohibited, as is smoking, drinking or eating. No pets, strollers or baby carriages are allowed either. You may bring a camera or camcorder into the buildings and shops, but you will be asked to put them away in their cases during any program or tour lecture. Cranky children will have to be likewise stowed, preferably beyond earshot of your fellow visitors.

Getting There

From southside Hampton Roads, Williamsburg is a fairly quick shot north on Interstate 64 W. (yes, the road is the western leg of I-64, but you're actually heading north — go figure), and the only congestion you're likely to encounter is at the Hampton Roads Bridge-Tunnel that connects Norfolk to Hampton. Once you've spurted through the tube, it's a pleasant 45-minute drive. Interstate exit signs are clearly marked. Take the Busch Gardens Exit for that destination, or follow the signs a few more miles north pointing you to the College of William & Mary to reach the Historic Area.

Attractions

Wherever do we begin? The 173 acres occupied by **Williamsburg's Historic Area** is chocka-block with 18th-century public buildings, homes, crafts shops and over 90 acres of gardens and greens. If you're a true history buff, we suggest you first go to the **Visitors Center**, which is located on Route 132Y off the Colonial Parkway. Here you can see the film *Williamsburg — The Story of a Patriot*, which is shown continually throughout the day. Shuttle buses also leave every few minutes from the lower level that will take you directly to the Historic Area, so you'll not have any parking headaches. For a full tour, you will need to purchase an admission ticket, available at the Visitors Center.

We'll start at the **Governor's Palace**, the place where everyone wants to have their picture taken. The residence of seven royal governors and the first two governors of the Commonwealth of Virginia, the restored interiors and formal gardens are simply gorgeous. Walking down Palace Green will take you to **Duke of Gloucester Street** (Dog Street in local language), where Colonial milliners, silversmiths, wigmakers, bakers, blacksmiths and more set up shop 300 years ago. All are staffed by contemporary craftspeople donning authentic wardrobe who will be pleased to answer any of your questions and sell you a few wares priced at today's dollar.

The trail down Duke of Gloucester ends at the front steps of the **Capitol**, where the principles of self-government, individual liberty and responsible leadership were developed by Virginia's patriots. If you hike across the green on the pedestrian pathway, you'll come to a popular photo opportunity . . . the **Public Gaol** on Nicholson Street. Here you can fling your arms into the wooden shackles while your partner snaps away.

Two fine museums are also located within walking distance. **The DeWitt Wallace Decorative Arts Gallery** houses more than 8,000 objects from Colonial Williamsburg's permanent collection of 18th-century ceramics, furniture, metals, maps, prints and textiles. The **Abbey Aldrich Rockefeller Folk Art Center** offers changing exhibits of American Folk art. Both museums require a separate ticket for admission.

On the opposite end of Duke of Gloucester from the Capitol, you'll be able to stroll through **Merchant's Square** and then onto the campus of the **College of William & Mary**. You'll feel smarter just touching the weathered brick walls of these truly handsome buildings, home to the second oldest college in the country.

Restaurants

You can dine or eat-on-the-run. The choice is yours. We prefer the Colonial taverns for their warm, fuzzy feeling and consistently excellent menus. There are three in the Historic Area. **Christiana Campbell's Tavern** was one of George Washington's favorites, with skillet fried chicken, pecan waffles and Southern spoon bread. **Josiah Chownings Tavern**, adjacent to the Courthouse, is a typical Colonial alehouse, favored for its sandwiches, Brunswick stew and Welsh rabbit. At night take in the Gambols — Colonial games, entertainment and "diversions." Lastly, there's **King's Arms Tavern** on Duke of Gloucester Street where peanut soup with Sally Lunn bread is a must to start, followed by Virginia ham or prime rib. To make reservations at any of the taverns, call 229-2141 or (800) TAVERNS.

For contemporary dining with all the graciousness of Southern hospitality, our unanimous vote goes to a tie. First, we highly recommend **The Regency Room** at the Williamsburg Inn. Divine breads, prime rib, seafood and veal match beautifully with the extensive wine list. Sunday brunch here is one you'll talk about for weeks. Reservations are definitely required for dinner, 229-2141. Next is the **Trellis**, located in Merchant's Square and the creation of renowned Executive Chef Marcel Desaulniers, host of his own TV show, "Death by Chocolate," which should give you a clue as to what to order as your feast finale. The mesquite-grilled fare and regional specialities like Chesapeake Bay seafood and Smithfield ham laced with divinely delicate sauces can not be imitated. The prix fixe seasonal supper is always a superb choice, but a limited number of à la carte main dishes are available. Whether you opt for a table in the intimate Vault Room, Grill Room or Garden Room, or linger in the Cafe or outdoor bistro, your meal will be a delight. Call early to reserve the room of your choice: 229-8610.

Shopping

Now we're getting warm. Williamsburg is host to some of the finest discount shopping this side of the recession. Comfy shoes are the basic entry requirement at the world-famous

Williamsburg Pottery, located 5 miles west of Williamsburg in Lightfoot. From a roadside shed on a half-acre lot, the Pottery has sprawled to more than 200 acres, with more than 30 structures including a passive solar building the size of eight football fields. This book isn't long enough for a laundry list of what goodies you can snap up for tiny prices. China, glassware and stemware, furniture, lamps, wicker and, of course, pottery is just the beginning. It also has a wonderful gourmet food section, and the largest wine selection in the state of Virginia.

Stuff those newspaper-wrapped goodies from the Pottery in your trunk and drive back towards town to the **Williamsburg Outlet Mall**. The one-story bargain mecca is so popular that it expanded to its full-blown size of more than 60 factory outlet shops, all arranged in a cross pattern with the food court in the middle of the "X." For ladies, there's the Dress Barn, Hit or Miss and Bruce Alan Bags, Etc. For men, head to Bugle Boy, Cape Isle Knitters and S&K Famous Brands. Join forces to browse The Kitchen Place, The Paper Factory, Book Hutch and Solid Brass of Williamsburg. Grab a sugar hit from the Fudge Factory, jump on in the car and head to . . .

Berkeley Commons, just a hop down Richmond Road towards town. We are now talking top-of-the-line, bottom-of-the wallet type shopping mania. Calvin Klein, J. Crew, J.G. Hook, Jones New York, Coach, Anne Kline, Liz Claiborne, Geoffry Beene, Brooks Bros. . . . need we say more? The entire U-shaped outlet center is charming and especially attractive with its savings to 70 percent off the original hefty price tags that designer wear demands. The only eatery here is the Pelican Cafe. They make a wonderful sandwich platter, reasonably priced, with just enough fuel to keep your motor going to one last discounter center.

Patriot Plaza Outlets, just down Richmond Road from Berkeley Commons, is a show-off . . . not just with its handsome architecture, but with its shops and showrooms. West Point Pepperell, Lenox, Villeroy and Boch, Gorham and Dansk all have their outlets here. But don't leave without us. We'll be between Ben & Jerry's and the Ralph Lauren shop.

All along **Richmond Road** are other small centers with wonderful crafts and gift shops. Back in town, there's **Merchant's Square** in the city's center. Here are some exquisite shops offering fine apparel for women (Binn's, Casey's and Laura Ashley) and for men (Beecroft and Bull, Ltd.). For kids, don't pass up Uncommon Toys, and everyone will enjoy relaxing in the wonderful Rizzoli Bookstore. Sign of the Rooster for folk art, Quilts Unlimited and Needle-crafts of the Nicholson-White House are also on the must-see list.

On your way back to Hampton Roads, there are two other stops you should make . . . Yorktown and Jamestown, which, along with Williamsburg, define the Historic Triangle. See our next section for details.

For More Information

For more than you'd even really want to know about Colonial Williamsburg and beyond, call (800) HISTORY. The free call will earn you a complimentary copy of the Vacation Planner, with all the details for full enjoyment of this special place. You should also pick up a copy of *The Insiders' Guide to Williamsburg, Jamestown and Yorktown*, which, as you hopefully already know from this book,

will give you the true "inside" scoop on the area.

Jamestown/Yorktown

Two of the most historic sites in the country are within an easy hour's drive from the Norfolk/Virginia Beach area. If you're already planning a trip to Williamsburg, they are definitely worth working into your itinerary. However, it is feasible to zip up for a fast-paced day and tour both Jamestown and Yorktown.

Jamestown, founded in 1607, is the site of the country's first permanent English-speaking settlement. The early years were tough on the settlers as humid summers, cold winters, hungry mosquitoes and unfriendly Indians thwarted their settlement efforts. Jamestown endured, however, and became Virginia's first capital. After the Colonial capital moved to Williamsburg in 1699, Jamestown ceased to exist as a community. Today it is the site of a painstaking, ongoing restoration.

Nearby Yorktown is a scenic town on the banks of the York River. Its claim to fame is being the place where the British threw up the white flag in 1781 and ended the Revolutionary War. Yorktown was established in 1661 and is filled with history.

Getting There

Take Interstate 64 and head west. Go through the Hampton Roads Bridge-Tunnel and keep going. If you're not familiar with the area, it's easiest to head for Yorktown first and start your tour there. Take Route 17 N. (J. Clyde Morris Boulevard) in Newport News. Look for signs steering you toward the Yorktown Visitor Center run by the National Park Service.

Monumental Taste

There is no better place to enjoy a special and unique seafood dinner than in the original birthplace of America's freedom.

Nick's Seafood Pavilion

Water Street
Yorktown
(804) 887-5269

When you finish at Yorktown, take the scenic Colonial National Parkway to Jamestown. This 23-mile wooded stretch directly links the Yorktown Visitor Center with Jamestown Island. Along the way you'll see historic markers, picnic areas and magnificent views of the James and York rivers. In spring and fall the scenery is spectacular. Keep a light foot on the gas pedal. The parkway is part of a federal park, and the speed limit is only 45 m.p.h.

If you're returning to the Norfolk/Virginia Beach area from Jamestown, get on Route 5 and take it to I-64 E.

Attractions

Both the Yorktown Battlefield and Jamestown Island are part of **Colonial National Historical Park**, which includes the parkway that connects them.

In Yorktown, start your tour at the **Yorktown Visitor Center**, 898-3400. Admission to this National Park Service site is free. Get oriented with a 15-minute film, pick up maps and check out the exhibits. Our favorites are George Washington's canvas battle tent preserved behind glass and a replica of a British warship. Children love prowling through the ship. Older ones will enjoy dioramas depicting the Revolutionary War through a boy's eyes.

Be sure to take a drive through the battlefields where you'll see earthworks, a historic house and the surrender site. There are markers along the way and free maps to guide you. For $2 you can rent a tape with a narration of what you're seeing. The tape comes with its own cassette player. There are numerous places to get out of the car and inspect the battlefields. The visitors center is open daily.

The **Yorktown Victory Center** is on Old Route 238, 887-1776. It was built by the Commonwealth of Virginia and is operated by the state-run Jamestown-Yorktown Foundation. Outside is a re-creation of a Continental Army camp. Interpreters also bring to life an 18th-century farm as they garden, dip candles and prepare wool and flax. Inside the center are interesting exhibits pertaining to the

Revolutionary War and the events leading up to it. There also is a 28-minute film that focuses on the people who lived during the Revolution. There is an admission fee for anyone who lives outside Williamsburg and James City and York counties. The best deal is a combination ticket to the center and Jamestown Settlement in Jamestown. The center is open daily. In April 1995 it wrapped up a nearly $4 million expansion that included new exhibits.

Another interesting site in Yorktown is the **victory statue**, which was ordered by the Continental Congress in 1781 but not started until 1881. The statue is downtown. Note the inscriptions in the base and the lightning rod on top.

To get completely away from the Revolutionary War stop by **The Watermen's Museum** on Water Street, 887-2641. It pays tribute to the crabbers, fishermen and oystermen who work the Chesapeake Bay and its tributaries. The museum is housed in a 1935 Colonial Revival wooden house floated across the York River in 1987 to its present site. It features an excellent collection of artifacts, photographs and literature about watermen. Outside are work boats and other traditional tools of the trade. There is a small admission fee. The museum generally closes in winter.

From a dock outside the Watermen's Museum, you can board a **Chesapeake Bay Deadrise** for a day-long fishing trip or an evening river cruise. The traditional waterman's boat requires a minimal number of passengers and runs from Memorial Day through October. Call ahead for times and prices, 879-8276.

While in Yorktown you may want to check out the York River beach in downtown Yorktown and also drive past some of the town's historic homes, businesses and churches. The town celebrated its 300th anniversary in 1991. Its oldest remaining building is the **Sessions House**, built in 1692.

In Jamestown there are two main places to see. The Jamestown-Yorktown Foundation runs Jamestown Settlement. Jamestown Island is part of the Colonial National Historical Park. Start your tour at either place.

At the **Jamestown Settlement**, which is just off Route 31, you'll see costumed participants pretending to be settlers living in a re-created fort. Docked along the James River are full-size replicas of the three ships that brought the first settlers in 1607. There also is a museum with displays on English colonization, the Powhatan Indians and the settlement's early years. A 20-minute film gives a good overview. There is a charge to visit the Settlement, which is open daily; call 229-1607. The best deal is to buy a joint ticket that also admits you to the Yorktown Victory Center.

There also is a fee to drive onto **Jamestown Island**, which is a National Park Service site, 229-1733. However, if someone in your car has a Golden Age Passport from the U.S. Park Service, everyone in the car gets in for free. Once on the island you can see a 15-minute film in the visitors center and look at displays of 17th-century artifacts. Outside are 3- and 5-mile drives that loop through the island. You can either join a guided tour or pick up brochures for a self-guided tour. Costumed glassblowers and potters on the island represent the island's first industries. The only 17th-century structure still standing at Jamestown is the 1639 Church Tower. Otherwise you see ruins of the original settlement and foundations of early buildings.

The Hampton Harbor Tour: A Three-Hour History Lesson

From 1716 to 1718, Blackbeard the Pirate and his 700-man crew robbed anything sailing in and out of the Hampton Harbor. That activity ended when some British heavies stabbed, shot and beheaded him. From the *Miss Hampton II*, you can see the ivy-covered tree that held the pole with Blackbeard's head, along with other scintillating bits of history that await discovery along the shores of the Chesapeake Bay.

The *Miss Hampton II* is a 65-foot cruise boat that leaves the Downtown Hampton Visitors Center each April through September to travel along these historic waters. In a speedy three hours, the boat cruises from its port to the Norfolk Naval Base and offers a panoramic view of the Bay's waterfront from both its upper and lower decks. This is a great excursion for the kids . . . not only can they soak up a little history, they can chow down on the ship's delish cheeseburgers, as well.

Sliding out into the Bay, you'll see the outline of Newport News, where Christopher Newport set up his store and spread his "Newport News." On the site where the Strawberry Banks Hotel now sits, Captain John Smith and his strawberry-loving crew often landed to satisfy their sweet-tooth and aid the healing of their scurvy. Then you'll see Old Point Comfort, named because of the comfort it gave to Smith's crew and today known as Fort Monroe, landmarked by the renovated Chamberlain Hotel.

Kids love the odd little island of Fort Wool. It is here that Robert E. Lee helped supervise the building of the Fort, and where Andrew Jackson came to vacation. Sitting next to the South Island of the Hampton Roads Bridge-Tunnel, Fort Wool played a major role in the battle of the *Monitor* and *Merrimac*. Cruise boat guests are invited to take their lunch or snack onto the island for a picnic and stand on historic ground.

The Norfolk Naval Base is the last leg of the tour with its views of the warships, guided missile cruisers and nuclear-powered subs. Whether looking up to see helicopters and planes, down into the Bay waters to watch watermen at work, or checking out the coastline, the Hampton Harbor Tour is a delight for all ages.

For more detailed information, call the Hampton Visitors Center at 727-1102 or (800) 244-1040.

Restaurants

If you want to eat in Jamestown your only options are the snack bar at the Jamestown Settlement or the picnic lunch you hauled along. There is no food available on Jamestown Island, but drinks are sold outside the **Glasshouse**. For a real treat, ride the ferry from Jamestown to Surry County and eat at the **Surry House** on Route 10, which is renowned for its country cooking, 294-3389. The half-hour trip on the state-owned ferry is great fun and provides a terrific view of the ships docked at Jamestown. For departure times and prices call 229-4193.

There are several restaurants in Yorktown. The most famous is **Nick's Seafood Pavilion** on Water Street, 887-5269. Founded in 1940, the restaurant has an elaborate decor and excellent seafood. More informal restaurants include the **Yorktown Pub** at 540 Water Street, 898-8793, **Sammy & Nick's Family Steak House**, 11806 George Washington Boulevard, 898-3070, and **The River Room** of the Duke of York Motor Hotel at 508 Water Street, 898-5270.

Shopping

There are gift shops at the various historic sites. For art try the **On the Hill Creative Arts Center** in Yorktown at 121 Alexander Hamilton Boulevard. This is a cooperative gallery of local artists. Nationally known folk artist **Nancy Thomas** also maintains a Yorktown gallery at 145 Ballard Street that feature many of the angels that have gained her acclaim. **The Yorktown Shoppe** on Main Street has a variety of gift items.

For antiques **The Galleria Antique Mall** on Route 17 in Yorktown is the place to stop. This 40,000-square-foot antique mall has 130 dealers selling everything from art nouveau to precious European antiques. The mall also runs several weekly auctions. It is at 7628 George Washington Highway in Yorktown and is open daily. Another possibility is **Swan Tavern Antiques** at 300 Main Street.

Accommodations

Your best bets are the approximately 85 motels and hotels in or near Williamsburg or the **Duke of York Motor Hotel** overlooking the York River in Yorktown, 898-3232.

For More Information

Write the Williamsburg Area Convention and Visitors Bureau at P.O. Box 3585, Williamsburg, 23187 or call (800) 368-6511 or 253-0192. For a detailed guide, our sister book, *The Insiders' Guide to Williamsburg, Jamestown-Yorktown*, is the way to go.

Richmond

There is so much to do in Richmond and surrounding counties that you could spend days here. It's one of our favorite cities to visit. With nearly 20 museums and 30 other interesting places to visit, we still haven't seen all of it yet.

Ever since PBS showed its documentary on the Civil War several years ago, Richmond has been invaded by history buffs from around the world. But there's more to see here than the city's Civil War heritage; Richmond boasts great architecture in its historic neighborhoods, excellent museums and fine restaurants.

Getting There

Head straight up Interstate 64 W. and keep going for about 90 minutes. To get downtown take the Fifth Street exit to Broad Street and maneuver through the city from there.

Attractions

If you're fascinated by history of the War Between the States, start at either the **Richmond National Battlefield Park Visitor Center** or the **Museum and White House of the Confederacy**. The center at 3215 Broad Street, 226-1981, has exhibits, a film and employees to guide you toward the city's numerous battlefields. It is open daily and admission is free.

The Museum and White House (former home of Confederate President Jefferson Davis) have the world's largest collection of Confederate memorabilia. Both are fascinating, so plan on spending several hours. They are at 12th and E. Clay Street, 649-1861, and are open daily. There is an admission fee.

Other must-sees include the **Richmond Children's Museum** at 740 N. Sixth Street, 643-JIDO, and the **Science Museum of Virginia** at 2500 W. Broad Street, 371-1013. Both are hands-on places all ages will enjoy. The **Virginia Museum of Fine Arts** at 2800 Grove Avenue, 367-0844, has a vast art collection from all periods. The science museum is open daily. The other museums close on Monday. All charge admission fees.

Two other museums that are favorites of ours are the **Edgar Allan Poe Museum** at 1914 E. Main Street, 648-5523, and **The Valentine Museum** at 1015 E. Clay Street, 649-0711. The Poe museum pays tribute to Richmond's native son. It is housed in Richmond's oldest building, a stone house built in 1737. The Valentine Museum focuses on the life and times of old Richmond and has one of the country's best costume collections. Both are open daily and charge admission fees.

Richmond's newest attraction is the $26 million **Valentine Riverside**, which opened in 1994 on the site of the historic Tredegar Iron Works along the James River. The iron works once supplied Confederate troops with weapons. Today this history park and museum complex lets visitors become time travelers who interact with scenes from 300 years of Richmond's history. Plan on spending a lot of time here. For information, call 649-0711.

For a peek at Richmond life in the 18th century, sit in on a docent tour of **St. John's Church**. This is where Patrick Henry made his "give me liberty, or give me death" speech, and the tour guides give just about as rousing an oratory. The church is at 2401 E. Broad Street in Church Hill and is Richmond's oldest church; call 648-5015. Outside is the burial spot for Edgar Allan Poe's mother, colonist George Wythe and several Virginia governors.

You also might want to check out the **State Capitol** at Ninth and Grace streets. The building was designed by Thomas Jefferson and built in 1788. The grounds include fountains and statues of famous Virginians. The Capitol is open daily.

For outdoor activities wander along the **James River** downtown along Tredegar Street or along **Monument Avenue**, named for its many historic statues. **Maymont** is a 100-acre Victorian state with a mansion, elaborate gardens and petting zoo. The paths along its grounds attract wildlife lovers, joggers, parents strolling babies and lots of other people. Maymont is at 1700 Hampton Street, 358-7166. You also may want to wander through some of Richmond's historic neighborhoods such as **The Fan, Church Hill** and **Jackson Ward**.

One fun event to attend in Richmond is the **Bizarre Bazaar**, held two times a year — The Christmas Collection show in December held at the Virginia Fairgrounds' Strawberry Hill and the Spring Market show in April at The Richmond Centre. Both offer an array of unusual gifts, gourmet foods, quality crafts, artists, seasonal decorations and gifts, imported items . . . the list continues. Started in 1975, the shows now attract more than 20,000 people a year. For more information, call (804) 288-7555.

Another event we'll drive to Richmond for is the giant **flea market** held the first weekend of every month at the Virginia Fairgrounds, 228-3200. The **state fair**, held every September, is another reason to drive to the capitol city.

About 20 miles outside Richmond is one of our favorite places to go — **Kings Dominion, 876-5000**. This 400-acre theme park is open from spring through fall with more than 40 fun rides. It is at Interstate 95 N. and Route 30. Plan to stay a whole day, and be sure to bring your bathing suits and towels for the nifty water park that's included in the admission price.

Restaurants

You'll find lots of restaurants in the Shockoe Bottom area, Carytown, Fan District and around Virginia Commonwealth University (VCU). Also, suburban Chesterfield and Henrico counties have many good places to eat. Recommendations from Richmond residents include ethnic dinners at the **Greek Island**, 10902 Hull Street in the Genito Forest shopping center in Chesterfield County, 674-9199, and the **Island Grill** at 14 N. 18th Street, 643-2222. This Shockoe Bottom restaurant cooks French food with a Caribbean flair. The trendiest spot in

town is **Havana '59** at 16 N. 17th Street. This tropical oasis hearkens back to Cuba's carefree pre-Castro days right down to the deck of cards on each table. The food has a Cuban salsa flair; call 649-CUBA. For fine dining try **The Frog and the Redneck** at 1423 Cary Street, 638-FROG, which blends regional French and American specialties. Reservations are recommended, particularly on weekends.

Our usual stopping off place is the **Texas-Wisconsin Border Cafe**, 1501 W. Main near VCU, 355-2907. It has a fun, funky atmosphere, fiery chili and great burgers. If we're in the mood for fresh fish we head to **Blue Point Seafood** downtown in the Sixth Street Marketplace at 550 E. Grace Street, 783-8138.

Shopping

For find boutiques and specialty shops, park your car and walk through **Shockoe Slip**, **Carytown**, **Sycamore Square** or the **Shops of Libbie and Grove**. The **Sixth Street Marketplace** is a festival marketplace that runs along several downtown blocks. There also are several malls in suburban areas.

Accommodations

There are many downtown and suburban hotels and motels in all price ranges as well as bed and breakfasts. If you're looking for something elegant try the **Jefferson Hotel**, built in 1895 and splendidly restored in the 1980s. It is on Franklin and Adam streets, 788-8000. **Linden Row Inn** at 100 E. Franklin Street, 783-7000, was created from seven restored antebellum townhouses and is a lovely choice for lodging.

For More Information

Write or visit the **Metro Richmond Convention and Visitors Bureau**, 550 E. Marshall Street, Richmond 23219, (800) 365-7272 or 782-2777. You can pick up brochures there or at the Richmond Visitors Center at Robin Hood Road and the Boulevard, 358-5511. For more extensive information, check out *The Insiders' Guide to Greater Richmond*.

Tappahannock

In the mood for a day of antiquing and filling up on home cooking? Then Tappahannock is the place to go.

With fewer than 9,000 residents in the city and neighboring Essex County, this is a small but charming community on the banks of the Rappahannock River.

Getting There

Jump onto I-64 headed west. Go through the Hampton Roads Bridge-Tunnel and turn north on Route 17 through Yorktown. It takes just over two hours to get to Tappahannock from Norfolk/Virginia Beach.

Attractions

Eating and antique hunting are always at the top of our list. However, there are other things to do while you're here.

To soak up the small-town atmosphere start with a walking tour. Maps are available at the **Tappahannock-Essex County Chamber of Commerce** on the courthouse square. It is open from 8:30 to 4:30 weekdays. To get the map in advance call 443-5241 or write the Chamber at Box 481, Tappahannock 22560.

Your walk will take you past an **1800s customs house**; the **Scots Arms Tavern**, built around 1680; an 18th-century **debtor's prison** and several historic **houses and churches**. Most are on four main streets that dead end at the river. Genealogy buffs can have a heyday in the historic **county courthouse**, which contains the oldest records in Virginia. The **Essex County Library** is another treasure trove of research material.

If you're yearning to get on the water, from May through October **Rappahannock River Cruises** runs all-day excursions. The *Captain Thomas* leaves Hoskins Creek in Tappahannock at 10 AM and returns at 5 PM every day but Monday. Be sure to bring the binoculars for some spectacular glimpses of bald eagles, which nest in the cliffs along the Rappahannock.

During your boat trip you'll stop at **Ingleside Plantation Winery** in the Northern Neck. This is Virginia's third-largest winery. You can purchase an excellent buffet lunch or bring your own to enjoy. Either way, you'll get a tour and a chance to sample the fruits of the winery's labors.

The *Captain Thomas* also docks at **Saunders Wharf** near Wheatland, a Federal-style farmhouse built in 1810 that is 12 miles from Tappahannock. For $3 you can wander through the gardens and house as well as its wharf where there's a museum of river history. Wheatland has the Rappahannock River's only remaining wharf from last century when 33 steamboats plied the waters.

The 150-passenger boat is enclosed and runs rain or shine. There's a snack bar on board. Tickets cost $18.50 with children younger than 14 going along for half-price. For information call 453-2628 or 333-4856. Reservations are a must.

If you enjoy a ride in the country you may want to drive to the Ingleside Winery. Another option is the 45-minute trip to **Stratford Hall**, the birthplace of Robert E. Lee and other members of his famous family. This lovely manor house was built about 1730 and is open for tours. It is on Route 214 off Route 3 and is open daily, 493-8038.

Restaurants

Now we get to the real reason we like to visit Tappahannock — **Lowery's Seafood Restaurant**. Since 1938 the Lowery family has dished up some of the best seafood and home cooking around. From the homemade vegetable soup to the coconut cream pie, everything tastes like Mom's cooking if she'd known how to do it this good. The menu is huge and reasonably priced. Entrees run the gamut from seafood platters to steaks and sandwiches. Be sure to try to soft-shell crabs if they're in season.

The back of Lowery's is a mini-museum that houses a 1910 Cadillac, a 1926 Chrysler and miscellaneous memorabilia. There's also Jake the mynah bird. Kids love this place because after eating they get to fish in a wishing well and trade their catch for a prize.

Lowery's is at the intersection of Route 17 and Route 360. It serves breakfast, lunch and dinner daily. Call at 443-4314.

Another dining option is **Ferebee's** at Church Lane and Price Street, which is gaining a reputation for its huge servings and excellent food. It is open for lunch and dinner, 443-5715.

Shopping

Shopping also is high on our list of things to do in Tappahannock. There are about a half-dozen antique shops in the area. Most are right on Route 17 — the main drag — or on Queen Street.

One of the top is the **Nadji Nook** on Queen Street. This place is overwhelming. Its two floors are stuffed with everything from fine furniture to vintage clothing, cooking utensil and glass doorknobs.

Another must-see shop is **A to Z Surplus** on Route 17 near Lowery's. Furniture is the name of the game here with other collectibles thrown in for good measure.

Other shops to check out are **Hodge-Podge** and **Hoskins Creek**, both on Route 17. **Queen Street Ltd.** and **Magnolia** are well-stocked shops on Queen Street.

Accommodations

There are a few budget motels in the area. But your best option is the **Linden House Bed & Breakfast**. This restored planter's home outside town is on the National Historical Register. It was built in 1750 and features five porches for relaxing. Beautifully appointed rooms are in both the main house and a two-story coach house. The 200-acre grounds include an English garden. Call (800) 622-1202 or 443-1170.

Smith Island

Smith Island in the Chesapeake Bay is Maryland's only inhabited offshore island. It actually is a chain of marshy islands with a fascinating history. Pirates once hid their boats in the tricky waters surrounding this archipelago while waiting to raid passing ships.

Dissenters from the Jamestown colony settled here in the 17th century, eventually forming the three villages of Ewell, Rhodes Point and Tylerton. Today,

Ewell, the island's largest town, is sometimes referred to as its capital. Here, anglers catch hard and soft-shell crabs and send them to the mainland to serve markets throughout the world. The life of these islanders is often harsh but is guided by a strong religious faith. Joshua Thomas established the Methodist church here and on several other Chesapeake Bay islands during the late 1800s. It continues to be the only organized religion on the island today.

Getting There

Cruises to Smith Island leave from the Chesapeake Bay/Smith Island KOA Campground in the Smith's Point area of Reedville. To get there take Route 17 N. to Tappahannock. Get on Route 360 and take it to Highway 652. Go east on 652 until it becomes 644, then turn northeast on 650. This sounds complicated, but signs for the **Smith Island Cruise** provide adequate direction. The drive takes about 2½ hours from Hampton Roads.

Once you've made it to the boat dock, you'll board the *Captain Evans*, which leaves at 10 AM and pulls in at Ewell around 11:30. You'll have several hours to roam at will before the 2 PM departure. Current round-trip rates are $18.50 for adults and $8.75 for children 12 and younger. Children younger than 3 are free. Groups of 25 or more can get a group rate that includes the cruise, luncheon and island bus tour. During warmer months trips are made everyday but Monday. For information about the cruise or camping at **Smith Point KOA** call 453-3430.

Smith Island cruises also depart from Crisfield, Maryland, just north of Virginia's Eastern Shore. To get there take Route

13 N. to Route 413, 4 miles south of Princess Anne. Crisfield is just 12 miles west of Smith Island. Trips on the *Capt. Tyler II* leave at 12:30 PM daily in warmer months and arrive back at the dock at 5:15 PM. Current prices are $17, free for children younger than 6 and half-price for children up to age 12. An all-you-can-eat seafood meal on the island costs $11.45, half-price for children older than 6 and $1 for those younger. Packages are available that include the cruise, island tour, lunch and a stay at a Crisfield motel. Group rates also are available. For reservations call (410) 425-2771.

Attractions

The main attraction, of course, is the island, which was settled in 1657 by British and Welsh citizens and today has 500 residents. Legend has it that Capt. John Smith sailed up the Chesapeake Bay to the island in 1608 and named it after himself. He described the island in his log by saying: "Heaven and earth seemed never to have agreed better for man's commodious and delightful habitation."

The leisurely pace of life on Maryland's only inhabited island is a welcome change from the hustle and bustle of mainland existence. This is a place where you can put your feet up on a back porch railing and enjoy the soft breezes off the Chesapeake Bay. If it's spring, you might catch the fragrance of blossoming fig, pear, mimosa and pomegranate trees, which grow in all of the island's towns.

Once you're rested, there is plenty to do and see. A **walking tour** of Ewell will take you past Cape Cod-style homes, rustic country stores and the sunken remains of the *Island Bell I*, one of the earliest island ferries. **Goat Island**, across Levering Creek, is home to a herd of about 20 formerly domestic goats. Natives rely on the goats' movements toward the water's edge to obtain salt from the marsh grasses as a sign that rain or snow is imminent. Other attractions include **Pitchcroft**, the island's first settlement, and the wooden keel remains of the 60-foot *Bugeye C.S. Tyler*, built for islander Willie A. Evans. The Evans and Tyler names are among the most common surnames on this island where many residents are related.

You can also tour by foot or bicycle **Rhodes Point**, the island's center for boat repair. This small town originally was called Rogue's Point because of the pirates who frequented the area. Here, you can watch boats being made and repaired and see the ruins of some of the earlier vessels that plied their trade on the bay.

During your visit, you may notice how friendly everyone seems. Islanders in cars and trucks honk their horns and wave to greet every vehicle and pedestrian they meet. The hospitality is extended to a hefty population of healthy-looking stray cats, which seem to be everywhere.

Restaurants

The island has three dining choices in Ewell. **Bayside Inn Restaurant** at the island's dock, (410) 425-2771, and **Harbor Side Restaurant** at 20956 James Road, (410) 425-2201, both offer moderately priced and hearty family-style meals. The charming **Ruke's Seafood Restaurant and Store** on Caleb Jones Road, (410) 425-2311, sells inexpensive seafood platters along with burgers and sandwiches. Even if you dine elsewhere, spend a few minutes looking around Ruke's gift shop.

Accommodations

If you want to spend the night on the island, reserve one of the three guest rooms at the **Ewell Tide Inn**, 4063 Tyler Road, (410) 425-2141. Rates are reasonable, and breakfast is whipped up by the innkeeper and Culinary Institute of America grad Sheryl Allston. The menu features herbal teas, homemade yeast and fruit breads and the piece de resistance — an English muffin layered with ham, egg, cheese sauce and local crab meat all baked together in the oven. The inn also offers two sitting rooms and a large screened back porch for some true R&R.

Another option is **Bernice Guy's tourist home** at 2 Tyler Road, (410) 425-2751, which has been in operation for more than 30 years. Mrs. Guy rents two rooms for a bargain price that includes breakfast. The island's single motel, **Smith Island Motel**, on Smith Island Road, offers eight cozy air-conditioned rooms, color television and bicycle rentals, (410) 425-3321.

Visitors who prefer to sleep on the Virginia mainland can reserve cabins or tent or camper spots at the **KOA** near Reedville. There also are several bed and breakfasts in Reedville, which has some gorgeous turn-of-the-century mansions. Three to keep in mind are **Elizabeth House**, at the end of Route 360 on Reedville's main street, (804) 453-7016, **Cedar Grove**, on Fleeton Road, (804) 453-3915, and **The Gables**, also at the end of Route 360 on Reedville's main street, (804) 453-5209.

For More Information

Call the **Somerset County Tourism Office** and ask for a brochure about the island, (800) 521-9189. It includes a self-guided walking tour of Ewell along with maps, historical information and important tips on island etiquette. For example, the island is dry, and islanders don't appreciate public consumption of alcohol.

Northeastern North Carolina

One of our favorite getaway destinations is a trio of nearby North Carolina cities — Elizabeth City, Hertford and Edenton. They're part of the historic Albemarle region of North Carolina. All are within an easy hour's drive but are so different from Hampton Roads they make you think you've been on a long trip.

History is the main reason for journeying to this part of North Carolina, which once was a seat of Colonial government. You'll find one of the oldest house in the state here as well as many other historic structures.

Getting There

The most direct route is to take Route 17 S. out of Chesapeake. One road leading to this is Route 104, which is at the end of Interstate 464 in Chesapeake. If you get on 464 in downtown Norfolk and head towardChesapeake, just follow the Elizabeth City sign at the end.

Along the way you'll be surrounded by the **Great Dismal Swamp**. For miles you'll parallel the **Dismal Swamp Canal**, which was dug in 1793. Along the way are several picnic areas where you can gaze at this natural wonder. One of them has a boat ramp where you could put in a canoe or small boat. At the **Dismal Swamp Canal Visitor Center** outside South Mills you'll find a friendly staff, all kinds of North Carolina brochures and the coffee pot filled, (919) 771-8333. This state-run center has a 150-foot dock on the canal and picnic tables. In the warmer months dozens of pleasure craft tie up here as they take a break from traveling the Atlantic Intracoastal Waterway. The center is open Tuesday through Saturday.

Elizabeth City will be the first city you'll hit, followed by Hertford about 15 miles later and Edenton another 12 miles away. Your total distance traveled will have been no more than 75 miles. To really see these lovely towns, be sure to take the business exits off Route 17 S.

Attractions

History and scenic beauty are the big draws in this region, which was one of the first settled parts of North Carolina. Each city has its own charm, so try to visit all three.

Elizabeth City is on the Pasquotank River where the Dismal Swamp Canal ends. It was an Indian town until British colonists settled it in the early 1600s. The town was established in 1793 and has a population of about 14,000.

Downtown, which runs along the river, you'll find two **National Historic Districts** with 32 historic homes and sites. Walking tour maps and other brochures are available at the Elizabeth City Area Chamber of Commerce. It's on your way downtown at 502 E. Ehringhaus Street, (919) 335-4365. One unique aspect of Elizabeth City that's gained international fame is the **Rose Buddies**, a local welcoming committee that provides free refreshments, roses and information for boaters docking downtown.

Be sure to visit the **Museum of the Albemarle** on Route 17. This free museum provides an ideal overview for your visit to this region near the Albemarle Sound. Its displays range from Indian artifacts to those used by early settlers and watermen. Two treasures are beautifully restored city fire trucks dating from 1890 and 1917. The museum is a division of the North Carolina Museum of History and is open every day but Monday, (919) 335-1453.

Hertford may be the best-kept secret in this part of North Carolina. While its sister cities draw the most tourism traffic, Hertford is a real jewel waiting to be discovered.

You'll sense its charm when you drive onto Business Route 17 and find the roadway surrounded on both sides by the broad Perquimans River. Spanish moss is draped over broad-bottomed cypress trees, and the only S-shaped drawbridge in the country leads you right to the heart of this town with 2,000 residents. There you'll find an all-American downtown complete with dry goods store and soda fountain in the local drug store.

Established in 1758, Hertford has about 50 19th-century buildings, including an 1825 Federal-style courthouse containing North Carolina's oldest deed. A walking tour map is available from the Perquimans County Chamber of Commerce, (919) 426-5657. Downtown you'll find a plaque honoring native son Jimmy "Catfish" Hunter, who has retired from the New York Yankees and returned home to run the family farm.

Just outside town in Perquimans County is the **Newbold-White House**. Built in the early 18th century, this two-story brick home is a well-preserved example of residential architecture. The house is open from March through December, Monday through Saturday, (919) 426-7567.

Edenton is built around Edenton Bay and the head of the Albemarle Sound. It's often touted as one of the prettiest towns in the South and was the center of Colonial government in North Carolina. This town of 5,000 has a wonderful historic district that's perfect for strolling. You'll find street after street of homes dating from the 18th and 19th centuries. The **Chowan County Courthouse**, built in 1767, has a green that runs right to the bay.

To start your tour visit the **Historic Edenton Visitor Center**, housed in a pink Victorian house at 108 N. Broad Street, (919) 482-2637. It's open every day but Monday. You can watch a slide show, pick up maps and brochures or sign up for a guided tour of five 18th-century buildings. Included are **St. Paul's Episcopal Church**, begun in 1736; the **courthouse**; the **Cupola House**, a Jacobean-style residence dating from 1758; the **Barker House**, built in 1782; and the **James Iredell House**, built in 1773 and the home of the former U.S. Supreme Court Justice it's named for.

Restaurants

In Elizabeth City you can find all your basic fast-food chains. For some local flavor try **Mulligan's Downtown Grille** at 200 N. Poindexter Street for sandwiches, soups and salads, (919) 331-2431. Seafood and other sandwiches are on the menu at the **Marina Restaurant** at the Camden Causeway, which overlooks the river, (919) 335-7307. **Zack's Mighty Mint** at 102 E. Ehringhaus Street specializes in barbecue and fried chicken, (919) 338-8870.

In Hertford, Carolina-style barbecue is the local standout. Local favorite

White's Barbecue recently moved to a new building on Route 17 and changed its name to **Captain Bob's**, (919) 426-5064. Don't worry; the famous barbecue and seafood are still just as good. **Jimmy's Barbecue**, the other longtime Hertford favorite, has several locations. The original is on Edenton Highway, which is the same as Route 17 Business, (919) 426-5014. Jimmy's packs in the locals for barbecue and seafood.

In downtown Hertford, you can get a grilled sandwich at the fountain in **Woodard's Pharmacy**, 101 N. Church Street, (919) 426-5527. Top it off with a limeade or milk shake. Even if it's not lunch time stop in for a dip of Ben & Jerry's ice cream. You'll be amazed at the price — only 40¢. A recent addition to downtown Hertford is the reopened **Daddy Ruth's Hertford Cafe**, 127 N. Church Street, (919) 426-5593, which specializes in Southern homecooking. Be sure to leave room for homemade pie or the outstanding bread pudding. Outside town on Snug Harbor Road, **Anglers Cove Seafood Restaurant** specializes in seafood and is decorated entirely in nautical memorabilia. Call (919) 426-7294.

In Edenton the **Dram Tree Restaurant** at 112 W. Water Street comes highly recommended, (919) 482-2711. Barbecue fans may want to check out **Lane's Family Barbecue** on East Church Street, (919) 482-4008.

Shopping

You'll find some antique shops along Route 17 and in Elizabeth City and Edenton. Outside Elizabeth City in Camden is the **Watermark Craft Co-op**, which features the works of more than 700 craftspeople. It is on Highway 158 E.

and is open daily from May through December and closes on Sunday during winter months.

In downtown Hertford, you'll find a traditional downtown with a hardware store, pharmacy and other basic businesses. Check out **Darden Department Store** at 109 N. Church. It's been there since the late 19th century and is a classic dry goods store. Besides clothes, you'll find everything from baseball mitts to zippers and shoe polish.

One recent addition to downtown is **The Bibliopath Bookshop & Bindery**, an offshoot of a Norfolk bookstore. This is a used bookstore with more than 50,000 volumes. Records, antique furniture and other treasurers are among the wares.

Accommodations

Bed and breakfast homes are a wonderful way to soak up the local flavor. In Elizabeth City you'll find **The Culpepper Inn**, a 1935 Colonial Revival style house with a swimming pool. It has 11 guest rooms and is at 609 W. Main Street, (919) 335-1993. **Elizabeth City Bed & Breakfast** has two historic buildings, one a home built around 1898 and the other a fraternal lodge that dates from 1847. The buildings are at 108 E. Fearing Street in the midst of the historic district walking tour, (919) 338-2177. **Arbor House at Fairlea** is another bed and breakfast. This southern Colonial home is filled with antiques and has a sun porch for relaxing. It is at 1803 Rivershore Road, (919) 331-5538.

Hertford has three delightful choices. At the **Beechtree Inn**, outside town just off Snug Harbor Road, guests can stay in either the 18th-century main house or a cozy cabin built around the early 19th century. Both are filled with period reproduction furniture made by the owners. The property includes a collection of 19th-century smokehouses, dairies and other outbuildings, (919) 426-7815.

Fans of plantation houses will feel right at home at **1812 on the Perquimans**. This home with wonderful double verandas is outside town off Route 17 on a working farm on the Perquimans River. The owners have had their early 19th-century home in the family for generations and still cook in a kitchen connected to the main house only by a screened porch. Guests can borrow bicycles, a sailboat or a canoe, (919) 426-1812. **The Gingerbread Inn** at 103 S. Church Street also has a bakery. It is a Victorian home on the historic walking tour, (919) 426-5809.

Edenton has several wonderful bed and breakfasts. **The Lords Proprietors Inn** at 400 N. Broad Street has three restored homes right in the historic district. There are 20 guest rooms in homes that feature parlors and gracious front porches, (800) 348-8933. Guests are served both breakfast and dinner.

Granville Queen Inn also is in the historic district at 108 S. Granville Street, (919) 482-5296. Furnishings from around the world provide the theme for guest rooms ranging from the Queen's Cottage to the Egyptian Queen bedroom.

The Captain's Quarters Inn puts a new twist on the bed and breakfast idea by offering two-night "sail and snooze" specials that include a three-hour sail on the Albemarle Sound. Dinner is also served at this 1907 home in the historic district, (919) 482-8945.

Governor Eden Inn at 304 N. Broad Street is a neoclassical-style home in the historic district that also welcomes guests, (919) 482-2072. **The Trestle House Inn** is on a private estate on Soundside Road outside Edenton. Built in 1972 it features exposed redwood beams milled from old railroad trestle timbers. Guests can fish in the inn's private lake or wander its extensive grounds, (919) 482-2282.

Outer Banks

There's a magically wonderful change in your personality as you are swept up onto the Wright Memorial Bridge and then to the downhill coast to the wonderland we call the Outer Banks. We think it might have something to do with the calming vapors rising from the Currituck Sound, those strange and wonderful mesmerizing molecules that envelope all those nasty little hyper brain cells and numb them into a peaceful little nap that lasts as long as you stay on these fragile barrier islands. With its laid-back attitude, long stretches of clean beaches and acres of protected flora, fauna and wildlife, to visit the Outer Banks, from Corolla on the northern tip to Ocracoke at its southernmost extreme, is to shed the burdens of civilization without giving up any creature comforts or amenities. From accommodations to restaurants, shopping to historical sightseeing, this is a destination that has no equal on this earth.

Getting There

From southside Hampton Roads, steer the car packed with beach chairs, bikinis and coolers onto Interstate 64 E. Take the Battlefield Boulevard N. exit (Route 168) and drive straight ahead to the 168 Bypass to Nags Head. Don't worry if you miss the bypass, it connects back to 168 on the other side of the Great Bridge area. Head straight on down 168, which will turn into Rt. 158 about 30 miles from the beach. (That's when those magic powers start taking over.) Aim for that mystical Wright Memorial Bridge and . . . bingo, lottery winner . . . you're in paradise. North Carolina's Outer Banks is only about 70 miles south of Hampton Roads, but depending on traffic, it can take you from 1½ hours to too long to tell . . . but who cares? Summer weekends are especially crowded on the two-lane stretches of 168, so plan your time accordingly.

Attractions

The beach.

Other attractions: It does rain occasionally in the Outer banks, so here's where we would be forced to go if we couldn't splash in the Atlantic Ocean.

Use the 60-foot granite pylon on a mammoth dune as a compass as you travel down the 158 Bypass road towards Kill Devil Hills. If you pretend it's December 17, 1903, you might just witness Wilbur Wright launch the world's first motorized flying machine off this dune and stay airborne for a full 12 seconds. This is where aeronautical history was birthed, and you can visit the re-created airstrip and rustic camp where Wilbur and brother Orville put the Outer Banks on the map here at the **Wright Brothers Memorial**. If you're here in June, you'll find yourself in the midst of modern examples of that original flying machine as they buzz through the air in the annual **Wright Brothers Fly In and Airshow**. There is a small entry fee at the National Park Service-run historic site, but it's well worth it for all ages.

You'll see this popular attraction even before you reach MP (Mile Post) 12 on Route 158 Bypass in Nags Head. It's the famous **Jockey's Ridge** . . . one mile long,

12,000 feet wide and rising to 140 feet above sea level. It's 140 acres of playground for the physically fit, where you can hike to the top to catch spectacular views of the Atlantic Ocean on one side, the Roanoke Sound on the other. Kite-flying is a primo activity, and you can purchase some of the zaniest kites at **Kitty Hawk Kites** right at the foot of Jockey's Ridge at a cute little shopping center called the **Kitty Hawk Connection**. The center is also where those with a death-wish can sign the release form that will give them the stomach-churning pleasure of hang-gliding, monitored by experienced instructors. You have to make a reservation for the thrill of it all, so call 441-4124 if you dare.

For a more down-to-earth experience with nature, why not try out the new $1 million **Manteo Bike Path** that starts just past Pirate's Cove and ends up by the William B. Umstead Bridge over Croatan Sound. This winding ribbon of smooth black asphalt, connected by patches of sidewalk and wooden bridges, runs north of Route 64 and weaves its way past the **Fort Raleigh National Historial Site**, the **Elizabethan Gardens**, businesses and homes on Roanoke Island. It's a leisurely way to pedal, safe from traffic, and an equally pleasant pathway for in-line skaters and joggers, too.

Traveling south on 158 towards Hatteras, you'll come to the quiet little town of Rodanthe. Here is the **Chicamacomico Life Saving Station**, restored to the glory it enjoyed back when it guarded the northern coast of Hatteras for 70 years. Established by the U.S. Government in 1874, a nonprofit organization has spearheaded its preservation, and every week during the summer months (usually on Thursdays, but you can stop at the information center right at the start of Highway 12 in Nags Head to ask for specifics on all NPS activities) you can watch as volunteers re-enact a lifesaving rescue of a shipwrecked crew.

Restaurants

Practically every restaurant on the Outer Banks offers three distinctive courses: seafood, seafood and seafood. We can almost guarantee that you will not be disappointed with any of these courses, and all you must choose is in what kind of atmosphere you want to join the clean plate club. As all Insiders, we have our favorites, and these are the three we highly recommend.

In the heat of the beach action is a quirky little place called **Awful Arthur's**, that sits right across from the Avalon Fishing Pier at MP 6 on the Beach Road in Kill Devil Hills. If you don't have a brimming platter of their Alaskan crab legs washed down with Bass Ale straight from the tap, you might as well not even bother to come to the Outer Banks. It's casual, it's crowded and it's the best place to dive into the world of steamed seafood to slather with full-strength melted butter. If you pass on dessert, use those dollars to buy an Awful Arthur's T-shirt. It will mean that you're part of the in-crowd. You can reach them at 441-5955.

Point your car north towards the village of Duck and wheel into **Blue Point Bar and Grill**, 261-8090, in The Waterfront Shops that dangle over the Currituck Sound. The 1940s-style diner will serve you unusual seafood dishes in the nouvelle manner, along with some sinful desserts whipped up fresh daily. Hosts John Power and Sam McGann pack the place seven days a week for both lunch and dinner, and if you're claustrophobic, you might make a beeline for the

A group of pleased Outer Banks anglers

outdoor dining deck. It's almost a necessity to call ahead for reservations at this more-than-popular little spot.

If you're suffering sushi-withdrawal, check out **Tortuga's Lie** in Nags Head. Wednesday night is sushi night here, and, judging from the juggling to get a table, it's a sure sign of a global culinary invasion in this notoriously seafood town. Give 'em a jingle at 441-RAWW.

Several our other favorites are **Penguin Isle** in Nags Head, **The Rundown Cafe** in Southern Shores, **1587 Restaurant** in Manteo and **Chili Pepper's** in Kill Devil Hills.

Shopping

One of the first signs that there is definitely a shopping experience in your Outer Banks future is **The Marketplace Shopping Center** you'll see on your left as you travel in on 158 towards the beach. Here there's an immaculate **Food Lion** for all the nibbles and cold drinks you'll require, along with some nifty shops.

There's also a cinema here showing first-run favorites.

Farther north in Corolla, you should visit the **John de la Vega Gallery**. This intriguing place houses beautiful artwork, some of our favorite done by Mr. de la Vega himself. It's a quiet, calming stop, and the perfect respite from the more hustle-bustle shopping experience. While in this area, you'll also want to visit the **Corolla Light Village Shops**, the **TimBuck II** shopping area and the **Bell Tower Station**. Be sure to watch for the wild horses that roam through the Corolla area. They're descendants of Spanish mustangs and the focus of a well-organized protection effort. Don't feed or pet them, please; just admire them for their beauty.

Duck Village, to the north of the main Outer Banks strip, is a shopper's heaven, with a plethora of small shops with gew-gaws and gimcracks to fine art and clothing you'll not likely find anywhere else. You can weave in and out of one darling shopping plaza to another, like **Scarborough Faire**, with the Island Book-store, Ocean Annie's for singular jewelry, pottery and gifts, Smash Hit, a great place for tennis and golf attire, and Elizabeth's Cafe and Winery, where you'll find the best wine selection on the Outer Banks, served with a charming menu and an equally charming atmosphere. Whip into the Duck **Waterfront Shops** for bargains at Barr-ee Station, handcrafted fashions at Donna's Designs and Marine Model Gallery with its wonderful model ships. A last must-stop is **The Lucky Duck** in Wee Winks Square. You'll not be able to resist the urge to touch every little thing in the place, including home accessories, cards, toys and games.

In Kitty Hawk, a trip to **Daniel's** is mandatory for all the beach stuff you need that you might have forgotten, as is a stop at **Gray's Department Store**, one of the oldest and most favorite shops for clothing and accessories. In Kill Devil Hills, you'll find **The Dare Centre**, anchored by a **Belks** department store with all the fine clothing, cosmetics and shoes you might want. Also located in this new center are a **NY Bagels** and **Petrozza's**, where the Italian cook in your group can find nirvana with their already-prepared dishes as well as their selection of goodies for you to do the cooking.

You'll also find a new **Kmart** and **Wal-Mart** where, despite our conflicting feelings over seeing this type of commercialism entering the Outer Banks scene, you can find everything you might even think you need while on vacation. In Nags Head, **Glenn Eure's Ghost Fleet Gallery** is a fascinating art gallery where, if you're lucky, you'll find the gracious owners, Glenn and Pat, on hand to tell you all about the featured works. If you must have your mall-fix, there's the **Outer Banks Mall** with a nature store, Radio Shack and Lady Dare featuring beautiful styles for the fuller-figured woman, and Soundfeet Shoes for your Reeboks and Nikes. Fairly new on the shopping circuit is **Soundings Factory Stores** with everything for home and family at discount prices. Pfaltzgraff Collector's Center, London Fog, Jones New York and Rack Room Shoes are all here, among many others.

And, don't forget Manteo for shopping — or for a great break from the beach scene. Our absolutely favorite stop in this small town is **Manteo Booksellers**, one of the best book stores we have even seen. You'll want to browse here all day (which is encouraged by the friendly and knowledgeable manager, Steve Brumfield), and your only problem will be not blowing your entire vacation budget on books. When you're finished here, spend the rest of the day ambling around town. You'll find a wonderful woman's clothing store, **Shallowbags**, several gift shops, one of which we adore called **My Secret Garden**, a great candle shop, fine jewelry, nautical gifts, a florist along with eateries like **1587 Restaurant**, a relative newcomer with some of the best cuisine on the Outer Banks and a great wine list to boot, **Clara's Seafood Grill**, **Poor Richard's** sandwich shop, and the **Green Dolphin Pub**.

Don't leave Manteo without visiting the famous **Christmas Shop**. Its rooms are filled with tinkling lights, ornaments, and gifts of every description. Right next door is the **Weeping Radish**, where authentic German beer is brewed right on the premises. If there is a heaven after a hard day of shopping, it's sipping this nectar of the gods then wandering across the courtyard to the new German bakery to indulge in a just a little something.

One evening, you might want to come back to this small town to see a showing of a first-run movie at **The Pioneer Theatre**, the oldest, continually running, family-owned movie theater in the country. Admission is only $3 for adults, and the popcorn and other goodies will only put you out another $1 or so (we always think they've undercharged us, everything is so cheap). After the movie, stroll along the Manteo waterfront — romantic and free at the same time.

As in any resort climate, there are also zillions of souvenir and beachy type shops that line both the Beach and Bypass roads, along with other shopping centers that seem to spring overnight right out of the sand. Strolling through any of them will earn you the right to bag a T-shirt, bathing suit or a new pair of flip-flops. Most of these pocket centers have places where you can grab a burger, sandwich or platter of shrimp for the stamina to get on to the next shopping adventure.

Accommodations

You do realize, we hope, that to try to pick out just a few of the worthy accommodation on the Outer Banks is almost as hard as picking out the above restaurants. But, being the Insiders that we are, here goes . . .

Our top nod goes to a brand new bed and breakfast in Manteo called the **White Doe Inn**. For beauty, pampering and peace, you can't find a better choice. Call for reservations at (919) 473-9851, (800) 473-6091. Another favorite in Manteo is the **Roanoke Island Inn**, situated on the waterfront, (919) 473-5511. In Nags Head, two of our favorites are the **Surf Side Motel**, (919) 441-2105, and the **First Colony Inn**, (919) 441-2343.

For More Information

There are so many other fascinating places to wander on the Outer Banks that to discover every one you will need *The Insiders' Guide to North Carolina's Outer Banks*. In it you can get a full rundown of places like Manteo, Hatteras Island, Ocracoke Island, Oregon Inlet and Corolla, along with so many other wonderful hidden treasures just waiting for you to uncover. The 1995 edition is the 16th edition of this popular book, so don't miss getting your copy!

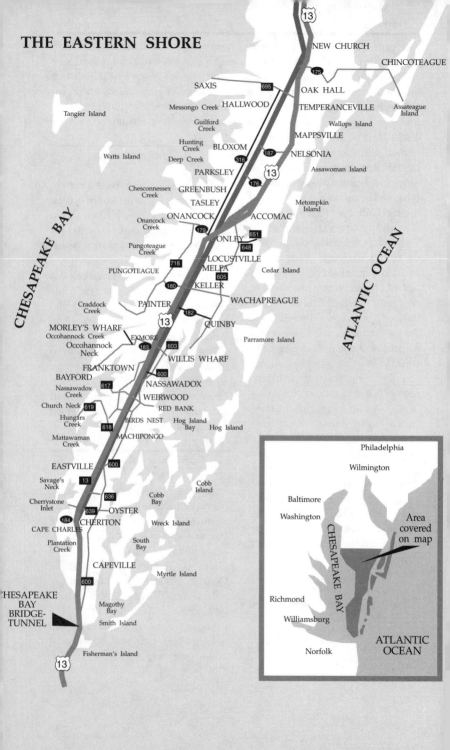

Eastern Shore of Virginia

EASTERN SHORE COMMISSION

A NATURAL EXPERIENCE.

Virginia's Eastern Shore

...is a quiet place. Here you'll find solitude in our rich natural settings. Colorful waterfowl rustic workboats and scenic islands where the pirate Blackbeard once sought refuge.

Enjoy salt water fishing at its best. Roam miles of unspoiled, uncrowded beaches. Camp in natural settings; swim in the Chesapeake Bay or the Atlantic Ocean; hunt for many species of wildlife and waterfowl; or search for bargains at numerous antique shops, gift shops and auctions.

Best of all, you can do it at your own pace, in your own time and when you need it most.

Virginia's Eastern Shore is a 70-mile long peninsula separating the Chesapeake Bay from the Atlantic Ocean. U.S. 13 , our major highway, extends from the Maryland line at the north to the Chesapeake Bay Bridge-Tunnel at the southern tip, providing access to all the area has to offer.

Since we trace our beginnings back to 1603, we have a rich, abundant history. We have monuments, blacksmith shops and debtors' prisons complete with whipping posts.

America's oldest continuous court records, in Eastville Courthouse, date back to 1632. The Courthouse complex, including the old Debtor's Prison, provides a fascinating look into the past.

There are churches built by the earliest settlers, and homes that have been lived in continuously for hundreds of years. Many are open during our annual Historic Homes and Garden Tour in April.

The Tourism commission welcomes the opportunity to assist you further as you plan your visit. for more information, call or write: VIRGINIA'S EASTERN SHORE TOURISM COMMISSION, Post Office Drawer R, Dept. CBB, Melfa, Virginia, 23410, (804) 787-2460, FAX (804) 787-8687.

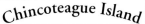

B&B'S OF VIRGINIA'S EASTERN SHORE

CAPE CHARLES

Cape Charles House
804/ 331-4920

645 Tazewell Ave., Cape Charles, VA 23310

Charming hospitality, restored Colonial revival home in town, furnished with antiques. Gracious gourmet "nouvelle" breakfast; private baths. History, antiques, galleries, beach, chartered fishing, golf, bikes, afternoon tea, wine & cheese. Paties, mettings and boating guests welcomed, with pick-up.

Sunset Inn B&B
804/ 331-2424
1-800-331-3113

108 Bay Ave., Cape Charles, VA 23310

Waterfront escape in our 1915 Victorian home overlooking Chesapeake Bay in historic Cape Charles. Breeezy porch. Spectacular sunsets. Walk the beach, relax, unwind. Full breakfast, central A/C, private baths, hot tub, TV's, bikes.

CHINCOTEAGUE

The Main Street House
804/ 336-6030
1-800-491-2027

4356 Main Street/P.O. Box 126, Chincoteague, VA 23336

Lovely 100 yr. old Victorian home. A/C rooms furnished with antiques - situated on Chincoteague Channel. Spectacular sunsets viewed from screened porch. Former Wildlife Refuge Manager. Member BBAV.

Island Manor House
804/ 336-5436
1-800-852-1505

4160 Main Street, Chincoteague, VA 23336
An historic landmark offering hospitality amid a charming Federal-style setting. A/C. Furnished with antiques. Breakfast/afternoon tea. Rose garden/brick courtyard. Fountain, garden room, fireplace. Receptions, private parties, meetings available. Open all year.

Miss Molly's Inn (1886)
804/ 336-6686
1-800-221-5620

4141 Main St., Chincoteague, VA 23336
This charming Victorian is now a painted lady, situated on the Chincoteague Bay. All 7 rooms (5 with private bath) have A/C and are furnished with antiques. Guests are served a full breakfast and a traditional English afternoon tea with Barbara's "world famous" scones. Marguerite Henry stayed here while writing famous "Misty of Chincoteague." Mobil travel guide quality rating.

The Channel Bass Inn
804/ 336-6148
1-800-221-5620

6228 Church St., Chincoteague, VA 23336
This elegant Inn is now owned by Barbara and David Weidenheft, also owners of Miss Molly's Inn, a long time Chincoteague favorite. The 5 spacious rooms, including one suite, are graciously appointed and have private baths. Traditional English afternoon tea and gourmet breakfasts are served in the large dining room. A great romantic getaway.

Year of the Horse Inn
804/ 336-3221
1-800-680-0090

3583 Main St., Chincoteague, VA 23336
Guest rooms with private baths and air conditioning. Private deck overlooking intercoastal waterway. 100 ft. pier for guests to fish or crab. Boating and picnic facilities available.

EXMORE / BELLE HAVEN

Bayview Waterfront B&B
804/ 442-6963
1-800-442-6966

35350 Copes Drive, Belle Haven, VA 23306
Old Eastern Shore home with beautiful, expansive views of Occohannock Creek and Chesapeake Bay. 140 acres of creekshore, farmland and woods to hike and explore. Pool, dock, beach, library, croquet, bicycles, many antiques and family heirlooms. Full breakfast. No smoking inside.

Martha's Inn
804/ 442-4641
1-800-99-MARTHA

12224 Lincoln Ave., Exmore, VA 23350
A three story brick residence featuring an unusual circular staircase and dining room. Enjoy the peace and quiet of this Georgian home. A full country breakfast is served to suit your schedule. Fishing, hunting available. Moderate rates. Open all year.

The Gladstone House
804/ 442-4614
1-800-BNB-GUEST

12108 Lincoln Ave., Exmore, VA 23350
Elegant 19th Century Georgian home. Gracious southern hospitality is extended to our guests, as well as pampering with coffee served at their bedroom door. Centrally located between Chincoteague & Cape Charles. Spacious appointed bedrooms with private baths and TV's Central A/C. House phone. Visa, MC, American Express.

LOCUSTVILLE

Wynne Tref Bed & Breakfast
804/ 787-2356

28168 Drummondtown Road/P.O. Box 96 Locustville, VA 23404
18th Century Colonial suite with private bath. Approximately one mile from ocean. Rent a boat to fish or explore the barrier islands. Near restaurants, gift and antique shops. Open April to November.

ONANCOCK

Colonial Manor Inn B&B (1882)   804/ 787-3521
84 Market Street, Onancock, VA 23417

Built 1882. Centrally located on Virginia's Eastern Shore in historic waterfront town on the Chesapeake Bay. Shops, restaurants, Tangier Island Ferry, all within walking distance. Visit us - you'll be glad you did. Open year round. Children welcome. Smoke free environment.

76 Market Street B&B   804/ 787-7600
Onancock, VA 23417

Restored Victorian in downtown Onancock. Leisurely walk to harbor, restaurants or the boat to Tangier Island. Three air conditioned rooms with private baths. Full breakfast. Come by boat or by car.

The Spinning Wheel Bed & Breakfast   804/ 787-7311
31 North Street, Onancock, VA 23417

1890's Folk Victorian in historic waterfront town. Walk to restaurants, shops, harbor, "Cruise to Tangier Island Package"! Five guest rooms each with private bath, queen bed, quilts and antique spinning wheel, A/C. Full served breakfast. Golf and tennis availabe at private club. Bicycles. AAA and BBAV Approved. Visa/MC.

PARKSLEY

The Homeplace Bed & Breakfast   804/ 665-6522
24234 Mary Street P.O. Box 66, Parksley, VA 23431

Privately owned and operated restored elegant Victorian home (c. 1903) is located in the charming hometown of the Eastern Shore Railway Museum. Relax in the ambiance of our antique filled parlor. Sumptuous full brakfast and afternoon tea served daily. Two A/C rooms available.

WACHAPREAGUE

Burton House & Hart's Harbor House   804/ 787-4560
Wachapreague, VA 23480

"Little City by the Sea" fishing village! Two Victorians side-by-side. Ten guest rooms furnished with antiques. Full generous country breakfast. Biking, birding, boating, antiquing. Waterfront cabins and marina. Brochure.

WILLIS WHARF

Ballard House Bed & Breakfast   804/ 442-2206
Route 660, Willis Wharf, VA 23486

Old fashioned hospitality at Grandma Jo's. A homey atmoshpere where pets and children are welcomed with well-behaved parents. Nature trails, entrance ramp, hot tub, attic playroom, bottomless cookie jar and more. Vegetarian and low fat menus available.

For Additional Information, Write:
Bed And Breakfast Association Of Virginia's Eastern Shore,
108 Bay Ave., Cape Charles, VA 23310

A WONDERFUL PLACE TO LIVE

The peninsula may be narrow, but it offers scenic view of woodlands, fields and picturesque towns. Then the road will sweep around a marsh or over a bridge to a small shetered harbor where the boats rock gently at their moorings.

With miles and miles of shoreline, we offer numerous opportunities to view a spectacular sunrise or a peaceful sunset.

Easy To Find, Hard To Forget

To reach U.S. Route 13 from the North, take I-95 or the New Jersey Turnpike; from Baltimore/Washington, take U.S. Route 50 east; from Virginia Beach, Norfolk and all points south, you'll arrive via the 17.6 mile long Chesapeake Bay Bridge-Tunnel, a marvel of the modern engineering world.

Were located approximately 170 miles from Baltimore and 65 miles from Salisbury, Maryland. Richmond (VA) is 165 miles away and the Norfolk / Virginia Beach / Hampton Roads area is a short 60 mile drive. From Williamsburg's Historic area we can be reached in just over two hours.

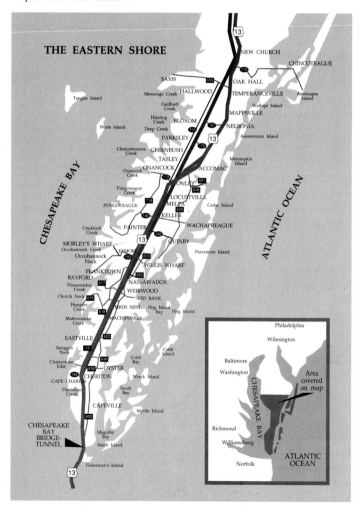

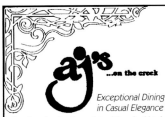

Attractions And Points Of Interest

Kerr Place   Onancock, VA
Historic Home (c. 1799) And Musuem
(804) 787-8012
Open Tue.- Sat. 10-4

Eastern Shore Railway Museum

Ask About Train Excursions

Open Weekdays 10:30-4, Sundays 1-4
2 Miles West of U.S. 13 on Parksley Road
Parksley, VA 23421

804-665-6271

STATE PARK

A *natural* part of your
Eastern Shore visit

- Swimming
- Boating
- Camping
- Fishing

3 miles north of the
Chesapeake Bay Bridge-Tunnel
For more information, call the
park at (804) 331-2267
Call the Eastern Shore of
Virginia Tourism Commission
about other attractions in the
area at (804) 787-2460.

DCR
Department of Conservation & Recreation
CONSERVING VIRGINIA'S NATURAL AND RECREATIONAL RESOURCES

Inside
The Eastern Shore

This remote peninsula between the Chesapeake Bay and Atlantic Ocean is one of Virginia's best-kept secrets. "God's country" is what one person we know affectionately calls the Eastern Shore.

The 70-mile-long shore is the southernmost part of the Delmarva Peninsula that encompasses parts of Delaware, Maryland and Virginia. Physically it is linked to the commonwealth only by the Chesapeake Bay Bridge-Tunnel that runs from Virginia Beach to Cape Charles. But historically the Eastern Shore has been an important part of Virginia since it was settled in the early 1600s. Before that time Native Americans were the main inhabitants, and their influence remains in the names of such locales as Nassawadox and Pungoteague.

The Shore's nearly 45,000 residents live in one of two counties — Accomack and Northampton. Both are agricultural centers renowned for growing sweet potatoes, azaleas and tomatoes. The Shore's abundant seafood harvest includes cherrystone clams and flounder.

There are numerous attractions throughout the Shore, but the most prominent are the Chincoteague National Wildlife Refuge and the Assateague Island National Seashore. Both are on Assateague Island, a barrier island that harbors wild horses and deer and is a bird-lover's paradise. The Eastern Shore has many other draws besides Assateague Island — outstanding hunting and fishing, historic homes and even a NASA museum. Many visitors come to chow down

on fresh clams and crabs, unwind at country inns and just get away from it all. Summer is when beach-bound tourists flock to the Eastern Shore, but don't rule out the other seasons. Even in winter the Shore has its own special beauty, and generally mild weather lets you enjoy everything but swimming and sunbathing.

The best source of tourism information is Virginia's Eastern Shore Tourism Commission, P.O. Drawer R, Melfa, Virginia 23410, (804) 787-2460. The commission produces a comprehensive travel guide for the entire region. It shares quarters with the Eastern Shore of Virginia Chamber of Commerce. The office is south of Melfa on Route 13. Stop by on weekdays from 8:30 to 5 PM and arm yourself with a slew of brochures. Another resource is the Chincoteague Chamber of Commerce, P.O. Box 258, Chincoteague, Virginia 23336, (804) 336-6161. The Chincoteague Chamber promotes its island community and has an office on Maddox street near the entrance to Assateague Island. It is open on weekdays.

The Commonwealth of Virginia runs a welcome center near the Maryland line on Route 13 in New Church. In warmer months it is open daily, but during the winter it shifts to limited hours, 824-5000.

To guide you on your trip, buy a copy of *Off 13 — The Eastern Shore of Virginia Guidebook*. Kirk Mariner, a minister and Eastern Shore native, first wrote this excellent book in 1987 to provide insight into the approximately 40 communities

Locustville Academy is the only local surviving school from the 1800s.

that make up the shore. The book gives specific directions to steer you off Route 13, the shore's boring main drag. On back roads you'll discover quaint fishing villages and historic towns with white clapboard homes.

Because there is so much to see and do on the Eastern Shore, try to stay several days here. We've included some suggestions to send you on your way.

Getting There

There's only one way to drive from Virginia — up Route 13 and over the Chesapeake Bay Bridge-Tunnel. You get on it in Virginia Beach off Northampton Boulevard. The tunnel toll is $10 each way, but don't sweat it, and consider the trip part of your adventure.

Also known as the Lucius J. Kellam Jr. Bridge-Tunnel, this 23-mile structure divides the Chesapeake Bay from the body of water known as Hampton Roads. It was completed in 1964 after 3½ years of rigorous construction. The American Society of Civil Engineers was awed enough

to name the bay bridge-tunnel the outstanding engineering achievement of the year. It is the longest bridge-tunnel in existence and is one of the Seven Wonders of the Modern World.

At the lowest point, the tunnels dip down 90 feet under the water. Arriving at the end of the bridge-tunnel, you start your Eastern Shore adventure in a wildlife refuge that is home to deer and other creatures.

Construction should start this year on a second set of bridges that will merge into the roadway's two tunnels. The completion date for this $250 million project is set for 1999. With traffic on the bridge-tunnel swelling by 7 percent a year, the project is designed to keep pace with future growth.

When traveling along the current three bridges and two tunnels, take a break and fish from a 625-foot fishing pier along the way. Or just stop and admire the Chesapeake Bay from the overlook on the man-made Thimble Shoal Island about 3 miles out in the bay. The rest

Photo: Virginia's Eastern Shore Tourism Commission

stop includes a restaurant and gift shop and some interesting bridge-tunnel trivia to test your knowledge. For bridge-tunnel information call 331-2960 or 624-3511.

Once you're on the Eastern Shore, Route 13 leads you up the middle of the peninsula and into Maryland. Although this is the quickest route, it speeds you right by some of the most scenic parts of the Eastern Shore. And, you'll never see water unless you get off the highway. Except for a few stately manor houses, along Route 13 you'll mostly pass fireworks stands, small homes and an occasional McDonald's or gas station. Pull off Route 13 toward towns such as Cape Charles, Wachapreague, Accomac, Onley and Parksley and you'll be treated to charming downtowns, fishing villages and restored houses several centuries old.

Pick up a copy of the free "Scenic Roads in Virginia" map published by the Virginia Department of Transportation and you'll see an easy way to take in the local scenery. Just over the bridge-tunnel at Kiptopeke you can veer off onto Route 600, which parallels Route 13. It will end at Route 180 and give you the choice of going to the left toward Pungoteague or right toward Wachapreague. Either way will steer you onto other backroads that lead to Accomac or Onancock. Both are picturesque towns, and from either one you can quickly get back on Route 13. The scenic route is marked in green on the map.

Don't hesitate to venture off the main highway. The Eastern Shore is so narrow that you can't get too lost. And, if you do, your jaunt is likely to take you past creeks and notable architecture. You'll have no trouble finding a helpful resident to guide you back on course. Some travelers who frequently zip up

Route 13 on their way to Maryland and points north always drive at least part of the trip on backroads.

In Chincoteague (pronounced shin-co-teague), there's only one way onto the island — over a causeway that takes you right to Main Street. Turn left and then right on Maddox Boulevard and you'll head right to Assateague Island. Most of the island's businesses are on these two streets.

Attractions

Chincoteague and **Assateague islands** are the hands-down winners as major attractions with their 40 miles of pristine beaches and wild horses. On Assateague, Mother Nature is chief planner, and you'll find no beachfront condos to spoil the view. In 1994 more than 1.4 million visitors came to these two barrier islands. Some vacationed here for the beach; others came to bird watch or escape city life. Many visitors are drawn by the idyllic life painted by author Marguerite Henry, who wrote the popular *Misty of Chincoteague* series starting in 1947.

Assateague, an uninhabited barrier island with a 37-mile beach, is in both Virginia and Maryland. However, all the island is in the public domain as either the **Chincoteague National Wildlife Refuge** or the **Assateague Island National Seashore**. The wildlife refuge was established in 1943 by the U.S. Fish and Wildlife Service as a wintering area for migratory birds and today has more than 250 varieties. The refuge is on the Virginia end of Assateague. Also on the Virginia side of the island is **Assateague Island National Seashore**, managed by the National Park Service. The island's undeveloped seashore is the only place on the Eastern Shore to plunge into the Atlantic Ocean.

Most of the other shoreline has marsh grasses and barrier islands separating the mainland from the ocean. Many of these uninhabited islands are owned by The Nature Conservancy and some can be explored if you have access to a boat. On the Maryland side of Assateague there is a state park that has the only camping spots on the island.

Admission onto Assateague from Virginia costs $4 a carload. Get there by driving over a short causeway from Chincoteague. Once on the island you can hike, swim, picnic and birdwatch. You can walk or ride your bike onto Assateague for free along a path that runs by the main road. It's about 3 miles to the beach. There are numerous trails on the island, so be adventurous and tromp through marshes to look for waterfowl or hike the quarter-mile to the island's red and white 19th-century lighthouse. Most of the island is accessible only by foot or bike. Drag along your binoculars and camera. On one visit we spotted deer, herons, pelicans, ducks, swans, geese and the wild horses that are Assateague's most famous inhabitants.

Two visitor centers on the Virginia side of the island provide maps, information and occasional guided walks and talks. To contact them call 336-6122 or 336-6577. From spring through fall, **Island Cruises Inc.** of Chincoteague shows off local scenery with guided boat tours on *The Osprey*. Reservations can be made at the **Refuge Motor Inn** by calling 336-5593 or 336-5511. **Assateague Adventures**, another local company, provides lectures and tours on Chincoteague and Assateague islands. Topics include ecology, decoy carving and wildlife photography. Participants can opt for package programs that come with lodging by calling (800) 221-7490.

Chincoteague bills itself as Virginia's only resort island. One regular we know who vacations here several times a year says Chincoteague has "a special spirit" that keeps drawing her back. Traditionally Chincoteague was a fishing community renowned for its oysters. Chincoteague is only 7 miles long and 1.5 miles wide and is considered the gateway to uninhabited Assateague. Chincoteague is a charming island loaded with motels, gift and craft shops, beds and breakfasts and seafood restaurants. Main Street is a fun place to wander with its shops selling decoys, T-shirts and crafts. There are two museums here, the **Oyster and Maritime Museum**, 336-6117, celebrates Chincoteague's heritage while the **Refuge Waterfowl Museum**, 336-5800, focuses on artistic decoys. Both are on Beach Road just before the Assateague entrance.

Five miles outside Chincoteague on

Insiders' Tips

On the Eastern Shore directions are based on two things — whether you're going bayside or seaside. Bayside is west toward the Chesapeake Bay. Seaside is east toward the Atlantic Ocean. Bayside is characterized by numerous creeks that lead to the Chesapeake Bay. Seaside is outlined by marshes and barrier islands that protect the Eastern Shore from harsh ocean waves.

Route 175 is the **NASA/Wallops Visitor Center**, 824-1344, 824-2298. This high-tech museum highlights the U.S. space program, particularly the balloon and rocket experiments carried out across the road at the Wallops Flight Facility. Wallops is affiliated with NASA's Goddard Space Flight Center. Displays include space suits, a moon rock and rocket-launching films. Admission is free.

Heading south from Chincoteague on Route 13, be sure to check out **Parksley**. This nicely restored Victorian town is centered around the **Eastern Shore Railway Museum**, 665-RAIL. Opened in 1989 in a restored 1906 train depot, this small museum is crammed with 3,000 artifacts and showcases memorabilia from the old New York, Philadelphia and Norfolk line that once ran through town. Outside are several train cars, including a 1927 observation car and a 1933 lounge car. The museum closes on Mondays. In the works are plans to open the Accomack Northampton Antique Car Museum adjacent to the Railway Museum.

Affiliated with the Railway Museum is the **Worcester Accomack Northampton Daycoach** (W.A.N.D.), which hooks up the antique train cars several times a year and hauls passengers from Parksley to other Eastern Shore towns. One popular trip is a Santa train ride in December. For information call (800) 852-0335 or 665-6271.

For a dose of history stop by **Accomac** and walk through the downtown area where you'll see a 1784 Debtor's Prison and more restored Colonial architecture than anywhere in Virginia except Colonial Williamsburg. There is a walking tour map available.

Onancock is another picture-perfect village with enough historic structures to warrant a walking tour. The many restored homes include **Kerr Place**, 787-8012. This Federal mansion was built in 1799 and is owned by the Eastern Shore of Virginia Historical Society, which opens it to the public Tuesday through Saturday. This grand house reopened in March after extensive restoration that returned to its original colors, many of them surprisingly bright. It costs $3 to tour Kerr Place (which is pronounced Carr Place). Also in Onancock is **Hopkins & Brothers Store**, one of the oldest general stores still operating on the East Coast, 787-4478. Its merchandise includes dry goods as well as arts and crafts. It also has a restaurant that serves seafood and steaks. In warmer months a boat ferries passengers from the store's dock to **Tangier Island**.

In **Locustville** you can see **Locustville Academy**, the shore's only surviving school of higher education from the 1800s. Although it's usually closed, you can arrange to go inside by calling 787-7480.

In **Willis Wharf** during mid-fall and early spring visitors can tour an oyster house to learn the fine art of shucking. Or they can spend the day on a typical farm. In 1993 longtime farmers Phil and Barbara Custis began welcoming city slickers to their sprawling **Custis Farms** near Willis Wharf. Visits include a hayride, lunch and the chance to observe the Custis' cultivating potatoes, planting azaleas or doing other seasonal work. Call (800) 428-6361 or 442-4121 to arrange group tours.

In **Wachapreague** visitors can watch fishing fleets come in or arrange their own fishing trip. History and genealogy buffs will enjoy **Eastville**, where the courthouse holds the oldest continuous court records in America dating from 1632.

Cape Charles is a Victorian town created as a railroad terminus along the Chesapeake Bay. Its downtown features several antique shops. A walking tour map will guide you along attractive residential streets. For a treat stop by **Charmer's Antiques** on Mason Avenue to visit the country store museum next door. Both are owned by Charles and Margaret Carlson, who are happy to show off their collection. The museum is open only by request but is worth asking about if you love Americana. Inside are hundreds of typical general store items, and none are for sale. You'll find a well-worn butcher block, brass cash registers and shelves lined with hundreds of patent medicine bottles.

At the southern end of the Eastern Shore are **Kiptopeke State Park** and the **Eastern Shore of Virginia National Wildlife Refuge**. Both are popular spots for bird watching. The refuge has an excellent visitors center with hands-on exhibits of a pelican's bill, whale bones and other biological artifacts. At a big window overlooking a salt pond, you can use the refuge's binoculars, telescope and birding guides to test your knowledge of the 294 bird species spotted at the refuge. There's also a short educational film as well as a display of duck decoys. Outside is a walking trail that leads through a maritime forest of loblolly pine, shrub thickets and holly.

The wildlife refuge is a major rest stop for migrating birds. Birding is at its best here from September through May. The refuge is open from dawn to dusk, 331-2760.

Nearby Kiptopeke, which opened in 1992 at an old ferry stop, is Virginia's newest state park. Its 375 acres border on the Chesapeake Bay and include areas for swimming, picnicking and camping. There also is a boat ramp. The water here

is shallow, making this an ideal family swimming spot. For information call 331-2267.

While driving around the Eastern Shore, be sure to admire its unique historic architecture. There are more than 400 buildings that date from before 1865. The Eastern Shore has its own indigenous architecture — the big house/little house/colonnade/kitchen-style that was common by the end of the 1700s and is unique to the Shore. These houses evolved when someone built a home, added on another part and then another until you had an incredibly long house with varying roof lines.

To tour some of the Eastern Shore's landmark homes time your visit with **Historic Garden Week**. Usually on the fourth Saturday in April, owners of some of the shore's oldest homes fling open their doors for visitors. The Eastern Shore day is part of a week of historic home tours throughout Virginia sponsored by garden clubs. This event is nationally known and extremely popular. For details on the Eastern Shore tour call 678-5352 or 787-7955. A $15 ticket lets your tour six grand houses and one garden. Individual admissions cost $4. A box lunch is available at Hungars Episcopal Church in Bridgetown for $5.50.

Included on the 1995 tour were Kerr Place; Eyre Hall built in 1765 and owned by a descendent of the builder; Holly Brook, a late 18th-century plantation house; Chatham, an 1818 brick house; Roselawn, built in 1981 in a gracious style; Lochwood, a 1942 house based in a mid-18th-century design; and One College Place's English garden.

For three years the Eastern Shore chapter of **Habitat for Humanity** has sponsored a spring tour of some splendid private gardens as a fund-raiser. The event is usually held in June on a Sunday afternoon.

Eastern Shore residents are big on festivals and go all out with native foods like fried sweet potatoes and steamed clams. You'll get a bonus if your visit coincides with one of these fun events. The biggest crowds come for the Eastern Shore Chamber of Commerce's May **seafood festival** in Chincoteague, which is by advanced tickets only, and the **Volunteer Fireman's Carnival** in Chincoteague in July. This is when Assateague's wild horses are rounded up to swim over to Chincoteague for a benefit auction. Other fun events are **marlin and flounder tournaments** in Wachapreague in May and July, the **spring and fall festivals** in Parksley in June and October, **Chicoteague's Oyster Festival** in October and **Waterfowl Week** in November at the Chincoteague National Wildlife Refuge.

Recently two additional festivals in October have given offshore residents new reasons to visit. The highlight of the **Eastern Shore Harvest Festival** is gorging on such native delicacies as crab cakes, devils on horseback (oysters wrapped with bacon), sweet potato biscuits with country ham, sweet potato pie and barbecue. Each year the two-day **Eastern Shore Birding Festival** draws a flock of nature lovers for workshops on everything from photographing birds to attracting them to their yards. During the festival, wildlife artists display their specialties while ornithologists, naturalists and conservationists share insight into their work. The festival centers around Kiptopeke State Park with events scattered throughout the Eastern Shore.

One part of the Eastern Shore you can't get to by car is **Tangier Island** in the Chesapeake Bay (see the sidebar in this chapter). This island is inhabited mainly by watermen. To get there hop on boats that leave from Onancock, Reedville or Crisfield, Maryland.

Restaurants

As you can guess, seafood is the cuisine of choice on the Eastern Shore. You won't find it any fresher so take advantage of it and eat your fill of steamed clams, soft-shell crabs and flounder. Your restaurant options include:

AJ's ON THE CREEK
6586 Maddox Blvd.
Chincoteague 336-5888

AJ's serves seafood, steaks, pasta and veal in one of the shore's most elegant atmospheres.

ARMANDO'S
10 North St.
Onancock 787-8044

Armando's is the trendiest place on the Shore. Its Argentine owner specializes in homemade pasta, seafood and divine desserts. On weekends Armando's swings with live entertainment.

One tradition of longtime Chincoteague vacationers is winding up the day with ice cream. Popular spots are Muller's at 4034 Main Street, 336-5894, Mr. Whippy at 4121 Main Street, 336-6313, and Island Creamery Ice Cream at 6243 Maddox Boulevard, 336-6236.

Insiders' Tips

BEACHWAY RESTAURANT
6455 Maddox Blvd.
Chincoteague   336-5590

The Beachway gives seafood a different twist by serving it in crepes or bouillabaisse. The Beachway has a reputation for luscious desserts.

CHINCOTEAGUE INN
Marlin St.
Chincoteague   336-6110

This venerable seafood restaurant has a terrific waterfront location. P.T. Pelican's Bar is outside on the deck.

E.L. WILLIS & CO.
Willis Wharf Rd.
Willis Wharf   442-4225

This casual seafood restaurant is housed in a converted general store. New owners recently expanded the traditional lunch hours to also serve dinner.

ETTA'S FAMILY RESTAURANT
5644 Eastside
Chincoteague   336-5644

For some regular Chincoteague visitors, no trip is complete without a meal at Etta's. Open April through October, Etta's seafood keeps vacationers coming back for more. The restaurant is in a prime location overlooking the Assateague Channel and its lighthouse.

GARDEN AND THE SEA INN
New Church   824-0672

Continental and regional cuisine are the standouts at this elegant country inn. Dinner menus are designed around seasonal local seafood and produce. Reservations are recommended.

FORMY'S BARBECUE
Rt. 13, Painter   442-2426

This is one of our regular stops for excellent Carolina-style barbecue with cole slaw, baked beans and other fixings.

The "que" is especially good fired up with Formy's "secret sauce."

HOPKINS & BROTHERS STORE
2 Market St.
Onancock   787-4478

Seafood and steaks are the main fare of this waterfront restaurant located in a general store built in 1842. It was moved to its present location at Onancock's wharf in 1966.

THE HUNGRY DUCK
Market and North Sts.
Onancock   787-8700

Steaks, Virginia ham, chicken and pasta are the mainstays of this restaurant, which opened in late 1994. The weekend specialty is prime rib. Breakfast is dished up on Saturday and Sunday. Otherwise only lunch and dinner are served.

LITTLE ITALY RESTAURANT AND PIZZA
10237 Rogers Dr.
Nassawadox   442-7831

Italian native Franco Nocera introduced authentic cuisine from his homeland to the Shore several years ago. Lasagna, eggplant dishes, fried calamari and pizza are the house specialties. You'll also find calzone, stromboli and homemade tiramisu on the menu. The restaurant is just off Route 13 at the stoplight on the way to Nassawadox.

LJ STREET SPORTS BAR & RESTAURANT
20250 Fairgrounds Rd.
Onancock   787-2144

Food and fun go hand-in-hand in this new restaurant just outside Onancock. Besides steaks, ribs, seafood and sandwiches, you'll find pool, Ping Pong, electronic darts and a big-screen TV tuned to sporting events. The restaurant is open for lunch and dinner with a band on weekend nights.

MARIA'S FAMILY RESTAURANT

Beach and Maddox Rds., Chincoteague 336-5040

Whether you're hungry for breakfast or pizza, Maria's has it on the menu. This casual spot offers everything from seafood to excellent Italian dinners. It's open from breakfast to late-night dinners.

MEMORIES

3341 Ridge Rd.
Chicoteague 336-3412

Nostalgia buffs will be in heaven here. From the picture of Elvis in the window to the pink-and-black interior, this former drive-in is rooted in the 1950s and '60s. Besides the burgers and fries you'd expect, the menu features fresh seafood and homecooked specials such as chicken and dumplings. One diner proclaimed Memories' oyster fritter sandwich "the biggest and best I've ever eaten." Seafood platters, steaks and homemade desserts round out the offerings.

THE OWL RESTAURANT

Rt. 13, Parksley 665-5191

This 40-room motel/restaurant specializes in country cooking and homemade pies.

SOMEPLACE ELSE

Rt. 13
Cape Charles 331-8430

This roadside restaurant is known for its fresh seafood and prime rib dinners.

STEAMER'S SEAFOOD RESTAURANT

6251 Maddox Blvd.
Chincoteague 336-5478

Steamer's opened in 1992 and features freshly steamed crabs, clams and shrimp.

STING RAY'S CAPE CENTER RESTAURANT

Rt. 13
Cape Charles 331-2505

This may look like a truck stop, but it offers a full menu of fresh crab, flounder and its famous, fiery Sting Ray Chili. Take note that the chili is only on the menu when owner Ray Haynie is there to properly spice it. This combination gas station/restaurant, dubbed "Chez Exxon" by the locals, is surprisingly elegant, with a menu that often includes lamb and chocolate torte. It's also a popular breakfast spot.

TAMMY AND JOHNNY'S

Rt. 13
Melfa 787-1122

Throw health concerns to the wind and dig into some of the best fried chicken you'll ever find. Locals come from miles away to eat at this local drive-in. Other standouts include fried corn-puffs and sweet-potato fingers. Basic burgers and fries also are on the menu.

THE TRAWLER

Rt. 13, Exmore 442-2092

One of our favorite places to take a break along Route 13, The Trawler has excellent seafood and is famous for its she-crab soup and irresistible sweet potato biscuits. Several times a year The Trawler transforms itself into a dinner theater.

WOLFF'S SANDWICH SHOPPE

Rt. 679, Atlantic 824-6466

Located in an old market, Wolff's old-timey charm is highlighted by Oscar the cockatiel. Sandwiches range from fresh-ground burgers to crab cakes and meaty subs. Wolff's also has clam strips and fish platters and serves both breakfast and lunch. It's a popular hangout for nearby NASA workers.

WRIGHT'S SEAFOOD RESTAURANT

Atlantic 824-4012

Located just a few miles outside

1995 Special Events

April 15-16 — Chincoteague Decoy and Art Festival
April 29 — Historic Home and Garden Tour (various locations)
May 3 — Chincoteague Seafood Festival
May 6 — Spring Lawn Sale in Onley
May 5-14 — Wachapreague Spring Flounder Tournament
June 3 — Parksley Spring Festival
June 21-July 8 — Onancock Fireman's Carnival
July 8-9 — Annual Marlin Tournament in Wachapreague
July 14-29 — Chincoteague Fireman's Carnival
July 15 — Onancock Harborfest
July 19-Aug. 5 — Wachapreague Fireman's Carnival
July 22 — Chincoteague Blueberry Craft Festival
July 26-27 — Chincoteague Pony Penning and Auction
Aug. 12 — Annual Heritage Festival in Eastville
Aug. 19 — Wachapreague Annual Fish Fry
Sept. 30 — Cape Charles Fall Festival
Oct. 4 — Eastern Shore Harvest Fest, Kiptopeke
Oct. 7 — Nandua Autumn Lawn Sale (tentative date)
Oct. 7-9 — Eastern Shore Birding Festival, Kiptopeke
Oct. 7 — Chincoteague Oyster Festival
Oct. 14 — Parksley Fall Festival

Chincoteague, Wright's sits right on the edge of Watts Bay. Its large seafood selection runs from flounder to clams. Wright's popular all-you-can-eat specials team up steamed crabs with fried chicken, ribs or other entrees. Although Wright's is in the country there are big billboards to guide you.

Accommodations

Whether you prefer family motels with a pool, country B&Bs or exclusive inns, you'll find many options on the Eastern Shore. The majority are in Chincoteague, but accommodations are scattered all along the Shore. Some are in small towns; others in rural areas. In the past few years there has been a profusion of new B&Bs in restored historic homes,

giving the Shore one of Virginia's largest concentrations this quaint style of accommodation. Many open year round; some only operate from spring through fall. All are antique-filled havens perfect for relaxing. If you're traveling with children, be sure to admit this fact right off the bat. Some B&Bs and inns welcome children only over the age of 10 or 12.

To help with your selection, the tourism commission has available a pamphlet called " Bed & Breakfasts of Virginia's Eastern Shore."

Bed and Breakfast Inns

BALLARD HOUSE BED & BREAKFAST
Rt. 660, Willis Wharf   442-2206
The owners of this Victorian home

welcome families. Children can explore Grandma Jo's attic filled with toys and books. They can crab off a wharf, play on a tree swing and walk along a nature path. Guests also can watch movies on cable TV or a VCR and sing together around a piano. They enjoy a full breakfast, afternoon tea and midnight snack. The cookie jar also is filled and waiting. There are four guest rooms with shared bathrooms. Pets are accepted. The Ballard House is accessible to handicapped guests.

BAY VIEW
35350 Copes Dr.
Belle Haven   442-6963 or (800) 442-6966

If you're fascinated by country living and Eastern Shore architecture, consider this bed and breakfast. Its main house was built in the early 1800s and has been added on in the big house/little house/ colonnade/kitchen-style known only on the Eastern Shore. Bay View sits on the banks of the Occohannock Creek in view of the Chesapeake Bay. It is in the country outside Exmore and Belle Haven. The innkeepers have had the house in their family for several generations. There are two guest rooms. Amenities include a swimming pool, tennis court, a dock for crabbing and 140 acres of woods for hiking as well as a full breakfast. Children are welcome.

BURTON HOUSE
11 Brooklyn St.
Wachapreague   787-4560

The owners of this bed and breakfast also run the adjacent Hart's Harbor House. This restored home, c. 1883, and its sister house are the only B&Bs in Wachapreague, a fishing village that bills itself as "Little City by the Sea." Both overlook the marshes leading to the Atlantic Ocean. The Burton House provides seven lovely rooms, with private half-baths.

The inn serves a full breakfast and has bicycles available. Cabins also are for rent.

CAPE CHARLES HOUSE
645 Tazewell Ave.
Cape Charles   331-4920

Opened as a bed and breakfast in 1993, this restored Colonial revival home is in the heart of Cape Charles near the Chesapeake Bay. Guests are treated to gourmet breakfasts, afternoon tea and wine and cheese as well as rooms with private baths

CHANNEL BASS INN
6228 Church St.
Chincoteague   336-6686

This elegant inn is now owned by Barbara and David Wiedenheft, also owners of Miss Molly's Inn, a longtime favorite in Chincoteague. Traditional English afternoon tea and gourmet breakfasts are served in the dining room. The Channel Bass is a great romantic getaway. The five spacious bedrooms, including one suite, are graciously appointed and have private baths.

CHESAPEAKE HOUSE
Tangier Island   891-2331

Comfortable rooms, full breakfasts and a family-style seafood dinner are designed for island visitors. Prices are downright cheap. The dining room is also open to the public. This longtime inn is open April through October.

COLONIAL MANOR INN
84 Market St.
Onancock   787-3521

Built in 1882, the inn has welcomed guests since 1936, longer than any other Eastern Shore establishment. It has 14 guest rooms and is on the main street of historic Onancock. Children are welcome at this relaxing, homey inn.

EVERGREEN INN

Pungoteague   442-3375

This is an 18th-century Georgian manor house on the Chesapeake Bay. The inn has two guest rooms with private baths and fireplaces. There are 25 acres of grounds, including a beach and dock for crabbing or fishing. Guests can borrow a paddleboat, canoe or bike. A full breakfast is served.

THE GARDEN AND THE SEA INN

New Church   824-0672

This elegant country inn opened in 1989 and recently gained new owners. The inn was built in 1802 as Bloxom's Tavern and is 15 minutes from Chincoteague. There are five guest rooms with private baths and some have whirlpools. Guests enjoy complimentary beverages, hearty continental breakfasts and afternoon tea. The elegant dining room, which is open to the public for dinner, features exceptional cuisine using regional foods. The inn has earned both a three-star Mobil rating and a three-diamond rating from AAA. It is open from April through October.

THE GLADSTONE HOUSE

12108 Lincoln Ave.

Exmore   442-4614, (800) BNB-GUEST

Get away from it all at this three-story brick Georgian-style home that started welcoming guests in 1994. Two guest rooms feature private baths. Amenities include a four-course breakfast plus coffee served in the guest rooms.

HART'S HARBOR HOUSE B & B

Wachapreague   787-4848

Owned and operated by the same folks who bring you the Burton House (see above entry), this c. 1870 home has been lovingly restored. It is furnished with antiques and overlooks barrier islands and thousands of acres of salt marsh. The inn offers three spacious rooms, each with a private bath. Breakfast is served, and bicycles are available.

HOLLY BROOK PLANTATION

Rt. 13, north of Eastville   678-5057

Built in the early 1700s this venerable home is owned by the Association for the Preservation of Virginia Antiquities. It is built in the big house/little house/colonnade/kitchen style. Holly Brook started accepting overnight guests in 1992.

HOMEPLACE BED AND BREAKFAST

Parksley   665-6522

This restored elegant Victorian home, c. 1903, is located in the charming hometown of the Eastern Shore Railway Museum. Relax in the antique-filled parlor. Full breakfasts and an afternoon tea are served daily. Two air-conditioned rooms are available.

Insiders' Tips

When calling the Eastern Shore, remember it has the same 804 area code as the Hampton Roads area of Virginia. From Hampton Roads it is a toll-free call to Cape Charles at the southern tip of the Eastern Shore. Beyond there a long-distance fee is charged, and 804 must be dialed as part of the phone number.

ISLAND MANOR HOUSE
4160 Main St., Chincoteague   336-5436,
(800) 852-1505

This home in the heart of Chincoteague was built before the Civil War by two men who later married sisters. To accommodate both families they split the house in half and moved the front part next door. The restoration that created the Island Manor House several years ago reunited the two houses with an airy garden room. There are eight guest rooms, some with private baths. A full breakfast and afternoon tea are served.

THE MAIN STREET HOUSE
Main St., Chincoteague   336-603
(800) 491-2027

This Victorian home is right on Chincoteague Channel. Its screened-in porch offers spectacular sunset views, and there are several guest rooms. The owner is a former wildlife refuge manager with lots of information to share. Breakfast is continental-plus with heartier fare on weekends.

MARTHA'S INN
12224 Lincoln Ave.
Exmore   442-4641, (800) MARTHA

Built in 1936 by the owner's parents, this stately Georgian-style home recently started welcoming bed and breakfast guests. The three-story features full country breakfasts. Outside are three acres of grounds. The inn is open year round.

MISS MOLLY'S INN (1886)
4141 Main St.
Chincoteague   336-6686, (800) 491-2027

This bed and breakfast is where Marguerite Henry stayed while writing part of *Misty of Chincoteague*, which was published in 1947. Miss Molly, the daughter of J.T. Rowely who built the house in 1886, lived here until the age of 84. The Victorian house is in the heart of Chincoteague and overlooks Chincoteague Bay. It is open from mid-February through New Years. Guests can enjoy full breakfasts and afternoon tea in the gazebo. There are seven guest rooms, five with private baths.

NOTTINGHAM RIDGE
Cape Charles   331-1010

With 100 acres bordering the Chesapeake Bay, this Colonial home has its own beach. Guest rooms have private baths. Breakfast is served on the porch overlooking the bay with wine and cheese offered in the evenings. Sunsets here are spectacular.

PICKETTS HARBOR BED AND BREAKFAST
Cape Charles   331-2212

This bed and breakfast has a private Chesapeake Bay beach. It offers full country breakfasts, and some guest rooms have private baths. It is open year round.

PUNGOTEAGUE JUNCTION BED AND BREAKFAST
30230 Bobtown Rd.
Pungoteague   442-3581

This 1869 house with a wraparound porch has two guest rooms. The bed and breakfast serves a full breakfast and offers dinners upon request. Children are welcome and will find toys waiting for them.

SEA GATE BED AND BREAKFAST
9 Tazewell Ave.
Cape Charles   331-2206

Built in 1861, this home is in walking distance of the Chesapeake Bay beach in historic Cape Charles. The bed and breakfast offers porches for relaxing, bikes for touring the town, full breakfasts and afternoon tea.

76 MARKET STREET
BED AND BREAKFAST
76 Market St.
Onancock   787-7600

This restored Victorian home is in Onancock's historic residential district and is an easy stroll from the harbor. It is owned by a town native and features three guest rooms with private baths and full breakfasts.

THE SPINNING WHEEL
BED AND BREAKFAST
31 North St.
Onancock   787-7311

This restored 1890s folk Victorian home is just off the main street of historic Onancock. Among its antique furnishings are several spinning wheels, which give the inn its name. Five guest rooms each have private baths. Guests enjoy full breakfasts served in bed or the dining room. They can opt for golf and tennis at a private club. Bicycles are available for exploring the town. The inn is open May through October.

STILLMEADOW
7423 Bayside Rd. (Rt. 618)
Franktown   442-2431, (800) 772-8397

Built in 1895, this restored house has three guest rooms with private baths. The home is near Nature Conservancy property and Nassawadox. It has a well-stocked library for visitors as well as a piano. Bicycles also are available. Full breakfasts and afternoon tea are served.

SUNSET INN BED AND BREAKFAST
106 Bay Ave.
Cape Charles   331-2424, (800) 331-3113

This vintage home overlooks the Chesapeake Bay and offers guests the chance to unwind on the porch, bicycle and swim. The porch is a great spot for watching sunsets. The inn has two guest rooms and two suites and serves a heavy continental breakfast. It is open year round.

SUNSET INN
Tangier Island   891-2535

The sunsets are spectacular from this beachfront home on Tangier Island. Guests have a choice of rooms in the main house or cabins outside. It is open year round.

THE WATSON HOUSE
4240 Main St.
Chincoteague   336-1564, (800) 336-6787

This Victorian home in the heart of Chincoteague has six guest rooms with private baths and provides full breakfasts served in the dining room or on the veranda. The inn offers afternoon tea and equips guests with free bicycles and beach chairs. It has earned AAA's three-diamond rating.

WINDER HOUSE
Atlantic   824-4090

This turn-of-the-century home is 8 miles from Chincoteague. Its hosts serve a full country breakfast.

WYNNE TREF
Locustville   787-2356

This is a traditional 18th-century Eastern Shore home a mile from the Atlantic Ocean. Its name means "White House" in Welsh. There is one suite for rent. Guests are served a hearty continental breakfast.

YEAR OF THE HORSE INN
3583 Main St.
Chincoteague   336-3221

This Colonial-style inn was built in the 1940s and was Chincoteague's first bed and breakfast. It is right on Chincoteague Sound and has a 100-foot

Photo: Virginia's Eastern Shore Tourism Commission

In the spring and fall, the Shore boasts some of the world's highest bird counts.

pier for crabbing or fishing and a deck overlooking the intercoastal waterway. Several guests rooms have balconies and all have private baths and beautiful views. One has a kitchenette, and there is a two-bedroom apartment available. Guests renting rooms are served a continental breakfast.

Motels

There are many nice motels to choose from on the Eastern Shore. The following are some to consider.

ANCHOR INN
534 S. Main St.
Chincoteague   *336-6313*
There are 40 rooms, some of them efficiency apartments. The motel has a boat harbor, launching ramp and fish cleaning and storage areas. There is a swimming pool. Rooms have refrigerators and some are handicapped accessible.

ANCHOR MOTEL
Rt. 13 in Nassawadox
and Onley   *442-6363, 787-8000*
(800) 283-4678
The Nassawadox motel has 36 rooms and the Captain's Deck restaurant. The Onley location has 32 rooms and four efficiency apartments. The motels accept pets.

ASSATEAGUE INN
6570 Coach Ln.
Chincoteague   *336-3738*
This motel's 27 rooms, most of them suites, overlook a peaceful-looking salt-water marsh behind tall pine trees. Amenities include a pool picnic area, HBO and a spa.

BIRCHWOOD MOTEL
3650 Main St., Chincoteague   *336-6133*
Located in the heart of Chincoteague, this 40-room motel has a swimming pool, crabbing pier, picnic area and playground.

CAPE MOTEL

Rt. 13, Cape Charles   331-2461

There are 16 rooms at this hotel 6 miles from the bridge-tunnel. It has free HBO, an outdoor swimming pool and a picnic area with grills.

CAPTAIN'S QUARTERS

Rt. 13, Melfa   787-4545

There are 22 rooms, some with kitchenettes and handicapped accessibility. Pets are accepted.

COMFORT INN

Rt. 13, Onley   787-7787

There are 80 rooms, some of which are handicapped accessible. There is a swimming pool and meeting room.

DRIFTWOOD MOTOR LODGE

Beach Rd.
Chincoteague   336-6557
     (800) 553-6117, Ext. 11

Located at the causeway to Assateague Island, the Driftwood has 52 rooms with balconies and patios. Rooms come with free HBO and refrigerators. There is an outdoor swimming pool and bikes for rent. The motel has an elevator to upper-level rooms. Restaurants are within easy walking distance.

DAYS INN CAPE CHARLES

Rt. 13
Cape Charles   331-1000, (800) 331-4000

This is one of the nearest motels to the Chesapeake Bay Bridge-Tunnel. It has 103 rooms, a swimming pool and accepts pets. There also is a meeting room.

ISLAND BELLE MOTOR LODGE

Beach Rd.
Chincoteague   336-3600

One of the island's newest motels, it is located just beyond the causeway to Assateague Island. There are 50 rooms, including some that are handicapped-ac-

cessible. There is an outdoor pool and a meeting room. The lobby has a display of more than 600 handbells.

ISLAND MOTOR INN

4391 Main St.
Chincoteague   336-3141, (800) 832-2925

All 60 rooms have a view of Chincoteague Bay as well as small refrigerators. You'll find both a heated indoor pool and an outdoor pool plus a fitness center with a hot tub. Amenities include a meeting room, fishing and crabbing pier, deep-water docking and an elevator.

THE LIGHTHOUSE MOTEL

224 N. Main St.
Chincoteague   336-5091

There are 25 rooms, some with refrigerators and microwaves. Handicapped facilities are available as are an outdoor pool and a screened picnic area.

THE MARINER MOTEL

6273 Maddox Blvd.   336-6565
Chincoteague   (800) 221-7490, Ext. 4

Located between downtown Chincoteague and Assateague Island, the Mariner has 92 rooms and an outdoor pool. It has a meeting room, is handicapped accessible, has a laundry facility and refrigerators in some rooms. Outside are picnic tables and a pony.

REFUGE MOTOR INN

Beach Rd.
Chincoteague   336-5511
     (800) 544-8469, Ext. 14

This 68-room motel is near the causeway to Assateague Island. It has an indoor/outdoor swimming pool, fitness center and hot tub. The inn recently expanded and added suites. Outside are several Chincoteague ponies. There are bicycles for rent, a playground, grills and picnic tables. Rooms have small refrigerators and some are handicapped accessible. There is a meeting room, laundry facilities and a gift shop.

THE SEA HAWK MOTEL
Maddox Blvd.
Chincoteague   *336-6527*

There are 28 rooms, some of them efficiency apartments, along with two cottages. Amenities include an outdoor pool, playground and picnic area.

SEA SHELL MOTEL
3720 Willow St.
Chincoteague   *336-6589, Ext. 3*

The 40-room motel has several efficiencies and apartments. All rooms have refrigerators. There is an outdoor pool and a screened-kitchen and eating area. A play area has picnic tables and grills.

SUNRISE MOTOR INN
Maddox Blvd., Chincoteague   *336-6671*

This motel is less than a mile from the entrance to the Chincoteague National Wildlife Refuge and the Assateague National Seashore. Amenities include an outdoor pool, picnic area with grills and a playground. Complimentary tea and coffee are offered each morning.

SUNSET BEACH INN
Rt. 13, Kiptopeke   *331-4SUN*

This 83-room motel is within shouting distance of the Chesapeake Bay Bridge-Tunnel. It has a restaurant, outdoor swimming pool and one of the best-kept secrets on the shore — a wonderful beach right on the Chesapeake Bay. There are beach chairs and colorful umbrellas for guests to use.

WATERSIDE MOTOR INN
544 S. Main St.
Chincoteague   *336-3434*

Guests at this 45-room motel can use a private pier for crabbing or fishing. Rooms have small refrigerators, coffee makers and HBO. There is an outdoor pool. Some rooms are handicapped accessible.

Photo:Richmond Newspapers

Saltwater fishing is a popular pastime all along the Eastern Shore.

WACHAPREAGUE MOTEL & MARINA

Wachapreague   787-2105

This 30-room motel sits along the marsh that leads to the Atlantic Ocean. It is a popular spot for fishermen who like to get an early start at the marina across the road. Rooms come with a small refrigerator and coffee maker, and some have kitchenettes. Pets are welcome, and some rooms are handicapped accessible.

House Rentals

If you really want to spread out and stay awhile, rent a house. There are about 800 of them available on Chincoteague alone. **Chincoteague Island Vacation Cottages**, 336-3720, (800) 457-6643, handles all types of rental property that you can have for a weekend or all week. Many homes have great waterfront locations. Other companies renting property include **Island Property**, (800) FI-NALLY, **Vacation Rentals**, 336-5490, and **Island's Pride Cottages**, 336-6345 or (301) 865-5842 in the off-season.

Camping

If camping appeals to you, there are several private campgrounds in Chincoteague. **Maddox Family Campground** offers the closest camping to Assateague Island, 336-3111 or 336-6648. **Toms Cove** overlooks Assateague Island and has fishing piers and a boat ramp, 336-6498. Another waterfront campground is **Inlet View**, 336-5126. For a public camping spot try **Kiptopeke State Park** at the southern end of the Eastern Shore near the Chesapeake Bay Bridge-Tunnel. The park is right on the Chesapeake Bay, 331-2760.

Shopping

Chincoteague's Main Street is lined with crafts and gift boutiques and has the Shore's greatest abundance of gift shops. You'll find work by many local artisans, including decoy carvers whose work is known nationwide. One famous local product is **Pony Tails** saltwater taffy. A visit to the Pony Tails factory often includes a chance to see taffy and fudge being made. A stop at Chincoteague's **Ben Franklin 5 & 10** will make you nostalgic for the good old days.

Chincoteague isn't the only place to spend your hard-earned cash, however. Most Eastern Shore towns have traditional downtowns with interesting antique and gift shops. There are about 20 antique shops scattered throughout the Shore. For basic necessities, there are two strip shopping centers along Route 13 at the Four Corners area near Onley. Not too far away is a new shopping center anchored by a **Kmart**.

To take home a taste of the Eastern Shore visit the **Blue Crab Bay Co.** at 108 Market Street in Onancock. This 11-year-old company creates a variety of specialty foods and runs a booming national mail-order business. Its customers include Macy's, Marshall Field's and Disney World. Blue Crab Bay has a retail store on Onancock's main street that sells gift baskets, seasonings, canned clams and other Eastern Shore delicacies.

Several other shops also could be considered attractions. Near Melfa on Route 13 is **Turner Sculpture** where artists William and David Turner cast bronze animal sculptures. Their work is world-renowned and housed at such places as the Brookfield Zoo in Chicago and Philadelphia Zoo. Prices in the shop range from $25 to $35,000. Browsers are welcome.

In Oak Hall check out the **Decoy Factory**, the world's largest maker of decoys. Visitors can watch woodworkers carving native waterfowl. They also can purchase their own decoys.

The **Painter Gallery** on Route 13 in Painter showcases a variety of fine arts with changing exhibits from various artists. The gallery also houses the studio of Dr. Joseph D. Adams, a noted poet and artist. The Gallery frequently sponsors poetry readings and writer's workshops. It's open Wednesday through Saturday from mid-May through early August.

Eastern Shore Pottery on Route 13 near Capeville is filled with a mind-boggling array of pottery. You'll find salt-glazed pieces as well as Mexican, Southwestern and Indian works. Bird baths, fountains and other decorative items also are in stock. The pottery is open daily year round.

Recreation

The great outdoors beckons on the Eastern Shore. The Eastern Shore's tidal marshes attract more than 250 species of waterfowl and shorebirds. In fact, the United Nations has named the **Virginia Coast Reserve** along the Eastern Shore as one of the few remaining Biosphere Reserves left in the world. In spring and fall the Shore boasts some of the world's highest bird counts.

Hunters enjoy seasons for deer, dove, duck and 12 other animals. **Fishermen** can go bayside or seaside for their catch. Their prime season stretches from May through November and includes everything from sea bass to shark and red drum. There are many **charter boats and headboats** that take you out with a crew that grew up fishing off the Shore. You also will find small boat rentals.

Wachapreague, the flounder capital of the world, has the greatest number of charter boats. However, Cape Charles, Chincoteague and other coastal towns also have rental boats available. Virginia's Eastern Shore Tourism Commission publishes a helpful hunting and fishing guide.

Bird watching, hiking and **bicycling** are other popular outdoor pastimes. **Camping** is available at Kiptopeke State Park and several private campgrounds (see the separate section above). Recently **Occohannock on the Bay**, a Methodist summer camp for children, started welcoming adult groups and individual campers to its grounds along the Occohannock Creek, 442-5713 or 442-7836.

Real Estate

If your trip to the Eastern Shore has you longing to put down roots, check out the real estate offerings. City dwellers most likely will think they stepped back 20 years in real estate prices. Browse through any Eastern Shore real estate brochure and low asking prices attached to snapshots of idyllic homes will make you ready to haul out your checkbook. Many fine houses sell for well below $100,000.

Whether you're looking to retire, buy a weekend cottage or settle down permanently, you'll find plenty of options. You can choose from property on the bayside, seaside, in small towns or in the country. You can settle on an existing house or buy land to build your dream home.

With more than 400 buildings dating from before 1865, the Shore has one of Virginia's largest concentrations of historic homes. You can still purchase the big house/little house/colonnade/kitchen-style homes typical of the late 1700s. Other

Yesterday's Island

Tangier Island. The name alone conjures up images of a faraway isle just waiting to be discovered. As the most remote spot in Virginia, a trip to Tangier Island is a memorable experience.

Constant erosion has reduced this island in the Chesapeake Bay to only a mile wide and 3 miles long. Although it is part of Accomack County on the Eastern Shore (and shares its 804 area code), the island is 14 miles west of the Shore and 17 miles east of Reedville in the Northern Neck of Virginia.

History

Legend has it that Capt. John Smith discovered Tangier Island in 1608 and that Indians traded the island in 1666 to John West for two overcoats. The first permanent settler, John Crockett, arrived in 1686 with his sons and their families. By the 19th century there were 100 residents — half of them Crocketts. The island was used primarily to graze livestock.

During the Revolutionary War the British used Tangier Island as a base for raiding American ships. Pirates also found it a great hideaway. After the war, the island's population started to grow as watermen settled here. From 1808 through 1858 up to 10,000 people swelled the island each summer for Methodist camp meetings. The British again occupied the island during the War of 1812, and 12,000 troops used it as a base to plunder Virginia and burn Washington, D.C.

Since 1866 Tangier's residents have depended on the Chesapeake Bay for their livelihood, with crabs being the primary catch. The island boasts that it is the soft-shell capital of the world, and when you arrive by boat you'll spot the soft-shell crab "farms" along the shore where the crabs shed their shells.

In researching this section, we found the November 1973 issue of *National Geographic*, which featured a detailed article on life on Tangier Island. Although more than 20 years have passed, little has changed on the island.

Getting There

You have several choices for arriving on Tangier. If you have your own boat, you can sail from Onancock, Saxis or Crisfield, Maryland, on the Eastern Shore. From the western shore of Virginia, you can leave from Reedville. At Tangier, you can dock at Parks' Marina, 891-2567.

Commercial boats ferry visitors from three locations: Onancock, Reedville and Crisfield, Maryland. Narrators clue you in on details about the Chesapeake Bay and life on Tangier Island. The trip over is a pleasant one, with sea gulls or geese flying overhead and fisherman at work in the bay.

In Onancock, you can hitch a ride on the *Captain Eulice* at Onancock Wharf right by Hopkins & Bros. Store. Tangier Island Cruises operates the 90-passenger boat from June 1 through September 15 every day but

Sunday. The boat leaves at 10 AM and arrives in Tangier 1½ hours later. The return trip starts at 1:30 PM, bringing you back to Onancock by 3 PM. Round-trip tickets cost $17.50, half-price for children between 6 and 12. Preschoolers ride free. For information call 891-2240, 787-8220 or (410) 968-2338 for group reservations. Although reservations aren't required for individuals, call in advance if it's peak tourist season.

Tangier Island Cruises also owns the *Steven Thomas*, which docks at Crisfield, Maryland, about a 50-minute drive from Onancock. The 300-passenger boat leaves daily May 15 through October from City Dock on Main Street. The boat departs at 12:30 PM and arrives at Tangier at 1:45 PM. You'll have a few hours to wander around before heading back at 4 PM. The cost is $18 for adults with anyone younger than 12 riding for free. Reservations are recommended for groups of 20 or more. For details call (410) 968-2338 or 891-2240.

For a no-frills trip, you can hop on the mail boat that leaves Crisfield Monday through Saturday at 12:30 PM. It heads back to the mainland from Tangier at 8 AM the next day. The mail boat plies the waters year round and also is operated by Tangier Island Cruises. The cost is $10 each way. Don't expect any official narration except for your conversation with the captain, a Tangier native. If you take the mail boat, plan to spend the night on the island. Call (410) 968-2338 or 891-2240 for details.

From the western shore of Virginia, the *Chesapeake Breeze* ferries passengers from May through October 15. It starts out running on weekends and ends with the same schedule. From mid-May through early October it sails daily. The boat leaves from Reedville, a Victorian fishing village, at 10 AM and returns about 3:30 PM. The trips takes 1 hour and 45 minutes. The cost is $18.50 for adults. Children between 4 and 13 ride for $9.25. Reservations are a must. Call Tangier & Rappahannock Cruises Inc. at (804) 453-2628.

One other option is to catch a Tangier Island Cruises boat from Portsmouth that stops at Tangier Island on its way to Crisfield. The boat trip takes about four hours. The $235-per-couple cost includes accommodations in Crisfield and several meals. The boat returns the next day. During the summer the boat usually makes about five excursions from Portsmouth. More trips begin in Chrisfield. Call 410-968-2338.

For a quick trip to Tangier Island from the Eastern Shore, you can charter a plane. Call Chesapeake Aviation Inc. in Melfa at 787-2901.

Attractions

The island itself is the main draw. What you'll find is a tightly knit fishing community with nearly 700 residents, many of them related. About a third of the residents share the Crockett surname. Other common monikers are Parks, Pruitt and Thomas. The island is no more than seven feet above sea level with a small beach that's being swallowed by erosion. The terrain is flat, with 80 percent of it covered with marsh, wetlands and water. In the summer you won't find much shade or many cool breezes so bring along a hat and sunscreen.

Tangier residents are clustered in three communities known as "ridges," connected by roads that are little more than paths. Although there are a few cars on the island, most people get around on foot, bicycle or motorized golf carts. You'll find one school with 120 students in kindergarten through grade 12. There is a post office and two grocery stores.

Except for the tourists, crabbing and clamming are the ways most families earn their livings. Residents are descended from generations of hardy watermen. Their isolation gives them a distinct accent that still rings with the Elizabethan tones of their forebears.

Most people stay only a couple of hours on the island, which gives enough time to grab a seafood lunch, wander through gift shops and stroll through the communities. Waiting at the dock will be tour guides who'll give you a spin through the island on golf carts for about $2 a person.

Since up to 500 people a day storm the island in the summer, you may want to time your visit for spring or fall. Another way to avoid the crowds is to spend the night and see what Tangier is like once the boat crowd leaves. This will give you time to soak up the atmosphere, kick back and go to the beach.

Accommodations

There are two choices for overnight stays. Since 1940 the Chesapeake House has welcomed guests from April 15 through October 15. Its eight rooms are comfortable and have shared baths. Rates include big family-style seafood dinners and breakfast. The Chesapeake House is run by Tangier native Hilda Crockett and is near the boat dock. Call 891-2331.

If you want to stay right on the water, try the Sunset Inn. Owner Grace Brown has about 10 rooms, including several cottages. All are air conditioned with private baths. The Inn is open year round. It has a wonderful view of the bay and its spectacular sunsets. Call 891-2535.

Dining

You'd better like seafood if you're eating on Tangier Island, although you will find a few sandwiches on some menus. Most restaurants are open only from April through October. Options include the Chesapeake House, Fisherman's Corner, 891-2571, and the Islander, 891-2249. The Waterfront is a small restaurant on the dock.

period homes, such as those from the Victorian era, can be bought for a song. Older houses tend to be less expensive than newer construction of similar square footage. You'll find both handyman's specials and beautifully restored homes among the older property.

Like anywhere else, when you're looking for a home or some land, location is the key. As you'd expect, waterfront locations carry a higher sales price than land-locked property. Property facing the Chesapeake Bay is more popular and more expensive than waterfront property on the Atlantic Ocean side of the Shore. This is because navigable creeks give direct access to the bay. The seaside, with its wonderful views and spectacular sunrises, is bordered primarily by marshes and tidal flats. This makes boat access to the ocean possible only in high tide and a few deep-water areas.

There are more than 30 real estate companies on the Shore. Although there is no multiple listing service, there is a strong Realtors' board. Most agents are tapped into what's available on the market. A few of the companies are:

Century 21-Eastern Shore Properties Inc., Chicoteague, 336-3121

Crockett Realty, Onancock, 787-2031

ERA Richard Hatfield Realty, Chincoteague, 336-6000, 800-666-1372

Kirkwood Properties, Exmore, 442-3224

Lassiter Realty, Accomac and other towns, 787-1305

Mason-Davis Co. Inc., Accomac and other towns, 787-1010

Parr Properties, Onley, 787-7277

Whitman Realty Inc., Accomac and other towns, 787-1999

Other Services

Medical Care

NORTHAMPTON-ACCOMACK MEMORIAL HOSPITAL
Nassawadox 442-8000

Founded in 1928, the 158-bed hospital is the third-largest employer on the Eastern Shore. The hospital has the Eastern Shore of Virginia's only emergency department and a full range of medical services.

Education

EASTERN SHORE COMMUNITY COLLEGE
Melfa 787-5900

This 600-student community college offers two-year degrees in such areas as electronics engineering and business technology. It also offers one-year certificates in such fields as automotive repair and drafting. Through interactive televised courses students can earn B.S. degrees in nursing and other fields from Virginia four-year colleges. They also can complete two years of study at the community college and then transfer to a four-year institution to complete their degrees.

Inside
Real Estate and Neighborhoods

What you're certain to discover when you enter the wonderful world of Hampton Roads real estate is the voracity of neighborhood spirit, a spirit that can reach the level of territorial supremacy previously attributed solely to the primitive tribes of Mongolia. City dwellers, oceanfront habitants and rural pioneers all claim their lifestyle to be the ultimate in residential superiority. Which puts new homebuyers in our market in a delightful quandary . . . what would you like in your backyard? The Atlantic Ocean or Chesapeake Bay? A manicured golf course? How about acres with a stable, or maybe the urban hustle-bustle of late-night restaurants and cultural centers?

After you've answered that question, the next decision is style. New construction or resale, townhome, ranch, high-rise condo or Southern Colonial — pick your favorite and you're sure to find it at the right price. So right, in fact, that if you hail from the West Coast, New England or Washington, D.C., you'll be pleased to learn that the median price of homes in Hampton Roads averages close to half of what you're used to. So, not only will you find a lot more house for your homebuying dollar, you'll also save loads of time in your work commute. No matter where in which city you choose to live, 30 minutes in rush hour is about all the time it will take to get from your pajamas to your desk.

There are a few general rules of real estate in Hampton Roads. First, the closer to water, the more expensive the property. Because we've been blessed with not only the ocean and the bay, but zillions of rivers, tributaries, creeks, inlets and lakes, your chance to land a waterfront property is fairly good. The price of the property rises proportionately with the size of the body of water it overlooks. So a home on the Atlantic Ocean might carry a price tag of $500,000 to more than a million dollars; a cedar-shake contemporary on the Chesapeake Bay, around $200,000; a resale rancher on a marshy creek an average of $150,000.

The second rule is that a resale home in an older, established neighborhood generally sells at a lower square-foot cost than a new construction home in a new, planned community. A recent comparison of homes sold in Virginia Beach reveals a median price of $85,000 for resale and $105,000 for new construction. What you get for that extra $20,000 is brand new everything, well worth the investment if you're not an adept do-it-yourselfer. Yet, plenty of people feel the trade-off in terms of knowing the "personality" of the neighborhood is well worth the cans of paint and elbow grease that might be required.

The final rule is that you really should have a definite focus on the style, community lifestyle and price of the home

Photo: Richmond Newspapers

Homebuyers have a wide selection of homes to choose from in Hampton Roads.

you're looking for. Faced with the alternatives of restored period homes, slick condo high-rises, beachy cottages, tract houses, city townhomes and country farmettes, the best advice is to first take a couple of days for a "just looking" tour through our different communities and neighborhoods. By contacting a relocation specialist within any of our major realty companies, you can be inundated with brochures, magazines, maps, city-by-city information and market details to confuse you even further. These relo specialists are used to your confusion, however, and are expert at helping point you in the direction of your new home-to-be, as well as being fountains of information for rentals, day care, job referrals for spouses, school systems, recreational opportunities and anything else that will help your family settle in to your new community. (Of course, this book will answer many of those questions, too!)

While nothing can really beat the advice and counsel of a well-informed Insider, there are a slew of homebuying magazines that can serve as a wish list in narrowing your search. *Home Search,*

Harmon Homes, Real Estate Digest and *For Sale By Owner* are the leaders in resale properties, and are all available free at local grocery and convenience chains. For new home construction, *New Home,* published by the Tidewater Builders Association, is the definitive volume for those interested in a brand-new home in a new community. Our local newspaper, *The Virginian-Pilot/Ledger-Star,* publishes "Real Estate Weekly" each Saturday. This tabloid-sized edition is a wealth of information, covering both resale and new construction, along with weekly updates on area lenders' mortgage rates and helpful editorial content.

All in all, real estate is big business in Hampton Roads. Home to numerous regional headquarters and, of course, the world's largest military base, people are constantly packing the vans for moves in and out of our market. To serve them, nearly 5,000 Realtors are at work around the clock, shifting folks between neighborhoods and between cities, across town, across country and even across the world. Because of the competition, any one of these go-getters you choose will more than likely bend over backwards to ensure your satisfaction. And, whether your chosen Realtor hails from a small, independent firm, or a nationally affiliated company like ERA, Century 21, The Prudential or Re/Max, you can trust each one knows the business and the market he or she represents. If you do need assistance in making that Realtor choice, contact the Tidewater Board of Realtors, serving Norfolk and Virginia Beach, 340-9700, or the Portsmouth-Chesapeake Board of Realtors, serving Portsmouth, Chesapeake, Suffolk and Franklin, 397-4613.

Real Estate Companies

To make your initial search a bit quicker, here's a sampling of the major real estate firms serving Hampton Roads:

WILLIAM E. WOOD & ASSOCIATES

16 Offices
Relocation   *464-0022*
TDD (Hearing Impaired)   *363-2557*

The region's largest real estate company, you'll find a William E. Wood & Associates sales office in practically every popular neighborhood in Hampton Roads. Boasting a sales force of over 400, it began as, and remains, a locally owned and operated firm, with specialists in resale, new construction, relocation, commercial and bank-owned properties. They also have a strong property management division that handles a wide variety of rental properties.

GSH REAL ESTATE

12 Offices
Relocation   *490-6530*
TDD (Hearing Impaired)   *(800) 828-1120*

An equally strong independent firm, GSH Real Estate has provided more than 40 years of service to the community. Four hundred sales associates strong, GSH offers resale and new construction sales, re-

location services and property management, including resort rental properties. Each of its offices has a book with color pictures of every VA/HUD property available, updated daily. The firm also offers escrow and title services. It is a member of The Dozen, a selective and prestigious group of independent Realtors across the country that meets annually to share new ideas and service innovations.

LONG & FOSTER

11 Offices
Relocation   *420-0000*

The largest real estate company in Virginia is a relative newcomer to the Hampton Roads market, but its hometown agents are both well known and respected. Help for resale and new construction, along with relocation services, is available at any of the Long & Foster offices.

CENTURY 21

District Office   *499-0164*

More than 20 independently owned and operated Century 21 offices are at work in Hampton Roads, offering top-notch advice on resale, new construction, investment and property management services. You can even shop for a house in Greenbrier, Pembroke and Lynnhaven malls at the Century 21 At The Mall offices that are staffed during mall hours. Because of their national affiliation, any of this network of Century 21 offices can provide excellent relocation information for moving in or out of the area.

ROSE & KRUETH REALTY CORP.

6 Offices
Relocation   *499-3330*

One of the strongest companies around for new construction, Rose & Krueth is known for its excellent marketing materials and can provide one of the most comprehensive relocation packages around these parts, including a video. An efficiently run organization, it also offers resale and rentals.

WOMBLE REALTY

6 Offices
Relocation   486-8052

For nearly 30 years, Womble Realty signs have been seen in Hampton Roads' finer neighborhoods. While not as large as some of the major hitters in the market, Womble agents are considerate and helpful to a fault, and excel in resale, new construction, commercial properties and property management.

THE PRUDENTIAL/DECKER REALTY

4 Offices
Relocation   422-2200

Known for its representation of some of Virginia Beach's most exclusive properties, The Prudential/Decker Realty holds its own with the "big boys," especially in higher-end sales. It is an especially friendly firm, with well-respected agents and an excellent reputation for resale and new construction sales as well as relocation services.

NANCY CHANDLER ASSOCIATES

2 Offices
Relocation   623-2382

If you're interested in Norfolk's West Side, this is a great company to hook up with. While listings cover the entire market (due to some long-term agents who have strong roots in the upper-end marketplace), the neighborhoods of Ghent, Larchmont and Lochaven are Chandler strongholds. This close-knit group of real estate professionals offers excellent service for resale, new construction (especially downtown townhomes), property management and relocation services. With its acquisition of the Coldwell Banker affiliate in Chesapeake, Chandler has expanded its scope of operations to take advantage of the flourishing Chesapeake marketplace.

COLDWELL BANKER

Gifford Realty	583-1000
Harbor Group Real Estate	484-4400
Helfant Realty Inc.	463-1212
Jeanne West & Associates	481-6181

All five of the Caldwell Banker affiliates in Hampton Roads were strong independent companies before changing banners. Joan Gifford's company excels in medium-priced housing and rental properties. Gifford, a past president of the Norfolk Division of the Hampton Roads Chamber of Commerce and a past director of the National Association of Realtors, is herself a real estate landmark in the community. Dorcas Helfant, who can lay claim to the honor of being the first woman to serve as president of The National Association of Realtors, has long been respected for her commitment to the advancement of integrity in the industry, and Jeanne West is synonymous with the sales and marketing of finer homes in Virginia Beach. Harbor Group claims Portsmouth as home and is one of the most knowledgeable firms for home buyers in this Hampton Roads city.

> If you're new to the area and curious about what county you live in, stop wondering. Chances are good you don't live in one. Virginia is the only state where cities are not located in counties.

Insiders' Tips

RE/MAX

Advantage	436-4500
Associates	498-7000
Central	490-7300

The independently owned and operated offices of the Re/Max network are known for their aggressive marketing of properties and the longevity of their experienced agents. Naturally, their relocation specialists are excellent, as are their resale and new construction agents.

OTHER SELECTED INDEPENDENT REAL ESTATE FIRMS INCLUDE:

Realty Consultants, 499-5911. New construction and resale in Virginia Beach.

Leading Edge Realty, 671-3343. New construction experts.

Realty Executives, 456-9500. New construction and resale in Virginia Beach.

Marshall-Ewald Realty, 463-2600. Personable firm specializing in Virginia Beach resales.

Judy Boone Realty, 587-2800. A family-owned and managed company headquartered in Norfolk's Ocean View.

Pyle Realty, 491-1600. A Landmark company specializing in Virginia Beach properties.

Cooke & Neff Realtors, 622-5075. Known for representation of higher-end properties, the firm is most widely recognized for their rental and insurance divisions.

Mary Lee Harris Realty, 498-7775. The leader for primo properties at Virginia Beach. If you're looking for top-of-the-line, Mary Lee is your connection.

Builders

If you want to direct the moving van to a never-been-lived-in new construction single-family home, townhome or condominium, here's the basic scoop on the builders who have made their mark

in Hampton Roads. Together, they have literally changed the face of our area, developing innovative communities and neighborhoods that incorporate some of the most novel features of homes being built all over the country, adapted to the tastes of Hampton Roads homebuyers. The reason for their success is their commitment not only to the highest standards in the building industry, but to buyer satisfaction as evidenced by their competent customer service divisions. A purchase from any of these fine companies is a sure bet.

While flipping through the pages of any local real estate publication, you'll see these names again and again.

THE FRANCISCUS COMPANY
620 Village Dr.   *425-8391*

Frank Spadea is the captain of this huge ship, one that is known primarily for its innovative townhome communities. He's a hands-on kind of builder, involved in every detail from master-planning to window detail, and it shows. Franciscus is recognized for demanding the most picky property management teams to watchdog their properties, meaning that all common grounds are meticulously maintained and repairs are promptly attended to. Current developments include The Country Club Collection, three unique condominium communities on Chesapeake's Greenbrier Golf Course, Les Chateaux in Great Bridge and Laurel Green in the Las Gaviotas Golf Course community.

NAPOLITANO ENTERPRISES
3012 Scarlett Oak Ct.   *340-8847*

Vince Napolitano continues his family's tradition of building homes and condominium communities that dovetail with the needs of local buyers. A past president of the Tidewater Builders Association, Napolitano is one of the most visible and vocal advocates for excellence in building design and has steered his company to be voted one of the top-five builders in Virginia by *Builder Magazine*. Napolitano products are known for their contemporary architecture and volume. Check out Beacon Point in Riverwalk and single-family homes in Greenwood at Greenbrier and The Crossings in Western Branch, all in Chesapeake.

R.G. MOORE
4480 Holland Office Park   499-8501

The granddaddy of builders and developers in Hampton Roads, R.G. Moore has touched practically every new community built in this area for the past 40 years. His single-family homes stick to the traditional on the outside, but incorporate open, contemporary floor plans inside. There's no wall in his office wide enough to accommodate all the awards he's won from area building organizations, and there's no sign that his quest to be the biggest and best has any chance of slowing. He's a feisty kind of guy who wants things done the way he knows will give his buyers the most bang for their buck. If you're looking for real value, check out an R.G. Moore home in Willow Ridge at Redmill Farms East, Southern Woods and Water's Edge in Ocean Lakes in Virginia Beach and Winding Creek and Hidden Cove at Long Point in Portsmouth.

DONALD L. MOORE
4480 Holland Office Park   499-8501

While he shares an office with dad, R.G., Donald Moore is a card-carrying member of the new age of builder, creating intimate communities that each have a personality that physically and emotionally sets them apart from the norm. The first local developer to introduce the three-story townhome concept in his applauded Aeries By The Bay, he continues to introduce innovative interior space-planning features and unique exterior designs that wow from first sight. A young man with a golden touch, both for industry awards and customer satisfaction, you can find his exceptional single-family homes in The Crossings in Western Branch and condominium communities in the drop-dead gorgeous Royal Court Estate Condominium and Haygood Estate Condominium in Virginia Beach and The Garage Townes at Miar's Farm in Western Branch.

HEARNDON CONSTRUCTION CORP.
2010 Old Greenbrier Rd.   523-2569

Chesapeake is home turf for Hearndon Construction, who has taken Hampton Roads by storm in recent years with their superior single-family developments on some of their home city's prime real estate. Primarily known as developers, the organization was listed a few years back as one of the "Giant 400" builders in the nation in a list compiled by *Professional Builder Magazine*. To see their work, check out the Chesapeake communities of Wellington and Cedarwood.

CHESAPEAKE HOMES, INC.
717 Battlefield Blvd.   482-2233

When Chesapeake Homes just glances in the direction of a piece of property, you know you'll have a community of exceptionally affordable single-family homes on that site in a blink of an eye. Under the leadership of Bert Reavis, the communities that define the outskirts of Chesapeake are now home to hundred of young families who look to this exceptional building team for transitional styling, innovative technology and well-designed, well-priced homes. Check out their newest endeavors, Stonegate and Wellspring in Chesapeake and Seasons at Glenwood in Virginia Beach. They're sure to be sellouts.

Custom Builders

For one-on-one builders, Hampton Roads can boast some of the best custom crafters in the business. These guys — and, proudly, women too — take your ideas, a few bricks and Palladian windows and turn out one beautiful product on whatever home site you've been lucky enough to snap up. While space does not permit listing all the custom builders in our market, these few are the most well known by peers and clients, and each is a vital force in the Tidewater Builders Association, our most powerful trade organization dedicated to the highest standards of professionalism and craftsmanship in the building industry.

LARRY HILL,
L.R. HILL CUSTOM BUILDERS
481-6748

Two-time chairman for this area's ultimate home show, Homearama, Larry Hill does it all, from design to financing, using the best subs and materials around.

BOB JOHNSON,
RESIDENTIAL CONCEPTS LTD.
363-9050

A third-generation builder, Bob Johnson has a handle on wide-open spaces within a traditional exterior. He takes on only 25 to 30 super custom home projects a year, so reserve his time early.

CLIFF BERNARD,
BERNARD BUILDERS LTD.
547-9549

This man knows style and how to build it. And, along with wife, Carolyn, they make a fantastic dream team in the design and meticulous construction of every home they touch.

JOE ROBINSON,
JOE ROBINSON CUSTOM
CONSTRUCTION CO.
547-2772

For more than 20 years, Joe Robinson has won enough design and quality construction awards to fill every wall he's built. His kitchen designs are to die for.

STAN EURE,
STAN EURE CUSTOM BUILDER
424-3616

Here's a man who, along with wife and partner Jan, dares to take a risk in presenting the newest, most innovative products available in the home building industry. Their "Environmental House" entry in this area's recent Homearama met with rave reviews, combining transitional design with the highest technology in energy efficiency and recycling innovations.

The list of highly qualified and respected custom builders goes on and on. If you're tossing around the idea of a home built just-for-you, a call to the Tidewater Builders Association will give you the background info on your many qualified builder choices in our marketplace. Call them at 420-2434.

Hampton Roads Neighborhoods

Remember that territorial thing we mentioned in the introduction to this chapter? It would be total suicide to even attempt to pick and present the best places to live in Hampton Roads, given the diversity of lifestyle alternatives the region has to offer. All we can do is to give you a general lay-of-the-land, pointing out some of the most popular communities, new and established, and then you're on your own. The neighborhoods that we'll address specifically are those that have a distinctive flavor, either sophisticated urbanite or country chic, that sets them apart from the rest. Your final neighborhood decision will most probably be based on your family's requirements, like school systems, proximity to the workplace and budget. Let's take the Insiders' armchair tour from one end of the region to the other.

Norfolk

THE WEST SIDE
While it's no longer appropriate to call this the "Land of the Yuppies," deep down we know it's true. Running almost the full length of the city on the side where the sun sets, Norfolk's West Side is home to older, established neighborhoods with true old-fashioned neighbor-helping-neighbor spirit.

FREEMASON DISTRICT/ GHENT/GHENT SQUARE
This is where the "Downtowners" migrate and mingle. The Freemason district is as close to city living as you'll find in the area, what with cobblestone streets and the Hampton Roads version of row houses. New affluence meets old money in the condominiums enveloping the area, like Harborplace, the Tazewell complex, the Pier and Archer's Walk. There's not much turnover in this deep-rooted neighborhood, so you'll need a lot of luck to snag one of these properties.

Ghent and West Ghent are two other older, well-established neighborhoods, the former sprinkled liberally with spacious apartment buildings and rehabbed condominiums. West Ghent is where you'll find many of the grand old houses . . . three-story jobs that can accommodate young, professional families with kids and pets to spare.

For new construction with that old-timey feel, Ghent Square is the place, a planned urban development with a mix of traditionally styled townhomes and single-family residences. The 65-acre urban pocket features large expanses of brilliant green common areas, so while homes may be packed tight, the feeling of spaciousness pervades. It is definitely an address you'll be proud to claim.

LARCHMONT/EDGEWATER
Within walking distance to the ever-sprawling Old Dominion University, these two back-to-back neighborhoods are

Ghent, An Insiders' History

While there certainly is a lot that's new in Ghent, there's a whole lot more that's old. This popular community in Norfolk's west side can boast almost more historical roots than anyplace else in the territory.

Though there's heated debate as to where the name Ghent actually originated, most agree it was to commemorate the Treaty of Ghent that formally ended the War of 1812 when it was signed in Belgium. Version one traces the name to Jasper Morgan, a plantation owner that gave his home the name in 1821. Version two gives all the credit to Commodore Drummond, who carried a copy of the Treaty of Ghent on his ship to Norfolk and so named his plantation in 1830.

Whomever started it all, little did they know what was to follow. In 1890, the publication *Norfolk's Industrial Advantages* reported that Ghent property was sold at $1,400 an acre, and no homes could be built that cost less than $7,500 . . . a mega-home in that time. John Graham accepted the challenge and erected Ghent's first home at 502 Pembroke Avenue, and by 1892 was paying welcome calls to neighbors Horace Hardy (442 Mowbray Arch), Richard Tunstall (530 Pembroke), Fergus Reid (502 Pembroke) and William H. White (434 Pembroke Avenue).

The majority of the streets in Ghent were named in honor of principals in the Ghent-Norfolk Company, a subcorporation of three syndicates formed abroad after the Civil War to develop Virginia's rich resources. Today you can stroll down Bossevain Avenue (after a Dutch banker), Stockley Gardens (after the same Dutch banker's birthplace in Northampton County) and Olney Road (for Richard Olney, who later became secretary of state for President Cleveland).

In the heart of Ghent Square, sits the Terminal on the Square that houses the Fred Huette Foundation, a horticultural society. The charming building first knew life more than a century ago as the Norfolk-Portsmouth ferry terminal concession building. While the terminal building itself was torn down in 1964, the concession building was taken apart, piece by piece, each one carefully numbered and matched to a diagram. In 1974, the Housing Authority took all the pieces out of the warehouse and set upon solving the most difficult jigsaw puzzle ever created . . . somewhere along the line, somebody lost the carefully diagrammed plans for the building's reconstruction. But here it is today, restored to better than its former glory, and serving as a central landmark in this vibrant community.

Ghent also claims a few of our country's firsts in the wonderful world of food. Bosman & Lohman, liquidated in 1924, was the largest peanut company in the world in its earliest days and is credited with introducing commercially sold peanut butter to the United States. James G. Gill added a two-bag coffee roaster to his wholesale grocery store in 1902 and begat the Norfolk-based First Colony Coffee and Tea Company, and Abe Doumar is said to have invented the very first ice cream cone, introduced at the St. Louis Fair in 1904. Abe must have loved ice cream, because he created a machine to make the cones and kept it at Doumar's, the restaurant that bears his name, where it is still operational today.

where you'll find a congenial mix of professors, young business folk, students and, along the bordering Elizabeth and Lafayette rivers, corporate presidents. The older homes are shaded by huge, mature trees, and the quiet streets are usually packed with kids on in-line skates with mom and dad biking alongside. With homes priced from the mid $100s, it's a great place to relocate if you want to find yourself surrounded by friendly, well-educated residents who take pride in maintaining the integrity of one of Norfolk's most coveted neighborhoods.

LOCHAVEN/MEADOWBROOK/ NORTH SHORE POINT

We'll be moving on up when we tour through these premier neighborhoods, home to gracious Colonials, Georgians and Cape Cods, many of which hug the banks of the Elizabeth and Lafayette rivers.

Many of these superb residences are known by the families who built them, and you'll pay the average price of $250,000 to even consider these addresses. What you get in return, however, is an exceptionally stable neighborhood, with a large, manicured lot and, if you're lucky, a backyard with a river view.

TALBOT PARK/BELVEDERE

These neighborhoods have Granby Street as their dividing line, with the more moderately priced Belvedere on the east. More and more younger people are finding jewels in the rough in many of these older homes and choosing these neighborhoods over the Ghent sisters for convenience and value. Many of the Talbot Park residents claim the Elizabeth River as a neighbor; Belvedere's border ends on the ever-calm Lafayette River.

LAKEWOOD/LAFAYETTE SHORES

Across the river you can get a glimpse of the docks that belong to the residents of Lakewood, a relatively small pocket of lovely and oh-so-exclusive Colonial and Tudor homes set among quiet, heavily treed streets. Across Willow Wood Drive is a brand-new executive community of exceptional custom homes called Lafayette Shores. This gated 66-acre community boasts the last remaining waterfront home sites available in the city, and many corporate leaders have snapped up the offer and are now in the process of building their dream homes.

OCEAN VIEW

Until a few years ago, the only thing Ocean View could offer was the beauty of the Chesapeake Bay and rickety old beach cottages. Today, it's starting to be another story, as sparkling new condominium and single-family communities are taking advantage of the valuable, if previously neglected, real estate. Of particular note is Pinewell By The Bay, an emerging community of single-family homes that rests on the bayfront. While prices average in the $250s, you'll get a lot more home for the dollar than any you could find on the oceanfront in Virginia Beach. For a less expensive investment with a built-in marina, Bay Point offers townhomes and condominiums starting in the $60s. At the end of Pretty Lake Avenue, Bay Point takes advantage of its magnificent views of both the Chesapeake Bay and Little Creek Inlet.

Portsmouth

OLDE TOWNE

With the largest number of authentic homes dating from the Colonial period between Charleston, South Carolina, and Alexandria, Virginia, Olde Towne residents share the spirit of renovation along with a sense of history. While prices average in the low $200s, these homes are less expensive than their Norfolk counterparts, even though they are just a quick tunnel ride under the Elizabeth River apart. The 62-acre residential area supports its heritage with a passion, and a stroll down the clean, quiet rebricked streets illuminated by antique electrified gas lamps proves that no neighborhood can ever be too old to restore to its past glory.

STERLING POINT/GREEN ACRES

From the Elizabeth River, you can see the docks of the residents of Sterling Point, and the river's tributaries will take you to many Green Acres backyards. Both neighborhoods were developed in the 1950s and have that rancher-type feeling, but lots are large and well-treed and streets are remarkably litter-free. Green Acres borders on the Elizabeth Manor Country Club and hubs around Green Lake in its center. Homes here hover around the $150,000 mark, with waterfront prices at $300,000.

CHURCHLAND

Where Portsmouth's up-and-comers call home, Churchland is almost like a small city unto itself, served by a flotilla of shopping strips, groceries and movie theaters. One of its neighborhoods, River Shore, is a neat-as-a-pin brick rancher community, blessed with heavily wooded lots. If you can snag a waterfront property here, you'll have a breathtaking view all the way to Newport News.

Along Carney Creek, a small Western Branch of the Elizabeth River, is Hatton Point, with fairly new homes that each have their distinctive personality. While most of the interior homes are ranches, some of those that border the water are truly magnificent. Home resale prices in both neighborhoods begin around $100,000.

For luxury condominium living, Churchland has Cypress Cove that offers residents their own boat slip on the Elizabeth River and Carney Creek. Credited with being the first condominium development in Portsmouth, prices average $140,000.

Just past Churchland on your way north, you'll run into Western Branch, an old-line neighborhood that's currently enjoying a spurt of new life and new construction. Of note is The Crossings, a brand new community of single-family homes priced from the mid $100s. If you're looking for a new home in an old-fashioned neighborhood, this might just be your ticket to the mortgage company.

Chesapeake

Chesapeake has a split personality. One face is that of old-line, deeply entrenched Chesapeake natives like those of the Great Bridge and Deep Creek areas. Flip the coin and you'll see the youthful expression of newly developed neighborhoods like River Walk and Greenbrier. Together they make for a city bulging at the waist from too many good meals . . . of incoming industry, migrating families and the retailers who serve them.

Because homes in this awakening city are simply more affordable than their comparable counterparts in Virginia Beach, the call of the once-rural Chesapeake has reached deafening proportions, especially to builders who firmly believed that the outskirts of Virginia Beach was the true mecca. But, throw in an acclaimed golf course, oversized home sites and developers who know how to squeeze a great home out of a tiny dollar, and you've got one of the hottest real estate markets in the region.

GREENBRIER

Twenty years ago, a group of investors had the vision to turn what was once fertile farmland into one of the fastest-growing commercial and residential areas on the East Coast. Today, it's a community of 3,500 homes and growing, along with a championship golf course, gorgeous shopping mall, numerous spanking-new strip centers and hundreds of offices and industrial plants.

Just 15 minutes from Norfolk via the interstate, the Greenbrier corridor, especially along the golf course, offers single-family homes where young families can spread out and grow. One of the newest and last communities to be built here is Emerald Greens, with homes constructed by some of the area's premiere builders. While prices are somewhat hefty, plan on $250,000 average, what you'll move into is scads of square footage with a backyard view of a manicured fairway or green.

For more streamlined condominium living, sneak a peak at The Country Club Collection by The Franciscus Company. Realistically priced from the $90s, this is a trio of condo complexes bordering the golf course, one of which is certain to meet your living standards.

RIVER WALK

Another Chesapeake phenomenon, River Walk on the Elizabeth spans 300 acres between Great Bridge Boulevard and the Intracoastal Waterway. While it seems light years away, it's only 10 minutes from the business district in Downtown Norfolk. Here you'll find private enclaves of custom homes, like Mystic Isle, Quiet Cove, Laurel Haven and Watch Island. Those seeking a more streamlined way of life will delight at the varied condominium alternatives, from Inlet Quay to Beacon Point to Creek Side, all set in heavily wooded sites. Condos start at around $120,000 with remaining custom home sites from $40,000 before the house. You can stop at River Walk's Information Center to pick up some exquisite marketing propaganda and browse through their library of available home plans.

GREAT BRIDGE

The school system is superb, the people downright neighborly. This is Great Bridge, the granddaddy of Chesapeake neighborhoods. Sprinkled with solid ranchers and farmhouse Colonials,

On a monthly average, more than 12,000 homes are listed for sale in southside Hampton Roads by local Realtors, even more when you throw in those for sale by owner and new construction offered by area builders.

Insiders' Tips

the many individual neighborhoods that make up this corridor are blessed with large, heavily treed lots and super out-in-the-country smells. But, if you're thinking "rural," you're wrong. Here's where you'll find Chesapeake General Hospital, financial branches and food places of every description, and shopping strips galore. If you're thinking on settling in a neighborhood that has a handle on mixing the old with the newfangled, Great Bridge is the place.

"Out There"

Those of us who grew up in the big city still find it hard to believe that people would actually want to live "out there" in Chesapeake. But we're not who some very savvy builders and developers were targeting. Past Great Bridge, in one direction you'll drive into the new communities of Forest Lakes, Cheshire Forest and Cedarwood, all master-planned neighborhoods with varying levels of single-family custom homes. Do a U-turn and drive in another direction to Etheridge Manor and Dominion Boulevards and run into Country Mill, Mill Run and River Pines, all offering exceptional, if similar in architecture, single-family homes at remarkably low prices, from the low $100s. If you want to start off big while still preserving your pocketbook, here's where to look.

Virginia Beach

The Gold Coast

There's but so much Atlantic Ocean, and all of its beachfront that isn't reserved for hotels is owned by the tanned and hearty of Virginia Beach's Gold Coast, that diamond strip of golden real estate that stretches from streets numbered in the 40s north about 50 blocks to the turn

at the Chesapeake Bay. Mostly, we're talking wind-weathered cottages, but there are a few sparkling contemporaries strewn about, as well as a token mansion or two. Buying one of these beach-hugging beauties is almost out of the question, as turnover is almost nil, but if you're in a renting kind of mood, many go for reasonable tariffs during the winter season. At the other end of the oceanfront is Croatan, just south of Rudee Inlet, which has become more and more popular for year-round residents, many of whom have erected monolithic contemporaries to worship the sun. Trés expensive (got an extra mil?), but worth the drive through.

Bay Colony/Princess Anne Hills

There's one "I-could-live-there!" home after another in these premier neighborhoods that are just steps away from the Gold Coast. Many of these sprawling mini-estates border on Crystal Lake and Linkhorn Bay, and their price tags float upwards accordingly. Home to many upper middle-management and corporate executives, entry into the life of the Beach's rich and famousdom will set you back no less than $250,000 for a pleasant starter home, a hair's breath past $2 million if you're on a roll. This is a very active real estate market, however, with many old-timers fleeing to the carefree condominium lifestyle, so if this is the sort of lifestyle you crave (the garden club is a must, daahling), go for it.

The Great Neck Corridor

Just minutes from the ocean, close to business centers and boasting a strong school system, the Great Neck corridor lays sole claim to the most affluent per capita demographics in the city. While you can start in a condo you can move into for the $90s, count on higher end single-family homes to set you back up to a mil. Along Great Neck Road, you can turn into such coveted neighborhoods as Broad Bay Point Greens (that owns one of the best golf courses around) to Wolfsnare Plantation or Alanton, and loads of small pockets of affluence in between. Waterfront naturally commands the highest price tag, and many of the secluded mini-mansions have been built to take advantage of the inlets of Lynnhaven and Linkhorn Bays. For single families in this prestigious area, have at least $170,000 in your back pocket.

THE LITTLE NECK CORRIDOR

Let the chips keep falling. We're talking the highly desirable neighborhoods of Kings Grant, Middle Plantation and Little Neck Cove — all upper middle-class magnets for those who feel comfy in a sprawling home with lots of lawn and, perhaps, a waterfront vista of the Lynnhaven Bay or Western Branch of the Lynnhaven River. While many Realtors urge that this is an excellent opportunity to snap up a waterfront property, better have your financial ducks in a row for the $250,000 plus bucks these beauties will demand.

KEMPSVILLE

Now we're talking suburban spread. The first real Virginia Beach suburb, the Kempsville area keeps getting larger and more popular, what with neighborhood additions like Fairfield, Dunbarton and Indian Lakes, and with neighbor community Salem Woods a short hop down the road. A quick zip to the interstate, you're still a ways from the oceanfront, but you are in the belly of retail heaven with strip centers galore lined up with specialty stores to serve your every indulgence. All in all, the Kempsville area is a

solid market. Even Sweet Pea Whitaker, Mr. Boxing, owns a home in Bellamy Manor. To be a next door neighbor, $250,000 should do the KO.

THE PEMBROKE CORRIDOR

Leave it to Virginia Beach to toss the old with the new and come up with a dish that suits everyone's taste. For older, established and very desirable addresses, you can check out Thoroughgood, the Haygood area and Lake Smith. Whip down to mucho affordable Aragona Village and then swing the pendulum to the newest star in Virginia Beach's crown, Church Point. All you need to create a new neighborhood today is 260 acres of prime real estate, then invite the region's premiere builders and crayon out huge lots into pockets called The Mews ($200,00 and up), The Commons ($300,00 and up) and The Quays (up to $1 million). This really is one handsome private residential development, and worthy of a serious look by affluent buyers.

CHESAPEAKE BEACH

To the north of Church Point, and kissing the Chesapeake Bay, is the home to many beachcombers who prefer yards of sand, not grass. A weird architectural mix of high-tech condos, townhomes, old beach cottages and stark cedar contemporaries, both home styles and family backgrounds melt into one under the hot Hampton Roads sun. What residents share, regardless of their home's selling price ($75,000 to $200,00+), is their explicit love for the casual beach lifestyle. If you're a sand-in-your-shoes kind of person, this is one great place to hang your flag.

GREEN RUN/HOLLAND ROAD CORRIDOR

Green Run, the first PUD (Planned

Urban Development) in the area, has come by hard and tough times. Single-family homes, townhomes and condos share the cul-de-sacs and curved streets that were the master plan of GSH Real Estate's Oscar Ferebee in the 1960s. Today, new construction developments like Parkside Green, Woods of Piney Grove, Holland Pines, Princess Anne Crossings and Landstown Meadows call new homebuyers farther down Holland Road and entice them more by offering solidly built, value-priced homes starting in the high $90s. While this particular area may seem way off the track for many urbanites, the area creeps right up to the Virginia Beach City Municipal Complex and is just a stone's throw from the connecting interstate system.

CYPRESS POINT/GLENWOOD

The link that connects these neighborhoods is golf — beautifully manicured championship golf courses, all encroached by single-family homes and condos that beckon with their country-club, resort-feeling lifestyle. Both target families on the way up (and empty-nesters on the reverse downward spiral) and offer pockets of glamour to varying degrees. Many different builders have opted on prime home sites in these two popular neighborhoods, so plan on a full day to inspect the fully decorated model homes in each.

Inside
Retirement

The retirement market is a growing one for Norfolk, Virginia Beach and surrounding cities. Some older residents have lived most of their lives here. But many have returned in later years — lured by the Atlantic Ocean, Chesapeake Bay, moderate climate and reasonable taxes. Most older newcomers have relatives in the area or passed through here during their military careers and decided to make it home.

Living in the area are more than 84,000 people age 65 and older. Lifestyle options for them are varied — from totally independent living to gracious retirement communities and assisted living and nursing home care. There also are many services and activities geared toward keeping older residents active and independent.

SEVAMP Senior Services

If you're a newcomer who's over age 60, don't hesitate to learn about the Southeastern Virginia Areawide Model Program Inc., or SEVAMP Senior Services as it's commonly known. SEVAMP was incorporated in 1968 as a nonprofit organization. In 1972 it was one of 10 national programs for the aging selected for a federal grant. A year later SEVAMP became the region's Area Agency on Aging.

SEVAMP's goal is to help older residents live independently so they can be involved in the community and enjoy their lives. SEVAMP can issue a photo identification card that will get you discounts at numerous businesses. If you need transportation, SEVAMP vans can take you to doctor's appointments, geriatric day care and SEVAMP recreational

Photo: Virginia Division of Tourism

The sun and sea — an ageless prescription for good health.

programs. Rides must be arranged in advanced.

SEVAMP, a United Way agency, also operates several senior centers that provide hot lunches and all kinds of activities. It offers job counseling, training and placement for people over 55. Through its Retired Senior Volunteer Program, it matches residents with more than 225 nonprofit organizations needing help. SEVAMP has a licensed geriatric day-care center as well as health screening, legal services and home care services. For information call 461-9481.

Other Services

Senior centers can provide a vital outlet for older residents. One of the largest is the Norfolk Senior Center at 924 W. 21st Street, which is a SEVAMP affiliate. One of 11 senior centers in Norfolk, it opened 25 years ago in the Ghent area. The center has classes ranging from crafts to ballroom dancing. It brings in a variety of speakers, runs a gift and thrift store, and operates two adult day-care centers for those who cannot be home alone. A van takes center participants on shopping trips, to festivals and on other outings. The center also has a Senior Wellness Center that screens for medical problems. For information call 625-5857

Virginia Beach has five senior centers providing a variety of services and activities. Call 471-5884. It also has the M.E. Cox Center for Elder Day Care. Call 340-4388. Adult day care also is available from the Beth Sholom Home of Eastern Virginia, 420-2512.

Chesapeake has two senior centers. For information call 543-9211, Ext. 265. Suffolk has two senior centers. Call 925-6388.

Portsmouth provides three senior centers. The largest at 305 High Street is run by the city's Department of Parks and Recreation. The department sponsors a variety of senior activities, including Chesapeake Bay cruises, parties and day trips. To receive a quarterly schedule call the senior center at 398-3777.

One popular Norfolk program is The Ghent Venture, which has educational sessions for anyone age 50 and older. It started in 1982 and is sponsored by seven churches and one synagogue in the Ghent area of Norfolk. Sessions run for six weeks at First Presbyterian Church and regularly draw big crowds. Participants come between 10 AM to 2:30 PM on Thursdays to take a variety of free classes — from lap quilting and mah jongg to foreign languages and money management. The program includes interesting book reviews and lectures. A hot lunch is available or participants can brown bag it. To receive a course schedule call 640-8566.

Other option are the city-sponsored recreational courses (see the Schools section) as well as those offered by area colleges. State-supported institutions such as Old Dominion University, Norfolk State University and Tidewater Community College let state residents older than 60 take one course a semester for free. To do this you must have been a Virginia resident for at least a year and pay taxes in the state. You can sign up on the day the class starts and attend the session if it isn't full. For information contact the registrars' offices at the colleges.

Virginia Wesleyan College, ODU and Atlantic University are among the local participants in Elderhostel. This popular program lets people 60 and older attend colleges around the country for a week. They live on campus and enjoy classes that range from history to music appreciation. Prices are so reasonable that some people go Elderhostel-hopping for a few weeks and make that their vacation. For a catalog write Elderhostel at 7575 Federal Street, Boston, MA 02110 or call (617) 426-8056 or (617) 426-7788.

If you need legal assistance, one possibility is the Tidewater Legal Aid, which helps older low-income residents through its Senior Law Center. Call 627-3232.

Community Service

If you have a few hours to spare, many nonprofit groups will welcome you with open arms. You may find your niche counseling business owners through the Service Corps of Retired Executives (SCORE) by calling 441-3733. Or you might lean more toward volunteering in a hospital, kindergarten, museum or literacy program. The Retired Senior Volunteer Program keeps tabs on these opportunities. Call 393-9333 in Portsmouth, 539-6385 in Suffolk, 622-6666 in Norfolk, 436-8178 in Chesapeake and 473-5238 in Virginia Beach.

Other clearinghouses for volunteers include the Volunteer Connection of South Hampton Roads at 624-2400 and the volunteer program of the City of Norfolk at 441-2584. Feel free to directly contact any organization that interests you. Chances are good the staff can find a job to suit your time and talents.

Local chapters of the American Association of Retired Persons also keep up with volunteer possibilities as well as providing other services to anyone over age 50. There are chapters in Chesapeake, Norfolk, Portsmouth, Suffolk and Virginia Beach. To find out about local AARP chapters call 625-4577. For information on AARP's Senior Community Services Employment Program call 625-7001. This service helps find part-time jobs for people older than 55 who need additional income.

Wellness Programs

Some area hospitals have programs geared toward older adults. Chesapeake General Hospital has the Seniors Health Resource Center, which has fitness, recreational and educational programs. Call 482-6132. The Chesapeake hospital also has an Older Adult Mental Health Program that includes inpatient services. Call 482-6143.

DePaul Medical Center in Norfolk has the Gerontology Institute, which does assessments and peer counseling and has a resource center. DePaul's Classic Care Program offers health screenings, support groups and help in filing insurance claims for members over age 55. One popular program is Friday night dinner at the hospital. Meals cost $3, and there usually is a piano player or other entertainment. Call 889-5976.

In Portsmouth Maryview Medical Center has a Senior Advantage Program that includes wellness workshops, help with insurance claims and social events. Call 398-2273. Its affiliated Maryview Psychiatric Hospital has a Senior Day Program that provides activities and respite care for older adults. Call 398-2537.

Sentara Leigh Hospital operates the Sentara Select Plus program for the Sentara Health System hospitals in the region. The program includes free classes, health screenings, educational programs and social activities. Call (800) 736-8272.

The YMCA of South Hampton Roads sponsors an Active Older Adults Program that includes exercise classes, a walking group, monthly socials, lectures and trips. The program also provides volunteer opportunities. Call 622-9622.

If you're into fitness, check with area malls. Many have mall walking groups who meet regularly to stride through the climate-controlled environments. Some malls also sponsor occasional breakfasts and programs for their walkers.

Lifestyles — Housing Options

Housing options range from total independence to varying degrees of assistance. Buying a single-family home, a condominium or townhouse certainly is an option. Throughout the region you'll find a variety of prices and neighborhoods that ranges from historic to brand new. If you like a great view — and don't mind paying for the privilege — scout out some of the possibilities along the Chesapeake Bay, the Atlantic Ocean and the Elizabeth River.

Apartments are also worth considering. You'll find some that particularly appeal to older residents, including the Hague Towers and Pembroke Towers in Norfolk and many apartment buildings in the Wards Corner area of the city.

There also are numerous subsidized apartment that rent for reasonable fees. However, many of these require lengthy waits to get in and have strict guidelines on income levels. Among the apartments designed for people on limited incomes are John Knox Towers and Stonebridge Manor in Norfolk and Chesapeake Crossing in Chesapeake.

If you prefer a retirement community that lets you live independently but offers numerous amenities, right now there are two to choose from in South Hampton Roads. And, if you don't mind traveling a little farther, there are others in Williamsburg and Newport News. In a few years the Christian Broadcasting Network plans to build a luxury retirement community on its grounds in Virginia Beach.

Before settling on a retirement facility, take time to explore it and get to know residents and staff. Eat a meal or two to see if you like the food. Check out the recreational activities and learn what your options are should your health suddenly decline. If you are considering a continuing-care community that charges a large entrance fee, make sure you know what is covered and what percentage is refundable if you decide to leave.

WESTMINSTER-CANTERBURY IN VIRGINIA BEACH
3100 Shore Dr., Virginia Beach   496-1100

Westminster-Canterbury is the hands-down winner for the best location of any area retirement community. It is built right on a beach overlooking the Chesapeake Bay and has 16 acres of grounds. This 14-story complex features 335 apartments as well as a health care center. Westminster-Canterbury opened in 1981 as a joint venture of the Presbytery of Eastern Virginia and the Episcopal Diocese of Southern Virginia.

It is open to any person age 65 or older who can live independently. Apartments range in size from studios to two-bedroom units. Most have full-sized kitchens. The smallest studio apartments sometimes are available immediately. Expect to wait from one to five years for larger apartments — the bigger the apartment the longer the wait.

Amenities include one prepaid meal a day, weekly maid service, bed and bath linens, 24-hour security, indoor swimming pool, whirlpool, steam room, gardening areas and a full roster of activities. As residents need more help, they can move to assisted living and a nursing home that are part of the facility.

Admission to Westminster-Canterbury requires paying a sizable entrance fee that guarantees lifetime occupancy in an apartment, the Assisted Living Center or Health Care Center. In addition, residents pay monthly fees. The amount of both the entrance fee and monthly fees depends on the size of the apartment. There is a limited amount of financial assistance available.

FIRST COLONIAL INN
845 First Colonial Rd.
Virginia Beach   428-2884

If you're interested in an independent retirement community but don't want to pay an up-front fee, First Colonial Inn is a definite option. It is strictly a rental community for retired people. The 185 apartments in this three-story building in the Hilltop area range in size from studios to two-bedroom models. There sometimes is a short wait to move in, especially if you want a larger unit.

Besides independent living, First Colonial Inn also has 21 personal care apartments that provide assistance with bathing, dressing and medications.

First Colonial Inn opened in 1985 and is managed by Excel Retirement Communities of Fort Worth, Texas. Amenities include three meals a day in the dining room, twice-monthly maid service and laundering of linens and towels, as well as transportation to nearby shopping centers, banks and doctor's offices. Most apartments include full-sized kitchens. There are many recreational activities from which to choose.

Residents pay only a monthly rental that includes some meals. Apartments also come with kitchens. Some units are available immediately, others sometimes require a wait of a few months.

ATLANTIC SHORES
RETIREMENT COMMUNITY
1398 Gibraltar Ct.   426-0000
Virginia Beach   800-2774

This retirement community is so new, it's not even open. Construction started in late 1994, and model units are already available for inspection. Even though the first occupants won't arrive until 1996, some have already paid 10 percent of their entrance fee to guarantee them room at Atlantic Shores.

Atlantic Shores is being developed by Rauch & Co. of Chicago and Lifecare Services Corp. of Des Moines. The community is on 200 acres near the Dam Neck Navy base. It is adjacent to Red Wing Lake Municipal Golf Course and is a mile from the Atlantic Ocean and its beaches.

Plans call for both multiunit buildings and detached villas with garages. The first phase will have about 340 units, many of them villas. For residents who later need more care, Atlantic Shores plans to offer assisted living and intermediate and skilled nursing services. Amenities will include a fitness center, indoor swimming pool and tennis courts.

There are sizable enrollment fees. Since the project is a cooperative, buyers will have equity in their unit. They also will pay monthly service fees.

Continuing Care

There are more than 60 nursing homes in the area — far too many to discuss here. In the past couple of years there has been a boom in assisted living facilities. These can bridge the gap between independent living and nursing home care by providing gracious surroundings and supplemental help for older residents.

The staff of assisted living facilities typically help with bathing and dressing, transportation to doctor's offices, dispensing medicine and recreation. All meals are served in the dining room, and residents are expected to dress in street clothes. Elegant common areas are brightened by chintz curtains and potted plants, while residents' rooms are personalized with furniture from home.

After spending months exploring this assisted living option for an ailing parent, we can forewarn you that you will be confused. Licensing varies from facility to facility, and you must be careful you're not comparing apples and oranges. It's crucial you know how ambulatory the resident must be. Some centers are licensed only for residents who walk independently or with a walker. Others will allow residents to be in wheelchairs. However, at some centers residents must get into wheelchairs by themselves. At other centers employees can assist them into wheelchairs.

Among the possibilities to consider are Brighton Gardens and Marian Manor Retirement Community in Virginia Beach, and Ghent Arms and Leigh Hall in Norfolk. All are privately owned except Marian Manor, which is affiliated with a Catholic church. Sentara Health System has Sentara Villages in Norfolk, Virginia Beach and Chesapeake as well as several nursing homes. Sentara provides a Senior Assessment Center to help determine what type assistance — from meal delivery to nursing home care — older residents need. It has an Alzheimer's unit in one of its nursing homes. Call 463-0100.

Another helpful option is the Hillhaven Rehabilitation and Convalescent Center, located at 100 Hampton Boulevard in Norfolk. It has short-term care with intensive physical and occupational therapy, as well as long-term nursing care. Call 623-5602. There also are affiliated centers in Virginia Beach and Suffolk.

Inside
Child Care

If you're from out of state, you may be surprised to see how loosely some day-care providers are regulated in Virginia. The commonwealth is one of only three states that completely exempts a care-giver from regulation if she (or he) keeps no more than five unrelated children in the home. In addition, she can also tend to her own children and any number of others who come only before and after school. Virginia also is one of only 10 states that does not regulate church-sponsored day-care centers.

That's not to say you won't find some excellent family day-care homes or church centers. It just means parents must do their homework, ask a million questions and trust their instincts when checking out potential providers. Once you select a care-giver, be constantly on the lookout for potential problems. From experience, we know child care can work smoothly one day and fall apart the next. Try to keep an option in the back of your mind, and be ready to move quickly if your instincts say you need to make a switch.

When it comes to child care, your best sources of information are other parents. Hunt them down and ask for suggestions on who to call. Be sure to jot down the names of any providers they recommend avoiding.

There are numerous licensed child-care centers in the area that meet state standards on staffing, curriculum, safety and nutrition. To find out about them contact the Virginia Social Services De-partment. Its Eastern Regional Office is in Virginia Beach; call 473-2100.

Another good resource is the Child Care Resource and Referral Center of The Planning Council. This Norfolk-based nonprofit organization has its own Child Care Assurance Program (CCAP) that involves on-site inspections of family day-care homes. For a nominal fee, parents can receive a listing of CCAP- and state-approved providers. Before paying the fee, check to see if your employer has arranged with the center to provide information to workers for free. Call 627-3993.

In the region, about 70 day-care centers and 400 home providers belong to Places and Programs for Children (formerly the Tidewater Child Care Association). This nonprofit group was formed in 1974 to upgrade child care. The local association offers ongoing training to child-care providers. It also conducts inspections to make sure homes and centers meet standards for health, safety and nutrition. Call 397-2981.

Fewer than 10 area child-care centers and preschools are certified by the National Association for the Education of Young Children. The association has standards that are stricter than the state's. For a listing of area members call (800) 424-2460.

Another resource is the Better Business Bureau of Greater Hampton Roads, which publishes an advisory publication on child-care services. The free publication defines various types of child-care options and gives tips on picking a provider. It also includes information on more than 50 child-care centers that responded to a questionnaire. For a copy send a large self-addressed, envelope with two stamps on it to the BBB at 3608 Tidewater Drive, Norfolk 23509.

Military families can help solve their child-care dilemmas by calling the Navy Family Service Center. The center can steer you toward child-care centers affiliated with area bases. You also can find out about military-approved providers who can accept only military or Department of Defense dependents. Call 444-4359.

Some parents have had luck locating good child care through the classified section of *The Virginian-Pilot/Ledger-Star*. So many family day-care providers advertise here that there is a separate Babysitting/Child Care section in the classifieds (category 5085).

For suggestions on child-care centers pick up a copy of *Tidewater Parent*, a monthly tabloid newspaper. This free, locally produced newspaper is loaded with ads from care givers. And, it frequently runs helpful articles on child care. You can usually grab a copy at grocery stores, child-care centers, consignment stores and just about anywhere else parents gather. For more information call 426-2595.

Parents whose children have developmental disabilities may want to contact the Child Development Resources. The nonprofit organization is headquartered near Williamsburg but serves children and their families throughout the region. Call 565-0303.

Extended Care

For before- and after-school care, try the YMCA of South Hampton Roads. It offers on-site service in many public el-

ementary schools and some middle schools. Besides supervised recreation, children get snacks and homework assistance while their parents receive peace of mind. Fees average about $40 a week. The YMCA also has a well-respected summer camp program for school-age children that suits many working parents' schedules. It starts right at the end of school and offers 11 weeks of swimming, crafts and other activities. Call 547-YMCA in Chesapeake, 622-YMCA in Norfolk, 398-9348 in Portsmouth, 934-YMCA in Suffolk, and 456-YMCA in Virginia Beach.

In Norfolk the YWCA of South Hampton Roads provides extended care from September through May in several schools. Fees are based on income. Call 625-4248.

You'll also find before- and after-school care at many private schools (see the Schools chapter). Some private schools also have fun summer programs that make life easier for parents whose work continues year round. Cape Henry Collegiate School, Norfolk Academy and Norfolk Collegiate School are among those with elaborate summer offerings.

One of the most popular summer programs is the Zoo Camp run by the Virginia Zoo in Norfolk for elementary students. There are six one-week sessions. Younger students stay a half-day while those in fifth and sixth grade can participate in full-day programs. Campers explore such topics as rain forests, insects and animal care. Call 624-9937.

Students age 8 through 16 can focus on marine life during one-week camps sponsored by the Virginia Marine Science Museum in Virginia Beach. For information call 437-4949. Old Dominion University also offers sea camps for students ages 5 through 16. Demand has picked up in recent years for these camps that feature frequent field trips to collect marine organisms. For information call 683-4285. For many local children, the highlight of the summer is attending sailing camp at ODU, whose sailing team is frequently top rated in the country. For information call 683-3372.

There are three terrific choices for the artistically inclined. Virginia Beach Center for the Arts runs one-week camps that last either a half-day or a full day. Most classes are for ages 6 to 12 but there usually is one session for preschoolers. Typical courses range from photography to painting and cartooning. Call 425-0000. The d'Art Center in Norfolk also runs art camps for children aged 6 through 10. During one-week sessions students focus on specific activities such as painting or working with clay. Call 625-4211. The Chrysler Museum sponsors half-day sessions two days a week for elementary students that blend museum tours with hands-on creativity. Call 622-1211, extension 268.

Another possibility for summer camp is the Jewish Community Center in Norfolk whose Shalom Children's Center runs two four-week camps for ages 2 through 13. Older children can choose from drama and sports camps while younger ones explore activities ranging from art to swimming. Call 489-1371.

To help explore all the summer options, the *Tidewater Parent* publication sponsors a free summer camp trade show each February. For details call 426-2595.

Preschools

As far as preschools go, there are many excellent ones. Again, your best bet in finding the one that is right for you is to talk to other parents. Look around your neighborhood — or the area near your office — to see what schools are nearby.

Many preschools are in churches. Others operate independently. Numerous private schools for older children also have a preschool program (again, check the Schools chapter).

Although some preschools stick to the traditional half-day program, many are melting under pressure from two-career parents. You'll find a number of schools that have started extended-day programs. Some also have summer fun days or camps that go beyond the September to May school year.

Even at preschools with half-day programs, working parents may be able to find another parent to keep their child after hours. There are care givers whose main business is caring for children after preschool ends at noon. Ask the schools for recommendations and try to hook up with other parents for carpooling.

Once you've come up with a list of preschool possibilities, call for brochures and tuition schedules. Then take your time visiting the schools and getting to know the teachers and directors. You may want to go without children at first so you can concentrate on asking key questions. Once you narrow your list down, take your child and spend some time soaking up the surroundings. If you're like us, you and your child may go to the same schools two or three times before making a final decision.

For some of the most popular preschools, the wait to get in can be long. So start your search as early as you can — at least a year ahead of time is not unreasonable. Be aware that some locals register their children at birth for a couple of the most prestigious preschools. Of course, there are plenty of newcomers who've lucked into a slot when a family suddenly moved from the area. So don't give up hope.

Hint: Among the preschools with the longest waiting lists are the Child Study Center run by Old Dominion University in Norfolk, 683-4117, the Stratford Preschool in Virginia Beach, 460-0659, and the First Presbyterian Church Preschool in Norfolk, 625-0667.

Nannies

Finding in-home child care is a definite option. If you place a classified ad in the Help Wanted section of *The Virginian-Pilot/Ledger-Star*, you'd better have a telephone answering machine. The one time we tried it, the calls easily topped 100, and only a few of those sounded like anyone you'd want to hire.

Although there are parents who've found excellent care-givers through the classifieds, many prefer to use a service to do the screening. There are several that are active in the area.

We've had good personal experience with AuPairCare. It is headquartered in San Francisco and provides European nannies ages 18 to 25. The au pairs, both young women *and* men, work an average of 45 hours a week, live with families as family members, and can stay in this country 13 months. Since AuPairCare is the largest au pair provider in the area, it has several local counselors to work with families and au pairs. The weekly cost averages $180 for any number of children. Call 482-0231 or 1-800-4AUPAIR.

If you prefer a United States citizen for a nanny, one source of help is All-American Nanny Ltd., 422-9600. This Virginia Beach-based company primarily draws nannies from the Midwest and places them along the East Coast. Rates range from $150 to $400 weekly depending on the number of children and amount of housework required. Another local nanny option is the Nannies & More Agency, 366-9441, which connects parents with au pairs, live-in nannies and those who come just during the day.

Babysitting

If you're new to the neighborhood, right now is the time to start cultivating that teenager or college student down the street. There seems to be a dearth of people in that age group, and finding reliable babysitters can be a ruthless business. In fact, don't be shocked in that friendly neighbor who welcomed you with brownies refuses to reveal the name of her sitter.

We've had great success hiring workers at our child-care center for occasional babysitting. But since we once called a dozen teens before snaring a sitter for a fairly impromptu Saturday night outing, we try to keep a long list of good prospects. Soon, you too may be asking any responsible teen or college student whether he or she babysits. The going rate is about $3 an hour.

One resource is Old Dominion University's excellent Child Study Center. If you mail a written notice of what type help you're looking for (regular, occasional, weekend), it will be posted on a bulletin board in the center. Be sure to specify where you live. Send information to Child Study Center, ODU, Norfolk 23519-0136. You also can tack notices in Webb Center, ODU's student center, as well as at other local colleges. Tidewater Community College in Virginia Beach also has a Child Development Lab.

Since 1949, Baby Sitters of Tidewater Inc. has rescued countless newcomers from babysitting dilemmas. Many of them now rely on the service for all their babysitting needs. The business has passed from its founder, Emma Johnson, to her daughter-in-law, Clarice Johnson.

This is a word-of-mouth service that hires mainly retired teachers and nurses as well as grandmothers. You can hire a sitter for a day, evening, weekend or while you go on vacation.

For one or two children, Baby Sitters of Tidewater charges $4.25 an hour with a required minimum of four hours. There also is a $4 transportation fee if you live within 30 miles of the sitter. It costs $5 an hour for three to five children in the same family and slightly more for children from two families or groups of kids. Although there are about 75 sitters on call, try to book your sitter several days in advance. Call 489-1622 during the day.

Many churches, especially those with preschools, have mother's morning-out programs. This is usually a drop-in service for toddlers and lasts only a couple of hours one or two mornings a week. It can be a great sanity saver for stay-at-home moms and provide valuable interaction for children.

For sick children, Sentara Home Care Services will send a nursing assistant to tend to your children at home as long as their fevers are under 101 degrees. This is a definite option for working parents facing a lengthy siege of the chicken pox. Children should be registered in advance of illness. Fees are about $7 an hour between 7 AM and 3 PM on weekdays and slightly more at other times. Call 461-564

If you're visiting the area and need a break from refereeing sibling squabbles, your hotel may be able to supply a sitter. It is likely, however, that you will be referred to P-Nut Butter N Jelly Inc., a child-care service geared toward vacationers. It is run by licensed Virginia Beach child-care operator Kathy Beck and services about 100 area hotels. All its 80-plus sitters have gone through state background checks and had at least three references checked. Plan on at least a three-hour notice to hire a sitter — more during peak holidays or if big conventions are booked. The cost is $10 an hour. Call 491-7688.

*T*he best in education is yours to discover at Cape Henry Collegiate School. Founded in 1924 and educating 3 year olds through twelfth graders, Cape Henry is a national Blue Ribbon School (1993) and was voted the Best Private School at the Beach (1994, 1995). Focusing on the Academic, Affective, Artistic and Athletic growth of every student, Cape Henry produces well-rounded and independent thinkers. Call to get acquainted.

 Cape Henry Collegiate School
1320 Mill Dam Road • Virginia Beach • 481-2446

Inside
Schools

Whether you are searching for a kindergarten or a high school for your children, Hampton Roads has an abundance of choices. Each of the five cities in this area has its own public school system. In addition, there are numerous private and parochial schools. Many of them also offer preschool and extended care programs.

Public Schools

All public schools in the region are governed by school boards appointed by city councils. There is a movement in Virginia toward voter-elected school boards, and a few area cities have had their first elections.

In Virginia all 8th graders must pass the Virginia Literacy Passport Test, which is first administered in 6th grade. The test focuses on reading, writing and math basics. Students who fail the test receive special instruction. However, if they don't pass all three parts of the test by the 8th grade they cannot be promoted. Special education students are exempt from the test.

To enroll a student in a school district for the first time, you will need the child's Social Security number, a certified birth certificate, a completed physical examination form, an immunization record and a report card from the child's last school, if the child has attended one.

Kindergarten students must be 5 years old by September 30 to enroll. However, several districts let parents enroll students whose birthdays fall within a month or two after that cutoff. The exact date varies with the district. Kindergarten is not mandatory in Virginia, although we're hard-pressed to think of any parents who don't send their children to kindergarten. However, the state legislature is considering changing the law to require kindergarten attendance.

Public schools throughout the region tend to draw students from nearby neighborhoods. Bus service is provided for students living too far to walk to school.

All public schools offer a wide range of academics, sports and extracurricular activities. Programs are provided for gifted and talented students and those with special educational needs. In the region, there are strong links with the business and military communities. Some organizations adopt entire schools and channel a lot of energy into improving them. Others occasionally provide lecturers and tutors.

The school districts receive federal money to help educationally disadvantaged students. Head Start programs also are available. For information on them call 623-6974.

Virginia Beach Public Schools

Virginia Beach has the largest public school district in the region and the second-largest in Virginia. It has more than 75,000 students and nearly 5,000 teachers. The school district has a dropout rate of about 4 percent.

The school district operates 10 high schools, 14 middle schools, 52 elementary schools and six specialized centers. Since the city's population boom in the mid- to late-1980s, the school district has worked to alleviate overcrowding by building new schools throughout the city.

Kindergarten in Virginia Beach operates in two shifts. Students are assigned to either morning or afternoon sessions. Students in 1st grade and beyond attend school all day.

For students with special needs, the school district offers several programs. Gifted 1st graders can participate in school-based programs that challenge them. Those in grades 2 through 6 can attend the Old Donation Center for the Gifted and Talented one day a week. The center also has additional programs for those in grades 4 through 6 with talent in visual arts and dance.

Students needing additional help are assisted by reading resource teachers and other remedial instruction. Some schools offer special instruction for students who speak English as a second language.

The Virginia Beach district recently converted all its junior highs to middle schools for 6th, 7th and 8th graders. A variety of programs is offered for gifted and special education students.

Virginia Beach's high schools offer both regular and advanced studies. Those in advanced studies take high-level classes in math, science and language. They also are required to complete more courses to graduate. Advanced placement classes are offered in art, biology, calculus, chemistry, computer science, English, foreign languages, physics and United States history. High schools offer instruction in French, German, Latin, Russian and Spanish.

Alternative schools include the Career Development Center, which offers a core curriculum and vocational courses, and the Vocational-Technical Educational Center, which teaches numerous trades and job-training courses.

Adults 17 and older can attend evening classes at the Open Campus High School to earn their high school diploma or GED certificate. They also can study at the Adult Learning Center, which has some basic courses as well as more recreational ones.

VIRGINIA BEACH NUMBERS TO NOTE:

Superintendent's Office	427-4373
Office of Pupil Services	427-4791
Gifted/Talented Center	473-5043
Adult Learning Center	473-5091
Career Development	473-5058
Vo-Tech Ed. Center	427-5300
Open Campus:	
High School	473-5200
Recreational Classes	473-5091

Norfolk Public Schools

With more than 36,000 students, Norfolk has the second-largest school district in the region. There are five high schools, eight middle schools and 36 elementary schools. The district has 2,500 teachers and a dropout rate of 6 percent.

The Norfolk school district offers a number of special programs. More than 6,000 students participate in gifted courses. For students in kindergarten through the 5th grade, there is the Field Lighthouse Program. One day a week gifted students travel to Stuart Gifted School for specialized studies. The center is also where foreign-speaking children spend part of the day learning English.

Gifted 6th graders can challenge their creativity once a week with an in-school program designed for them. Students in grades 7 through 12 can take gifted alternative classes in math, science, social studies, communication skills and foreign language. Students eager for more learning can stay late or come on Saturday for the Arts & Sciences Gifted Extended Day Program. The curriculum includes Russian language, problem solving and architecture/engineering. Students whose interests lean towards high technology can get practical training at the NORSTAR Student Research Institute, which conducts space shuttle experiments and robotics projects. Those learning toward health careers can participate in the Magnet High School for the Sciences and Health Professions through Eastern Virginia Medical School.

Many programs are designed for special education students. The district runs St. Mary's Infant Home for severely disabled children and toddlers. The school district has a program for disabled preschoolers. Students kindergarten age and older are mainstreamed, if possible, with the help of resource rooms.

The Willard Model Elementary School is the school district's only model school. Since 1985 Willard has been a laboratory school designed to prepare students for the 21st century. It uses a lot of computers and a flexible staff to introduce innovative educational programs. Computers are now infiltrating all other schools in the district.

There are several specialized centers run by the school district. The Coronado School is for pregnant students. The Norfolk Technical Vocational Center helps students prepare for careers. The Madison Career Center also provides vocational training as well as adult basic education.

In Norfolk, adult education courses, which run the gamut from quilting to computers, are administered by the city's parks and recreation department. The reasonably priced classes are scheduled year round at the city's recreation centers and are some of the better bargains in town.

NORFOLK NUMBERS TO NOTE:

Superintendent's Office	*441-2107*
Adult/Vocational Ed.	*441-2957*
Gifted Programs	*441-2638*
Special Ed. Services	*441-2491*
Recreational Classes	*441-2149*

Chesapeake Public Schools

The Chesapeake Public School District gained acclaim in 1990 when it put a warranty on all its graduates. The gimmick guarantees that any employer can "return" a Chesapeake graduate to the school district if he or she fails to have mastery of basic skills. So far no one has taken the school district up on its offer to reeducate any deficient graduate.

The Chesapeake School District is the fastest growing in the state. It operates five high schools, seven middle schools and 26 elementary schools. It has more than 34,000 students and nearly 2,000 teachers. Its dropout rate is 3 percent.

Gifted and talented programs are available for those in grades kindergarten through 12. Younger students have in-school programs, while 5th and 6th graders go once a week to the Laboratory School for the Academically Gifted. There they do problem solving and learn more about math, science and computers. Middle school students can participate in gifted programs in most subject areas, while senior high students have advanced placement and honors courses.

Special education students attend their assigned schools. Those who can be mainstreamed are included in regular classes. Resource rooms and teaching assistance are available along with some self-contained classes. The Preschool Education Center is designed to help disabled children ages 2 to 5.

Among the school district's special centers are the Adult Education Center, which offers preparation for the GED as well as career-oriented classes for working adults; the Chesapeake Center for Science and Technology, which offers vocational courses training in such fields as engine repair and nursing; and the Alternative School for students whose discipline problems prevent them from attending their assigned high schools.

CHESAPEAKE NUMBERS TO NOTE:

Superintendent's Office	547-4114
Gifted Programs	494-7640
Vocational Ed. Programs	547-6013
Adult Education Program	548-6001
Special Ed. Programs	547-1321
Recreational Classes	547-6411

Portsmouth Public Schools

There are nearly 18,000 students attending Portsmouth Public Schools. The district has four high schools, four middle schools and 16 elementary schools. The school district has 1,148 teachers and a dropout rate of 5 percent.

Gifted and talented programs run from kindergarten through grade 12. Through the Spectrum Program for the Gifted and Talented, students can participate in a variety of programs. Recently the district started a Potential National Merit Scholars program for high-achieving 5th graders who are offered supplementary Saturday and evening sessions. The program will take the students through graduation and each year bring in a new group.

Kindergarten through 2nd grade students are offered the Explorer program that supplements everyday studies. Twice a month gifted and talented instructors also come to the schools for special programs. Grades 3 through 5 have the Search program, which takes students to one of the district's five gifted and talented labs for a full day of studies once a week. The Discover program takes middle school students to a weekly lab and supplements their program with workshops and seminars. High school students have both honors and advanced placement labs and can participate in a special program in conjunction with the College of William & Mary in Williamsburg.

The school district offers a variety of special education programs. Some are based in regular classrooms; others involve resource rooms or special education centers. Preschools and early elementary students can get special help at the DAC Center for Learning.

Among the school district's special centers are the Emily Spong Center, an alternative school for elementary students with discipline problems, and New Directions, a similar school for secondary students. The S.H. Clarke Vocational Training Center offers hands-on training in practical trades while the Adult Learning Center offers adults the chance to earn their GED or take computer classes or other helpful courses.

PORTSMOUTH NUMBERS TO NOTE:

Superintendent's Office	393-8742
Adult Ed. Program	393-8822
Special Ed. Program	393-8658
Vocational Ed. Program	393-8869
Gifted Programs	393-8483
Recreational Classes	393-8481

Suffolk Public Schools

To keep pace with growth in Suffolk, the school district opened two new high schools in 1990 and did a massive renovation of its older schools. In the transition, three of the city's old high schools became its middle schools. Its three former middle schools became new elementary schools, giving the city a total of 10 primary schools. The school district has more than 9,400 students, 625 teachers and a dropout rate of nearly 6 percent.

About 10 percent of the student body is involved in gifted programs while another 9.5 percent participates in special education services. Gifted and talented programs start in kindergarten. Through the Student Trial Enrichment Program (STEP) students in kindergarten through 3rd grade meet once or twice a week for special creative thinking programs in their schools.

Gifted students in grades 4 through 8 can attend the QUEST Center at John F. Kennedy Middle School once a week. Topics of study include space exploration, Japan and foreign languages. These students also can take special art and music classes designed for gifted students. In high school teachers offer gifted students special units designed for them. Students also can take advanced placement and honors courses. They can earn college credits at Paul D. Camp Community College by taking such advanced courses as calculus and western civilization.

The school district has programs for disabled students ranging in age from 2 to 21. Offerings include the Parent Resource Center, which trains parents and educators to work with the disabled. There is a preschool program for handicapped children. Elementary and upper level programs for more severely disabled and special education students are consolidated at several schools. As many students as possible are mainstreamed.

The school district operates the P.D. Pruden Vo-Tech Center, which trains high school students during the day for careers in 16 areas, such as cosmetology, horticulture and data processing. The Pruden Center is a joint project of the Suffolk School District and neighboring Isle of Wight County School District. At the same facility the two districts also operate the Center for Lifelong Learning. Evening programs let adults earn their GED and learn skills such as welding or word processing. They also can take fun courses on decorating cakes and troubleshooting their VCR. The school district also cosponsors a school for practical nurses at Obici Memorial Hospital.

With the help of a grant from the Planters Peanuts plant in Suffolk, the school district operates The Planters Reach-A-Parent Center. This resource center has materials and workshops that help parents improve their children's skills. It is open afternoons in Booker T. Washington Elementary School.

SUFFOLK NUMBERS TO NOTE:

Superintendent's Office	925-5000
Special Ed. Programs	925-5579
Planters Reach-A-Parent Center	925-5727
Pruden Vocational-Technical Center	925-5590
Recreational Classes	925-6328

Magnet Schools

There is only one regional magnet school in south Hampton Roads — the Norfolk-based Governor's School for the Arts, 451-4711. The school provides intense training in dance, music, theater, visual arts or other performing arts for nearly 300 public school students. The program is sponsored by the Virginia Department of Education and public schools in Chesapeake, Norfolk, Portsmouth, Suffolk, Virginia Beach and nearby Franklin, Isle of Wight County and Southampton County.

The school, which started in 1987, is one of five regional magnet schools in the state and the only one focused on the arts. Graduates have gone on to such prestigious schools at Yale, Princeton and Juilliard.

Magnet school students take academic courses at their home high schools in the mornings. They then hop on buses and congregate in Norfolk for afternoon arts studies. Dancers, artists, singers, musicians and actors meet at various locations such as Old Dominion University and Norfolk State University. In 1992 the school raised funds to renovate a downtown building as the home of its theater department. Plans call for consolidating more of the Magnet School in the building as funds become available.

Norfolk Public School students can participate in the Magnet High School for the Sciences and Health Professions. It was founded in 1986 and sends 80 Norfolk high school students to study five days a week at Eastern Virginia Medical School.

Suffolk participates in the Tidewater Governor's School for Science and Technology. The school, which started in 1993, is a three-week summer program for students in Suffolk and Isle of Wight and Southampton counties.

Private Schools

Stroll through some of the region's nicest neighborhoods on an early fall morning and you may wonder why clusters of students are gathered on different corners. Chances are they are waiting for buses headed for their various schools.

Gathered in one block may be the public school students. A few streets away you may see the group waiting for buses from Norfolk Academy or Norfolk Christian School. Rounding the corner may be the parent driving the car pool for a private elementary school with no bus system.

In these neighborhoods the mix of public and private school students is pretty even. And there's not a lot of rivalry between the students. In the afternoon you're likely to see a cross-section of the older children playing street hockey. Younger ones may gather for a game of soccer in someone's yard as their parents wind down by chatting with neighbors.

If you're interested in private or parochial schools there are more than 50 to choose from. Some are only for primary school students; others can take children from preschool through graduation. You'll find both religious and secular schools. Among the secular schools are some with private owners and others run by independent boards. There are schools with dozens of organized sports and extracurricular activities and others with just a few offerings.

Despite these differences all schools pride themselves on their small class size and emphasis on excellence. Upper level schools all tend to have college-preparatory curriculums. Tracking down the right school for your child can be a time-consuming but rewarding process. The ideal is to start your search a year ahead of time, but when that's not possible you can jump start the process with a lot of legwork.

Your best resources are other parents who have been down the same road and settled on schools for their children. Grill as many of them as you can for their insight. Then call the schools and ask for information packets. After perusing them spend time in the schools talking to administrators, teachers and students. Be aware that admission policies vary greatly. Some schools have open admissions but others are very selective, and there may be competition for a limited number of slots.

Be sure to check into accreditation since it varies widely. Some schools have no accreditation. Others are accredited by the selective Virginia Council for Private Education and the Virginia Association of Independent Schools. Schools with these designations are also recognized by the state Board of Education. Other schools are accredited by the Association of Christian Schools International, the Southern Association of Colleges and Schools, the Virginia Catholic Educational Association and the American Montessori Society.

To get you started, we have included a sampling of private schools that is by no means all-inclusive. Since tuition varies widely depending on grade level, call schools for specific information. Remember that transportation, before-school care and other special services cost extra. And, most schools charge an enrollment fee. When comparing schools, be sure you know exactly what the tuition covers. To avoid throwing your budget out of whack, find out if there are any mandatory funds or fees.

Some schools offer tuition discounts for families enrolling more than one student or for military families. A few have some aid available for financially strapped families.

Among the area private schools are:

ATLANTIC SHORES CHRISTIAN SCHOOLS

1861 Kempsville Rd.
Virginia Beach   479-1125
1219 N. Centerville Tnpk.
Chesapeake   479-9598

This Christ-centered school was organized in 1985 and has a preschool through high school program that includes a college-preparatory curriculum along with training in music and sports. There are two campuses — one in the Kempsville area for elementary student and an 18-acre complex a mile away for secondary students. Enrollment in the preschool and elementary program is 315. There are 170 secondary students. Besides Virginia Beach, students come from Chesapeake, Portsmouth, Suffolk and nearby parts of North Carolina. Extended care is available for grades K-6, and there are both half-day and full-day kindergartens.

BAYLAKE PINES PRIVATE SCHOOL

2204 Treasure Island Rd.
Virginia Beach   464-4636

Started as a preschool in 1951, this school now also takes students through the 7th grade. It is located at the entrance to the upscale Baylake Pines neighborhood but draws some of its 445 students from as far away as Norfolk and Chesapeake. The academically oriented school features a traditional curriculum grounded in phonics, reading, math and science that also promotes creativity. Students begin French lessons in kindergarten and science labs in 2nd grade. There are both all-day and half-day kindergartens.

BAYVIEW CHRISTIAN SCHOOL AND DAYCARE

707 E. Bayview Blvd., Norfolk   588-5687

This Christian school was founded in 1979 by Bayview Baptist Church and is adjacent to the church in the Ocean View area. The school's 100 students run the gamut from preschoolers to 8th graders. Although most are from Norfolk, many live in outlying cities and have parents working at the nearby Norfolk Navy Base. Before- and after-school care is available. For working parents there's also a summer program and child care available on non-school days. The Bible and Christian teachings are integrated into all areas of study.

CAPE HENRY COLLEGIATE SCHOOL
1320 Mill Dam Rd.
Virginia Beach   481-2446

With more than 700 students, this is the largest private school in Virginia Beach. Cape Henry was started in 1924 and has a 30-acre campus. Its individualized learning programs are for preschoolers as well as high school seniors. Middle school and upper school students are required to complete some community service work. There are both half-day and full-day kindergartens. The upper school focuses heavily on college preparatory studies with some honors and advanced placement classes available. Younger students also have some accelerated classes. The Academic Enrichment Program helps students who may have trouble maintaining the academic pace. There is before- and after-school care for younger students and an all-day summer program. Buses bring students from Virginia Beach and parts of Norfolk and Chesapeake.

CATHOLIC HIGH SCHOOL
4452 Princess Anne Rd.
Virginia Beach   467-2881

The only Catholic high school in south Hampton Roads opened in 1994 on a 16-acre site. It has a long history, however, since the new school replaced 44-year-old Norfolk Catholic High. The school has an enrollment of 400 in grades 9 through 12 and concentrates on a college-preparatory curriculum in a Catholic environment. Community service is emphasized, and graduates must complete 80 hours of volunteer work.

CHESAPEAKE BAY ACADEMY
5721 Sellger Dr., Norfolk   459-2300

The academy has a specialized curriculum for students with learning disabilities, attention deficit disorders and other special learning needs. The school was organized in 1988 and uses an individualized, multisensory approach for students in kindergarten through 8th grade. Its student body averages about 50 students who come from as far away as Williamsburg.

COURT STREET ACADEMY
447 Court St., Portsmouth   393-2312

Founded in 1966, this academy offers a traditional curriculum for preschool through 8th grade. For the academy's nearly 200 students, the emphasis is on the mastery of basic skills. The kindergarten program lasts a full day. Before- and after-school care is available. Although the school is in Court Street Baptist Church, it is not directly affiliated with the church. Transportation is available for students in Portsmouth and parts of Chesapeake and Suffolk.

FIRST BAPTIST CHRISTIAN SCHOOL
237 N. Main St., Suffolk   925-0274

Started as a kindergarten more than 25 years ago, the school is affiliated with First Baptist Church. It has more than

Insiders' Tips

Norfolk Academy, founded in 1728, is Virginia's oldest independent secondary school. It is the 13th-oldest secondary educational institution in the country.

100 students in preschool through 5th grade. Most come from Suffolk. The school provides a Christian-based education and has both half-day and full-day kindergarten programs. There is before- and after-school care, and vans will take children to and from public school.

GHENT MONTESSORI SCHOOL
610 Mowbray Arch, Norfolk   622-8174

Founded in 1978 this school is housed in a building designed for the Montessori approach, which lets children move freely around their rooms working on a variety of projects. Students can start as young as 2½. The school has steadily expanded its program to older students and now goes through 6th grade. Enrollment is about 110, and students come from throughout the region. Classes combine several ages of students so younger ones can observe older ones, who get a chance to teach what they've learned. To appreciate the Montessori style, parents are encouraged to enroll children before they are 4 years old. On occasion, upper level slots go to students not previously in Montessori studies. Full-day and extended-day programs are available.

GREENBRIER CHRISTIAN ACADEMY
311 Kempsville Rd., Chesapeake   547-9595

This academy was founded in 1982 and goes from kindergarten through high school. It is situated in the fast-growing Greenbrier area on a 20-acre campus and draws its 710 students from Chesapeake, Suffolk, Portsmouth and Virginia Beach. Greenbrier has a full-day kindergarten and before- and after-school care available for younger students. The school sponsors specialized summer camp programs in sports, computers and remedial studies. Integrated with the school's basic curriculum are Bible studies.

HEBREW ACADEMY OF TIDEWATER
1244 Thompkins Ln.
Virginia Beach   424-4327

The academy, which opened in 1955, offers a general and Judaic education for students in preschool through 7th grade. Its 200 students come from throughout the region, including the Peninsula. Besides emphasizing a core curriculum of science, math and language, students take daily classes in Hebrew, the Torah and Jewish history, laws and customs. The school has a program for students with learning difficulties. Kindergarten is a full-day program. Transportation and before- and after-school care are available.

HOLY TRINITY SCHOOL
154 W. Government Ave.
Norfolk   583-1873

This school in the Ocean View area was founded in 1934 and has 240 students. It provides a Catholic education for students in kindergarten through 8th grade and has both before- and after-school care available.

NANSEMOND-SUFFOLK ACADEMY
3373 Pruden Blvd., Suffolk   539-8789

Founded in 1966 for grades 1 through 7, the academy added an upper school in 1970 and now educates preschoolers through high school seniors. The academy is on a 50-acre campus and has an enrollment of about 900. Most students come from Suffolk, but the academy also attracts students from Portsmouth, Chesapeake and nearby counties. The academy stresses a college-preparatory curriculum, offers honors and advanced placement courses in high school and sponsors several athletic teams. Extended care is available for younger students. Transportation is also available.

NORFOLK ACADEMY
1585 Wesleyan Dr., Norfolk   461-6236

With a founding date of 1728 and an enrollment of about 1,170, this is the region's oldest and largest private school. Students can enroll in 1st grade and stay until they graduate. Liberal arts and college preparatory work are stressed as well as community service and independent study. In the upper school there are advanced placement courses. There are 40 extracurricular activities, an emphasis on fine arts, and dozens of athletic teams. Buses bring students from Norfolk, Virginia Beach, Chesapeake and Portsmouth. Before- and after-school care is available for grades 1 through 6. There is a diverse summer program for all ages that includes sports camps and sessions on archeology, theater and marine science.

NORFOLK CHRISTIAN SCHOOLS
255 Thole St., Norfolk   423-5770

From their start as a grammar school in 1952, these schools have grown into three schools in Norfolk as well as a Virginia Beach campus. The schools are evangelical and nondenominational and go from preschool through high school. There are more than 600 students who come from throughout the region. There are both half-day and full-day kindergartens. Special programs are available for students with learning disabilities and those who need accelerated studies. The upper and lower Norfolk schools are about a block apart. The Virginia Beach school, at 1265 Laskin Road, is limited to kindergarten and 1st grade. Transportation is available.

NORFOLK COLLEGIATE SCHOOL
5429 Tidewater Dr., Norfolk   625-0471
7336 Granby St., Norfolk   480-2885

Founded in 1948 as a kindergarten, Norfolk Collegiate has grown into a complete school system with academic programs that take students through high school. There are two campuses with about 600 students who come from throughout the region. The lower school is on nine acres on Tidewater Drive, while the middle and upper schools are on five acres on Granby Street. Kindergarten is a full-day program. The school stresses a college-preparatory curriculum, and advanced studies are offered to high school students. Transportation is available. The school has a varied summer program.

PARKDALE PRIVATE SCHOOL
321 Virginian Dr., Norfolk   583-5989

Although this school only goes through 2nd grade, we're partial to it since we have had a child enrolled in preschool. Parkdale started in 1957 as Barbara Jacobs School and has nearly 100 students. Its proximity to Norfolk Naval Base draws students from throughout the region. There is before- and after-school care for students as old as 14 and transportation for them to and from nearby public schools. Parkdale also has a summer camp program.

PORTSMOUTH CATHOLIC ELEMENTARY SCHOOL
2301 Oregon Ave., Norfolk   488-6744

Since 1970, this school has provided a Catholic education. Its 245 students range from preschoolers through 8th graders. The school has a full-day kindergarten and both before- and after-school care.

PORTSMOUTH CHRISTIAN SCHOOL
3214 Elliott Ave., Portsmouth   393-0725

Biltmore Baptist Church started this school in 1965 as a church ministry. It added a grade a year until it built up a Christian program for kindergarten through 12th grade. Enrollment is about 528, and students come mostly from

Photo: Cape Henry Collegiate School

A student at Cape Henry Collegiate takes part in her art class.

Portsmouth, Chesapeake and Suffolk. There are both half-day and full-day kindergartens. Extended care is offered through the 4th grade.

RYAN ACADEMY

844 Jerome Ave., Norfolk   583-RYAN

Ryan Academy started in 1988 on the site of a former private school that dated back to the 1950s. Its 140 students include kindergartners through high school seniors. The academy has an Alternate

Learning Center and resource rooms for students with learning difficulties. It has an all-day kindergarten. Transportation is available.

STAR OF THE SEA CATHOLIC SCHOOL

311 Arctic Crescent
Virginia Beach   428-8400

Founded in 1958 and affiliated with St. Mary's Star of the Sea Catholic Church, this school has about 300 students who come primarily from Virginia

Beach. It emphasizes a Catholic education for students in preschool through 8th grade. There is a full-day kindergarten.

ST. PIUS X SCHOOL

7800 Halprin Dr., Norfolk   588-6171

Established in 1958, this parochial school is for kindergarten through grade 8. Enrollment is 515. The school has both half-day and full-day kindergartens and after-school care available.

STONEBRIDGE SCHOOLS

4225 Portsmouth Blvd.
Chesapeake   488-7586

Stonebridge was founded in 1980 to offer a Christian, nondenominational, college-preparatory curriculum. Its 220 students come primarily from Chesapeake, Portsmouth, Suffolk and Virginia Beach. There are two campuses. The lower school is on Portsmouth Boulevard in the Western Branch area; the middle and high schools are in Faith Baptist Church on Jolliff Road. There are half-day kindergarten classes for 4-year-olds and a full-day program for 5-year-olds.

Extended care is available, and transportation is an option for students in Virginia Beach and the Great Bridge area of Chesapeake.

TRINITY LUTHERAN SCHOOL

6001 Granby St., Norfolk   489-2732

The school has programs for 175 students, preschoolers through 5th grade. It was established in 1945 and offers a Christian education. It has both half-day and full-day kindergartens as well as before- and after-school care.

VIRGINIA BEACH
COUNTRY DAY SCHOOL

2100 Harbor Ln.
Virginia Beach   481-0111

Started in 1975, the school offers classes for preschool through 6th grade. It has a four-acre campus and an enrollment of 130. Students come primarily from Virginia Beach and Chesapeake. There are both half-day and full-day kindergartens. Extended care is available, and there is a summer program. Transportation is available.

Photo: Cape Hrenry Collegiate School

Students are becoming more educated through computer technology.

VIRGINIA BEACH FRIENDS SCHOOL
1537 Laskin Rd.
Virginia Beach 428-7534

Organized in 1955, this is Virginia's only Quaker school. It promotes the values of community, equality, harmony and simplicity. The school has an 11-acre campus and is for preschool through 8th grade. There are 110 students who come from throughout the region. Before- and after-school care is offered. There are both half-day and full-day kindergartens.

THE WILLIAMS SCHOOL
419 Colonial Ave., Norfolk 627-1383

Housed in a historic home in the residential Ghent area, this school was founded in 1927. It has about 115 students in kindergarten through 8th grade, with most coming from Norfolk and Portsmouth. The school prides itself on its environment, which nurtures individuals while giving them a solid grounding in basic studies.

Inside
Colleges, Universities and Adult Education

Doctor. Lawyer. Executive chef. Name almost any career you are interested in, and chances are you'll find a degree in it offered somewhere in Hampton Roads. There are six major colleges and universities based in the five-city area. In addition, the region's large military population has attracted a number of out-of-area colleges that offer undergraduate and graduate degree programs here. And, if that's not enough, there are four other colleges on the Peninsula within easy driving distance — Christopher Newport University, the College of William & Mary, Hampton University and Thomas Nelson Community College.

If you're holding down a job and thinking of earning a degree on the side, you'll find that easy to do here. All colleges offer evening programs, and some also have early morning and weekend sessions that cater to working students. Locally, Old Dominion University is a pioneer in bringing classes to students at suburban education centers and through telecommunications.

In Hampton Roads there are also more than 50 private career colleges and schools that train mechanics, computer technicians, cosmetologists, travel agents and chefs, to name a few of the possibilities.

For residents with a lifelong love of learning, reasonably priced adult education programs can teach them to tap dance, paint or become a tennis ace. Most of these fun classes are run by city parks and recreation departments. However, some are offered through the continuing education departments of area schools and colleges. Most programs publish quarterly guides giving class times and fees. Among the city programs, Norfolk Parks and Recreation Department stands out for its Lakewood Dance and Music Center, which has an excellent curriculum for both adults and children.

Colleges and Universities

Major colleges and universities based in the area that are accredited by the Southern Association of Colleges and Schools are:

EASTERN VIRGINIA MEDICAL SCHOOL
Norfolk   446-5600

Established in 1973, Eastern Virginia Medical School is one of only three medical schools in Virginia. The school is operated by the Medical College of Hampton Roads from a campus in Norfolk. However, its students and medical residents use 30 area hospitals and clinics as their training ground. From its first class of 24 medical students, the school has grown to an enrollment of about 475 students who come from Virginia as well as other states. Each year EVMS sponsors 20 residency programs, a psychology internship, and fellowship programs that attract about 300 physicians. Besides the M.D. degree, EVMS grants a doctorate in clinical psychology and biomedical sciences through cooperative programs with area universities. It also offers a master's degree in art psychotherapy.

EVMS receives some state funding but depends heavily on support from area cities and private donations. In fact, the school got its start when area residents raised $17 million in the late 1960s and early 1970s to start the school. Having a medical school in Hampton Roads has brought a full range of sophisticated medical services — including heart transplants and in-vitro fertilization — to the region. The school has also greatly increased the number of physicians working in the area.

EVMS is noted for its Jones Institute for Reproductive Medicine — the first in-vitro fertilization clinic in the United States. In 1981 the Institute helped produce the country's first in-vitro baby. Since then more than 1,500 in-vitro babies have been born with the Institute's help. It has the world's highest pregnancy rate among in-vitro programs and draws patients from across the country. Housed in a $12.5 million building, the Institute has an international reputation for treating reproductive problems. In 1994 it gained international acclaim for its genetic engineering, which produced a healthy child for a Louisiana couple who were carriers of the deadly Tay-Sachs disease.

Another major program of EVMS is the Diabetes Institutes, which has dedicated itself to finding a cure for diabetes. It also operates both outpatient and in-patient treatment programs for area residents with diabetes.

NORFOLK STATE UNIVERSITY
Norfolk   683-8600

Founded in 1935 as a division of Virginia Union University, Norfolk State has grown into one of the country's five largest historically black colleges. It has an enrollment of more than 8,600. Students come from throughout the United States and 35 foreign countries.

In 1944 NSU became part of the Virginia college system and in 1979 gained university status. Today it has nine schools, 32 departments and 72 degree programs. NSU offers seven associate, 50 bachelors, 15 master's degrees and one doctoral degree. Degree programs include education, nursing, journalism and social work. There are 13 varsity sports, including football and basketball.

In 1986 NSU established the Ronald I. Dozoretz National Institute for Minorities in Applied Sciences, which recruits top high school seniors across the country to study science. In 1994 it instituted a master's degree in science and recently started its first doctoral program, which is in social work.

NSU is renowned for its marching band and Army ROTC program. It has the country's second-largest female ROTC cadet enrollment and its total ROTC enrollment is the largest in Virginia for a nonmilitary school.

Besides its 130-acre campus in Nor-

Old Dominion University was founded in 1930.

folk, NSU operates a graduate center in Virginia Beach with Old Dominion University.

OLD DOMINION UNIVERSITY

Norfolk 683-3000

Founded in 1930 in Norfolk as a branch of the College of William and Mary, ODU became independent in 1962. In 1970 the state-supported institution gained university status. It has an enrollment of about 17,000. Students come from across the United States as well as 80 foreign countries. ODU offers 85 bachelor's degree programs, 53 master's programs and 16 doctoral degrees.

ODU is one of Virginia's top Ph.D. research institutions and receives about $13 million annually in research grants and contracts. ODU's proximity to NASA Langley Research Center in Hampton has helped it become the leader among Virginia universities in NASA research contracts. ODU recently formed a partnership with the Continuous Electron Beam Accelerator Facility (CEBAF), a massive nuclear physics project that opened in Newport News in 1994. The university is expanding its physics faculty to meet its goal of having one of the country's premier physics programs.

ODU already is recognized worldwide for its Department of Oceanography, which offers two graduate degrees and includes the Center for Coastal Physical Oceanography. ODU's Applied Marine Research Laboratory conducts environmental studies for regulatory agencies and private organizations.

At ODU, degree programs include business, education, science and English. There are 16 varsity sports, including basketball, sailing and soccer. Recently both ODU's sailing and field hockey teams have been ranked No. 1 in the country.

Besides its Norfolk campus on Hampton Boulevard, ODU operates the Old Dominion University Peninsula Center in Hampton and an off-campus program in Portsmouth. It is a partner in the ODU-NSU Virginia Beach Graduate Center. Many courses are offered at the satellite locations, which utilize both on-site instructors and teleconferencing. ODU widely uses telecommunications.

REGENT UNIVERSITY
Virginia Beach   523-7400

Founded in 1977 as CBN University, this private graduate school gained a new name in 1990. Regent shares an 800-acre campus in Virginia Beach with The Christian Broadcasting Network. Its 800 students come from across the United States and 20 countries. They can earn any of eight master's degrees in business, communication, counseling, education, government, law, ministry and theology.

Regent is the only university in South Hampton Roads to offer a law degree. All its classes are taught from a Christian perspective.

Although Regent is accredited by the Southern Association of Colleges and Schools, its law school is seeking accreditation from the American Bar Association. The school currently has provisional status from the ABA.

TIDEWATER COMMUNITY COLLEGE
Chesapeake	547-9271
Portsmouth	484-2121
Virginia Beach	427-7100
Norfolk	683-9414

Started in 1968, Tidewater Community College provides training and higher education throughout the region. It has campuses in the Green Run area of Virginia Beach, the Churchland area of Portsmouth and the Great Bridge section of Chesapeake. In 1993 TCC started offering a few classes in downtown Norfolk and is building a full campus there that will open by 1996. TCC also offers off-campus programs at area high schools, military bases and other locations.

With more than 18,000 students — the majority of them part-time — TCC is the second-largest public community college in Virginia. TCC offers two-year associates degrees as well as occupational training in 90 different programs. In addition to academic courses in English, math and business, TCC offers training in such fields as truck driving, landscaping and welding. Some TCC graduates transfer to four-year colleges while others launch right into their careers. The college recently has moved aggressively into computer and Internet training through continuing education courses that have attracted a loyal following.

VIRGINIA WESLEYAN COLLEGE
Norfolk/Virginia Beach   455-3200

Sitting astride the Norfolk-Virginia Beach city line, Virginia Wesleyan was founded in 1966. It has a 300-acre campus and a student body of about 1,500. Students come from 31 states and 22 foreign countries. The private college is affiliated with the United Methodist Church and offers a liberal arts curriculum.

Virginia Wesleyan students can earn

Insiders' Tips

Tidewater Community College is the clearinghouse for all grammar hotlines in North America. If you're stumped by punctuation or grammar problems, dial TCC's hotline at 427-7170 on weekdays. A helpful English professor will try to make your prose perfect.

Students on their way to class at Virginia Wesleyan College.

bachelor's degrees in 35 areas, including business management, communications and physics. They can participate in varsity sports, including basketball, baseball, soccer and tennis.

The college's adult studies program schedules classes early in the mornings, at night and on weekends. It is aimed at working adults eager to return to college and earn a degree. To keep college within working students' budgets, tuition is half-price for evening classes. One popular offering is an alternative certification program for professionals who want to become teachers. Participants must have degrees in either math, science, English, history or a foreign language. By taking three concentrated courses, student teaching for a semester and passing the national teacher's exam, they can be certified to teach.

Other Opportunities

Educational options abound in Hampton Roads. Here is a sampling of what is offered in the region:

• A master's degree in transpersonal studies from Atlantic University. The private university is affiliated with the Virginia Beach-based Association for Research and Enlightenment and the Edgar Cayce Foundation. It also offers an independent studies program. Call 428-1512.

• Courses in law enforcement, data processing, English and business at the Suffolk branch of Paul D. Camp Community College. At this public college, associate's degrees are available in some fields with certificates offered in more technical fields. Call 925-2283.

• An associate's of applied science degree in business management from Commonwealth College. This proprietary, two-year college has branches in Norfolk, Virginia Beach and Portsmouth. Its programs include computer science and ho-

tel and restaurant management. Call 626-3247.

• An associate's degree from ECPI Computer Institute in Virginia Beach. The proprietary school offers training in such fields as computer programming, word processing and accounting. Call 490-9090.

• A two-year culinary arts degree from Rhode Island-based Johnson & Wales University. The University has a Norfolk branch of its College of Culinary Arts that trains chefs. It also offers a series of excellent one-night community classes for people who love to cook. Call 853-3508.

• Graduate courses at the Hampton Roads Graduate Center run jointly in Virginia Beach by the University of Virginia and Virginia Tech. Among the offerings are engineering degrees and teacher recertification. Call 552-1890

Other outside colleges and universities offering degrees here are: Central Texas College, City Colleges of Chicago, Embry Riddle Aeronautical University, Florida Institute of Technology, George Washington University, King James Bible College, Saint Leo College, Tabernacle Baptist Theological Seminary and Troy State University.

Inside
Hospitals and Health Care

If you want to see what health looks like carried to its most robust level, look no further than the medical community of Hampton Roads. Apparently armed with a powerful vaccine against the symptoms of recession, hospitals throughout the region are expanding, cutting-edge specialized programs have been introduced, and world renowned volunteer programs have reached new proportions.

On the expansion front in just the last couple of years, Norfolk's Children's Hospital of The Kings Daughters has completed a $73.5 million, eight-story, 387,000-square-foot addition that has more than tripled the hospital's size, including a new emergency room. CHKD's neighbor, Sentara Norfolk General, has completed a mammoth six-story addition that houses the Sentara Cancer Institute along with expanded facilities including emergency services. Eastern Virginia Medical School completed its $12.5 million Jones Institute for Reproductive Medicine, a 60,000-square-foot facility that hosts the incredible in-vitro fertilization program that gave our nation the first successful birth using the in-vitro technique, and has added more than 1,500 more healthy births to that record in the past 13 years.

In recent years Chesapeake General Hospital joined the expansion list with a $30 million, 50-bed addition. Maryview Medical Center has invested $13.6 million to expand its emergency room and

The Children's Hospital of The Kings Daughters is the only full-time pediatric hospital in Virginia.

renovate a surgical suite, lobby and intensive care unit. DePaul Hospital recently completed a $10 million, three-year project to create a new critical care pavilion and ambulatory surgery center to complement its new laser center and renovated rehabilitation center. Portsmouth Naval Hospital is several years into a $154 million expansion that will replace the aging hospital with a new 464-bed facility, scheduled for completion in 2001.

While all these millions prove that the medical community of Hampton Roads certainly knows how to spend a buck, it shows that it also knows the humanitarian value of offering time and talent to benefit those less fortunate around the world. Headquartered here, the organization called Operation Smile International has donated reconstructive surgery to tens of thousands of indigent children in developing countries. Begun by local surgeon Dr. Bill Magee and his wife Kathy in 1983 and comprised of volunteer surgeons, physicians, nurses, dentists, social workers, psychologists, speech therapists and other good-hearted medical professionals, Operation Smile flies off several times a year with hundreds of these volunteers from around the country to travel in teams to Africa, South America, Vietnam and the Philippines. Here they have performed life-changing operations on more than 7,500 children who would face a future of permanent disfigurement from such things as cleft palates and lips, burn scars and club feet, plus given medical care to tens of thousands more. When not in the operating room, they provide educational support and training to health-care professionals in these struggling countries.

Also working to educate the medical communities of faraway countries like Egypt, Greece, Israel, Jordan, Syria and Turkey is another nationally applauded volunteer organization, Physicians for Peace. Formed in 1987, teams of U.S. physicians and health care specialists travel several times a year to the Middle East to further their mission of "international friendships and peace through medicine." Its founder, Dr. Charles Horton, was honored in 1992 by Jordon's King Hussein for the acclaimed medical missions of his organization.

And, there's more. The Children's Hospital of the Kings Daughters not only expanded its own facilities here in Hampton Roads, but also in a land many moons away. It has forged a relationship with the former Soviet Union Ministry of Health that has led to the very first officially sanctioned U.S./Russia health-care association, as well as a critically needed neonatal intensive care unit at a children's hospital in Moscow.

While all this information should swell the pride of any newcomer to our area, the outstanding leadership of our emergency and trauma-care network will likewise be a comfort to any short-term visitor. Considered one of the best emergency care networks on the East Coast, we are an integral provider of Virginia's trauma-care system, rated number two in the nation. Sentara Norfolk General's Level I trauma center and burn/trauma units, along with the Nightingale medivac helicopter, join Level II emergency rooms throughout the region. Numerous urgent care centers for minor emergencies and emergency medical services councils that oversee the area's rescue services are all considered absolutely top-notch.

So, from a bee sting to bypass heart surgery, influenza to in-vitro fertilization, any medical assistance that might be required is not only here, but is at the highest levels available anywhere in the United States.

Here are the hospitals that form one of the finest medical networks in the country.

Norfolk

CHILDREN'S HOSPITAL
OF THE KINGS DAUGHTERS
601 Children's Ln. 668-7000

Built in 1961, CHKD, Virginia's only freestanding, full-service pediatric hospital operates as a regional referral center for pediatric specialists focusing on cancer, cystic fibrosis, orthopedics, craniofacial and urological reconstructive surgery. CHKD opened its 387,000-square-foot expansion in 1994 that includes the region's first pediatric emergency room. The hospital is licensed for 186 beds and has a 38-bed neonatal intensive care unit.

One of the first of its kind in the country, CHKD's Transitional Care Unit has 12 beds for stable, ventilator-dependent children. CHKD has more than 50 outpatient programs, including ones for sickle cell anemia, lead poisoning, cystic fibrosis and child abuse. A new neurodevelopmental center houses a variety of disciplines, including neurology and speech pathology. Children's Home Health provides home infusion therapy for children on intravenous medication and apnea monitors for high-risk infants, as well as private duty nursing services and access to necessary medical equipment.

Associated with the hospital are the Barry Robinson Center for emotionally disturbed and learning disabled children and the Discovery Care Centers in Greenbrier, Chesapeake, Ghent and Military Circle in Norfolk.

DEPAUL MEDICAL CENTER
150 Kingsley Ln. 889-3400

A 366-bed, acute-care teaching hospital for Eastern Virginia Medical School, DePaul was founded in 1855 by the Daughters of Charity of St. Vincent de Paul and is affiliated with the Charity National Health System, the nation's largest not-for-profit health care provider.

Its "Centers of Excellence" include The Cancer Center, a 30-bed unit selected by the American College of Surgeons as a teaching hospital cancer program; The Center for Birth, offering single-room maternity care (the latest concept in family-centered maternity service); The Diabetes Center, one of the most comprehensive in the region and the inpatient component of the Diabetes Institutes of Eastern Virginia Medical School; The Heart Center; The Eye Center, which offers laser procedures; and The Gerontology Institute, which offers a comprehensive range of services for those 65 and older.

Just opened is DePaul MedExpress, a quick and convenient service for minor emergencies within the confines of the Center's emergency facilities. It's the place to go for colds, cuts or minor mishaps that do not require full-blown emergency room treatment.

LAKE TAYLOR HOSPITAL
1309 Kemspville Rd. 461-5001

A 332-bed, long-term care/chronic disease hospital, Lake Taylor is governed by the Hospital Authority of Norfolk and managed by Riverside Health System. The hospital, which is more than 100 years old, is the only one in the state that offers chronic disease care including AIDS treatment.

Included in the facility is a 104-bed wing providing intensive recuperative care for patients with long-term chronic diseases and a 229-bed nursing facility for long-term residents who require either skilled or custodial care.

NORFOLK COMMUNITY HOSPITAL
2539 Corprew Ave.   *628-1400*

Opened in 1915, this 202-bed facility offers specialized services including therapeutic counseling, nuclear medicine, stress testing, outpatient surgery, a peripheral vascular lab and a renal dialysis center.

NORFOLK PSYCHIATRIC CENTER
Granby St. at Kingsley Ln.   *489-1072*

With inpatient and day-treatment programs for adults and adolescents, this 62-bed psychiatric hospital provides therapy for individuals, groups and families. Along with recreation, occupational and expressive therapy, a chemical dependency recovery program, detoxification facility and rehabilitation program for those addicted to alcohol and drugs are offered by NPC.

NDC+ MEDICAL CENTER
850/880 Kempsville Rd.   *461-5900*

A well-respected independent urgent care facility with expertise in dermatology, gerontology, neurology, rheumatology and internal medicine, NDC+ also offers a full menu of occupational medical services, including pre-employment examinations, executive physicals and Worker's Compensation treatment. A full-service laboratory and x-ray facility is on-site. NDC recently affiliated with Sentara Health System.

SENTARA LEIGH HOSPITAL
830 Kempsville Rd.   *466-6000*

An acute care facility established in 1903, this 250-bed, all private-room hospital operates a 10-bed pediatric unit and new Family Maternity Suite featuring 16 suites for LDRP (labor/delivery/recovery/postpartum).

Special services include cardiac catherization, an expanded imaging center with nuclear medicine, CT scanning, MRI, telemetry, one-day surgery, breast diagnostic center and 24-hour emergency room.

The hospital's Physical Therapy Specialty Center specializes in back, orthopedic and sports medicine; the Mobile Medical Diagnostic Services Unit provides x-rays and EKG's to nursing homes and retirement communities as well as mammography to businesses. Of note is Tel-Med, a telephone tape library with information on more than 200 health-related subjects.

SENTARA NORFOLK GENERAL HOSPITAL
600 Gresham Dr.   *628-3000*

Our largest, and considered by many to be our best, Sentara Norfolk General is a 644-bed, acute care facility and the primary teaching hospital for Eastern Virginia Medical School.

The 105-year-old hospital provides the broadest spectrum of services, including a Level I trauma center, Nightingale medivac helicopter service for southeastern Virginia and northeastern North Carolina, regional burn center, The Heart Pavilion, The Sentara Cancer Institute, hospice, high-risk pregnancy center, Women's Health Pavilion, kidney and heart transplants, renal dialysis, Kidney Stone Center of Virginia, Imaging Center, Lions Sight and Hearing Center, Eating Disorders Center of Virginia and Sleep Disorders Center of Virginia.

The hospital manages the School of Allied Health Sciences, which trains nurses and professionals in eight fields, and is affiliated with the Jones Institute for Reproductive Medicine, the Institute for Plastic and Reconstructive Surgery and Specialized Urologic Surgery.

Portsmouth

FHC OF PORTSMOUTH
301 Fort Ln.   *399-3300*

FHC operates The Pines Residential Treatment Center, The Phoenix at Portsmouth Psychiatric Center and Crawford Day School. It offers specialized comprehensive mental health care programs for adults and children.

MARYVIEW MEDICAL CENTER
36 High St.   *398-2200*

Part of the Bon Secours Health Systems, Inc. of Marriottsville, Maryland, Maryview is a 321-bed, general hospital that offers a wide variety of technologically advanced diagnostic inpatient and outpatient services. It includes many "Centers," including the newly remodeled Family Birth Center, the Martha W. Davis Cancer Center, Cancer Treatment Centers of America (CTA), Plastic Surgery Center, MRI Center, Eye Center and Breast Center. It also operates three Maryview MedCare Centers, freestanding urgent care facilities.

Included in a recent $13.6 million expansion and renovation project are a new ambulatory surgery pre-operative and recovery area, sterile processing and outpatient testing, a new Intensive Care Unit and an expanded emergency department.

Adjacent to the general hospital is Maryview Psychiatric Hospital, a 54-bed facility that provides psychiatric and chemical dependency treatment for adults and adolescents. Along with a Women's Treatment Program and a Pain Management Program that includes The Headache Institute, the facility offers the innovative "Turning Point" program for patients in the early to middle stages of chemical dependency.

PORTSMOUTH GENERAL HOSPITAL
850 Crawford Pkwy.   *398-4000*

Three hundred and eleven beds strong, nonprofit Portsmouth General provides acute care, diagnostic and educational services. It provides full service obstetrical care featuring private rooms, birthing rooms, a newborn nursery operated by Children's Hospital of The Kings Daughters along with Lamaze classes, Stork Night/hospital tours, sibling awareness classes and other programs and support groups for parents.

Other specialty areas include the Center for Sight, a surgical center dedicated to the diagnosis and treatment of eye disease; The Cardiac Fitness Center, an inpatient rehabilitation program; and Homelife Health Care. Community outreach programs include the Diabetes Education Program, the Better Breathers Club (for those with chronic lung disease) and Mended Hearts (for heart surgery patients). It is affiliated with The Urgency Care Center at 2425 Taylor Road in Chesapeake.

PORTSMOUTH NAVAL HOSPITAL
Foot of Effingham St.   *398-5000*

The oldest naval hospital in the United States and the second-largest naval hospital in the country, the 500-bed Portsmouth Naval Hospital offers superlative health care to the military community, including active duty, their dependents and retirees.

Suffolk

OBICI HOSPITAL
1900 N. Main St.   *934-4000*

A 243-bed medical center, Obici offers an affiliated three-year registered nursing school and one-year LPN school along with diagnostic and acute care services.

Special services include neuro-ophthalmology, a Psychiatric Care Center, a Women's Health Center, cardiac catherization lab and cardiac rehabilitation, comprehensive radiology department, mobile MRI and mobile lithotripsy, rehabilitation medicine, outpatient surgery and a 24-hour emergency department.

Virginia Beach

SENTARA BAYSIDE HOSPITAL
800 Independence Blvd.   *363-6100*

Obstetrics, diabetes center, intensive and coronary care, surgery, physical therapy, radiology, nuclear medicine, emergency room and community classes are offered at this 250-bed, acute care facility. Special services include The Family Center, a fully equipped birthing center and comprehensive educational center for expectant and new parents, and The Children's Health Center.

VIRGINIA BEACH GENERAL HOSPITAL
1060 First Colonial Rd.   *481-8000*

Home to the Tidewater Perinatal Center for high-risk pregnancies, Virginia Beach General is a full-service, 274-bed hospital. It provides a full range of technologically advanced services, including a Level II intensive care nursery, open-heart surgery, diagnostic cardiology, nuclear cardiology, cardiovascular therapy and coronary care. Along with intensive care and critical care units, it offers an excellent emergency room.

Special centers at VBGH include the Cardiac Fitness Center, the Sleep Disorders Clinic, the Heart Institute, the Department of Neuroscience, the Coastal Cancer Center, the Ambulatory Surgery Center and Birthing Center.

In a cooperative venture with Riverside Health System, Tidewater Health Care, parent corporation of VBGH, operates a 60-bed long-term care facility called Windermere on the hospital campus.

VIRGINIA BEACH PSYCHIATRIC CENTER
1100 First Colonial Rd.   *496-6000*

This private, 78-bed facility provides comprehensive psychiatric and substance abuse services for children, adolescents, adults and families. Among its many services are free support groups, outpatient referrals, day-treatment services and in-patient services.

It also offers the Mental Health Crisis Line, which has qualified professionals who provide free, confidential consultations 24-hours a day, seven days a week.

Emergency Services

Whether a Hampton Roads resident or a visitor to our medically astute community, if a crisis requires ambulance service, you can be assured of attention from the best in the business. Every member of our phenomenal ambulance crews has taken at least 125 hours of training and has been certified by the state of Virginia as an Emergency Medical Technician. Even more training can be claimed by cardiac technicians and paramedics.

Because speed of response is critical in emergency situations, you might just find a fire truck wheel up to your door. Not to worry. All Hampton Roads firefighters have been extensively trained as "first responders," and if they are the closest emergency vehicle to your given address, they will be first on the scene.

If your situation does not warrant calling out our emergency angels, you will most likely find a freestanding acute care facility or hospital emergency room close to where you are. Regardless of where you go, or who you might need to call, we advise that you take not only personal identification, such as a driver's license and medical insurance card, but a list of current prescription medicines and respective dosages for any examining physician.

Physician Matchmakers

If you are new to the area, asking co-workers or neighbors about the physicians and dentists of choice is an excellent way to make the doctor-connection. If you would like more information, however, there are several referral services that are on standby to answer any of your questions about the selection process for a physician for the members of your family.

Feel free to call any of the following for no-charge, no-obligation information:

Norfolk Academy of Medicine	622-1421
Portsmouth Academy Medicine	398-4100
Virginia Beach Medical Society	481-4516
Chesapeake Medical Society	547-7800
Sentara Hospitals Physician Referral Service	(800) SENTARA
Ask A Nurse, Riverside Health Systems	398-4454
Doctor Connection, Virginia Beach General/ Portsmouth General	481-8888
Physician Finder Maryview Hospital	398-2131
Health Care Connection Chesapeake General	547-7800
Tidewater Dental Society	627-8534
Tidewater Optometric Society	490-4015
Health Departments	
Norfolk	683-2700
Portsmouth	393-8585
Chesapeake	547-9213
Virginia Beach	431-3500
Suffolk	925-2300

Inside
Business and Industry

One symptom of our country's economic roller coaster that Hampton Roads traditionally has not been accustomed to dealing with is the negative G's of the downward force of recession. After all, we've always been strapped tight in our seats by the comforting power of our strong military presence. Even in the 1980s, while we watched those news clips of distraught laid-off workers, we happily skipped from one thrilling business ride to the next, and added nearly 200,000 civilian and military jobs during those years. In fact, during that dismal period, Hampton Roads grew faster than 90 percent of the nation's metropolitan statistical areas, according to the Hampton Roads Planning District Commission.

Well, the carnival has closed. By the fall of 1990, the downsizing of service businesses, construction companies, banks and shipyards had come home to our own backyards. Even our military, facing the groundswell for national defense spending cuts, found that many get-a-job/keep-a-job ticket booths were slammed shut thanks to the Base Realignment and Closure Committee. Hampton Roads did fare better than many other communities, however. Even though 7,000 civilian jobs were lost due to BRAC closures, 11,000 new military positions were claimed thanks to relocations from operations in other areas.

While many economic ringmasters are convinced that it will continue to rain on Hampton Roads' parade, others are cautiously optimistic about the future. Even though a worldwide 25 percent military force reduction (that's 500,000 jobs) looms heavy on the horizon, our position as host to the world's largest Navy base — and heavy concentration of other military installations — could well mean the additional infusion of military personnel from closed bases around the world. And, that hope is what gives us all, civilian and military, an outlook entrenched in a better tomorrow.

With all that discussion of gloom out of the way, we flip the page to the good news about the Hampton Roads business and industry scene. Sharp prognosticators that we are, we've been fortifying our economic base with a hotbed of back-office operations and the "fulfillment" industry. Enter mega-companies like United Services Automobile Association (USAA) with a corporate complex in Norfolk. Household International Inc. put down credit card processing roots in Chesapeake — where it employs 1,400 — to neighbor its Household Finance Corp., 700 employees strong.

Adding even more computers and telephones is our "fulfillment" industry. Think Lillian Vernon Corp. and the QVC Network (the shopping channel). The retail front claims more than 133,000 workers, and general service sector employees number 191,000 at last count.

Over the next several years, the construction industry will be enjoying a hayday unseen in decades. This, due in part to the approval for development of shopping complexes from Norfolk's MacArthur Center to Virginia Beach's "34th Street Project" to Chesapeake's Greenbrier Market. It will indeed be a very, very good time to be in the concrete business in Hampton Roads.

But for employment giants, look to the sea. To Newport News Shipbuilding which counts more than 25,000 workers on its payroll, Virginia's single largest private employer. To the Port of Hampton Roads, the East Coast's busiest, where 75 shipping lines ship an estimated $9 billion in annual exports that give another 115,000 residents a place to hang their hard hats. Then, of course, there's the military, with more than 100,000 active duty personnel. Add in local, state and federal government employees and that number swells to over 272,000.

We can't talk sea-biz without applause for the thriving cash crop of our watermen. Virginia's seafood business is a $442 million industry, and we can claim an annual haul of 103 million pounds of oysters, clams, crabs and finfish, making us the third most productive fishing region in the country.

The sea brings us industry from other lands as well. A global melting pot for international business, more than 60 foreign-based firms have set up Hampton Roads operations just in the last decade, bringing the list of foreign-owned or operated firms to 125. From Japan: Canon Virginia, Mitsubishi Kaisei Virginia/Kaisei Memory Products, Inc. and Sumitomo Machinery Corp. of America. From Germany: Stihl Inc., whose U.S. headquarters is in Virginia Beach. In Chesapeake, find Volvo Penta Production, Inc. And look no further than your local Food Lion to find the Belgian connection.

Speaking of food, we can't neglect to recognize our agricultural community. While we city folk find their ways mysterious, they alone are responsible for maintaining the productivity of our fertile farmlands, first nurtured nearly 400 years ago. Peanuts, soybeans, corn and livestock thrive in our temperate climate and support landowners with generations of farming in their blood.

Unfortunately, our suburban sprawl has encroached upon much of the rich soil formerly earmarked for cash crops, dwindling the usable acreage and putting many farmers out to pasture. Many other farmers who work in the shadow of the city are getting urban-smart, however, inviting us onto their land for pick-your-own strawberries and veggies. If you're a newcomer, or visiting during a harvest season, this is one down-country experience that is a treat for the whole family.

And lastly, there's tourism, a $1.5 million Hampton Roads industry.

If you're a visitor to our region, we want you to know that you are supporting more than 40,000 full- and part-time workers who hustle to spit-polish our more than 40 historic sites and museums, three theme parks and as many state parks. We thank you, and the 4 million others, who choose our area as a vacation spot every year.

Want to take an advanced course in Hampton Roads business? Follow through this brief city-by-city tour of the industry that supports our pro-business environment backed by the state's right-to-work laws:

Norfolk

Traditionally the region's financial center, Norfolk claims the main offices for most of the region's stock brokerage offices, along with the regional headquar-

Mr. Peanut

In 1913 Italian immigrant Amedeo Obici decided to move his fledgling Planters Nut and Chocolate Co. from Pennsylvania to Virginia. He chose Suffolk as a prime location and borrowed $25,000 to finance the relocation.

Obici's new Suffolk processing plant put him in the heart of Virginia peanut country, and Suffolk soon touted itself as "The Peanut Capital of the World."

In 1916 Planters offered a $5 prize to the person submitting the best sketch for a corporate logo. The winner was a 14-year-old Suffolk boy who created a peanut person with arms and crossed legs and labeled it "Mr. Peanut." Later a commercial artist added a monocle, top hat and cane to give the mascot his distinctive look.

Today Planters is owned by RJR Nabisco. The Suffolk plant, whose 500 workers roast and package nuts, is part of the company's Planters Division. Fourteen cast iron statues of the dapper Mr. Peanut line the fence outside a new plant that opened in 1994. The one built in 1913 was recently demolished. While there is a small museum in the building, it is not open to the public. Mr. Peanut aficionados can check out his memorabilia in a display in the basement of Riddick's Folly, a historic home in downtown Suffolk. It is open 10 AM to 5 PM Tuesday through Friday and 1 to 5 PM on Sunday. Admission is free. There's also a Mr. Peanut statue in the heart of Suffolk at Main and Washington streets.

MR. PEANUT

MR. PEANUT ®

ters for major banks like First Union, in the rose-colored monolith that soars on the edge of the Elizabeth River. NationsBank, in the 21-story office tower that forms the nucleus of the Downtown area, has bank offices and a credit card operation that employs nearly 1,500 workers.

Rising two-stories higher than the NationsBank building is the gorgeous Marriott Hotel and adjacent Waterside Convention Center, and opened in April of 1993 is Harbor Park, a state-of-the-art ball park facility that is home to the Norfolk Tides AAA baseball club. Also on the downtown waterfront, The National Maritime Center, NAUTICUS, a multi-million dollar world-class marine showcase of interactive exhibits and displays along with working labs, and the Hampton Roads Naval Museum opened to applause in June of 1994.

Norfolk's Downtown visions continue in MacArthur Center, a $270 million shopping mall projected to open in 1997, anchored by such venerable retailers as Nordstrom. To house shoppers and visitors alike, city leaders are considering development of a new upscale hotel near the mall, along with the renovation and refurbishing of two other downtown landmark hotels, Howard Johnson and The Thomas Hotel.

To ensure Norfolk's economic future from one end of town to the other, the city's redevelopment authority has hired one of the nation's most renowned urban planning teams to design a new bayfront neighborhood out of a 90-acre redevelopment tract in East Ocean View.

Portsmouth

The mainstays of the Portsmouth economy are the government-operated Norfolk Naval Shipyard, the Portsmouth Naval Hospital, and a Coast Guard installation.

Portsmouth's industrial sector is anchored by Hoechst Celanese and Gwaltney of Smithfield, softened by the charm of Olde Towne, the city's successfully revitalized historic district with rebricked streets and quaint gas lamps.

Chesapeake

Once the rural agricultural hub of the region, Chesapeake has traded coveralls for pin-striped suits, tractors for computers, grain silos for glitzy shopping malls. The city's 10 bustling office parks play host to business concerns from 31 countries, with a large concentration of Japanese manufacturers. This influx of ready-to-spend workers has birthed numerous new retail shopping strips, restaurants and service related businesses, along with acres of new residential communities.

Not to let shoppers slip out of their sight, Chesapeake has just announced plans for another mega shopping experi-

ence, a $35 million complex dubbed Greenbrier Market to be built on 73 acres in the Greenbrier corridor. Noteworthy here is the inaugural appearance of Target, a discount mass-market retailer new to the Hampton Roads market. Projected opening of the complex is spring of 1996.

Suffolk

The most rural city in the region, "Surprising Suffolk" lays claim to more land than any city in Virginia. It is renowned for its amazing peanut crop (don't miss the Suffolk Peanut Festival!) and is also a strong manufacturing base for plants that produce Hills Bros. coffee, Planter's peanut snacks and Lipton Tea. QVC, the TV home shopping network, maintains a mammoth distribution center here, too.

Virginia Beach

With tourism and conventions an enviable mainstay of the Virginia Beach economy, this resort city has beached the total inner-tube mentality for the serious conquests of the manufacturing, distribution and service industries. With more office space than any city in Hampton Roads, plus wide open spaces primed for industry seeking inexpensive acreage and a reliable work force, Virginia Beach has landed such respected companies as Lillian Vernon, who continues to expand operations and employment opportunities.

Virginia Beach has showbiz in its blood, too. It is home to Pat Robertson's Christian Broadcasting Network, producers of the 700 Club, and to The Family Channel, one of the country's fastest-growing cable networks, now traded on the New York Stock Exchange. Three years ago CBN opened the $36 million Founders Inn and Conference Center.

CBN also is the parent of the Regent University complex.

To put the lock on tourists, enter the "30th Street Project," a $46 million shopping and entertainment complex recently proposed near the city's Oceanfront. Add to that a 20,000 seat amphitheater, tripling the size of both the Virginia Marine Science Museum and the Pavilion Convention Center and adding at least six new golf courses, and Virginia Beach watchers should be keep on guard for several years to come.

New business and industry does not find Hampton Roads by accident. There are several high-powered organizations whose sole mission is to aggressively pursue more and more business investment in our market. Anticipating reductions in Department of Defense spending in the Hampton Roads region, the impact of the current recession on employment, and growing competition in the global marketplace, our Chamber of Commerce has developed what it calls "Plan 2007," a blueprint for the region's future economy. At Virginia Beach, a group of business and professional leaders have formed "Virginia Beach Vision," an issue-oriented organization with a mission to study areas of community concern for Virginia Beach.

Matching the vision of our extremely active Chamber of Commerce, there's Forward Hampton Roads, the Chamber's umbrella marketing and information resource organization that supports valiant municipal and state efforts to seduce large corporations to the region.

For small business, there's no lack of assistance either. The Small Business Development Center of Hampton Roads

stands ready to provide business advice, counseling and assistance at no cost. The Entrepreneurial Center at Old Dominion University is a fertile incubator for emerging companies, offering administrative and office support in the formative years of development. Lastly, there's the state of Virginia supported Center for Innovative Technology, a superlative resource for business, utilizing a worldwide data base and academic network to help business solve technology-based problems.

For more information about the state of the Hampton Roads economy, we will direct you to the following sources:

DEPARTMENTS OF ECONOMIC DEVELOPMENT

Norfolk	441-2941
Portsmouth	393-8804
Chesapeake	523-1100
Virginia Beach	499-4567
Suffolk	934-2303

HAMPTON ROADS CHAMBER OF COMMERCE

Regional Headquarters	622-2312
Norfolk Office	622-2312
Portsmouth Office	397-3453
Chesapeake Office	547-2118
Virginia Beach Office	490-1221
Suffolk Office	539-2111

OTHER EXCELLENT INFORMATION SOURCES

Forward Hampton Roads	627-2315
Small Business Development Center of Hampton Roads	622-6414
The Entrepreneurial Center/ Old Dominion University	683-3000
Better Business Bureau	627-5651

Inside
Media

Hampton Roads residents are a very nosy bunch. We want to know what's happening and where, when and why. And, we want to be thoroughly entertained . . . 24 hours a day.

No problem. In fact, Hampton Roads is one of the most fiercely competitive media markets in Virginia. In just the radio category, we can boast more stations than markets twice our size. Flip on the tube and you'll find not only the big three, but more than 50 cable channels all fighting for your attention. In print, there are daily newspapers as well as scores of weekly specialty publications that appeal to everything from parenting to partying, marine life to metaphysics, home searching to higher consciousness.

No matter what you want to know about the heartbeat of Hampton Roads, it's as close as a flick of a button, a click on the Internet or the black and white of a tabloid. Whether it's a helicopter traffic report at six in the morning or a radio talk show at midnight, plug and play into Hampton Roads' media and, in no time at all, you'll sound just like a native.

Radio

Every market has its own favorite radio personalities that they love, and love to hate. We're no different. Local celebs have earned their notoriety by a) being outspoken, b) being on-air for more years than they, or anyone else, can remember, and c) being one taco short of a combina-

tion platter. WCMS's Joe Hoppel is our answer to Mr. Country-Western, and what can we say about Henry "The Bull" Del Torro, a real piece of work whose antics on and off air match wits with the hutzpa of the Energizer Bunny.

Beach music and Bach, hard rock and sharp talk, fast jazz and easy listening . . . it's all here on your dial in Hampton Roads.

The programming listed here for each station is current as of this writing, but stations jockeying for higher ratings have been known to change formats overnight.

FM Stations

WAFX 106.9

"Classic Hits 106" keeps the beat with, naturally, round the clock classic sounds of the '70s minus the hard rock, plus local news and traffic. Boogy, boogy.

WCMS 100.5

Country music, old and new, and one of the most listened-to stations in the market. When it comes to country, no one sings a sweeter song than WCMS. ABC, local news, traffic reports, continuous.

WDCK 96.5

More oldies for your listening pleasure, plus AP and local news. Continuous.

WFOG 92.9

Always a rating leader, with easy listening that's quite a relief from hard rock.

Add in a unique blend of vocal favorites, golden oldies and light jazz. AP, local news, continuous.

WFOS 88.7

The oldest high school radio station in Virginia, WFOS, operated by the Chesapeake school system, mixes classical programming with a touch of Big Band and jazz. Mutual Broadcasting System and AP. 6 AM to midnight.

WGH 97.3

"Eagle 97" is taking the market by storm with all new country. Local news (including frequent updates direct from WAVY TV, Channel 10), continuous.

WHOV 88.3

Operated by Hampton University, this eclectic student-staffed station broadcasts some of the best jazz around, with a little classical and hot salsa thrown in for good luck. Local news, 10 AM to 1 AM.

WHRO 90.3

The mainstay of this Public Broadcasting affiliate is classical music. Local news, continuous.

WHRV 89.5

WHRO's sister station, here you'll find all your NPR favorites, like "All Things Considered," the "National Press Club" and the popular "Morning Edition." Local news, traffic reports, continuous.

WKEZ 94.1

It's time for your favorite easy listening, Big Band sounds, 24 hours a day. AP, local news and traffic.

WLSV 96.1

Contemporary Christian music is featured here.

WJQI 94.9

Q 94.9 brings us the melodies of the '80s and '90s all day and night. Local news and traffic, too.

WQSF 96.5

Easy listening, plus AP, local news, continuous.

WLTY 95.7

Oldies are us. "Oldies 95.7" features AP, UPI, local news and traffic, continuous.

WMXN 105.3

CD 105 recently switched to a "smooth jazz" format.

WKOC 93.7

A blend of old guard, offbeat and easy listening defines "The Coast," one of only 34 stations in the country playing a new format called Adult Alternative, sort of a hip, thinking person's lite FM sound, NBC and local news. Don't even think of missing their infamous Grateful Dead Hour. What a hoot.

WROX 96.1

The comer in the ever-shifting Hampton Roads radio game, you'll hear an aggressive alternative rock format. "96X" mixes college-rock classics with newer cutting-edge artists. Look for this station to be blasting loud for the surf patrol in the Summer of '95! Continuous.

WNOR 98.7

If there's a stick to the good old rock and roller in town, it's FM 99. Classic and current rock, plus bad boy Henry "The Bull" Del Torro and sidekick Tommy Griffiths get your juices going in the morning. UPI, local news and traffic, continuous.

WNSB 91.1

Jazz, Big Band and blues from Norfolk State University as well as UPI news; 7 AM to 1 AM.

WNVZ 104.5

Z-104 is for the Top-40 gang. Contemporary hits, local news and traffic around the clock.

WODC 88.5

Local and satellite ministries, along with Christian music and children's programs.

WOWI 102.9

More than 50,000 ears are tuned into No. 1-ranked 103-JAMZ every weekday morning for The Supreme Team of Chase "The Commander-in-Chief of the Base," Stan "The Man" Verrett and Cheryl Wilkerson. This station is hip all day long with urban contemporary music.

WWDE 101.3

If you want to be an Insider, catch Dick Lamb and his Breakfast Bunch every weekday morning on 2WD. Captain Crunch will get you going, with adult contemporary music filling the rest of the station's 24-hour broadcast day. CBS, local news and traffic.

WYFI 99.7

Christian music and programming, BBN, local news, continuous.

WSVY 107.7

Black urban adult music surrounds national and local news throughout the day.

AM Stations

WBSK 1350

Black urban adult music. AP, NBN and local news, continuous.

WCMS 1050

Spins country hits just like her sister station on the FM dial. ABC, local news, continuous.

WESR 1330

Christian programming and music, along with AP news from 6 AM to midnight.

WGH 1310

All sports, all day. Sports trivia nuts love John Castleberry's show in the morning named "The Score" and won't touch the dial when Tony Mercurio talks jock talk in the 3 to 6 PM slot. Cowboys football, UNC-Chapel Hill and ODU bas-

---

"I want my buz-tv" is the award-winning cry of the year. Seen on WTKR, Channel 3, Saturday nights at 11:30 and Sundays at midnight, it's a half-hour of locally produced entertainment, zapped with slick graphics, hip set and that bob 'n' weave handheld camera work that makes it so "today." Hosted by former radio jock Robert James, you'll get a real Insiders peek at oh-so-current music, restaurants, movies, fashion and cultural events, along the highlighted "Buz-band" of the week . . . local talent in an in-studio performance. Prop up those eyelids and check it out . . . it's a real local award winner.

Insiders' Tips

ketball for those who can't get tickets to the games.

WJQI 1600

Adult soft contemporary music, just like sister station Q 94.9, from sunrise to sunset.

WLPM 1450

Suffolk's only radio station recently adopted a Christian format.

WKGM 940

Christian programming and music with Satellite Radio news. Sunrise to sunset.

WNIS 850

"The Big One" is talk radio in Hampton Roads. Rush Limbaugh, *Wall Street Journal* reports, CBS, Mutual and local news, continuous.

WNOR 1230

Catch the simulcast of "The Bull" on 1230 each weekday morning, then settle in for '60s and '70s hits for the rest of the day. UPI and local news.

WPCE 1400

Political and religious leader Bishop L. E. Willis calls the shots at this station for gospel programming. Sheridan Broadcasting. Continuous.

WPMH 1010

Inspirational music and programs. USA radio news. 6 AM to 9 PM.

WTAR 790

The oldest radio station in town, 790 holds the attention of music-weary Baby Boomers. The lineup includes G. Gordon Liddy, ESPN and NBC news, Dow Jones and local talk. Continuous.

WTJZ 1270

Black contemporary inspirational. Read "gospel." Plus NBN, sports and local news. Continuous.

Television

Along with enough channels to make your VCR groan, Hampton Roads is home to several major electronic media companies. International Family Entertainment, based in Virginia Beach, owns

The Family Channel, one of the top-10 cable channels in the country, which puts out popular original programming. IFM is, in turn, owned by Christian Broadcast Network (CBN) patriarch Pat Robertson and son Tim, and although it shares the CBN complex, it is a for-profit company totally independent of the nonprofit CBN.

CBN is a worldwide network of Christian stations, most famous for it's popular "700 Club," produced at state-of-the-art facilities in Virginia Beach. If you'd like to watch a live taping of the show and take a tour of the studios, just call 424-7777 for ticket availability.

We've listed the television stations below in order of appearance on your dial.

WTKR CBS/CHANNEL 3

The first television channel to sign on the air in Hampton Roads, CBS affiliate WTKR has been benched with the network's loss of NFL football. It does score big with its long-respected news reporting, anchored by media veteran Ed Hughes, with more than a quarter-century of broadcast experience. If you hate to wait for your evening news, WTKR starts off the evening news marathon at 4:30, along with the succinct "Eleven at Eleven," which gives sleepy-heads 11 minutes of uninterrupted news, weather and sports at the eleven o'clock hour.

WAVY NBC/CHANNEL 10

All your favorite NBC hits are here, from "The Today Show" to "Tonight with Jay Leno," along with a young, aggressive and well-respected local anchor team and an attractive bunch of news, weather and sports professionals.

WVEC ABC/CHANNEL 13

This is the place where local sports fans park each Monday night during foot-ball season to bring Al, Dan and Frank into their TV locker rooms for "Monday Night Football." It's also the place where the Godfather of local news anchors, Jim Kincaid, shares his insightful "notes" on current events and responds to viewers' letters at the conclusion of the 5:30 PM broadcast. Kincaid's folksy delivery, backed by his decades of solid, international news reporting experience, epitomizes the station's themeline of "The Spirit of Hampton Roads."

WHRO PBS/CHANNEL 15

Our Public Broadcasting affiliate and champion of exceptional children's, educational and how-to programming. Catch Big Bird on "Sesame Street," the news team on "McNeil-Lehrer News Hour" and numerous specials on nature, the performing arts and more. WHRO has also produced many award-winning educational shows that have been seen around the country.

WGNT INDEPENDENT/CHANNEL 27

Catch your syndicated favorites on this independent station, along with The "700 Club" with Pat Robertson and troop. In fact, this is the station, formerly known as WYAH, where Dr. Robertson launched his television ministry career.

WTVZ INDEPENDENT/CHANNEL 33

While Channel 33 is an independent station, here's where you'll find your favorite programming from the FOX Network, including NFL football.

Cable TV

More than 50 channels zip right into your home when you're cable connected, ranging from MTV to good old CNN and A&E. HBO, Showtime and Cinemax are popular premium add-ons, and pay-per-view is slowly establishing a following, especially for sports freaks who are denied access to ultimate showdowns in regular programming. Several cable companies operate in Hampton Roads. Contact the one that services your city for specific rates and installation fees.

Cox Cable, Norfolk, Virginia Beach, Portsmouth, 497-2011

Tele-Communications of Virginia, Inc., Chesapeake, 424-6660

Virginia Beach Cable Television, Virginia Beach Oceanfront, 425-0586

Falcon Cable TV, Suffolk, 539-2312

Online

Whatever you can find in print, you can find online, courtesy of InfiNet, a joint venture of Landmark Communications Inc. and Wyvern Technologies. Computer users armed with a modem can venture out into cyperspace and gather tips and tidbits ranging from classified ads (even before they hit the newsprint!), to real estate info courtesy of local real estate companies, and to electronic shopping with the region's leading retailing entrepreneurs. For all the details on subscribing, call InfiNet at 622-4289.

Newspapers and Magazines

What flavor do you want? Hip-speak on the hot band that's playing this weekend? Who's making the social scene in big style? How to potty-train without angst? These, and answers to many other pressing questions, will be answered to the fullest in one of Hampton Roads' newspapers and tabloid magazines. From the plethora of specialized publications that come (and sometimes go) from our market from week to week, you can be sure that if you're thirsty for knowledge,

you'll not have any farther to go than your local grocery store's pickup rack to take a big drink. Here are the major pubs that appear with continuity, offering different spins on their respective themes and keeping all of us abreast of the newest, latest, hottest and most controversial subjects in the community.

Of special note to those who, because of disabilities, cannot see or hold printed material, Hampton Roads Voice is a free reading service heard on public radio station WHRV FM. The 24-hour service is supplemented by programming from Touch Network based in New York and provides daily readings of local, regional and national newspapers, special publications, monthly magazines and periodicals. Special equipment is needed to receive the closed circuit programming, and there is a waiting list. For more information call 489-9476 or 881-9476.

THE VIRGINIAN PILOT/LEDGER-STAR

The daily newspaper serving all of Hampton Roads, now with a full-color, highly graphic format.

What you might miss in *The Virginian-Pilot* in the morning, you'll catch in its afternoon sister, the *Ledger-Star*. Owned by Norfolk-based media giant Landmark Communications, it's basically the only "daily" game in town for both news lovers and advertisers. With the largest circulation of any daily newspaper in Virginia, *The Virginian-Pilot*, along with the *Ledger*, has a long tradition of excellence, with even a few Pulitzers to its credit. What it lacks for in competition is competently made up for in special interest supplements . . . community-oriented tabloids for each of the five Southside cities.

For TV couch potatoes, there's the "Green Sheet," the ultimate TV listing guide each Saturday. And, for those who must party, party, party, check out "Preview" each Friday for all upcoming performances and complete movie and theater listings and reviews.

Pin-striped suit types get a full dose of business news each Monday in "Business Weekly." Anyone house hunting must have the latest copy of Saturday's "Real Estate Weekly" for the latest on-the-market reports as well as updated mortgage information from local lenders.

Community tabloids that focus on the haps in a smaller spectrum, and are published along with both morning and evening editions include:

Norfolk   *The Compass*
Virginia Beach *The Beacon*
Portsmouth   *Currents*
Chesapeake   *Clipper*
Suffolk   *The Sun*

THE SUFFOLK NEWS-HERALD
*Daily newspaper for Suffolk
and surrounding areas*

A general interest newspaper, *The News-Herald* features local happenings along with major international news of the day. It's at racks throughout the city or by subscription.

PORT FOLIO
*Lifestyle Magazine, published
by Landmark Communications*

Don't let the fact that it's a free weekly fool you. This is the "bible" for those on the way up . . . and for those who are already there. Along with timely cover stories that highlight (or expose) a local personality or event, inside is a wealth of info about where to dine, to party and to meet the person of your dreams. Make sure you check out the first edition of every month. Inside is "Home," a voyeur's peek inside some of the most gracious and glamorous homes in the area. And, then there's

the monthly "Health & Fitness" special, packed with all the information to make you feel guilty if you're not running laps before work. All in all, it's a slick piece of work that never fails to come up with topical, fascinating tales about who's making news in Hampton Roads.

BYERLY PUBLICATIONS
Weekly community newspapers

Byerly has long been known for its commitment to the important little things in life, like what's going on next door. Cover to cover, these are decisively hometown papers, and a must for newcomers who want to get the full, and positive, picture of their new community. The Byerly publications include:

The Chesapeake Post, published each Wednesday
The Portsmouth Times, published each Thursday
The Virginia Beach Sun, published each Wednesday

VIRGINIA BUSINESS MAGAZINE

Here's a statewide publication targeted at our slice of corporate America. Special editorial sections on travel, hospitality and the medical industry, to name a few, are especially helpful to a newcomer trying to get a firm handle on the workings of our business community.

REAL ESTATE MAGAZINES

Even if you've snagged the best Realtor in town, there are a number of real estate publications to help you focus before jumping in the car for the major open house assault. All are free and multiplying at a rack at the grocery or drug store nearest you.

They include: *Home Search, Harmon Homes, Real Estate Digest, For Sale By Owner* and the Tidewater Builders Associations' *New Homes* and *Apartment Guides*.

Specialty Publications

There are numerous specialty publications in our market, each dealing with a specific hobby, avocation or interest. While some rise and fall within the blink of an eye, those that endue are all are free and available at racks throughout the cities of Hampton Roads. Some of the most popular still rolling off the presses at this writing include:

FLASH

This will tell you where to go and when to be there to make the music scene in town. With caustic rock notes, hot disc reviews, rock flash calendar and ads from the leading lyrical places in Hampton Roads.

VIRGINIA PATHWAYS

For those seeking guidance from a source other than the Insiders' Guide, this alternative monthly for holistic thought is for you. New agers will want to journey afar to snag the latest issue, filled with remarkably insightful dialog concerning higher consciousness of body, soul and spirit.

INSYTE MAGAZINE

Devoted to African-American culture and news, *InSyte* covers the gamut from movie and book review to fashion to political affairs.

TIDEWATER PARENT

Anyone living with a human person under three feet tall should tuck a copy of this pub in the diaper bag. Published monthly, it is the definitive guide to child-rearing in Hampton Roads, with articles aimed at education, constructive play and mommy-relief.

THE COMPASS ROSE

The boating services guide for Hampton Roads and the lower Chesapeake, don't leave shore with out it. Marinas, dockside dining guide and boat-accessible calendar of events are all here.

STARBOARD TACK

Sailing the Chesapeake and beyond is the theme song for this free tabloid available at local marinas, yacht clubs and waterlogged restaurants. It includes everything from the galley sink for the novice and experienced sailor.

Inside
Worship

There are more than 500 churches and synagogues in Hampton Roads — enough to fill nine pages of listings in the Yellow Pages directory. Worship options range from established mainline churches that are centuries old to nondenominational congregations started only a few years ago.

In recent years area churches and synagogues have seen a resurgence of young families coming back to the religion they abandoned during their teenage and college years. Many churches have been quick to respond to the needs of these younger members. Potluck family dinners, parenting classes, strong youth programs and free babysitting during committee meetings are just a few of the inducements that help keep the 30-something crowd hooked on religion.

Hampton Roads' religious heritage is more than 300 years old. In 1637 the Colonial government established the Elizabeth River Parish of the Anglican church. The parish's first church was built in 1641 at what is now Norfolk Naval Base and was called "Ye Chappell of Ease."

A 1637 entry in the records of Lower Norfolk County, which yielded Virginia Beach and other area cities, ordered that a "penance of the church" be carried out by a local resident. At the time church services in the county were held in private homes, but in 1639 Lynnhaven Parish church was built in what is now Virginia Beach.

Until the Revolutionary War began in 1776, the Anglican religion was the only one officially recognized in British-controlled Virginia. However, Rev.

Historic St. Paul's Church still holds a cannonball embedded in its wall from the British attack on Norfolk in 1776.

Frances Makemie introduced the Presbyterian religion to Norfolk while living here between 1684 and 1692. In Norfolk, First Presbyterian Church on Colonial Avenue traces its roots to The Church on the Elizabeth River, which was founded before 1678.

Today there is still an Anglican church in Newport News. But there are also dozens of other religions represented here — from African Methodist Episcopal Zion to United Pentecostal. Besides the basic Baptist, Catholic, Episcopal, Jewish, Lutheran, Methodist, Presbyterian and Unitarian churches, there are numerous nondenominational churches. The region also has congregations affiliated with the Friends, Greek Orthodox, Mennonite and Muslim religions. Jewish synagogues include conservative, messianic, orthodox and reformed congregations. Temple Beth El on the outskirts of Suffolk dates from the early 1900s and is noted for having a congregation composed of African-American Jews.

Congregations range greatly in size. Some have fewer than 50 members while others' rolls number in the thousands. Among the largest are First Baptist Church of Norfolk, Atlantic Shores Baptist Church and the Rock Church. All are in the Kempsville area of Virginia Beach

and Norfolk. First Baptist has 6,000 members and relocated to the suburbs from downtown Norfolk in 1970. Already cramped for space, it is planning to build on 45 acres in Chesapeake. Atlantic Shores is an independent Baptist church with about 5,000 members. Rock Church is nondenominational with about 3,000 members. Anticipating more growth, it is building a new 5,200-seat sanctuary. One of the fastest-growing congregations is Calvary Revival Church of Norfolk with 3,000 members.

One major influence on the area's religion is having The Christian Broadcasting Network based in Virginia Beach. CBN's world headquarters includes studios that broadcast worldwide the "700 Club" TV talk show hosted by Rev. M.G. "Pat" Robertson, CBN's founder. Robertson's home is on the Georgian-style CBN campus as is Regent University, the Founders Inn and Conference Center and the Family Channel cable network. Although CBN isn't affiliated with any one religion, it has hundreds of employees and many followers in the region who lean toward fundamentalist churches. Therefore, there are many churches in the populous Kempsville area near CBN.

If you're a newcomer, finding the right church involves visiting various ones to see what suits your needs. Get recommendations from friends and neighbors and scout out your neighborhood to see what churches are nearby. Then take your time attending services and classes and getting to know the members.

You can learn more about area churches by reading *The Virginian-Pilot/Ledger-Star's* Saturday religion page. Besides discussing topics of current interest, it includes listings of upcoming special programs and services at area churches. For recommendations on specific churches, contact the following offices of religious organizations:

Baha'i Faith	467-4008
Catholic Diocese of Richmond	588-2941
Church of Jesus Christ of Latter Day Saints	488-2239
Episcopal Diocese of Southern Virginia	423-8287
Lutheran Council of Tidewater	622-0125
Norfolk Baptist Association	463-6525
Presbytery of Eastern Virginia	423-2193
United Jewish Federation of Tidewater	489-8040
United Methodist Church, Norfolk District	473-1592

Some of the region's older churches have fascinating architecture and are a real treat to see. The downtown areas of Norfolk, Portsmouth and Suffolk have a concentration of massive church buildings dating from the late 19th and early 20th centuries. The following are some of the more historic churches.

Norfolk

•Christ and St. Luke's Church, Olney Road and Stockley Gardens, 627-5665. Originally known as Christ Church, this Episcopal church is noted for its Gothic Revival architecture. It was built in Ghent around 1910 at the end of the Hague and features an ornate square bell tower.

•Freemason Street Baptist Church, Freemason and Bank streets, 625-7579. Dedicated in 1850, Freemason Street Baptist is Norfolk's oldest Baptist church and a marvel of Gothic Revival architecture. Its architect was Thomas U. Walter of Philadelphia, who designed the United States Capitol dome as well as what are now the MacArthur Memorial and Hampton Roads Chamber of Commerce headquarters in Norfolk. When the church was built it was renowned for its steeple, which had dozens of weather vanes and was the tallest structure in town. After a storm blew it down in 1879, the steeple was replaced with only one weather vane.

•St. Mary's Catholic Church, 232 Chapel Street, 622-4487. This is Norfolk's oldest and most elaborate Catholic church. Built in the French Gothic Revival style, its majestic steeples are a downtown landmark. The current church was built in 1858 to replace one that burned. Inside are elaborate paintings, marble sculptures and stained-glass windows. One noted architect who visited the church in the early 1900s called St. Mary's "the best antebellum Gothic workmanship in the South."

•St. Paul's Episcopal Church, 201 St. Paul's Boulevard, 627-4353. The church was built in 1739 and is the city's oldest building. After the burning of Norfolk in 1776, St. Paul's was the only building left standing. The church still has a Revolutionary War cannon ball wedged in one exterior wall and retains its original box pews and Colonial appearance. It also is noted for its stained-glass windows. A bell tower was added in 1901. Outside, a brick wall surrounds a peaceful, burial ground shaded by giant live oaks. The sanctuary is usually open to visitors. A detailed brochure makes it easy to take a self-guided tour.

• Epworth United Methodist Church, 124 W. Freemason Street, 622-2970. Built in 1894, this massive downtown church is granite and sandstone with a bell tower that still chimes hymns several times daily. It is an outstanding example of the Romanesque Revival architectural style.

Virginia Beach

• Nimmo United Methodist Church, 2200 Princess Anne Road, 427-1765. This is a traditional white-frame church that sits in the rural part of Virginia Beach on the way to Pungo. It was built in 1791 on land purchased for five shillings from Anne Nimmo. Although the building has had several additions, it retains its original charm.

• Old Donation Episcopal Church, 4449 N. Witchduck Road, 497-0563. This is the only surviving Colonial church in what was Princess Anne County. Originally part of the Church of England, it affiliated with the new Protestant Episcopal Church of Virginia in 1785. Except for holding about one service a year, the church was abandoned for 40 years until 1882. The current building is the third one on the same site. It is a classic structure built in 1916. The church still owns several silver communion pieces from the early 18th century.

Chesapeake

• Oak Grove United Methodist Church, 472 N. Battlefield Boulevard, 547-2319. Founded in a home in 1770, this is one of the oldest churches in what was Norfolk County. It became a Meth-

odist church in 1840 and gained a permanent home two years later when a small structure was put on wheels and rolled a mile to the present location. The current church dates from 1852. The traditional white frame structure shares its design with Christ Church in Alexandria and Old St. John's Church in New York.

Portsmouth

• Emmanuel AME Church, 637 North Street, 393-2259. This is a historically black church whose congregation dates back to 1772 when it was a Methodist Episcopal Church. In 1871 the congregation affiliated with the African Methodist Episcopal Church. The red brick church dates to 1791. The interior features elaborate stained-glass windows and hand-carving, much of it created by slaves.

• Monumental United Methodist Church, 450 Dinwiddie Street, 397-1297. This was the first Methodist congregation in Portsmouth, and its roots extend to 1772 when Portsmouth residents heard the first Methodist sermon preached south of the Potomac. The church was built in 1876 after another building was destroyed by fire.

• St. Paul's Catholic Church, 518 High Street, 397-7066. Established in 1824, St. Paul's has had several buildings. This one is built of stone in an elaborate Gothic style with flying buttresses. The granite church was completed in 1897.

• Trinity Episcopal, 500 Court Street, 393-0431. The church dates to 1762. It sits on land designated in 1752 for a church when the city of Portsmouth was first laid out. Outstanding features include Tiffany windows, an 18th-century burial ground and a brick wall around the churchyard that dates to the 1820s. The church has a stained-glass window dedicated in 1868 in memory of those who died ". . . in defense of their native state, Virginia, against invasion by the U.S. Forces." Protests by the U.S. Navy forced the church to remove the window and edit its anti-Union message. The replacement window installed in 1870 is still there. However, the offending message is framed and resting on the windowsill.

Suffolk

• First Baptist Church, 237 N. Main Street, 539-4152. The church was organized in 1827 with its first building constructed a year later. The current brick church was built in 1890 in a typical style of the day with an elaborate sanctuary.

• Glebe Episcopal Church, 4400 Nansemond Parkway, and St. John's Episcopal Church, 828 Kings Highway, 255-4168. These two small churches are part of the same parish and are the only Colonial-era churches remaining in Suffolk. The Glebe Church was built in 1738 and replaced an earlier structure. St. John's Church was the third built on this site. It was completed in 1756 and remodeled in 1888 to the appearance it has today.

• Main Street Methodist Church, 202 N. Main Street, 539-8751. Modeled after a cathedral in England, this church was constructed in 1914. Its congregation dates to 1801, making it the oldest Methodist church in Suffolk. The red brick building has 14 stained-glass windows.

Photo: Portsmouth Convention and Visitors Bureau

The Portsmouth lightship was commissioned in 1915 to help mariners navigate through treacherous waters.

Inside
The Military

The minute you arrive in Hampton Roads you likely will know this is a military community. But in case you're not sure, here are some clues:

• If you flew in, chances are good that you spotted at least a few Navy uniforms on the plane.

• If you're driving into downtown Norfolk or Portsmouth, you'll see gray-hulled Navy battleships docked at ship repair yards. A hodgepodge of shipyard cranes stand at attention ready to lower supplies to workers.

• Cross the Hampton Roads Bridge-Tunnel from Hampton to Norfolk and you can glimpse ships anchored at Norfolk Naval Base.

• Look skyward in Virginia Beach and you'll probably spot a trail from an F-14 Tomcat or other fighter plane based at Oceana Naval Air Station.

• Arrive here by private boat, and you'll glide past miles of shipyards and Navy bases that hug the shoreline.

With this visual introduction, it won't take long to learn that Norfolk Naval Base is the largest Navy base in the world. Team it up with all the other branches of the Armed Forces located here — Army, Marine Corps, Air Force and Coast Guard — and you have the United States' largest concentration of military might.

Throughout the entire region there are more than 134,000 military personnel, 59,000 civilian Department of Defense workers and an estimated 44,000 military retirees. The region has seven of the country's largest military installations. Its 20 shipyards, which rely heavily on military business, are the United States' biggest concentration of repair yards.

Norfolk is headquarters for the North Atlantic Treaty Organization command that oversees the Atlantic area. Attached to the NATO command are military officers from the 16 member nations who come here to live and work.

In 1993 the Department of Defense spent more than $7 billion in the region, making the military the backbone of the economy. Virginia typically ranks at least third in the country in Department of Defense spending with the bulk of allocations going to Hampton Roads and Northern Virginia. On a per capita basis, Virginia is frequently first in defense expenditures.

The region's history is intertwined with that of the Revolutionary War, World War I, World War II and every other major war or conflict (see the History chapter). During Operation Desert Storm in 1990 and 1991, more than 40,000 military personnel shipped out to the Persian Gulf and stifled the local economy. Before the battle groups left, ship repair yards, ship chandlers and other local companies worked around the clock to gear up for war. When the war heroes returned in 1991, they were greeted by thunderous celebrations not seen here since the end of World War II.

With the federal Base Realignment and Closure Commission evaluating all aspects of the military to find ways to make it more efficient, Hampton Roads officials have united to preserve their region's military might. Hampton Roads made it through relatively unscathed during the military cutbacks recommended in 1994 and 1995. Only a few regional operations are slated to close, and Hampton Roads gained installations and personnel shifted from other parts of the country.

Local optimists believe the region will continue to benefit as obscure bases in other parts of the country are consolidated into larger operations like the ones we have here. The Hampton Roads Planning District Commission study gives some credence to that idea by showing that in 1971 less than 3.9 percent of the United States' armed forces were stationed in Hampton Roads. By 1990 that percentage had grown to more than 5 percent.

The region received good news in early 1993 when Norfolk became the training center for all joint military operations. This makes Norfolk's military community second in prominence only to the Pentagon.

The military gives Hampton Roads a unique flavor. Your neighbors will be people who have lived all over the world. However, they may move away within a few years to new duty stations. The comings and goings of large battle groups affect everything from rush hour traffic to business at area malls.

The following are the region's major military bases:

NORFOLK NAVAL BASE

This complex is in the Sewells Point area of Norfolk. It got its start in 1917 after when the U.S. government purchased 474 acres of the old Jamestown Exposition Site for a Navy base. Another 300 acres were soon added by filling in adjacent waterways, and the base has expanded from there.

The base's naval station is homeport for more than 90 ships. During the year there are about 5,000 arrivals and departures from the station's 15 piers. Nearby is a submarine base that has 25 subs homeported there. The Naval Air Station is home to about 40 aircraft squadrons. With an aircraft taking off or landing every three minutes, this is one of the world's busiest airports.

The Navy Public Works Center supports numerous shore activities, while the Fleet Industrial Supply Center keeps ships throughout the world stocked

What Does That Spell?

The military loves acronyms. Some local signs look like someone shook up a bunch of letters and let them tumble out. Here's a primer that will help you decipher this alphabet soup.

CINCLANT or CINCLANTFLT — Commander-in-Chief Atlantic Fleet.

FASOTRAGRULANT Det Oceana — Fleet Aviation Specialized Operational Training Group, Atlantic Fleet, Detachment Oceana.

FCTCLANT — Fleet Combat Training Center, Atlantic, Dam Neck.

NADEP — Naval Aviation Depot.

NAMTRAGRUDETS — Naval Air Maintenance Training Group Detachment.

NAS — Naval Air Station.

NAVFACLANTDIV — Atlantic Division of the Naval Facilities Engineer Command.

NAVPHIBASE — Naval Amphibious Base, Little Creek.

NSC — Naval Supply Center.

SACLANT — North Atlantic Treaty Organization's Supreme Allied Commander, Atlantic.

USACOM — U.S. Atlantic Command.

---

with more than 600,000 different items.

Other major commands include:

• The Naval Aviation Depot (NADEP), whose 2,900 employees work in 75 buildings doing maintenance, engineering and other services to support naval aviation.

• The Atlantic Division of the Naval Facilities Engineering Command (NAVFACLANTDIV).

• The Training Command of the U.S. Atlantic Fleet (TRACOM)

• The Fleet Training Center (FTC).

Located just down the road from the base are the headquarters for the Commander-in-Chief Atlantic Fleet (CINCLANT), which commands more than 136,125 personnel. The command supplies and services more than 197 ships and 1,405 aircraft.

Adjacent to the Atlantic Fleet headquarters is that of NATO's Supreme Allied Commander Atlantic (SACLANT). This command watches over ships and personnel in 12 million square miles of Atlantic Ocean — from the North Pole to the Tropic of Cancer and from North America to Europe and Africa. Next to the Atlantic Fleet headquarters is U.S. Atlantic Command (USACOM), whose major function is to train forces from various branches of the Armed Force as joint units so they can work together during times of war.

LITTLE CREEK
NAVAL AMPHIBIOUS BASE

This is the major base for the amphibious forces of the United States Atlantic Fleet. It is home to about 30 ships. The Norfolk base is on 11,000 acres next to

Help for Newcomers

The best source of information for new military families is Navy Family Services Center. It has a wealth of information and services for Navy and Marine Corp members and their dependents. The center has a Relocation Assistance Unit that has welcome packets and other information. If you get here ahead of your household goods, you can rent cookware, cribs, cots and other necessities.

Navy Family Services also has information on child care, jobs for spouses, counseling and many other services. The center is at 8910 Hampton Boulevard in Norfolk. Call 444-2102 or (800) FSC-LINE. To reach the center's 24-hour hotline, call 444-NAVY.

If you arrive here by flying into Norfolk International Airport, look for the Airport Information Booth. There usually is a Navy representative stationed there to answer questions and help get you going in the right direction. There also is a Navy Welcome Center in Janaf Shopping Center in Norfolk.

To help get you oriented read some of the free weekly or bi-weekly newspapers geared toward the military, available on base, in shopping centers and other public areas. *The Flagship*, published by local media giant Landmark Communication, is the official Navy publication. It is published every Thursday. Other military-related papers are *Soundings*, *Navy News*, the *Jet Observer* and *The Wheel*. Each Wednesday, *The Virginian Pilot* and *Ledger-Star* include a military page as part of their editions.

the Chesapeake Bay. It is the East Coast base for the Landing Craft Air Cushion craft (LCAC).

OCEANA NAVAL AIR STATION

This is home to the Navy's East Coast squadrons of F-14 Tomcats and A-6 Intruders. Twenty squadrons operate out of the 5,000-acre complex in Virginia Beach. This master jet base has a plane land or take off every two minutes.

FLEET COMBAT TRAINING CENTER, DAM NECK

This 1,100-acre oceanfront base has one of the best beaches in the area. Its real purpose, however, is to teach young recruits or boot camp survivors. It has a curriculum of more than 100 courses offered to about 15,000 sailors a year.

NORFOLK NAVAL SHIPYARD, PORTSMOUTH

In 1994 the shipyard celebrated its 227th anniversary, making it the country's oldest naval shipyard. It occupies a 5-mile stretch along the Southern Branch of the Elizabeth River in Portsmouth and has more than 200 buildings. The yard has the country's oldest dry dock, which opened in 1833. It employs about 7,700 workers who repair and improve everything from missile systems to berthing compartments on Navy ships.

NAVAL SECURITY GROUP ACTIVITY NORTHWEST

This activity operates on 4,500 acres in Chesapeake. It is a high-security intelligence base that monitors communications from around the world. Both Navy and Coast Guard personnel work here.

PORTSMOUTH NAVAL HOSPITAL

This is the oldest Navy hospital in the United States and is the second-largest one in the country. Its first patients were admitted in 1830. The 500-bed hospital has a full range of services and operates several clinics. This hospital is in the midst of a $330 million renovation and construction project that will include a new 464-bed hospital to be completed in 2001.

ARMED FORCES STAFF COLLEGE

The college is part of the National Defense University, which started in 1946. Its Norfolk campus prepares mid-career officers for joint and combined staffs duty during six overlapping sessions a year. Each has about 120 students who come for three months of intense study.

FORT STORY

This Virginia Beach Army base is located where the Chesapeake Bay meets the Atlantic Ocean at Cape Henry. It was created in 1917 and has 1,451 acres that include a great beach that is open to the public on weekends. The base is an in-stallation of the U.S. Army Transportation Center Fort Eustis in Newport News. Fort Story's military and civilian workers primarily maintain amphibious craft.

FIFTH COAST GUARD DISTRICT

The district is headquartered in Portsmouth and coordinates lifesaving efforts in the waters off Virginia, Maryland, North Carolina and the District of Columbia.

U.S. ARMY CORPS OF ENGINEERS

The Corps of Engineers' Norfolk District headquarters oversees several field offices around the state. The corps is involved in dredging and in issuing permits for construction in wetland and coastal areas. The office has more than 300 employees, most of them civilians.

CAMP PENDLETON STATE MILITARY RESERVATION

Camp Pendleton is used mainly as an air defense artillery range. It is in Virginia Beach on the oceanfront and is the Virginia National Guard's summer train-

A youngster poses for a shot with sailors at Norfolk Naval Base.

ing camp. Its 120 buildings can hold 1,700 troops.

PENINSULA BASES

Across the Hampton Roads Bridge-Tunnel are several other major bases that are included in the region's military complex. They are the Yorktown Naval Weapons Station in Yorktown, Langley Air Force Base in Hampton, Fort Eustis in Newport News and Fort Monroe in Hampton. Both Fort Eustis and Fort Monroe are Army bases. Newport News also has Newport News Shipbuilding, a private company that makes aircraft carriers and submarines. With more than 20,000 employees the shipyard is the state's largest private employer.

Inside

Service Directory

Community Service Information

BATTERED WOMAN'S HOTLINES
Norfolk	625-5570
Portsmouth	393-9449
Virginia Beach	430-2120
Eastern Shore	787-1329

DENTIST REFERRAL
Virginia Beach	481-4516
Norfolk	627-8534

INFORMATION CENTER OF HAMPTON ROADS
625-4543

POLICE
911

RED CROSS LANGUAGE BANK
Translators   446-7760, 446-7756

RESPONSE — SEXUAL ASSAULT SUPPORT GROUP
622-4300

TIDEWATER AIDS CRISIS TASK FORCE
626-1027

VIRGINIA FAMILY VIOLENCE HOTLINE
(800) 838-8238

VOLUNTEER CONNECTION
624-2400

UNITED WAY OF SOUTH HAMPTON ROADS
629-0500

UNITED WAY HELP LINE
627-1000

MEDICAL EMERGENCY
911

ASK A NURSE
398-4454

POISON CONTROL CENTER
(800) 552-6337

Physician Referral Services

Norfolk	622-1421
Virginia Beach	481-4516, 398-4454
Portsmouth	398-2131, 398-4454
Children	628-7500
Regional	(800) SENTARA

Regional Resources

BETTER BUSINESS BUREAU
627-5651

FORWARD HAMPTON ROADS
(Economic development)
627-2315

HAMPTON ROADS CHAMBER OF COMMERCE
Headquarters	622-2312
Chesapeake office	547-2118
Norfolk office	622-2312
Portsmouth office	397-3453
Suffolk office	539-2111
Virginia Beach office	490-1221

HAMPTON ROADS
PLANNING DISTRICT COMMISSION
420-8300

Retirement Services

AMERICAN ASSOCIATION
OF RETIRED PERSONS (AARP)
625-4577

SOUTHEASTERN VIRGINIA AREAWIDE
MODEL PROGRAM (SEVAMP)
461-9481

Surfing Information

SURFING REGULATIONS
428-9133

SURF REPORT
428-0404, 422-8823

Tourism Information

AAA OF TIDEWATER VIRGINIA
Chesapeake office   *547-9741*
Norfolk office   *622-5634*
Portsmouth office   *393-6471*
Virginia Beach office   *340-7271*
Emergency   *622-4321, 340-0533,*
                 397-5941, 547-9742

CHINCOTEAGUE CHAMBER
OF COMMERCE
336-6161

NORFOLK CONVENTION
& VISITORS BUREAU
441-5266, (800) 368-3097

NORFOLK VISITOR
INFORMATION CENTER
441-1852

PORTSMOUTH CONVENTION
AND VISITORS BUREAU
393-5327, (800) PORTSVA

VIRGINIA'S EASTERN SHORE
TOURISM COMMISSION
787-2460

VIRGINIA BEACH
DEPARTMENT OF CONVENTION
AND VISITOR DEVELOPMENT
437-4700, (800) 446-8038
For hotel reservations   *(800) VABEACH*

VIRGINIA BEACH VISITOR
INFORMATION CENTER
437-4888

Transportation Services

AMTRAK
(800) 872-7245

CHESAPEAKE MUNICIPAL AIRPORT
421-9000

HAMPTON ROADS AIRPORT
488-1687

HAMPTON ROADS BRIDGE-TUNNEL
Information line   *640-0055*

NORFOLK AIRPORT SHUTTLE
857-1231

NORFOLK INTERNATIONAL AIRPORT
857-3200

SUFFOLK MUNICIPAL AIRPORT
539-8295

TIDEWATER REGIONAL TRANSIT (TRT)
640-6300

Utilities

BELL ATLANTIC TELEPHONE
954-6222

COX CABLE
497-2011

FALCON CABLE TV
539-2312

VIRGINIA BEACH CABLE CO.
425-0586

HAMPTON ROADS
SANITATION DISTRICT
460-2491

VIRGINIA NATURAL GAS
466-5550

VIRGINIA POWER
858-4670

SOUTHEASTERN PUBLIC
SERVICE AUTHORITY
(Recycling)   *420-4700*

WATERWORKS

Chesapeake	*547-6352*
Norfolk	*441-2334*
Portsmouth	*393-8524*
Suffolk	*925-6390*
Virginia Beach	*427-4631*

TCI OF VIRGINIA
424-6660

Index of Advertisers

Index

ORDER FORM
Fast and Simple!

Mail to:	Or:
Insiders Guides®, Inc.	**for VISA or**
P.O. Drawer 2057	**Mastercard orders call**
Manteo, NC 27954	**1-800-765-BOOK**

Name _____

Address _____

City/State/Zip _____

Qty.	Title/Price	Shipping	Amount
	Insiders' Guide to Richmond/$14.95	$3.00	
	Insiders' Guide to Williamsburg/$12.95	$3.00	
	Insiders' Guide to Virginia's Blue Ridge/$14.95	$3.00	
	Insiders' Guide to Virginia's Chesapeake Bay/$14.95	$3.00	
	Insiders' Guide to Washington, DC/$14.95	$3.00	
	Insiders' Guide to North Carolina's Outer Banks/$14.95	$3.00	
	Insiders' Guide to Wilmington, NC/$14.95	$3.00	
	Insiders' Guide to North Carolina's Crystal Coast/$12.95	$3.00	
	Insiders' Guide to Charleston, SC/$12.95	$3.00	
	Insiders' Guide to Myrtle Beach/$14.95	$3.00	
	Insiders' Guide to Mississippi/$14.95	$3.00	
	Insiders' Guide to Boca Raton & the Palm Beaches/$14.95 (8/95)	$3.00	
	Insiders' Guide to Sarasota/Bradenton/$12.95	$3.00	
	Insiders' Guide to Northwest Florida/$14.95	$3.00	
	Insiders' Guide to Lexington, KY/$12.95	$3.00	
	Insiders' Guide to Louisville/$12.95	$3.00	
	Insiders' Guide to the Twin Cities/$12.95	$3.00	
	Insiders' Guide to Boulder/$12.95	$3.00	
	Insiders' Guide to Denver/$12.95	$3.00	
	Insiders' Guide to The Civil War (Eastern Theater)/$14.95	$3.00	
	Insiders' Guide to North Carolina's Mountains/$14.95	$3.00	
	Insiders' Guide to Atlanta/$14.95	$3.00	
	Insiders' Guide to Branson/$14.95 (12/95)	$3.00	
	Insiders' Guide to Cincinnati/$14.95 (9/95)	$3.00	
	Insiders' Guide to Tampa/St. Petersburg/$14.95 (12/95)	$3.00	

Payment in full (check or money order) must
accompany this order form.
Please allow 2 weeks for delivery.

N.C. residents add 6% sales tax _____

Total _____

Who you are
and what you think
is important to us.

**Fill out the coupon and we'll give you
an Insiders' Guide® for half price ($6.48 off)**

Which book(s) did you buy? _____

Where do you live? _____

In what city did you buy your book? _____

Where did you buy your book? ❏ catalog ❏ bookstore ❏ newspaper ad

❏ retail shop ❏ other _____

How often do you travel? ❏ yearly ❏ bi-annually ❏ quarterly

❏ more than quarterly

Did you buy your book because you were ❏ moving ❏ vacationing

❏ wanted to know more about your home town ❏ other _____

Will the book be used by ❏ family ❏ couple ❏ individual ❏ group

What is you annual household income? ❏ under $25,000 ❏ $25,000 to $35,000

❏ $35,000 to $50,000 ❏ $50,000 to $75,000 ❏ over $75,000

How old are you? ❏ under 25 ❏ 25-35 ❏ 36-50 ❏ 51-65 ❏ over 65

Did you use the book before you left for your destination? ❏ yes ❏ no

Did you use the book while at your destination? ❏ yes ❏ no

On average per month, how many times do you refer to your book? ❏ 1-3 ❏ 4-7

❏ 8-11 ❏ 12-15 ❏ 16 and up

On average, how many other people use your book? ❏ no others ❏ 1 ❏ 2

❏ 3 ❏ 4 or more

Is there anything you would like to tell us about Insiders' Guides? _____

_____

_____

Name _____ Address _____

City _____ State _____ Zip _____

**We'll send you a voucher for $6.48 off any Insiders' Guide© and a list of available
titles as soon as we get this card from you. Thanks for being an Insider!**